FRANCIS M. TYRRELL was ordained a priest for the dio-
cese of Brooklyn (now Rockville Centre) in 1942. He
holds degrees, including a doctorate in philosophy, from
Gregorian University and Catholic University. He has
served as an assistant pastor, Dean of Cathedral College, Professor of Philosophy, and since 1963 has been
Professor of Fundamental Theology at Immaculate
Conception Seminary. He is a writer, lecturer and
member of several professional organizations, including
the American Catholic Philosophical Association and
the Catholic Theological Society of America.

MAN: BELIEVER AND UNBELIEVER

MAN: BELIEVER AND UNBELIEVER

FRANCIS M. TYRRELL

Prof. of Fundamental Theology
Immaculate Conception Seminary
Huntington, New York

ALBA · HOUSE NEW · YORK

SOCIETY OF ST. PAUL, 2187 VICTORY BLVD., STATEN ISLAND, NEW YORK 10314

Library of Congress Cataloging in Publication Data

Tyrrell, Francis Martin, 1916-
    Man: believer and unbeliever
    Includes bibliographies.
        1. Apologetics—20th century. 1. Title.
BT1102.T9   239   73-20055
ISBN 0-8189-0283-3

Nihil Obstat:

Francis Glimm, S.T.L.
Censor Librorum

Imprimatur:

Walter P. Kellenberg, D.D.
Bishop of Rockville Centre
April 11, 1973

Designed, printed and bound in the United States of America by the Fathers
and Brothers of the Society of St. Paul, 2187 Victory Boulevard,
Staten Island, New York 10314, as part of their
communications apostolate.

2 3 4 5 6 7 8 9 (Current Printing: first digit).

FOREWORD

Although the foreword comes first, it is written last, if at all. An introduction announces plans and intentions for a work about to begin. A foreword is a retrospective glance at the work after it is completed. From that vantage point I would like to tell the reader where I think this book fits.

First of all, it belongs to Fundamental or Foundational Theology. It can be called an effort at a contemporary apologetic for the Christian faith. Apologetics is said to have fallen into disfavor. Yet as a theological function, it has been integral to the exercise of a reflective Christian faith since its first thematization in the New Testament. As Tillich insists, kerygmatic theology, which proclaims the Gospel message in systematized form, needs to be completed by apologetic theology, which relates that message to the contemporary situation. It responds to the questions put to Christian faith by the present age. For that reason it is the organ of theology most sensitive to and most affected by the evolving character of the human condition.

The apologetics of the recent past was a worthwhile effort to justify Christian faith in an age of rationalism which credited human reason with greater powers than it deserved. We can say that now and we have to adjust our apologetic sights accordingly. Former apologists, Catholics especially, thought of apologetics as an undertaking of reason logically prior to the commitment of faith and therefore to the theological enterprise itself. At present we are more inclined to see it as a task proper to theology. It is performed by a professed Christian believer who is seeking reflectively to understand and to appropriate his faith commitment in its foundations.

Like any science, theology, which claims to be the science of faith, is constituted by its method as well as by its subject matter. To say the least, its subject matter is unique and gives rise to the problem of language about God. On the other hand, its method has to take into account the capacities and limitations of man's power to know which every science must employ. For that reason, it will reflect the transformations in the uses of intelligence that scientific progress makes possible. In the 13th century, Aquinas appealed to Aristotle and his primarily deductive scientific method to serve his theological goals. Today Bernard Lonergan, for example, proposes a more empirically grounded method for theological investigation available to a 20th century man.

Actually Lonergan employs the transcendental method which he has brought to its highest point of refinement in his recent master-work on method in theology. It is the method I have used in this book, although it is Karl Rahner's version rather than Lonergan's that I have adopted. In fact, even a cursory reading of the later chapters will reveal the enormous debt which I owe to Rahner. It was he who enabled me to navigate the transition from a teacher of philosophy to an instructor in Fundamental Theology in the years immediately following the second Vatican Council.

In pursuing its apologetic aim, Fundamental Theology undergoes a somewhat similar transition. For the believer, without abandoning his personal commitment, must engage the unbeliever on ground which both share. Consequently the first stages of the theological quest for the foundations of faith is a work of philosophical reason in the service of theology but adhering to its own method and criteria. Even an appeal to sociology, psychology or other sciences must be philosophically interpreted. On that account theology starts out on common ground and on equal terms with those philosophies, world-views, human faiths, which do not appeal to a revelation from God as a source or guarantee of their truth and value. At that point it is the credibility of Christian theism as a world-view for contemporary man that is in question and which is judged by the standards of reason and not of faith.

Fundamental Theology, however, does not remain on the philosophical level at the threshold of faith. Its apologetic goal is to vindicate Christian faith as the adequate response to the most probing and basic questions of contemporary man. The complete performance of that task must evoke the total power of Christian faith which carries us far beyond the stretch of reason. For it is the whole vision of man and his world illuminated by faith which will furnish the most effective answers to the questions of modern man. Only it will be an adequate and faithful account of man and his world as God has revealed their meaning through His Incarnate Word.

Lonergan analyzes theological method on the basis of the functions which the theologian or reflective believer must perform if he is to be systematic and critical. In the performance of the total theological task, Fundamental Theology, as practiced here, focusses on Dialectics and Foundations and the shift between them. In Dialectics, the climax of the investigative operation, a decision is made between contending positions that is informed by the research, interpretation and historical judgment that have preceded it. In its fullest realization it takes the form of a full-blown Christian religious conversion, a surrender to the love of the Father revealed through the Son by the power of the Spirit.

In theological reflection, this involves various levels. Our attention is initially directed to that Absolute Other Who is the Personal Ground of our being in the world. The concern is to vindicate the Christian commitment precisely as theistic. Therefore, the contention of Dialectic expresses itself in a dialogue between Christian and other world-views. This leads the Christian believer to thematize his religious conversion reflectively and critically over against them as well as in function of them. He expresses his commitment foundationally, that is, in terms of a comprehensive context within which all of its specific meanings and decisions emerge.

The critical or self-justifying character of Foundations is based in the meticulous exercise of the transcendental method itself. By virtue of it, each inquirer is invited and enabled to come to an understanding and possession of himself in his social and historical setting. It is in this arena that the contest between Christian and other faiths occurs as rival interpretations of contemporary man's experience and understanding of himself and his world. On this basis Christian faith presents itself as more adequate than any other. It comprehends and therefore surpasses them in providing a fuller, more definitive explanation of human experience as well as in being more liberating and fulfilling of his self-transcending spirit. It is the norm by which their truth and value are to be judged.

The contents of this book took shape as a course in Fundamental Theology for seminarians. Its publication is the result of many concurring factors. Not least of these was the encouragement of many students who tested its merits against their own experience and critical judgment. I am grateful for their encouragement and their criticisms. Among the many who assisted at its birth, I must single out three who generously assumed a disproportionate share of the labor, Dennis Pope, John Budacovich, and Joseph Mirro.

I must pay tribute to the members of the Society of St. Paul at Alba House, especially Brother Jeffrey Mickler, SSP, and Father Anthony L. Chenevey, SSP, not only for bringing this work to published form, but above all for their unselfish dedication to the apostolate of the communications media.

Finally, I must acknowledge my indebtedness to my brother-priests on the seminary faculty. Especially under the leadership of our recently retired rector, Rev. Msgr. James F. Coffey, S.T.D., Ph.D., they have taught me what it is to live in a loving community of Christian faith.

Seminary of the Immaculate Conception
Huntington, New York   *Francis M. Tyrrell*

CONTENTS

Foreword   v

Introduction   5

CHAPTER ONE: The Contemporary Problem
          of Belief   13
1. *God and the Philosophers*   15
2. Hegel *and 'the Death of God'*   21
3. *After* Hegel: *Point and Counter-point*   24
4. *The Prophet of 'the Death of God'*   28
5. *Positivism*: August Comte   29
6. *Historicism*: Wilhelm Dilthey   31
7. *Psychologism*: Sigmund Freud   35
8. *Reflections on Projections*   38
9. *The Situation of Christians in A Post-Christian Culture*   41

CHAPTER TWO: Atheistic Humanism   51
Existentialist Humanism   51
   A. Edmund Husserl   51
   B. Martin Heidegger   54
   C. Jean Paul Sartre   58
   D. Maurice Merleau-Ponty   60
   E. Resume and Reflections   64
2. *Marxist Humanism*   66
   A. Soviet Orthodoxy   67
   B. Some Revisionists outside the Soviet Union   68
   C. Mao Tse-Tung: The 'Sinocizing' of Marxism   73
   D. Marxist Aggiornamento: Bloch and Garaudy   78
3. *Secular Humanism*   86
   A. John Dewey: A Democratic Faith   87
   B. Julian Huxley: Scientific Humanism   91
   C. Gerhard Szczensy: The Future of Unbelief   95
   D. Secular Humanism: Common Themes   100

CHAPTER THREE: Toward A Christian
          Anthropology—I   109
1. *Introduction*   109
2. Gabriel Marcel: *Existentialist Theism*   111
3. Maurice Blondel: *Philosopher of Action*   122
4. Pierre Teilhard de Chardin: *Convergent Evolution*   140
5. *Distinctive Stands and Common Conclusions*   162

CHAPTER FOUR: Toward A Christian
          Anthropology—II   169

1. *Transcendental Thomism: Movement and Method*   169
2. Joseph Maréchal: *Forerunner*   171
3. Karl Rahner: *Philosophical Foundations*   175
   A. Spirit in the World: Metaphysics of Knowledge   176
   B. Spirit and Matter; Intellect and Sense   180
4. Emerich Coreth: *Metaphysics of the Question*   187
5. Karl Rahner: *Hearers of the Word and Later Writings*   196
   A. Man before God and His Possible Revelation   197
   B. God's Freedom and Man's History: The Problem of Revelation   203
6. *From Philosophy to Theology: The Problem of Nature and Grace* 207

CHAPTER FIVE: A Christian Theological Anthropology   221

1. *Anthropology Is Theology*   222
2. *Christ: The Norm of Man*   225
3. *Man in the Light of Christ, His Norm*   230
4. *Salvation: God's Revelation and Man's Faith*   233
   A. Revelation and the History of Salvation   236
   B. Faith: Man's Response to God's Revelation   239
   C. Faith and Revelation in the Church: Community of Salvation   250
5. *Man, Christ and the Church*   254
   A. The "Anonymous Christian"   255
   B. Christianity and the Non-Christian Religions in the
     History of Salvation   262

CHAPTER SIX: Unbelief: Transcendental Malaise   281

1. *Faith and Freedom*   283
2. *The Intellectual Assent of Faith: "Restless Conviction"*   285
3. *Unbelief as an Existential Dimension of Faith*   289
4. *Man at Once Sinner and Justified: Protestant and Catholic
   Interpretation*   291
5. *Unbelief as a Consequence of Concupiscence*   294
6. *The Unbelief of the Believer*   298

CHAPTER SEVEN: The Christian-Humanist Dialogue   301

1. *Prelude to the Dialogue: The Role of Atheism,
   Positive and/or Negative*   301
2. *Conditions of the Dialogue*   306
3. *The Dialogue Itself*   309
   A. The Christian-Marxist Dialogue   311
   B. The Christian-Secular Humanist Dialogue   320
4. *Achievements and Prospects: A Resumé*   340

CHAPTER EIGHT: Christian Faith and the Future of

MAN AS BELIEVER: Christian Faith in
a Pluralistic, Evolutionary World 347

I. Christian Faith as the Divinely Guaranteed Norm of Multiple
  Human Faiths. *Unity In Diversity: One Truth, Many Faiths* 348
II. The Church and the World 354
  1. *A Theology of Christian Secularity* 355
  2. *Political Theology* 366
  3. *Theology of Liberation* 372
III. Christian Faith as the Vision of the Absolute Future of
  Man's Evolution 386
  1. *The Future as a Dimension of Christian Faith* 386
  2. *The Church and the Future of Man* 391
  3: *Man: His World and His Future* 399

Index 411

MAN: BELIEVER AND UNBELIEVER

INTRODUCTION

The problem of belief is the central issue of our age. Implicitly it is at the heart of the struggles and aspirations of every age, for it reflects man's current self-understanding and the meaning of his existence to which he is willing to commit himself. For centuries in the West that meaning and that self-understanding derived from faith in Jesus Christ and in the God Whom he revealed and Whom his Church preached. Divisions arose within the body of Christians about the nature and work of Christ, his God and his Church. But Christian faith in some form remained. What marks our age is not the inability of contemporary Western men to agree upon this or that tenet of Christian faith. It is rather their incapacity to be Christian believers at all, that is, to commit themselves to Christian faith as the meaning of their lives. For this reason our age poses the problem of belief in its starkest and most explicit terms.

Christian faith has lost its power over the mind and heart of Western man because he no longer is able to perceive its harmony with his experience of himself or to recognize in it the reflection of the self-image his experience has compelled him to form. In effect,

. . . the Christian concept of man has been devalued. It offers no point of contact to modern man, because his self-understanding is completely divergent from the Christian concept . . . The essence of Christianity is felt as alien to man's condition.[1]

The task of Christian apologetics is to face this fact honestly and then to lay the groundwork for justifying to our generation the perennial truth that there is no other name given under heaven than that of Jesus Christ by which man can become wholly human. Christian apologetics, then, must take the form of a Christian anthropology. It will have to provide an image in which modern man can readily recognize his own portrait and a self-understanding which harmonizes with his present experience, the bad as well as the good, and yet holds out a vision of his future in which he can hope. Thus there has been no radical change in the goal of Christian apologetics: namely, to show the credibility of Christianity. It is rather the means, the methods, and the attitude that have to be altered.

It is especially the attitude that has undergone the most drastic change. No longer the old polemics, the belligerent defensiveness, the insularity. The Counter-Reformation is behind us. Post-conciliar apologetics reflects the attitude of the renewed Church which regards itself humbly but seriously as "the sacrament of the unity of all mankind." (*Dogmatic Constitution on the Church*, 1.) We have passed "from anathema to dialogue." "Those others" are no longer our adversaries, but rather our dialogue partners. Thus a new attitude calls for new methods and approaches.

The new attitude represents more than a mere change of heart. On the part of Christians along with others, it reflects a deeper consciousness of the unity of mankind made possible by our entrance into a planetary age. Supersonic transportation, instantaneous world-wide communications, the atomic threat of annihilation that would spare no one and is therefore an equal peril to all, the opening of man's horizons toward outer space as a common human perspective, the accelerated movements of all peoples toward national and personal freedom and a share in the wealth that scientific technology promises to make available to everyone: all these have tended to fuse man's diverse cultures and to point toward that single human family we are fast becoming in fact. It is not at all surprising that Teilhard de Chardin, the prophet of man's converging future, should fascinate and appeal to the intellectuals of many traditions outside the Catholic fold.

There is, however, another reason why the attitude of the Catholic apologist had to change that is more interior to man's own consciousness. It proceeds from the recognition that there is no such person as the unbeliever in the pure state. There are only different kinds of believers. "Belief" and "unbelief" are relative, better, correlative terms, not merely because they co-exist in different persons with commitments that are mutually antagonistic. Rather, they co-exist in each person and in all. For Marxists, atheists, and secularists as well as Christians have made a fundamental option about the ultimate meaning of their lives. Therefore they are believers too and they face the common human problem: "the unbelief of the believer." Unbelief in this more universal context refers not to the state of the other: the non-Catholic, the non-Christian, the non-Marxist, but rather to the infidelity of the believer, whatever his commitment or system of beliefs.

The angle of approach of this book as an effort at Christian apologetics will therefore be that of dialogue. The dialogue partners will be especially those other believers we have customarily called "unbelievers" in the past: the atheists, agnostics, secularists; for they confront us with the problem of Christian belief most pointedly and forcefully. The common ground of discussion will be *"man"*; for we are all humanists. We agree on his unique worth. We disagree in the way we account for his worth, in terms of its ground and its goal. It is a case then of contending anthropologies. In the final analysis, however, the dialogue partner will be not so much "those others": the atheists, agnostics, and secularists, but the "unbeliever" in ourselves. Eventually he is the one each of us must face up to.

It will be an attempt at a Christian apologetics by way of a Christian anthropology. It is not for that reason a mere humanism. Man and his consciousness do not become the norm and the measure of God's revelation and of man's response to it in faith. Rather, God's Word revealed definitively in Christ and preached by his Church is the norm and measure of what it is to be human. Christ is *the* man and therefore the exemplar of what man is to be. For apologetics, which belongs to Fundamental Theology, man is the way to God in and through Christ. Thus Anthropology, Christology, and Theology are seen to coalesce in the vision of Christian faith. Our purpose here is to seek to justify that vision by showing its coherence with man's consciousness and understanding of himself and his world. It is not that Christian faith is tailored to fit man as we find him at present. Rather, we discover that man's consciousness and understanding of himself and his world point to Christian faith as providing the ground of their meaning and the source of their fulfillment.

We shall build our image and understanding of contemporary man from every source, Christian and non-Christian, that promises to make it more authentic and complete. For that reason the attitude of dialogue, of openness to others and the insights they can contribute, will be operative from the beginning, even though the formal use of dialogue with unreligious believers will occur only after the main work of composing a Christian anthropology has been done.

Notes and references

1 Gabriel Vahanian, **The Death of God** (New York: George Braziller Inc., 1961), pp. 7-8.

Bouillard, Henri. "Human Experience as the Starting point of Fundamental Theology," *The Church and the World.* Ed. Johannes B. Metz. New York: Paulist, 1965, pp. 79-91.
Bouillard, Henri. *The Logic of the Faith.* New York: Sheed & Ward, 1967.

Development of Fundamental Theology, The. Ed. Johannes B. Metz. New York: Paulist, 1969.
Dewart, Leslie. *The Foundations of Belief.* New York: Herder & Herder, 1969.
Dulles, Avery, S.J. *A History of Apologetics.* Philadelphia: Westminster, 1971.
Dulles, Avery, S.J. *Apologetics and the Biblical Christ.* Westminster, Md.: Newman, 1963.

Fransen, Piet, S.J. "Three Ways of Dogmatic Thought," in *Intelligent Theology,* I. London: Darton, Longman and Todd, 1967, pp. 9-39. Also in *Heythrop Journal* 4 (1963) pp. 3-24, and in *Cross Currents,* 13 (1963) pp. 129-48.
Fries, Heinrich. "Fundamental Theology," *Sacramentum Mundi,* 2, New York: Herder & Herder, 1968, pp. 368-72.

Kasper, Walter. *The Methods of Dogmatic Theology.* Tr. John Drury. New York: Paulist, 1969.

Latourelle, René, S.J. *Theology: Science of Salvation.* Tr. Sister Mary Dominic. Staten Island, N.Y.: Alba House, 1969.
Lonergan, Bernard. *Method in Theology.* New York: Herder & Herder, 1972.

MacQuarrie. John. *Principles of Christian Theology.* New York: Charles Scribner's Sons, 1966.
Metz, Johannes B., and Henrici, Peter. "Apologetics," *Sacramentum Mundi,* 1. New York: Herder & Herder, 1968, pp. 66-72.

Schillebeeckx, Edward, O.P. *Revelation and Theology.* 2 vols. Tr. N. D. Smith. New York: Sheed & Ward, 1967, 1968.

Tillich, Paul. *Systematic Theology.* vol. I. Chicago: University of Chicago Press, 1961.
Tracy, David. *The Achievement of Bernard Lonergan.* New York: Herder & Herder, 1970, especially cc. 1 and 10.

Walgrave, Jan H., O.P. "The Nature and Scope of Theology," *Louvain Studies,* 4 (1972) pp. 3-12.

The problem of belief
is the central issue
of our age. Implicitly
it is at the heart of
the struggles and
aspirations of every
age, for it reflects
man's current self-
understanding and
the meaning of his
existence, to which
he is willing to
commit himself.

1

The Contemporary Problem of Belief

To pronounce a definitive historical judgment on the age in which one lives would appear to be at best a dubious enterprise. One would seem to lack the necessary perspective from which to view the whole. Yet we are not lacking those who are daring enough to do so. Their number is large, their credentials impressive, the consensus among them is both strong and cumulative. Not only, they say, have we witnessed the decline of the Christian West, we have entered a period in our culture which can rightfully be called post-Christian inasmuch as it has become thoroughly secular. We live in the age of the "Death of God."

By now the proclamation of God's death by Nietzsche's Madman has become a literary commonplace. It is on the verge of entering the collective sub-conscious as one more unquestioned assumption. Yet an inquiry into the status of religious belief in our time cannot avoid either the phrase or the issues it dramatizes. Is Western culture really post-Christian, secular? Are we truly living in the age of the "Death of God"?

The answer to such questions is complicated by the diversity of western culture itself. What is true of Western Europe may not be true of the United States, or at least not yet. There has usually been a time lag in the past between the currency of philosophical fashion in Europe and in

America, since, as in the instances of existentialism and linguistic analysis, they have frequently been importations from abroad. There is also an interval between changing moods and convictions of intellectual leaders and the general acceptance of them on the popular level. Witness the Christian ministers of the recent past trained in the theology of Tillich or Niebuhr preaching to congregations who had scarcely heard of them or cared, and the more activist successors to their pulpits who are so far removed from their congregations by their commitment to an active role in the racial struggle. However, especially in the light of the ever broader reach of higher education and the rapid advent of world-wide instantaneous communications, the cultural diversity as well as the cultural time lags seem fated gradually to disappear.

The United States constitutes an odd, if not unique, phenomenon on the religious landscape of the western world. We puzzle the Europeans and even defy our own self-analysis. At a time when religious disbelief represents the dominant disposition of most of our neighbors across the Atlantic, we are still to a large extent a church-going people, granted that statistics now indicate a growing decline in recent years, and most of us are still willing to call ourselves Christians.

There was a dramatic upsurge in church attendance after World War II during the fifties and early sixties and a general rise in the influence of religion and religious leaders in our national life. This has been variously interpreted. The editor of a rather prestigious study of religion in America, published in the latter sixties, hailed the religious revival of the fifties as one of the Great Awakenings in the spiritual career of our people which

> constituted a general re-orientation of the whole social and intellectual climate of Western society, just as America's previous Great Awakenings had done . . . (And it) is by no means over yet.[1]

On the other hand, Gabriel Vahanian calls the same historical event an upsurge of religiosity, which is not authentic religious faith, but a caricature of it, a superstitious substitute for it, and in fact precisely a loss of faith in God.[2] He would insist that it is merely a further proof of the real death of

God in our times, for it depicted the degree to which Christianity has become acculturated, that is, a victim of the culture which it helped to create and which has progressed to the point where "God is admitted only as a lack."[3]

This difference in interpretation is important, because our interest here is not in the mere statistics of church-goers over non-church-goers, but rather the present state of western man's self-understanding and the degree to which belief in the reality of God and Christian Faith itself enter into its constitution. The well publicized drift of American youth away from institutional Christianity toward other forms: oriental religion, occultism, psychedelic explorations of the frontiers of consciousness, and more recently the "Jesus Movement" which deliberately avoids any link with the established churches, is one of the more pertinent indices of the direction western man is going religiously. But the historical judgment that we are living in a period that can rightfully be called post-Christian is based not so much on the immediate present or the problematic future, but rather on the steady movement of western culture in the past century and a half, a span of time that does provide a sufficient perspective for hazarding such a judgment.

God and the Philosophers

One of the most intriguing and illuminating literary events of this century was the publication of Ludwig Feuerbach's *The Essence of Christianity* with an introduction by Karl Barth.[4] Feuerbach was of course long gone, but Barth, the doughty champion of Neo-Orthodoxy, saw in the philosopher's atheistic reduction of Christianity a confirmation of his own diagnosis of human religion over against God's Word and Revelation. The theologian rejects the philosopher's assimilation of theology to anthropology, his identification of the divine essence with the glorified human essence, of God with man's self-awareness, emancipated from all actuality. But he sees this atheist faith as the logical implication of the man-centered theologies of Schleiermacher and his nineteenth century German Protestant colleagues which sought God as a datum of man's consciousness, or which would, in Feuerbach's terms, interpret religion, revelation and the relation to God as a predicate of man. Thus Barth appeals to Feuerbach to furnish a negative confirmation of his own insistence on the irreversibility of the downward movement from God to man in vindication of God's absolute sovereignty in His relationship with man. For any Christian who would desire to approach theology by way of anthropology, it is a salutary caution, even while it may be thought too sweeping in its rejection of any such attempt.

Barth's singling out of Feuerbach was typically the stroke of a genius. For Feuerbach is, on many counts, the pivotal figure on which the nineteenth century swung from a Christian toward a post-Christian attitude, a movement that would not be fully manifest until our own century. His role was less passionately played than those of Kierkegaard and Nietzsche, yet no less effectively. Like them his reputation and impact were to be lost after his lifetime, only to be recovered in ours.

The effect of *The Essence of Christianity* when it first appeared was apparently immediate and powerful. As de Lubac summarizes it:

> The impression made on people was of something final; of a perfectly clear revelation, as if the scales had at last fallen from all eyes; of a full stop put to discussions that had been going on for a thousand years and had suddenly become pointless; of an end to the illusion of religious faith and the adventures of idealist speculation. The solution to the human problem had been found; there was nothing left to look for.[5]

Feuerbach mediated Hegel for Marx. If he had done nothing more, he would have deserved immortality for this. His own system was to be definitively superseded by Marx's dialectical materialism, yet it was he who had already made atheism reputable, for many imperative, and whose humanism without God sounds so contemporaneous in the midst of the twentieth century. He looks small only because he stands between the giant figures of Hegel and Marx, but without him, it is less likely that they would have so hugely informed the future of our race.

For him as for many of the seminal thinkers of his time, Hegel had said the final and fateful word for Christianity and the God Christians had been worshipping. One is tempted to, and perhaps one should, begin the account of the death of God in western consciousness much sooner. But this story has already been well told and documented elsewhere[6] and a brief summary of it should serve our purpose. Moreover, to fit his own claims, Hegel does recapitulate that story in his own system and he has written its thunderous climax.

It need not have happened that way, but the death of God in the mind of western man began when the God of Christian revelation began to be transformed into the God of the philosophers. It need not have happened because it has been a profound Christian conviction that the God Who spoke to man in His Word has also spoken to man in His creation. But it did happen because well-meaning and even devout Christian men began to separate the God of their reason from the God of their faith. The great medievals, like Thomas and Scotus, did not make that separation; their faith informed their reason in all its explorations into God. But their successors effected the divorce, whether to defend the autonomy of faith as in Ockham or the autonomy of reason as in Descartes and the many who followed him.

It was certainly not impious to want to defend the freedom and the autonomy of human reason against what were too often the oppressive claims of religious belief. It was in fact inevitable if scientific and philosophical progress were to be made. But with special reference to man's knowledge of the true God there was a temptation that can only be called insidious and which could only be overcome by an unwonted humility and an untiring intellectual asceticism. In plain terms, the temptation was to idolatry, the special idolatry philosophers are prone to: of erecting one's own man-made conception of God in His stead, indeed of even believing that His infinite mystery could be localized or encapsulated in human thought.

The special form the process actually took was to use God, or rather the idea of Him, for limited human purposes: to provide a principle of explanation for a philosophical account of the world. Since in most instances the explanatory system itself suffered from various inadequacies—a hardly unexpected feature of successive attempts that can only be termed tentative efforts to universalize a growing but still rudimentary scientific understanding of the universe—the role assigned to God usually amounted to that of an explanatory function to fill gaps otherwise unaccounted for in the system. In all fairness, it must be confessed that the philosophers were only doing on their more sophisticated level what was being done wholesale on the popular level in preaching, catechizing, and in those places where what we call the pious wisdom of the people is exchanged, passed on, and taken for granted; and of course it is still widely being done.

A resumé of some of the more familiar names in classical modern philosophy suffices to make the point, though apologies are begged beforehand for rather crude simplifications which are nevertheless, I believe, substantially correct interpretations.

To start with the man commonly called the father of modern philosophy: Descartes needed God to bridge the gap between his enclosed ego and the substantially other material world, a veracious all-powerful God who would guarantee the spiritual mind's perceptual contact with material bodies as well as provide reassurance that the *Cogito* could extend its certain knowledge beyond self-validating acts of present consciousness. Malebranche invoked God as the universal cause and indeed the only cause that he could conceive in the Cartesian universe he inherited. Spinoza, anticipating Hegel, used God as the comprehensive principle of explanation, deducing his system with rigorous logic from the definition of the divine essence. Leibnitz depended on God to summon into existence the best of all the possible worlds, assuring its smooth operation by pre-ordaining the harmonious coincidence of monadic components conceived to be causally isolated from one another. Bishop Berkeley, in a world believed to consist solely of minds and their ideas, called on God to be the causal agent, who disposed those ideas in a stable universal order as well as to be the common bond among the disparate minds, accounting for the possibility of their intercommunication. Isaac Newton and the Newtonians like Clarke were employing God as the Divine Mechanic who had constructed the world machine and now kept it going. Locke, in a wholesome reaction to the Cartesians, refused to use God as a philosophical functionary and tried instead to defend reason's power to demonstrate His existence even from an empiricist's starting point. However, he was preparing the stage for Hume who exhibited in definitive fashion that an empiricist version of knowledge excludes any firm assertion of existential truth beyond the reach of experience and that any conviction of God's reality must rest on non-rational foundations, such as instinctive human belief.

Hume in effect put an end to the metaphysical exploitation of the God of the philosophers, at least as it had been practiced by those who preceded him. In this process he also appeared to demolish any hope of rational proof of God's existence even in the interests of Christian apologetics. It was Immanuel Kant who perceived the full force of Hume's critique and gave it lasting significance by incorporating its consequences into his own monumental synthesis.

Kant defended the validity of mathematical and empirical science against Hume's scepticism at the price of accepting a metaphysical agnosticism. Scientific laws and conceptions are reflections, not of the forms and flux of a mind-independent real order, but of the structures and dynamisms of the mind itself, operating within the phenomenal limits of sense experience. The idea of God and the other metaphysical ideas of the world and the self, exceeding the reach of sense-bound understanding, are only pretensions of human reason in the sense of constituting ideals of ultimate unity in our understanding which perpetually beckon the mind onward toward a horizon at which one never arrives.

Kant's powerful critique of the traditional proofs for the existence of God directly collided with the presentation by Wolff, Leibnitz and their rationalist predecessors, which was the current one of his time. It did not so directly come to grips with their more ancient formulation in the realist tradition of Aristotle and the scholastics. In any event, the effect was the same. It was generally accepted, and still is, that he had once and for all disposed of any possibility of demonstrating God's existence by philosophical reasoning.

For Kant, God's existence and attributes were still a matter of philosophical concern, but now as a postulate of the moral will or as an implication of aesthetic judgment. What man could not know, he was at least entitled to believe for moral or aesthetic reasons. This opening was to influence the shaping of many Protestant theologies of the nineteenth century.

Let us pause for a moment to reflect on what has been happening. Brilliant thinkers, not aloof aristocrats of the intellect, but rather influential citizens of their age, who not only resounded to but also helped to mold the intellectual fashion of their time, devote their minds to a philosophical exploration of fundamental human issues deliberately prescinding from the deliverances of religious faith or divine revelation. Operating within the limitations of their own intelligences as well as of their own cultural milieux, they reinterpret the inherited faith-understanding of God in response to the methodological demands of their speculations. Under progressive criticism, their explanatory systems are seen to erode and crumble, and with them the notion of God which had served those systems as intrinsic explanatory functions.

In reply to the scepticism that ensues, a new effort is made to rehabilitate the notion of God, now no longer as the terminus of ill-fated human reason, but as the object of human will, feeling, and faith. The subject of these misadventures is not the Self-revealed God of traditional Christian faith, but the construct of the series of human minds that had fashioned it for their own philosophical purposes. Yet all this has not occurred in a vacuum. Since these are the formative minds whose works become the classic expressions of their culture, they exercise a preponderant influence on the thoughts and convictions of their contemporaries and successive generations. Since their context is that of a nominally Christian culture, their interpretations of man, his world, and his God become part and parcel of that culture and thus the mirrors in which that culture sees itself and its beliefs. The fate of all becomes intertwined. In the minds of the many, the God of religious faith is identified with and shares the fate of the idea of God which has entered the cultural fabric.

HEGEL *and 'the Death of God'*

What Kant bequeathed to his successors, Hegel preeminently, was the conviction, constituting his "Copernican revolution," that in knowing the mind actively constructs what it knows. In successive stages, Fichte, Schelling, and Hegel brought this conviction to what must be regarded as its ultimate implications: the identification of total reality with creative thought. In the process, metaphysics had been reinstated, but it was a monistic metaphysics of the absolute identity of God, man, and the world. For Christian theism, involving belief in a God Who is transcendent as well as immanent to His creation, was no longer intellectually respectable.

Hegel eventually came to regard Christianity as the absolute religion, but even then it was still only the penultimate stage to his own philosophy in the self-realization of Absolute Spirit. Religion in general was as yet a symbolic representation of the reconciliation of all things in Spirit which was at once the goal and the ceaseless process by which that goal was being endlessly achieved. In the Christian doctrines of Creation, the Blessed Trinity, and the Redemptive Incarnation were symbolically expressed as well as revealed the principal stages and factors in this eternal process. Hegel's enduring relation in history to Christianity and the God of Christian faith, however, is rather negative than positive. It was he who more than any other one man paved the way for the death of God and furnished the weapons to those who performed the final deed. He gave them the slogan and the rationale for every antitheism and atheism after him. The slogan was: the Christian God can exist only at the price of the alienation of man. The rationale was the whole thrust of his philosophy, however his successors would choose to use it.

Hegel's philosophy is a phenomenology of human consciousness which he absolutized into a monistic metaphysics of Absolute Spirit. In the course of developing it, he provided not only the impetus to the demise of Christian theism but an enormously influential analysis of man in his subjectivity and historicity which is even at this moment still informing contemporary man's self-image and self-understanding. In that sense every current anthropology is post-Hegelian.

Hegel benefitted from Fichte's vindication of intellectual intuition against Kant. The latter had restricted intuition to the sensibility which receives its matter from the "thing-in-itself," though it furnishes the form of perception. For an intuition to be intellectual, it would have to be divine, since it would be creative of the very existence of its object. Fichte accepted the stipulation. The ego's reflective intuition of itself in act—precisely in the act of moral willing by which, following Kant, it is in fact the autonomous law-giving will that is acting—furnishes the empirical basis for his bold stand. In this grasping of consciousness in its very originating act, we apprehend not merely a finite subject, but the Absolute Subject in the act of positing itself and constituting an objective order over against, though encompassed within, its own total reality that will provide its moral task.

Kant's idealist followers rejected his dualism of man the knower and the "thing-in-itself" which furnishes the matter that the human mind structures and renders intelligible. The known is the in-itself real because knowing (with willing) constitutes the total reality of the known. This is so because human consciousness is radically absolute consciousness in act.

Hegel brought German Idealism to its most coherent and finished form in his philosophy of Absolute Spirit. All the real is identical with Absolute Spirit in the various stages of its eternal process of self-realization. Since everything that is is encompassed in Spirit, diversity comes about by a process of self-differentiation, and progress toward unity occurs by a corresponding process of self-recovery and enriching reconciliation. The model of this process on the absolute plane is found on the finite plane of human consciousness.

Human consciousness tends to be incurably realist, that

is, convinced that knowledge and other conscious processes relate one to things, objects, that are independently other. Reflection discloses the naiveté of this attitude by uncovering the dominant role which the subject has in constituting its conscious object. Yet the subject keeps searching for the other on whose firm reality it can depend and to which it can submit, only to have its search frustrated again and again· This is the stage of "the unhappy consciousness," vacillating between the unchangeable other in which it would anchor itself and the free changing self which would not be so bound. It is a necessary stage toward the fulfillment of self-possession and full wisdom: the reflective consciousness of the inter-related unity of all in the developing self-consciousness of Absolute Spirit. But it is a partial stage, arrested in the condition of alienation of the self. It is an indispensable step, but one which must be surpassed by the final reconciliation of subject and object in the enriched consciousness of their underlying unity.

Hegel believed strongly that history, and especially the history of religion, reflected the stages of the evolution of consciousness itself. The stage of "the unhappy consciousness" achieved its most complete historical expression in the socio-cultural and religious forms of the Middle Ages. For then the stage of human consciousness represented by Christian theism was given objective form in social structures and relationships. The absolutist hierarchical church and feudal society institutionalized the "master-slave" relation which Christian theism, according to Hegel, dictated as the only relation between God and man which it could conceivably tolerate. This was the social counter-part of "the unhappy consciousness," the inescapable predicament of the Christian, who was compelled by his faith to submit worshipfully to a God Who was an Absolute Other. Thereby he was required to accept alienation from his true identity as a permanent condition, to remain in the inauthentic posture of one perpetually denying his ultimate unity in and with the God Who is Absolute Spirit.

Hegel blandly conceded the historical inevitability of Christianity and its faith in a transcendent God in the ongoing evolution of human and universal consciousness. As we have remarked, he even asserted its uniqueness as the "absolute religion," in whose central doctrines the eternal truths adequately expounded in his philosophy are inadequately represented in imaginative and symbolic forms. To acknowledge the due course of man's spiritual progress, however, even the "absolute religion" had to be superseded by Hegelian philosophy, and the Christian God had to die that the true God Who is the totally immanent Absolute Subject might be born in human consciousness.

After HEGEL: *Point and Counter-point*

The disciples of Hegel diverged into a Left and a Right Wing: the former, which eventually included Feuerbach and Marx, rejecting his idealism, insofar as it identified reality with spirit; the latter, espousing his philosophy as furnishing the vesture in which Christianity could be clothed with intellectual respectability. Feuerbach was to accept Hegel's Absolute Spirit as the final and definitive version of the God of Christian faith, and in rejecting the first was convinced he was repudiating the other.

Søren Kierkegaard (1813-1855) knew better. He fought Hegel on two fronts. On the philosophical-theological level, he persistently combatted what he called "the System," which dominated the theological schools and intellectual centers of Germany and his own Denmark. He sharply chided Hegel for encompassing everything in his system except what was of absolute centrality and importance: the unique individual existent person. Neither the individual nor the truth to which he commits himself can be the mere ingredients of a system. The individual is unique and particular, irreducible to the universalizable components of a transcendental logic. Truth becomes his truth, not as the cold dispassionate deliverance of an impersonal reason, but as that meaning whose truth engages him with passionate earnestness. That truth which reveals him ultimately to himself and engages him in his deepest freedom is the Absolute Paradox of Christianity, the Incarnation. For here we do not have, as Hegel would propound, the entrance of universal Reason into the equally universal categories of Nature, but rather the union of the absolute mystery Who is God with man in that particular individual, Jesus Christ, Whose identity as God-man and redeemer can be embraced only after the leap of faith beyond the boundaries of reason.

Kierkegaard also fought Hegelianism as it was preached in the pulpits of the established Danish Church and reflected in the complacent lives of Danish Christians, whose respectable mediocrity he denounced as the antipode of genuine response to the Gospel of Christ. From the viewpoint of a distressed Christian, he diagnosed the same death of God in the consciousness of western man which Nietzsche was to herald as the great deed, still unacknowledged, that would usher in the age of Superman, humanity at last freed from the master-slave relation to the Christian God.

It was the atheists rather than the Christian theists who drew out the more consistent, certainly the more powerful implications of Hegel's thought, and it was thus not a startling step for a twentieth century religious thinker to invoke Hegel as a prophetic forerunner of "a gospel of Christian atheism" (Altizer). Hegel subverted the divine transcendence by making God wholly immanent to, insofar as God was constitutive of, the world process. By the same stroke he reduced man to a moment in the evolving self-consciousness of Absolute Spirit. This trend of divinizing man by absorbing him into the divine consciousness was reversed by Feuerbach, who humanized God by reducing Him to a projection of man, a summation of human consciousness. Hegel had defined the transcendent God of Christian faith as the fixation of human consciousness in a stage of alienation that must be dialectically succeeded by the recovery of the unified consciousness. Feuerbach, who ironically enough identified Christian theism with Hegel's syncretism, defined the God, who is absolute spirit into whom man is ultimately absorbed, as the alienation of the essence of man, projected outside himself and then worshipped as the ideal to which he aspired for his absolute fulfillment.

> Religion, at least the Christian, is the relation of man to himself, or more correctly to his own nature; but a relation to it, viewed as a nature apart from his own. The divine being is nothing else than

the human being, or, rather, the human nature purified, freed from the limits of the individual man, 'made objective—that is, contemplated and revered as another, a distinct being. All the attributes of the divine nature are, therefore, attributes of the human nature . . . Consequently, the object and contents of the christian religion are altogether human.[7]

Thus Feuerbach brought to its inevitable conclusion the process by which the idea of God was fashioned and refashioned to serve the needs and uses of human philosophy. It had reached its climax of arrogance when Hegel had equated his philosophy with the self-knowledge of God. Feuerbach gave the idol its true name, and its name was Man.

By reversing the God-man relationship and apotheosizing man, Feuerbach wrote the charter for every atheistic humanism that would follow. But his ideas would enter most decisively into the formation of western and world culture in the mind of the man who wrote in the last of his critical "Theses on Feuerbach": "The philosophers have only *interpreted* the world, in various ways; the point, however, is to *change* it."[8] Actually Karl Marx (1818-1883) was not repudiating Feuerbach. Rather he accepted his humanizing of God as definitive and was only insisting that one must pass beyond the "fiery brook" (*feuer-bach*) to bring the truth of atheism to social reality. His predecessor was judged and found wanting as a mere theoretician who even spoke of man as an abstract essence.

For Germany the criticism of religion is in the main complete, and criticism of religion is the premise of all criticism.

The basis of irreligious criticism is: **Man makes religion,** religion does not make man. In other words, religion is the self-consciousness and self-feeling of man, who either has not found himself or has already lost himself again. But **man** is no abstract thing of being, squatting outside the world. Man is the world of **man,** the state, society. This state, this society produce religion, **a perverted world consciousness,** because they are **a perverted world.** Religion is the general theory of that world . . .

The abolition of religion as the illusory happiness of the people is required for their real happiness . . . The criticism of religion disillusions man, to make him think and act and shape his reality like a man who has been disillusioned and has come to reason, so that he will revolve round himself and therefore round his true sun. Religion is only the illusory sun, which revolves round man as long as he does not revolve round himself.

The task of history, therefore, once the world beyond the truth has disappeared, is to establish the truth of this world. The immediate task of philosophy, which is at the service of history, once the saintly form of human self-alienation has been unmasked, is to unmask self-alienation in its unholy forms. Thus the criticism of heaven turns into the criticism of the earth, the criticism of religion into the criticism of right, and the criticism of theology into the criticism of politics.[9]

Marx agreed with Feuerbach that religion was a form of self-alienation, the projection of man's own essence into an alien being named "God," but he felt that he had not provided an explanation of the fact, either in its content or its method. It is not man abstractly conceived in his essence, but man the social being, man the worker who, emerging from nature and in union with his fellow-man, creates himself in the process of creating nature in his own image. Thus his work and the product of his work are an extension and expression of himself and he realizes himself in the social process of production by which he humanizes his natural world.

Religion for Marx then cannot be subjected to criticism in isolation from the socio-economic reality of which it is merely the superstructure and by-product. Religion as the alienating projection of man's hopes and aspirations to another world above this world and after this life is only the symptom of the more fundamental alienation of the socio-economic structure in which the worker is deprived by the profit system and its capitalist masters of the fruits of the very work in which he creates and realizes his authentic self by his labor. Thus the unmasking of the holy form of self-alienation of religion must lead to the more radical unmasking of the unholy forms of self-alienation built into the very structure of capitalist society and its economic system, founded on the exploitation of man's personal labor.

. . . The criticism of heaven turns into the criticism of the earth.

Religious distress is at the same time the expression of real distress and the protest against real distress. Religion is the sigh of the oppressed creature, the heart of a heartless world, just as it is the spirit of an unspiritual situation. It is the opium of the people.

The abolition of religion as the illusory happiness of the people is required for their real happiness. The demand to give up the illusions about its condition is the demand to give up a condition which needs illusion.[10]

Marx devoted himself primarily to the task of removing

the social conditions which require the religious illusion, but his animus was as strong against the illusion as against its cause. From his earliest years, he made his own the defiant cry of Prometheus, the mythical rebel against the divine monarch, Zeus: "I hate all gods!" Marx chose man against all gods, whom he lumped indiscriminately in the same company: Zeus, Hegel's Absolute Spirit, and the God of Christian faith. His vindication of man against all exploitation and alienation was magnificent. His atheism, on the other hand, was an emotional option of his youth, a faith accepted from the intellectual milieu in which his convictions grew and never afterward subjected to radical self-criticism.

The Prophet of 'the Death of God'

Friedrich Nietzsche (1844-1900) declared the truth of atheism and the advent of man as the only God with the same passionate earnestness with which Kierkegaard had proclaimed his faith in the God-man. As for Marx, Prometheus was his patron-hero also, but with a difference. It was not the proletarian masses, but the Super-men, (the "over men") an aristocratic elite of individualists, who would be the bearers of man's autonomy and his future greatness.

Nietzsche was himself by instinct an aristocrat and an individualist. He did not seek to liberate man by changing his social structures, but rather foresaw the emergence of a vanguard of emancipated spirits, who would lead the race toward its radically new and liberated state. Theism had been a failure of nerve by men of puny spirit. But as men had inevitably grown, the God of their minds had correspondingly diminished and decayed for want of being needed. But outmoded ideas often outlive their needfulness. The majority of nominal believers was still too blind or too cowardly to confront the truth that their God had died. The minority of unbelieving scoffers was too shallow or unperceptive to realize the colossal difference that the deicide in which they had collaborated must impose on the universe of man.

With vehement passion and poetic eloquence, Nietzsche preached the gospel of God's death and man's rebirth, straining to rouse the soul of his age to a clear consciousness of its new freedom and its unbounded promise. He was however a prophet not honored by his age; he was too far ahead of his time.

Borrowing from his philosophical mentor, Arthur Schopenhauer (1788-1860), Nietzsche eventually based his world-view, his reversal of traditional values and man's radical openness to novelty and grandiose possibilities, on the ultimate irrationality of the ground of existence: the Will to Power. Man himself was the only source of meaning and value and therefore was utterly unfettered by limiting frontiers of reason or morality.

Ironically Nietzsche founded this seemingly infinite freedom of man on one of the strictest systems of determinism that could only be adequately described by the myth of eternal recurrence. It was an ancient myth served up to meet his modern needs; the universe and man in it endlessly repeating themselves with exact sameness in an eternity of recurring cycles. It not only gave man a kind of immortality, it conferred on every act and every moment an infinite weight of significance; but only great souls could bear such knowledge and assume readily the burden of each existential moment. In such trial and travail, the race of Super-man is being born whose capacity to live each eternal moment to the full would be the measure of man's future of infinite greatness.

Positivism: Auguste Comte

Nietzsche's poetic vision of man as Prometheus unbound, as one who could not bear that there be any God but he, has evoked a profound response in the soul of our age, especially as it expresses itself in an existentialist mode. But one facet of the contemporary mind he did not share: its scientific temper and its concern for man's rational control of the world and planning of his own future.

The prophet of atheistic humanism which bases itself

on science was a Frenchman, less poetic but no less imaginative. Auguste Comte (1798-1857), called the founder of positivism, went Hegel one better. The latter had regarded his own system as the culmination as well as the summation of the principal metaphysical systems that had preceded him. In his renowned law of the three stages, Comte relegated all metaphysics conceived as the exclusive resort to abstract explanations to a transitional role between the more primitive theological stage and the final maturity of man's mind in the positive stage of explanation in terms of scientific law. Like Hegel, Comte believed that he had summarized in his law the necessary stages in the unfolding of human consciousness as well as the inexorable evolution of that consciousness in human history. Once again it all led to his philosophy as its definitive climax, though the pretentiousness of this claim seems somehow more modest in Comte's version.

The father of positivism resembles the founder of communism in his emphasis on social change as the key to human progress and the liberation of man from all forms of human bondage. Social reform was the unvarying aim of all his thinking, writing, and lecturing. Even his reclassification of the sciences with the new science of sociology as their summit was meant to serve that goal.

Having in his early teens abandoned his Catholic faith and belief in God without regrets, Comte thereafter made the exaltation of man the objective of his mind and his emotions. Comte understood the depth of the religious sense in man. He saw the need to provide for the role of affectivity as well as for inculcating moral ideals in any viable social reconstruction. With this in mind, he founded a positivist religion of humanity-worship, modelled on medieval Catholicism, with its secular saints and liturgy. It was never to achieve more than limited acceptance among his followers, especially in England where with its empiricist traditions his positivism was to receive its most decided welcome. Nevertheless, it was in its own way a logical step in the progressive installation of man in the place of the God who had died. It was also an earlier dramatization of the conflicting claims of the sacred and secular dimensions of human life in an increasingly secularized world and of the current concern over maintaining a vital residual sacredness in such an environment.

John Stuart Mill (1806-1873) popularized the thought of Comte for English-speaking people in the context of his own empirically oriented synthesis. But the major impetus toward a scientific humanism came rather from Charles Darwin (1809-1882) and his theory of biological evolution. The initial shock of the Copernican revolution propagated by Galileo had scarcely been felt outside the little cosmos of the Roman Curia, granted that it was eventually to be felt in every sector of man's universe. The full impact of the Darwinian revolution was felt almost immediately through-out the world of Christian faith. The remaining foundations of religious belief seemed to crumble under the relentless attack of the popularizers of evolution, like Thomas Huxley and Ernst Haeckel. The hypothesis of God seemed hope-lessly outmoded and superfluous in their deterministic uni-verse, all of whose components, including man, could be accounted for by evolution through natural selection from earlier, simpler forms. Man and his evolving intelligence alone seemed needed now to give an account of what had gone before and to plan the unbounded progress that lay ahead. There were flaws in their drab, neat cosmos, as a later physics was to disclose, but not until they had had their heyday. Meanwhile the new image of man in a god-less world was being hammered out.

Historicism: WILHELM DILTHEY

Evolution remains the master-idea which the nineteenth century bequeathed to ours. For that reason, although psychology, anthropology, and sociology were born in the last century and biology was radically renewed, history is the science which best communicates its mentality. Our acute consciousness of the temporal dimensions of our existence, of our historicity, we owe to these predecessors of ours, chiefly Hegel and Wilhelm Dilthey. Dilthey (1833-1911) is another of those thinkers whose considerable influence on the formation of our age is receiving belated recognition. Psychology and psychoanalysis, the philosophy of history, the history of ideas, and existentialism itself are all in some measure dependencies on his thought. It was his insistence on the specific difference in the method of the human sciences (*Geisteswissenschaften*) from that of the natural sciences (*Naturwissenschaften*) and thus his opposition to positivism, which would reduce the former to the latter, that made provision for the later distinctive development of history and the various human and social sciences that employ the historical method.

Dilthey extended Kant's question: "How are the sciences possible?" to include the human over and beyond the physical sciences, and he attempted to construct a "critique of historical reason." This was not a pure, but a concrete reason embedded in a consciousness which was as much willing and feeling as thought. Life itself is the starting point and content of his philosophy as it is the total object of consciousness itself, for life comes to consciousness of itself in the individual's act of living experience.

For Dilthey, however, the self is never alone but always involved in a living relationship with other subjects and the objects that constitute its setting. In fact, the first condition of the living consciousness is one in which there is concrete identity of subject and object, of perception and its contents. The impetus of consciousness is towards developing a total view or outlook to integrate its experiences and provide a measure for evaluating them.

This total view's elementary form is that of a world picture (*Weltbild*) which is neither stable nor reflective since it relies primarily on feeling. The stabilizing of feeling by reflective thought leads the way to a world outlook (*Weltanschauung*) by which meaning and pattern are objectivized, that is, the varied data of experience are integrated in a total structure of significance.

There are three types of world view: religion, art, and philosophy, inasmuch as will, emotion, or cognition respectively predominate in its formation, even though none of man's faculties is ever wholly lacking in any conscious act. Dilthey regards religion as more rudimentary than philosophy. It relies on a will act of faith in invisible super-natural agencies that underlie and explain visible natural manifestations of life. Philosophy on the other hand seeks to understand life in ultimate fashion by means of concepts that are universally valid. The search for an ultimate solution is bound to be endlessly unsuccessful, but the effort to find one is worthwhile, for each one yields some partial answer to the riddle of life. An important task of philosophy is to study the diverse world outlooks in their historical development.

Following Kant, Dilthey regards the primary function of philosophy as that of determining the logical method and structure of the sciences, which he extends to the human sciences. This is based on the Kantian conviction that what we know obeys the laws of knowing itself and therefore we are able to deal with and perceive the structure of the objective order. The fact that the human sciences deal with humanity, that is, the total human-social-historical reality, separates them from natural sciences. The latter deal with nature as an order of causal necessity known through outer experience; the former rely on inner experience of ourselves as free and self-directing agents and seek a pattern in human acts and events by discerning the aims and purposes which govern them and which thus establish their meaning. Human sciences differ from the natural in acknowledging the pur-posive pattern of human action and thereby the teleological character of its object. The movement of human life is from within outward, so that we can only understand human action and human creation as the objectivizing of inner attitudes and purposes. This applies not only to art but to every ex-pression of the human spirit which is given an external form, whether it be language, law, or religion.

The understanding of human acts and products is thus possible inasmuch as each one knows from his own experience the modes of expression by which life tends to objectify it-self. Dilthey believes that human nature is basically the same throughout history, and that there is constancy as well as variation in the modes in which human life expresses itself in different periods. However, since understanding is a kind of reflective re-living of what we or others have already lived, we are limited in our understanding to what is somehow contained "in that dynamic unity of life of which our individual life is a part."[11] Moreover, time is of the essence of our existence, and all the meaning in human life is bound up with its temporal structure. This understanding is, of course, not merely intellectual or cognitive, since the very life which it expresses and interprets is equally emotional and volitional. In this fact is founded the historical relativity of our understanding, since we are restricted in its scope by the boundaries of our culturally and time-conditioned experience of life. This essential temporality of human existence and understanding was to play a central role in the thought of Heidegger and other existentialists who felt the influence of Dilthey's thought.

Dilthey also contributed other themes to the existentialists that arise within his historicist philosophy. Thus, for him, man is the creator of the values that govern his life, since they actually arise only through human acts of valuing. He attacked the idea of eternal values, moral or otherwise, since such a conviction is a denial of man's genuine freedom and creativity. "The relativity of values is only the reverse of the coin of man's creative freedom."[12] However, he recognized in human existence itself an intrinsic value which is universal or objective, not as a metaphysical truth, but as an unvarying fact of historical experience.

> Because all other things have been considered as valuable only insofar as they maintained, protected, furthered and enriched human life, human beings themselves constitute the sole objective value which is manifested by the flux of history and the change of moral standards. Respect for individuality is the anchorage of moral judgments and is not subject to historical relativity.[13]

In this final position, we see what is perhaps the lasting significance of Dilthey for the problem of belief. He stressed as few men have the historical and cultural relativity of human existence and its values. Yet he deliberately rejected the relativism which leads to the extremity of the moral sceptic or nihilist. He left to his successors the image of man as the creator of his own values in each new stage of his evolution, yet he saw at least in their human creator the unconditioned value which escapes relativity. In a sense, he transcended relativism by first passing through it. To the degree that our faith is to be truly contemporary, we may have to duplicate his feat, since relativism is the characteristic temptation of our age which we must be willing to confront directly, if we would be in fact entitled to claim that we have overcome it.

Psychologism: SIGMUND FREUD

Sigmund Freud (1856-1939), the founder of psychoanalysis, must be acknowledged as the single individual who most powerfully influenced the formation of contemporary man's self-image. Paul Ricoeur has put it simply: "Our culture analyzes itself through him."[14] Although he lived most of his productive years in our century, he rightly belongs in this gallery of nineteenth century thinkers who made the most telling contributions to the formation of the twentieth century mind.

Freud was preoccupied with the problem of religion and emotionally convinced of its baneful character from his earliest years. In fact, his obsession with the problem of death and the validity of the Judaeo-Christian faith and his life-long compulsion to discredit the latter have been seriously suggested as deserving of separate psychoanalytic study.[15] His earliest published treatment of the religious problem was an essay written in 1907.[16]

> . . . we might venture to regard obsessional neurosis as the counterpart of religion and to describe this neurosis as a private religious system, and religion as a universal form of obsessional neurosis.[17]

Freud was to declare with reference to his *The Future of An Illusion* that he was concerned mainly with the ordinary man's understanding of religion rather than the most profound sources of religious feelings. Having granted that this was a legitimate restriction for the purposes of psychological study, it is nevertheless worthwhile keeping in mind when one evaluates the scope of his strictures on religion.

Freud situated his critique of religion in his over-all psychoanalytic study of culture and its origins. He belongs in the line of Feuerbach, Marx and Nietzsche insofar as he shares their reductionist approach of classifying religion as an illusory projection of human consciousness. His goal, like theirs, was to enable men to emerge from a more primitive or infantile state and thus develop in full freedom and autonomy to maturity and self-actualization. His method was more conjectural than empirical, relying, for example, in two of his three major studies of religion (*Totem and Tabu* and *Moses and Monotheism*), on provisional theories of current ethnology (as in *Totem and Tabu*), or on strongly personal interpretations of biblical data (as in *Moses and Monotheism*) to provide a basis of probability for hypotheses furnished by his highly cultivated psychological intuition.[18] Concerning the third of those studies (*The Future of an Illusion*), he was later to confess: "Now it already seems to me childish . . . I regard it as weak analytically and inadequate as a self-confession."[19]

In *Totem and Tabu*, he traces religion in its supposedly earliest stage of totemism, along with society and morality, to the primordial enactment of the Oedipal conflict, when at the stage of the primitive horde the sons slay and devour the father who has prohibited sexual contact with the females he himself monopolizes. The ritual meal at which the totem is slain and consumed is a memorial re-enactment of this event by which purification and catharsis of guilt-feelings are achieved. The combination of mourning and festivity expresses the ambivalent feelings of love and hatred toward the father. At a greater distance in time from the primal event, the prohibition against killing the totem animal and against incest becomes the initial code of morality, and the totem itself, as the substitute for the father, becomes a god to be worshipped and appeased. In later stages of religious evolution, totemism is left behind, but the sacrifice remains and with it the evermore majestic and transcendent Father-God to whom it is offered in propitiation.

Two events at the origins of Judaism and Christianity re-present the primal traumatic event: the highly conjectural murder of the prophet Moses and the Crucifixion of Christ. The former achieves the triumph of the monotheistic version of the Father-God, derived through Moses from Egyptian sources. The latter, by a transformation that includes a revival of the primitive rivalry of father and sons, achieves the apotheosis of the son in the place of the father. Thus,

> . . . a son-religion displaced the father-religion. As a sign of this substitution the ancient totem meal was revived as a form of communion, in which the company of brothers consumed the flesh and blood of the son—no longer the father—obtained the sanctity thereby and identified themselves with him.[20]

In *The Future of an Illusion*, Freud re-affirmed his interpretation of religion as a longing for the father. In his cultural infancy man is able to face the threatening forces of nature by imagining them to be beings like himself, though superior in power. They are likened to the father whom the child fears, but also reveres as his protector against danger. Thus the identification of the gods with the father has a personal as well as racial prototype. The functions of the gods progress with the progress of civilization itself. From protecting men from the terrors of nature through reconciling them to the cruelty of Fate which is even above the gods, especially to the inevitability of death, the gods are finally charged with motivating men to accept the restrictions which society imposes on them along with the inequities of social living. Christian monotheism as the highest development of religion in its unification of the multiple gods actually "had laid open to view the father who had all along been hidden behind every divine figure as its nucleus."[21]

Freud disavows the intention of assessing the truth value of religious doctrines. It is enough, he is convinced, to "have recognized them as being, in their psychological nature, illusions." He defines an illusion as a belief that is based on a wish-fulfillment. Religion is an illusion which originated in the infancy of the race and which still reflects the attitude of the dependent, helpless infant toward his father. It is, therefore, a human projection, entirely explicable in purely psychological terms, which has served mankind in a less mature past to preserve moral and cultural values. Freud believes that if man is to mature further, he must cast away from this basically neurotic escape into the infant's fantasy world of wish-fulfillment and honestly confront his real world with the only worthy instruments at his command: his reason and the progressive methods of science.

Reflections on Projections

The mighty figure of Freud concludes this view of the major thinkers and their thoughts that have not merely reflected, but have contributed most decisively to the cultural formation of contemporary western man. Our special concern has been to trace the declining influence of Christian theism in that process. We are in a position to reflect and even to respond tentatively by way of intiating dialogue with "unbelievers."

In the beginning we noted that the God of Christian faith tended to be confused in our culture with the ideas of God fashioned by certain influential modern philosophers and to share in the ill-fate of those decidedly imperfect human artifacts. The awareness of this ambiguity at the heart of the historical and cultural process we call the "death of God" has often been overlooked, or at least underestimated. However, we ought not overstate it either. The target of most of the anti-theists from Feuerbach to Freud was the God of Christian faith. Frequently enough they were off target. But their aim was sufficiently accurate to hit that deity in whom many Christians (to all outward appearances) believed: the almighty and beneficent Being Who subserved their needs and fitted their minds.

All of us believers are prone to a little idolatry, and perhaps we should be grateful for the iconoclasts who show us up. Yet the salient facts remain. The God Who died in the mind of the nineteenth century and thereupon in the soul of the twentieth century was an idol, a human construct, regardless of whose trademark it bears. The tragedy is the case of mistaken identity. What was lost was the keen sense of the mighty presence of Him Whose passing is more like the subtle movement of a soft breeze, along with the sensitivity to the divine Mystery which faith infuses into the unobstructed mind.

There is a common theme that unifies the thoughts of these adversaries of God, and a common complaint. The theme is that the God men believe in is, in every instance, a creation of man, on which he projects his own best attributes as well as his aspirations arising out of a life-situation which he often finds unendurable and from whose imperfections he would wish to be delivered. The complaint is that faith in God leads to the alienation of man. It demoralizes him by diverting him with what is unreal and illusory from this real world, which with all its imperfections is his exclusive place and his proper task. He is its only creator and by humanizing it, ordering it after the image of his own mind, he creates himself and achieves the only destiny that is available to him and worthy of him.

We have already echoed the theme in acknowledging that the God Who entered the culture and mind of the West was largely the product of its leading thinkers as well as of its popular lore. Yet Christian faith did not die altogether and the God of faith, though partially concealed behind man-made pretenders, lived on in the lives of countless believers. Was this God, too, merely a human projection? Is all theology, as Feuerbach would insist, only anthropology after all?

We shall attempt to show on the contrary that only a Christian theological anthropology can adequately ground man's self-understanding. But suppose we concede, for the sake of argument, that Christian faith in God does involve the psychological mechanism of projection. Indeed, there is little doubt that it enters to some depth into the belief formation of every believer. The sociology of knowledge, by laying bare the structures and dynamics characteristic of human perspectives, tends to manifest the relativity of all perspectives, of analyses of religion along with the religions analyzed. Thus, as Freud implicitly acknowledges of his own analysis of the religious consciousness,[22] the explanation of any human commitment as a projection does not preclude its claim to truth. Mathematics as one of the more obvious examples of human projection has nevertheless time and again proven its truth-value by its continually verified reflection of the structure of physical reality. This may be so

> . . . because man himself is part of the same over-all reality, so that there is a fundamental affinity between the structures of his consciousness and the structures of the empirical world. Projection and reflection are movements within the same encompassing reality . . .
>
> The same may be true of the projections of man's religious imagination. In any case it would seem that any theological method worthy of the name should be based on this possibility . . . The theological decision will have to be that, "in, with and under" the immense array of human projections there are indications of a reality that is truly "other" and that the religious imagination of man ultimately reflects.[23]

The explanatory hypothesis that the idea of God is a human projection which has become the predominant antitheistic theme since Feuerbach points to a more fundamental theme which, as we shall attempt to document further, is common to all anthropologies, theistic and anti-theistic alike. This is the universal admission that constitutive of and essential to being human is man's drive toward self-transcendence, his ceaseless and insatiable urge to surpass the self that he is at any moment and in any situation. At least since Hegel, this has been at the source of both his grandeur and his self-estrangement, of the infinite potentialities of his evolving historical consciousness and of the temptation to reside in the servile alienated condition of "the unhappy consciousness." Successive anti-theists, into our own time, have interpreted theism as an erroneous and inauthenticating objectification of the boundless horizon of human self-transcendence, whereas theists have recognized in the infinity of man's essential dynamism the subjective human correlate to the Infinite One Who can alone bring man to total and authentic fulfillment.

Thus it becomes clear that man's self-transcendence provides at once the common ground which unites and the crucial issue which divides modern anthropologies and humanisms into theistic and atheistic. The problem is still that posed by Feuerbach: is the God of theistic faith merely the projection of man's own essence, the objectivization of the ideals of his own creation toward which he strives in his constant quest for self-transcendence, or is God the Reality Who corresponds to the innermost aspiration of man's nature and Who is, therefore, the ultimate source of human authenticity? It is on this ground and about this issue that the dialogue which will be the substance of this book will take place.

The Situation of Christians in a Post-Christian Culture

We have been tracing the intellectual ancestry of the post-Christian culture in which we live. In the next chapter, we shall explore some of the more dominant intellectual currents of our own time in an effort to discern the faiths by which twentieth century man lives, the understanding of himself and his world to which he is willing to commit himself as the meaning or meaninglessness of his existence. What remains to be done in this preface to the dialogue is to portray concretely, at least in a few broad strokes, the predicament of the Christian believer in the post-Christian age.

It may seem that what we have been considering has had little relevance to the daily religious lives of average men and the transformation they have been undergoing. But as W. T. Stace observes in a similar context: "This modern world-picture envisaged by a few intellectuals is nevertheless the unconscious background of modern life."[24]

All too often, we who are Christian believers have tended to regard the men whose thought we have been studying as the great non-conformists. The disconcerting truth is that we are the non-conformists and they are the ones whose world-picture has come to form "the unconscious background" of the life-stance of the majority of our contemporaries.

Sociologists of religion have documented statistically the decline in the population of those who profess formal allegiance to the various Christian churches and sects.[25] We have already noted that this trend has advanced much further on the continent of Europe and in England than in the United States, that in fact the opposite tendency prevailed at least for the period following the end of World War II. At present the trend seems to be reversing itself, most significantly among the young and especially on the college campuses.

Yet even the relatively large percentage of church attendance and the considerable residual influence of religion in our national life are phenomena requiring some adroitness of interpretation. For it has been cogently argued that the churches have fulfilled a predominantly social function as the focus of community life for a largely mobile population which was deprived of the natural communities of the more stable traditional societies of Europe.[26] They also serve as an organ for establishing one's identity and status as one enters a more affluent sector of the society. It is maintained too that church affiliation has served as an affirmation of one's identity as an American: to be Catholic, Protestant, or Jew is to adopt one of the three socially sanctioned ways in which one expresses one's identity as an American and one's adherence to the dominant values of our society.

Thus religion becomes not so much the source of the people's values as the reflection of the common denominator of those widest values which have achieved social acceptance. In the mind of the average churchgoer, the doctrinal distinctions of the various faiths are blurred and reduced to nominal significance in contrast to the commonly held tenets of the civil religion, the American heritage or "way of life" which cuts across denominational differences.[27] The extent to which this is true (and even the most optimistic interpretation of the role of religion in American life would have to admit that it is largely true) is the measure of the acculturation of religion, the submitting of Christian faith to the emasculating demands of the culture and society which it has chosen to affirm rather than judge by the exacting norm of the Gospel.

The domestication of Christianity to secular purposes is merely the peculiar form the process of secularization has assumed in our country. On the continent of Europe it was a blatant secularism, often anti-clerical, if not anti-Christian in temper. In England dissent took the form first of non-conformity to the established church, but with the advance of de-Christianization, it has become more frankly a-religious and secularistic. It would appear that the United States is catching up with Europe in this respect as the enthusiasm which accompanied personal commitment to the distinctive beliefs of the various religious groups has waned with their leveling to a common denominator of beliefs.

Pluralism has always characterized the American religious scene, but now the force of the current is in favor of uniformity. In its best form it expresses itself in the ecumenical movement which strives for an authentic unity corresponding to the inner dynamism of Christianity. In its more popular and theologically unreflective form, it expresses itself in the dilution of essential doctrinal differences which are the very ground of the believer's distinctive commitment. Simultaneously, growing numbers, especially among the young as they progress in their education, find the churches, and in consequence the Christian faith as it is officially represented, relatively impotent and lacking relevance to their own personal problems and to the social problems whose solution, to their minds, evokes the noblest challenge and thus the purest human faith of our time.

It would be unfair to portray the religious institutions of our nation as totally subservient to the role of endorsing the popular will and our most widely accepted cultural values. There are enough counter-instances, as in the matter of birth control, abortion or advocacy of "open housing" and other social changes required for full racial equality, to disprove such a generalization. It would likewise be unjust to overlook the large number of believers who are committed with unqualified sincerity to the distinctive tenets of their churches and who would resolutely resist any compromise of them.

Nevertheless, it must be acknowledged with all candor that such believers are a diminishing breed. They are swimming against a rising tide. The dominant current of our culture, rather than supporting them, as it would have in the past, threatens to submerge them. The day of mass Christianity, of mass Catholicism is over, even on this continent. Social pressure no longer coerces the irresolute to adopt a Christian identity for protective coloration. It is perfectly respectable to be non-religious, and in certain circles, especially among the intellectuals, it is quite disreputable or at least eccentric to be anything else. It would appear that we are fast approaching in this country the situation which already obtains in most of Europe where believers pursue their distinctive commitments on the fringes rather than at the heart of the world in which they live.

Cultural Christianity, that is, the allegiance of masses of people to the Christian Church as the practically exclusive mode in which to maintain one's identity and social status in a predominantly Christian society as well as to confer meaning on one's own existence in a culture or world of meaning formed by an inherited Christian faith, is all but dead. There are some outposts, like Ireland, for example, where this may not yet be true, but in all of the larger and more influential nations that comprise the traditionally Christian West, neither the society nor the culture imposes a Christian identity on its members. Becoming or remaining a Christian has moved more and more towards being one option among others which must be freely made and sustained rather than being a status that is constantly impressed by the bias of the society and a heritage that is nurtured by the culture.

In nominally Christian countries, Christian believers have become, in Peter Berger's term, a "cognitive minority," by which he means

> a group of people whose view of the world differs significantly from the one generally taken for granted in their society . . . a group formed around a body of deviant "knowledge" (in the sense of) what is taken to be or believed as "knowledge."[28]

The minority status of Christian believers is due to "the demise of the supernatural" in our culture which is credited to the process of secularization that has affected not only social institutions as in the separation of Church and State, but man's consciousness itself.

The status of a cognitive minority is an uncomfortable one because we rely on others to confirm our own beliefs, to maintain their plausibility even in our own minds. Beliefs that are constantly being challenged, at least implicitly, by the majority of those around us, are in constant peril and, even in those of strong minds and conviction, in incessant danger of erosion.

> The predictable conclusion of the unequal struggle is . . . the progressive disintegration of the plausibility of the challenged "knowledge" in the consciousness of the one holding it.[29]

Assuming the continuation of the secularizing trend, believers as a cognitive minority will be facing more and more urgently the fundamental option of choosing to hang on or to surrender their cognitive deviation. The choice of hanging on involves the maintenance of a strong counter-community, equivalent to an intellectual ghetto. This lives in tension with the larger society from which it tries to keep itself closed off, and it must make strong claims on the loyalty and solidarity of its members. However, our society is not conducive to such a closed system of belief, but rather tends increasingly to favor an open system of commitments in competition and communication with one another. In addition, Christianity, and in particular Catholicism, is a universalist creed relying on social structures. Under such circumstances, maintaining defiance and deviation becomes less and less feasible as an enduring posture.

The opposite alternative is surrender. It is not labeled as such; rather it is called: translation into modern idiom, making faith relevant, demythologizing. The result becomes much the same: a gradual evacuation of all supernatural elements, a transmutation from so-called "other-worldly" to "this-worldly" terms: secularized Christianity. As this trend continues, it tends to escalate, since the stronger factor at all times is the secular culture to which the concessions are being made. In the end, it becomes self-defeating because the reasons for retaining the "Christian" label decreases as the distinction from a purely secular humanism becomes more and more tenuous, less and less defensible.

It is also subject to a kind of law of diminishing returns. Especially in a secular culture that is itself the victim of abrupt and often unpredictable shifts, the "timely" quickly becomes the irrelevant. Thus, for example, the "Secular City" celebrated by Harvey Cox as the contemporary locus of the Kingdom of God has become instead the focus of racial and youthful frustrations, and Cox has opted successively for a less secular theology of eschatological hope and then of playful celebration. Meanwhile, there have been out-croppings of supernaturalism under other than Christian auspices: astrology, Yoga, what have you!

Berger feels that there are other options than the ones he has canvassed. They involve different answers because they imply a rephrasing of the questions. Thus, they imply the priority of truth over timeliness as a value to be cultivated. For "genuine timeliness means sensitivity to one's socio-historical starting point, *not* fatalism about one's possible destination."[30] They also require an indifference to one's majority or minority status, tied to a creative belief that one can free oneself from the mass assumptions of one's time. For him this liberating function, as we have noted (cf. above p. 40), is performed by the sociology of knowledge. By explaining the social structures and dynamisms which support the plausibility of any commitment, this science tends to relativize not only religious but all commitments, including those of the secularist or atheist who attempts to explain away religious belief in the supernatural. What is more, the relativizing analysis is applicable even to the factual condition of contemporary consciousness inasmuch as it finds itself incapable of a belief in the transcendent or the supernatural. For after the empirical data descriptive of such a consciousness have received sociological diagnosis and the timeliness or relevance of belief in the supernatural for such a consciousness has been established, the more fundamental issue of the truth of such belief remains untouched and unresolved.

> One (perhaps literally) redeeming feature of sociological perspective is that relativizing analysis, in being pushed to its final consequence, bends back upon itself. The relativizers are relativized, the debunkers are debunked—indeed, relativization itself is somehow liquidated. What follows is **not**, as some of the early sociologists of knowledge feared, a total paralysis of thought. Rather, it is a new freedom and flexibility in asking questions of truth.[31]

And so, when truth rather than relevance is once again clearly seen to be the ultimate value, religious faith can get back into business again.

Knowledge, as a human function, has an ecstatic power. This is a manifestation of what we have already referred to (and shall continue to call attention to) as man's unique potency for self-transcendence. Erich Kahler has called this "spirit" and has identified it as the essential human quality: "man's faculty of going beyond himself, of transcending the limits of his own physical being."[32] Berger himself believes that within the empirically given human situation are certain phenomena called "signals of transcendence," which are found within the normal, everyday world of human beings but which appear to point beyond that reality. These are typical human situations, events, or gestures which provide the basis in our experience for an induction of faith and include ordering gestures, the phenomenon of play, and man's "unconquerable propensity to hope for the future." Faith interprets these as indicators or signs of a reality that is truly "other" or supernatural. Whatever the merit of his reasoning, Berger is assured that the most fruitful starting point for theology as the justification of religious faith is the study of man and his consciousness.

The study of man and his consciousness is the unavoidable point of departure for theology today because the contemporary crisis of faith can only be properly understood within the wider context of the crisis of culture of which it is a symptom. Anyone who doubts this ought to be convinced by the world-wide magnitude of the youth rebellion which is directed not only against the institutional church but against every established institution—political, social, as well as ecclesiastical.

At the root of this all-but-culturally-universal phenomenon is the significant shift in human consciousness, of man's perception of himself and his world whose own sources we have to some extent outlined in this chapter. Human consciousness in this sense develops in continual reciprocity with the culture in which it exists. It is at once the product of that culture and the producer of it.

For countless ages, cultural progress and therefore the corresponding developments in human consciousness were sparse and laborious. The scientific revolution initiated in the seventeenth century and the technological revolution that followed in the nineteenth and twentieth centuries radically changed not only our cultural environment, but human consciousness itself. Once again it was a matter of reciprocity, for it was human consciousness that produced those revolutions; yet except for the genuises that created them, it was the cultures that played the more active role in molding the consciousnesses of those who lived out their existences within them.

The pace of change has continued to accelerate with every decade, so that only a few years account for a new generation gap. The current "generation gap" can be understood as a familiar and intimately experienced sign of this more profound change. For the young are obviously those who will be influenced the most by the current condition and style of culture and reflective of its impact; their elders will have been formed in an earlier stage.

A perfectly intelligible interpretation of the widespread rebellion of youth is the uneasiness and dissatisfaction they feel, often sub-consciously, with a culture which reflects an earlier and obsolescent stage of consciousness and which they reject and want with typical impetuosity to change suddenly and violently. They desire institutions, political, social, and religious, that reflect the new human self-image and self-understanding which they experience in themselves and which most faithfully mirror the revised cultural situation in which Western man now lives. By the same token they are searching for a faith that is authentic in that it can ground and give purposive direction to the human persons they feel themselves to be. In the following chapter we shall describe some of the most influential faiths that contend for the allegiance of men in our age.

Notes and references

1 William G. McLoughlin, "How is America Religious?" in **Religion in America,** ed. by William G. McLoughlin and Robert N. Bellah (Boston: Beacon Press, 1968), p. x.

2 G. Vahanian, **The Death of God,** pp. 3-11.

3 Paul Ramsey, "Preface" to **The Death of God** by G. Vahanian, p. xxix.

[4] Ludwig Feuerbach, **The Essence of Christianity**, translated by George Eliot (New York: Harper and Row, 1957).

[5] Henri de Lubac, **The Drama of Atheistic Humanism** (New York: Sheed and Ward, 1950), p. 12.

[6] Cf. James Collins, **God in Modern Philosophy** (Chicago: Henry Regnery Co., 1959).

[7] Feuerbach, **The Essence of Christianity**, p. 14.

[8] **Marx and Engels: Basic Writings on Politics and Philosophy**, Lewis S. Feuer, ed., (Garden City, N.Y.: Doubleday, 1959), p. 245.

[9] "Toward the Critique of Hegel's Philosophy of Right," ibid., pp. 262-263.

[10] **Ibid.**, p. 263.

[11] Hajor Holborn, "Wilhelm Dilthey and the Critique of Historical Reason," in **European Intellectual History Since Darwin and Marx**, ed. by W. W. Wagar (New York: Harper & Row, 1967), p. 71. Cf. also, Anton Donoso, "Wilhelm Dilthey's Contribution to the Philosophy of History," in **Philosophy Today** Vol 12, (Fall, 1968), pp. 151-163.

[12] H. P. Rickman, **Wilhelm Dilthey: Meaning and Pattern in History** (New York: Harper & Row, 1961), p. 59.

[13] **Ibid.**, p. 58.

[14] Paul Ricoeur, "The Atheism of Freudian Psychoanalysis" in **Is God Dead?**, Series 1, **Concilium** Vol 16 (New York: Paulist Press, 1966), p. 61.

[15] Gregory Zilboorg, M.D., **Psychoanalysis and Religion** (London: Allen & Unwin, 1967), pp. 196-243.

[16] Sigmund Freud, "Obsessive Acts and Religious Practices" in **Collected Papers II**, (New York: Basic Books, 1959), pp. 25-35.

[17] **Ibid.**, p. 34.

[18] E. Jones, **The Life and Work of Sigmund Freud** (Garden City, N.Y.: Doubleday, 1963), pp. 280-281.

[19] **Ibid.**, p. 460.

[20] Sigmund Freud, **Totem and Tabu** trans. by James Strachey (New York: W. W. Norton & Co., Inc., 1950), p. 154.

[21] Freud, **The Future of an Illusion**, ed. by James Strachey, (Garden City, N.Y.: Doubleday, Anchor Books, 1964), p. 27.

[22] **Ibid.**, p. 52.

[23] Peter Berger, **A Rumor of Angels** (Garden City, N.Y.: Doubleday, 1969), pp. 58-59.

[24] W. T. Stace, **Religion and the Modern Mind** (Philadelphia: J. B. Lippincott Co., 1952), p. 97.

[25] Bryan Wilson, **Religion in Secular Society** (Baltimore: Penguin, 1969), A statistical study of the decline in formal church affiliation in England as contrasted with the situation in the United States.

[26] **Ibid.**, pp. 139-141.

[27] Will Herberg, **Protestant, Catholic, Jew** (Garden City, N.Y.: Doubleday, 1955).

[28] Berger, **A Rumor of Angels**, p. 7.

[29] **Ibid.**, p. 9.

[30] **Ibid.**, p. 33.

[31] **Ibid.**, pp. 52-53.

[32] Erich Kahler, **Man the Measure** (Cleveland: World Publishing Co.,

1943), p. 11.

Balthasar, Hans Urs von. *The God Question and Modern Man.* Tr. Hilda Graef. New York: Seabury, 1967.

Berger, Peter L. *A Rumor of Angels.* Garden, City, N.Y.: Doubleday, 1969.

Burkle, Howard R. *The Non-Existence of God. Anti-Theism from Hegel to Duméry.* New York: Herder & Herder, 1969.

Collins, James. *God in Modern Philosophy.* Chicago: Henry Regnery, 1959.

Collins, James. *The Emergence of Philosophy of Religion.* New Haven: Yale University Press, 1967.

Culture of Unbelief, The. Ed. R. Caporale and A. Grumelli. Berkeley: University of California Press, 1971.

Dilthey, Wilhelm. *Pattern and Meaning in History.* Ed. and with introduction by H. P. Rickman. New York: Harper & Row, 1962.

Duméry, Henry. *The Problem of God in Philosophy of Religion.* Tr. Charles Courtney. Evanston, Ill.: Northwestern University Press, 1964.

Evans, Robert A. *Belief and the Counter-Culture.* Philadelphia: Westminster, 1971.

Fabro, Cornelio. *God in Exile: Modern Atheism.* Ed. and Trans. Arthur Gibson. Glen Rock, N.J.: Newman, 1968.

Feuerbach, Ludwig. *The Essence of Christianity.* Tr. George Eliot. Introduction by Karl Barth. New York: Harper & Row, 1957.

Freud, Sigmund. *The Future of an Illusion.* Ed. James Strachey. Garden City, N.Y.: Doubleday, 1957.

Freud, Sigmund. *Totem and Taboo.* Ed. and trans. James Strachey. New York: W. W. Norton, 1950.

God Knowable and Unknowable. Ed. Robert J. Roth, S.J. New York: Fordham University Press, 1973.

Hegel, G. W. F. *The Phenomenology of Mind.* Tr. J. B. Baillie. New York: Harper & Row, 1967.

Is God Dead? Ed. J. B. Metz. New York: Paulist, 1966.

Lubac, Henri de. *The Drama of Atheist Humanism.* New York: Sheed & Ward, 1950.

Luijpen, William, and Koren, Henry J. *Religion and Atheism.* Pittsburgh: Duquesne University Press, 1971.

Mackey, James P. *The Problems of Religious Faith.* Dublin: Helicon Ltd., 1972.

Masterson, Patrick. *Atheism and Alienation.* Dublin: Gill & Macmillan, 1971.

Marx and Engels: Basic Writings on Politics and Philosophy. Ed. L. S. Feuer. Garden City, N.Y.: Doubleday, 1959.

New Questions on God. Ed. J. B. Metz. New York: Herder & Herder, 1972.

Nietzsche, Freiedrich. *The Portable Nietzsche.* Ed. W. Kaufmann. New York: Viking, 1954.

"Pastoral Constitution on the Church in the Modern World, *Gaudium et Spes,*" in *The Documents of Vatican II.* Gen. Ed. Walter M. Abbott. New York: American Press, 1966, pp. 183-308.

Persistence of Religion, The. Ed. Andrew Greeley and Gregory Baum. New York: Herder & Herder, 1973.

Presence and Absence of God, The. Ed. Christopher Mooney, S.J. New York: Fordham University Press, 1969.

Reid, John. *Man Without God.* An Introduction to Unbelief. Philadelphia: Westminster, 1971.

Religion in America. Ed. Wm. G. McLoughlin and R. N. Bellah. Boston: Beacon, 1968

Religion of the Republic, The. Ed. Elwyn Al Smith. Philadelphia: Fortress, 1971.

Thils, Gustave. *A "Non-Religious" Christianity.* Staten Island, N.Y.: Alba House, 1970.

Vahanian, Gabriel. *The Death of God.* New York: George Braziller, 1961.

Woods, Richard, O.P. *The Occult Revolution: A Christian Meditation.* New York: Herder & Herder, 1971.

/ 2 /

Atheistic Humanism

Existentialist Humanism

Existentialist Humanism, perhaps the most typical expression of the temper of the first half of this century, has been both theistic and non-theistic, when not explicitly atheistic. All Existentialists have been Kantian, even the theists, in denying human intelligence the power to demonstrate God's existence by objective rational methods. All of them have accepted "the death of God" bequeathed to them by the nineteenth century. The atheists do so by asserting it as a postulate for their consequent affirmations about man; the theists by acknowledging atheism as an alternative option to theism, though a mistaken one, since it rests on a refusal to make the free commitment to the One Who is the absolute ground of our personal being which a philosophical reflection on our free but participated being should uncover. Our first interest is in the former group because they articulate a faith for contemporary man that rivals Christian faith and repudiates it for being inauthentic.

A.   EDMUND HUSSERL

The most powerful forms of non-theistic Existentialism were born from the phenomenological movement and therefore must claim descent from its founder, Edmund Husserl (1859-1938). This claim has been disputed by those who say that the existentialists misread Husserl and employed his thought and method to establish positions contrary to his basic intentions. These counter-claims may never be definitively resolved since there appears to be an internal ambiguity in Husserl's own thought. In any event, the historical factuality of the parentage is certain, whether its legitimacy can be ascertained or not.

Husserl's phenomenological enterprise was the founding of philosophy as a strict presuppositionless science. He went about trying to accomplish this by a rigorously disciplined investigation of experience to lay bare the essential structures of that experience which the constructions of science and common sense themselves derive from and therefore must take for granted.

Husserl called for a "return to things themselves," but the "things" are no more the objects of our experience taken as things in themselves than they are the conscious subjects, conceived à la Descartes, as isolated or enclosed egos. It is rather experience or consciousness itself as the meeting place of subject and object, for knowledge is always "knowledge of." From Aristotle through Brentano, Husserl was led to rediscover and re-emphasize the intentionality of knowledge, its essential relatedness to an object. It is inescapably noetic—noematic in structure: that is, it is in every instance a subject's act (*noesis*) inherently co-related with an object (*noema*). This is the *phenomenon,* not in the sense of mere appearance, but as the originative and normative occurrence of experience to which every other form of knowledge is radically "reducible." The radical and presuppositionless character of the reduction is underlined in Husserl's resort to the "bracketing of being" which involves in his mind a setting aside of judgments, whether scientific or common sense, concerning the existential status assigned to it.[1] It is allowed to appear as itself in its immediate givenness.

> The whole secret of phenomenological method, as conceived by Husserl, is that it is a laborious process wherein objects are brought to "self-givenness" in intuition.[2]

Husserl goes beyond both idealism and realism in his notion of "constitution," whereby the consciousness grasps itself as "constituting" the meaning of the world. For consciousness of meaning is necessarily consciousness giving meaning.[3] Yet consciousness is intentional.

> The object or the thing (the world) is already given, essentially tied to consciousness by intentionality. In other words, the world gives itself to consciousness which confers on it its meaning.[4]

The world is always there as a pre-given for consciousness. The process of bracketing or the epoché achieves the reduction to the essential elements of immediate experience to allow the laborious explicit recovery of the process by which the pre-given world is constituted by consciousness in its developed meaning.[5]

The idealistic interpretation of Husserl tends to emphasize the transcendental reduction as yielding the "transcendental Ego," a pure impersonal consciousness at the root of individual experience which actively constitutes "the world" in all its determinateness and meaning. The existentialists, like Merleau-Ponty, focus on what they interpret as the trend of his later writings, such as *Philosophy and the Crisis of European Man*. In these he stresses the *Lebenswelt*, the immediate object of experience which is prior to any thought about experience and which is the necessary point of origin to which more developed forms of knowledge are to be reduced. In this interpretation, the phenomenological reduction leads us back from the derived world of science and common sense to the primordial world of lived immediate experience (*Lebenswelt*), shorn of its cultural accretions and developed interpretations. Here the emphasis, rather than on the Transcendental Ego and its constitutive activity, is on the intentional correlation between the subject and the world toward which it is ever referred in an active-passive attitude. Thus the world can only receive its meaning because of its relation to consciousness, yet the subject is itself constituted as subject on account of its active involvement with a world that is given to it as object. By the same token, the subject and human consciousness partake of the temporal and historical character of the world which is its constant intentional correlate.

B. MARTIN HEIDEGGER

Husserl's willingness to employ such themes in his later writings which appeared after the publication of Heidegger's *Being and Time* points to, though it certainly does not prove, an influence of his student's thought on his own. For in that work the younger man characterizes the essential mode of human existence as "being-in-the-world" (*in-der-welt-sein*)[6] and underlines the historicity of human consciousness.

Heidegger had been Husserl's assistant at the University of Freiburg and, at his mentor's request, succeeded to his chair of philosophy at his retirement in 1928. This was in spite of their growing disagreement on the task of philosophy. Heidegger was convinced of the fruitfulness of the phenomenological method and its necessity for philosophical work, but he could not accept the phenomenological reduction as a "bracketing of Being" or the study of man as a pure consciousness. For Heidegger, philosophy had to be the study of Being and therefore a phenomenological *Ontology*.

Thus the return "to the things themselves" urged by Husserl led Heidegger not to a "pure consciousness" as the primitive and irreducible context of experience, but to a pre-conceptual awareness which already discloses man as fundamentally related to his world. Rather than "bracketing Being" he is convinced that existence is inescapably present from the beginning as man's primordial experience of "being-in-the-world." This experience as integral is prior to the subject-object dichotomy which arises in consciousness out of man's precedent awareness of being-with and being-in-a-world. This structure is revealed not only in intuitive theoretical consciousness, which was Husserl's special area of investigation, but in the pre-cognitive awareness that accompanies man's practical concern with things and his relations with other persons.

Heidegger's primary objective therefore is an elucidation of Being, the perennial goal of philosophy's search for understanding and wisdom which has proven so elusive because so consistently misconceived and misdirected. It is in pursuing his objective that he elaborates his conception of man whom he understands always in the perspective of Being. His philosophy becomes inevitably an ontology of *Dasein* or human existence because it is in the existent which man is that Being comes to be unconcealed. Being (*Sein*) is that by which a being (*seiendes*) is. Truth (Greek: *a-lētheia* = un-concealment, non-oblivion) is the unconcealing, revealing of what a being is. Being is the process of unconcealment or revelation. Man, whose being is *Da-sein* (There-being), is that unique being to whom and for whom the revelation is made, who, as it were, provides the locus and thereby lets the Being-process take place.[7] It is in human thought that this response to Being occurs, though man is not capable of comprehending Being except in terms of beings. As a consequence he is open to the chronic threat of the forgetfulness of Being.

As against his compatriot, Karl Jaspers, Heidegger believes therefore in the possibility of an ontology of existence developed from an analysis of its essential structure disclosed in the concrete historical existence of man. Thus the exclusive access to being is by way of human existence which is intrinsically historical and therefore constituted by temporal modes of being. The investigation of Being necessarily takes the form of an historical hermeneutic or interpretation and the truth of Being is sought and found within man's history and as developed in the modes of his temporality. Thus the theme of man's historicity, so prominent in Hegel and especially in Dilthey, becomes absolutely central in Heidegger, who passes beyond Dilthey in making it constitutive of man's very existence as *Dasein*.

Dasein is disclosed to be finite transcendence whose ultimate meaning is time. It is transcendent because it passes beyond the level where beings are differentiated among themselves and in terms of the subject-object polarity (the ontic level) to the Being of beings, that is, to the being-process that lets them be what they are (the ontological level). This transcendence is finite because *Dasein* is not creative of itself or others, but finds itself in a world into which it has, as it were, been cast or thrown. It is constituted in function of its relations with the persons and things of this world and by its very essence is propelled toward death as the termination of its possibilities. Finally it is time that confers meaning on *Dasein* as finite transcendence insofar as it is the source of its unity and constitutes the modes of its being.

Basic to man's essentially temporal being is the disposition called Care (*Sorge*), which is an ontological structure of man's essence and not merely a psychological attitude. Accordingly man's very essence is disclosed in his fundamental posture of care or concern about the kind of being he is. As finite transcendence realizing itself in temporal modes, *Dasein* is a project, that is, a being who is continually being constituted by a drive beyond beings toward Being whereby he is constantly coming to be himself. As a project, man is always future oriented, engaged in a coming to himself, but he is also projected, that is, thrown, and thereby the self he comes to be already is as having been thrown, and thus it involves his past. What Heidegger is stressing here is the reciprocity of past and future.

(Man's) coming is to a self that already is-as-having-been to such an extent that its coming is a type of return; on the other hand, (man's being) is what it has been only as long as the future continues to come.[8]

Accordingly, man *is* not merely; as finite transcendence he exists (*ex-sistit*), he "stands out from." He stands out not merely from the world of things, but he can be said to stand out from himself to whom he can be related, for example, by self-understanding or self-misunderstanding, by self-integration or self-alienation. In other words, he is capable of being authentically or inauthentically, that is, of accepting himself for what he is and accordingly relating himself to others, or of forgetting or neglecting his true nature and thereby distorting his relations to the world in which he has his being. Thus, as essentially temporal, he is, unlike things, never complete, but in his very being always *underway* and on the conscious level laden in his freedom with the responsibility of constituting what he is to be by his decisions.

Moreover, from the outset his existence is a transcendence towards a world in which he is already constituted, but which he has the care of constituting in the reciprocal process by which he is himself ever being constituted. Therefore man as *Dasein* constitutes the world characteristically by illuminating it, by disclosing the various modes by which he is present and related to the things of the world. The modes of the presence of most things, especially those of nature, are to be merely at hand (*Vorhandenheit*). It is especially over against this mode of being that man's unique being as *Dasein* is distinguished (*Existenz*). However, man's concern with things is revealed in the first instance in their mode of being as utensils or tools serving the projects of his everyday needs (*Zuhandenheit*).

The paramount truth is that man is not merely a thing, his being is not that of just being at hand (*Vorhandenheit*). He is not only one instance of a class whose essence can be adequately accounted for by general statements. Rather he is that unique being who, thrown into existence in the world, finds himself with the ceaseless care of disclosing the identity and meaning of that world in the very process by which his own is being constituted. He is the shepherd, the tender of Being, the clearing in the forest of things in which the light of Being shines through. Only at the risk of inauthenticity, of untruth, can he settle back into the passivity of thinghood, into the anonymity of the crowd whose decisions are mass-produced by others and whose lives are propelled by other forces. He is responsible for his own life and, within his individual finiteness, for his own world. To be authentic and faithful to his own being, he must actively assume the care of both his life and his world and thus unveil the Being that each conceals. Moreover, he must do so in the face of their tragi-comic ambiguities and, ever and above all, in the lengthening shadow of his personal death whose final annihilation of the temporal project of his existence he directly confronts and freely incorporates into that very project.

Heidegger's hermeneutic of Being by way of *Dasein*-analysis has borne rich fruits in psychology, biblical theology, the philosophy of language and numerous other areas. In psychology it has contributed to the development of the school of existential psychoanalysis, specifically to the *Dasein*-*analyse* of Ludwig Binswanger and his associates. In biblical theology, Bultmann's monumental project of demythologization is a translation of the Christ-event and man's redemption into the contemporary idiom of Heidegger's portrait of human authenticity as delineated in his *Being and Time*. The post-Bultmannians, such as Fuchs and Ebeling, have chosen the later writings of Heidegger that have emphasized the revelation of Being to man especially in the primal understanding that articulates itself in language and the 'word' to provide a vehicle for interpreting the biblical word and the Incarnate Word as a saving revelation event for man which has historical roots in the Jesus of history.

Heidegger has steadfastly refused to identify Being with God, especially in the usual terms of His identification with *a* being, albeit the Supreme Being. The inquiry into God he regards as a theological and not a philosophical enterprise, and so he has remained silent about God. In this sense, he has challenged theologians to apply the fruits of his demolition of metaphysics as a merely ontic science of beings and his ontological disclosure of Being to the theological question. As we shall see, many thought it fruitful and worthwhile to attempt to respond to his challenge.[9]

C.   JEAN PAUL SARTRE

Foremost among those who have employed the phemonenological method in the exploration of existentialist themes are Jean-Paul Sartre and Maurice Merleau-Ponty. The converging and diverging lines that relate their two careers are an intriguing disclosure of how the similar projects of their lives as thinkers and men of action would follow arrestingly different paths. Both set out to prosecute Husserl's program of a rigorous phenomenology of human experience and its reduction to its primal components, and both, rejecting Husserl's transcendental idealism, would uncover human consciousness originally engaged in an existential involvement with the world. Yet their understanding of man, his consciousness, and his relation with his world would emerge as almost contrary positions.

Sartre proposed to carry forward the intentions of both

Husserl and Heidegger, whose thought he had mastered, but he departed creatively from the direction of each. He pushed the phenomenological reduction beyond the Transcendental Ego of Husserl and the *Dasein* of Heidegger to a pure consciousness which is prior to any ego. It is "being-for-itself" (*l'être-pour-soi*) which is sheer subjectivity or intending activity for which everything is object, including the ego. "Being-for-itself" is always intending what it is not by which it is alone defined. Of itself, it is devoid of content, it is "nothingness," since every content, anything that is merely itself, "being-in-itself" (*l'être-en-soi*), is object for it and therefore exterior to it.

Thus for Sartre, man is that being through which nothingness comes into the world. That is both the price and the glory of human consciousness which is ever conscious of what it is not insofar as it incessantly negates mere thingness or "being-in-itself" as its own being. As a result it is absolutely intentional, always orientated toward what is other than itself. As the *Dasein* for Heidegger, so the "being-for-itself" *ex-sists*, is perpetually transcending itself towards the other. Sartre expresses this in the axiom that Heidegger does not make his own: "Existence precedes essence." By it the French philosopher stresses the "nothingness" of consciousness, its lack of thingness or of the opacity of content. For it, essence is that which it is ever transcending, with which it is never coincident. Therefore, human consciousness as ex-sistence can never be founded in an essence, in a "being-in-itself," not even in an Ego; it can only continually found itself as a ceaseless project nihilating what is.

As founding itself and as founded in no-thing, consciousness is identical with freedom. It is not determined by any-thing, but rather everything can become involved in its project, in what it proposes to do and to be. To be determined would be to be reduced to the passivity of a thing. Consciousness is pure spontaneity, irreducible to the passivity of that which is merely itself, tending rather to regard all else as the passive object of its intention and of the meaning it would confer on it.

Man as consciousness can never settle into coinciding

with himself, much less coinciding with an idea of himself. He is always becoming, always engaged in the project of choosing the self he is to be. We are constantly being tempted to settle down into a secure, fixed identity: to be a waiter, a postman, to be a lazy person or an industrious one, but in every instance to be merely something. We are also tempted, as Heidegger himself had warned, to submit to the conventional standards and opinions of others, "what everyone thinks." But these are all forms of inauthenticity, of seeking to escape the inescapable burden of our freedom to which we are condemned as men.[10]

Inauthenticity or bad faith, the desire of a consciousness, the "being-for-itself," to escape the human condition and to achieve the stable security of things, the "being-in-itself" which is always what it is, its own cause and foundation, is one facet of the fundamental human project, which is to constitute oneself as an identification of both conditions of being. To unite the self-caused and self-founded being of things in their completeness and repose with the freedom and the capacity to confer meaning and value that is proper to "being-for-itself," in other words, to become God: this is the passion which ultimately constitutes man. "In-itself-for-itself" is impossible. Yet each man pursues this general human goal in the concreteness of his individual situation within which he continually improvises the project of his existence and his personality.[11]

Sartre is echoing a familiar theme: the inevitability and the futility of man's belief in God. He confers on it an added poignancy and intensity by diagnosing it as the passion which drives man toward divine self-identity as his fundamental human project. Like Feuerbach, he discovers the ideal essence of man in the projected idea of God. The tragic note peculiar to Sartre is that the ideal essence of man is an impossible dream.

D. MAURICE MERLEAU-PONTY

Sartre's latter years have been devoted to the attempt to reconcile his conception of man as the absolute individual subjectivity whose essence is freedom and his profound concern for the workers whose only salvation lies in the collective solidarity of the Communist Revolution. He has attempted the theoretical union of both these concerns in his *Critique de la Raison Dialectique*. It is disputable whether he has succeeded.[12] Some of the most incisive criticisms of this effort came from the pen of Maurice Merleau-Ponty (1908-1961), his friend and fellow editor of *Les Temps Modernes*.[13] Besides opposing certain concessions to a totalitarian relation between the Communist Party and the worker, the younger man brings to light his own fundamentally different views of man and the world.

Merleau-Ponty sees in Sartre's radical duality of "being-for-itself" and "being-in-itself" of man and things, an obstacle to the dialectical union of man and his world which he hoped to achieve. Sartre has made individual human consciousness an absolute which resists incorporation into a social unity except on the individual's own terms and which fails to transcend its own isolation and thereupon sufficiently ground the intersubjective relation which authentic social unity demands.

Merleau-Ponty's own basic philosophical commitment was in favor of the radical contingency of the human situation and against all absolutes, wherever they appear, even in the human subjectivity. Sartre has pushed the phenomenological reduction to the nihilation of every content in consciousness, including the Ego and the world. This movement of withdrawal was succeeded by a reverse movement of intentional engagement with the world in creative decision and action. Under the impact of criticism, including Merleau-Ponty's own, he was to strive for a consciousness "which is situated in the world and which through its negation posits things and englobes them in a dialectical appropriation."[14]

Merleau-Ponty's reduction led him in an opposite direction from a pure consciousness to an original human body-subject in which the subject and the world are mutually co-present. Rather than uncovering a translucent subject over against an opaque "being-in-itself," his reduction discloses our existence as a pre-conscious "being-in-the-world" which is primordially dark and obscure and which can never be wholly brought to light. Philosophical reflection can reveal this original obscurity, but it cannot ever overcome it completely. The philosopher has to acknowledge this ambiguity as indigenous to the human situation and therefore to forego any ambition to achieve completeness in his understanding of man or his world. In fact, any attempt to explain or understand must presuppose the subject's "being-in-the-world" as its antecedent. Though it can be recognized, it escapes explanation. As a result, man's condition is radically contingent and free; he does not derive his meaning from anything or anyone else. Rather in the social human world structured by language, he constructs meaning in a common human history which is itself contingent and open to novelty and to ever fresh interpretation.

The contingent free human subject resists every explanation, whether naturalistic or theistic. He would insist that a theistic view of man inevitably views his contingent freedom as dependent on God as the Necessary Being. To Merleau-Ponty's mind, this is precisely to do away with man's contingency by attributing it to a divine antecedent. In spite of this stand, he refused to be called an atheist. For atheism, or at least anti-theism or positive atheism, he would hold, is itself a theological rather than a philosophical position, since it accepts the theological problematic and removes itself from the province of the philosopher.[15]

When Merleau-Ponty died in 1961 he was engaged in an intriguing though still tentative revision of his thought which is adumbrated in the posthumous publication *The Visible and the Invisible*[16] and hinted at in several articles published before his death.[17] Suggested in these writings and working notes is a new "turn" in his thinking in the direction of a philosophy of Being, which bears certain resemblances to that of Heidegger. Contingency is no longer the final word about the human situation. The dialectical relationship of man and the world as the matrix out of which meaning arises is now situated within the more fundamental and primordial context of the unity of Being.

The intentional intimacy of man and the world receives even stronger emphasis, but now in terms of a precedent, pre-intentional unity of Being. They belong to each other (*en-être*), man to the world and the world to man, not only as essentially correlated, but as permeated by the same primal reality. This original unity of Being cannot be perceived or observed directly, since it is prior to the subject-object distinction and is rather the horizon or field within which subject and object, man and the world, are perceivable figures, knowable phenomena. Within that field man and his world intimately compenetrate so that man can be called the humanization of the world, the world having come to itself.

Thus the world can be said to have an "invisible" or "spiritual" side. This is man's own spirit which is in effect the revelation of spirituality as a primary possibility of the world. As "body-subject," however, it is still in his body that man is in the world, that the field of Being, in which their unity is rooted, is manifested. For "the flesh of the body" is the same as "the flesh of the world," they are in a relation of "overlapping."[18] The "perceived world" is the visible unity of the body as perceiving subject and the world, including the body, as being-perceived. "All this is finally possible and means something because *there is* Being"[19] which is related to the world as invisible to visible. Being, which is the common source of all that is visible and perceptible, subject and object, is not directly visible but rather co-appears in everything that appears, hiding itself as it constitutes the visibility of all that is perceived. By the same token, it acts in every activity and thus in the act of the perceiver. It is knowable therefore not directly or frontally but laterally. It is the field which makes the figures within it visible, but not being itself a figure, it is not itself directly visible.

We exist together in Being, we belong to the world and the world to us in the community of Being. We share a common knowledge and can communicate with each other because all of us have access to the same Being. Being speaks in all philosophies, past and present, which are therefore so many perspectives on the same Being. Thus despite their differences and their relativity, all philosophies cohere as perceptions of the same Being and are so many expressions of a philosophy which is immanent to the history of philosophy and which can rightfully be called "absolute."

The contingency of man's "being-in-the-world" as the primary source of meaning and therefore removed from explanation in terms of any prior cause, including God as the the Necessary Being, is no longer the final truth of Merleau-Ponty's philosophical reflection. The relationship of man and his world presupposes the more basic unity of Being within which it is situated. To the end he declined to incorporate the theological problematic within his philosophical enterprise, but his former objections to the existence of God, based on the contingency of the human situation, had lost their foundations in his more recent thought. His own later life along with certain ambiguous allusions in his writings suggest that, while rejecting the God of the philosophers, he may have opened himself to the God of Abraham, Isaac, and Jacob, and of Christ.

E. RESUMÉ AND REFLECTIONS

Does any coherent understanding of man as a form of human faith emerge from the study of these four men that can contribute to a productive dialogue with a Christian believer? It seems to me that there is.

In reaffirming the intentionality of human consciousness, Husserl not only revived an ancient insight, but gave it creative vigor in a thoroughly modern setting. Man is not isolated from the world in an enclosed consciousness so that contact between man and his world is a thesis to be justified. Rather, knower and known so compenetrate that their distinction calls for an uncovering and an elucidation. Knowledge is always "knowledge of," the knower is always towards and for another.

The three thinkers who followed Husserl at once released and redirected the creative force of this insight. For Heidegger, man is "being-in-the-world" and the bearer of its meaning. His existence is a temporal project whereby he ceaselessly comes to be by transcending the defined limits of himself and others towards the horizon of Being from which and in which their definitions and meaning are derived. For Heidegger this meaning and its source in Being are immanent to the temporal confines of man's lived experience of this world. Finiteness constitutes the evolving definition of man and the world, but the Light of Being, which shines in man to illuminate and reveal the meaning of every being, itself emerges from original concealedness. The mystery which Being is may indeed exceed the finiteness which defines the beings we experience.

Sartrian man as consciousness and freedom is essentially intentional. As "being-for-itself," he unceasingly transcends his current situation in the world of persons and things. He does so in the double movement of a negative differentiation from the world as "being-in-itself" and a positive commitment in freedom to the world, giving it meaning and value. His life is the futile project to become God, the absolute coincidence of free consciousness and thinghood. Yet futile though his life may be in its ultimate issue, man is irrevocably destined to the perpetual exertion of self-transcendence by which he is ever becoming himself.

For Merleau-Ponty, man is the body-subject who intimately shares "the flesh of the world." This is the world of culture and history, of language and social institutions, as well as the world of his physical environment. The individual arises out of his pre-conscious immersion in this world to constitute himself and the world-for-him in their reciprocal meaning within a linguistic human community. His existence is the very project whereby he comes to himself in the continual process of transcending himself within this community and this world. In his later years, Merleau-Ponty saw this world-constituting project that man is as a self-disclosure of Being which is the primal field within which the human project occurs and by which it is vitalized. Being is not itself directly known, but it co-appears as the field within which man and his world appear as figures which it situates and structures.

In all three, man is a finite project of self-transcendence transacted in a history with a world and within the human community. For Sartre the limits of this transcendence are defined negatively in terms of the futile objective of becoming God. For Heidegger and the later Merleau-Ponty, man enacts his project of transcendence within a field of Being, understood non-theistically and yet, in its elusive mystery, inconceivable in finite terms.

Marxist Humanism

Marxist Humanism is the contemporary faith which exerts the most powerful presence to the lives of the greatest number. For professed Marxists wield actual political control over vast portions of the earth's population. They are zealously engaged in a deliberate program of building the social and cultural environment for these multitudes according to Marxist norms, and the Marxist movement is propagating itself ever more widely on a militant wave of revolutionary fervor.

To be more precise, it is not Marxism, in the sense of the ideas of Karl Marx on man and society, but rather Marxism-Leninism which exercises this pervasive control over the minds and aspirations of so many. For in his own lifetime, the thought of Marx was being transformed and interpreted by his collaborator, Friedrich Engels, and other theoreticians of the socialist revolutionary movement, a process that is still going on today inside and outside of the socialist countries. Lenin gave this ideology a definitive formulation for Soviet Russia, the country in which Marxist Socialism achieved its first lasting triumph. Marxism-Leninism is at least nominally the ideological pattern of all other countries which have been brought within the Communist camp.

Despite strict control over the public expression of thought, the spread of Marxism-Leninism to various nations and cultures has led to a genuine pluralism in its interpretation and appreciation. The distinction between orthodox and revisionist is as valid among Marxists as that between conservative and liberal in democratic countries. It applies to differences within countries as well as to the official doctrines professed by the Communist parties of the various countries.

The Soviet Union claims ideological primacy over the

other Communist nations. This claim was most effectively exercised during the Stalinist era (1930-1956). It was challenged first by Yugoslavia, and then after the denunciation of Stalin in 1956, by the Chinese Communists and by the parties of the Eastern European bloc: the Chinese in the interest of their version of orthodoxy, the Eastern Europeans in the direction of a freer interpretation more comfortable to national and cultural distinctions. The repression of the liberal regime in Czechoslovakia has dampened the ardor of the non-conformists, but the literature of the new Marxists in these countries provides interesting variations on the basic theme of Marxist Humanism.

The interest of contemporary Marxists in the early writings of Marx with their humanistic concern was heightened by the impact of Existentialism after the second World War and by the more recent and still tentative dialogue with Christians. The effect of both these factors is felt principally outside the Soviet Union which has kept Western influence at a minimum. As a consequence the problem of man as a person and of his subjectivity has only recently received the attention of Soviet thinkers.[20]

A. SOVIET ORTHODOXY

The current Soviet view of man is based on the full corpus of Marx's works, along with the developments added by Engels, Lenin, and other later commentators. It repeats the Marxist tenet that man is an evolving historical being who creates himself by his work and is constituted essentially by his social relations. The mode of his production is the base which determines the superstructure of social and cultural institutions, including arts, religion, and philosophy, by which he expresses his humanity. Thus the individual is defined in terms of his relations with others and not in isolation from them. Therefore, it is not the individual man who creates himself but rather men taken collectively. Society produces the individual man, and in a conflict the interests of society always prevail.

Just as culture is determined by the material mode of

production which it reflects, so man's subjectivity or inner life of consciousness is a product and function of matter and derives from the objective social and cultural world which it reflects. His personality is similarly derivative and is more or less developed according to the culture of the society in which he lives and its capacity to support and nourish its development. Only a communist, classless society will be able to provide the optimum conditions, for only there will man be delivered from all causes of alienation and freed to develop his personal potentialities as essentially a worker or producer. In a capitalist society, man's individual existence is set into opposition with his human essence as a social being constituted by his work, since there the distinction of classes and division of labor alienate him both from his work and his social bond with others. The task of creating man in the fullest sense is thus the task of creating and building the communist society which will make "the new man" possible. Thus man, understood as the only god for man and the highest being in this universe, is the ideal man of the future communist society and the men of today can only realize the value of their own humanity by engaging in and subordinating themselves totally to the mission of building the communist society that will produce this ideal.

B. SOME REVISIONISTS OUTSIDE THE SOVIET UNION

Existentialism, especially in the thought of Sartre, has compelled the Marxists to confront the problem of man's individual subjectivity and freedom. The most interesting responses have come from Communists outside the Soviet and their variety is an enlightening disclosure of the wide range of views that has developed. In Poland Leszek Kolakowski (1927-   ) has attempted to reinterpret Marxism existentialistically. He places himself in opposition to every form of absolutism and monolithic thinking in his own socialist society. He distinguishes between *institutional Marxism,* conceived as a system of dogmatic formulae and practices which can only be revised by the established authorities, and *intellectual Marxism,* which is subject to constant internal criticism and revision in the light of evolving experience and its analysis. He proposes a "concept of the Left" as an intellectual attitude of "permanent revisionism toward reality," which can operate as a critique of absolutist tendencies in a socialist as well as in a capitalist society.[21] For his nonconformism, he has been expelled from the Polish Communist Party.

Kolakowski criticizes Marxists for having insufficiently developed an ethics. He vindicates the role of individual free decision and moral responsibility against the absolutes of historical determinism and political institutions. In doing so, he evidences an existentialist preference for the individual over against the institution. He and other Polish Marxists who have followed his lead have been criticized by Adam Schaff (1913-   ), an incisive defender of Marxist-Leninist orthodoxy who has nevertheless made original contributions to its developing philosophy of man. Schaff's principal argument has been directed against the views of Sartre himself who has both criticized Marxism from an existentialist viewpoint and attempted to combine the two philosophies, especially in his *Critique de la Raison Dialectique*. His Polish critic sees an internal contradiction in Sartre's project to reconcile his fundamentally asocial concept of the human individual with the Marxist notion of man's essence as "the ensemble of social relations." Against the French philosopher and his Polish disciples, he insists that "Marxism shows that the individual, in making independent decisions, . . . always does so socially, in the sense of the social conditioning of his personality."[22] Schaff acknowledges that Existentialism has raised significant questions in the area of personal responsibility and morality which the Marxists had neglected, but he is convinced that they can only receive an effective solution in the Marxist context of man's essentially social situation.

In spite of his antipathy to the "revisionists" in his own ranks, Schaff has not hesitated to admit and to criticize the presence of alienating forces within the socialist system, as well as to concede the absence within Marxism of an adequate account of the uniqueness of individual human personality. Moreover, he has advocated dialogue with other "humanisms" as a constructive exigency as well as an historical necessity for Marxists in an age of "peaceful coexistence."[23]

Other East European Marxists outside of Poland have contributed to the rich variety of contemporary Marxist thought. The Czechoslovak, Karel Kosik (1926-   ), has responded more affirmatively than Schaff to the existentialist challenge. He sees both Existentialism and Marxism in some instances succumbing to the temptation of seeing man from a partial view-point and therefore abstractly rather than concretely. The sciences necessarily deal with man from one or another aspect. Philosophy has the task of seeing man in his concrete wholeness, in his existential relatedness with the world of nature.

> To posit the existence of man is to make a statement not only about man, but also about the reality ouside of him: nature, out of which man developed and in which he exists, is in principle different from nature without man.[24]

The fact of human freedom presupposes that man is not merely a component of nature, subject to its laws, as the sciences rightly treat him from their limited perspective, but that he is also a precondition of natural processes and therefore involves more than being a factor subject to their laws. Concretely, man and the world always imply each other.

> If philosophy excludes man from its subject-matter, or reduces him, with respect to the reality outside of man, to either some aspect or product, then . . . it sooner or later loses its genuinely philosophical character and transforms itself either into a logical-technical discipline or into mythology,[25]

such as the logical positivists and Heidegger do respectively. Similarly to treat the question of truth independently of the problem of man's nature, as he believes Husserl has done, leads to a misunderstanding of both or an ignoring of their essential inner relationship.

> Since mankind's Being has a kind of structure through which the Being of extrahuman reality (nature) and that of human reality unfold themselves in a certain way, human history can be considered as a process in which truth differentiates itself from not-truth.[26]

Kosik rejects historical determinism as he does every

view that tends to deprive the concrete individual of his creative freedom or autonomy. Yet man's freedom is situated within history, they are inter-related, since "history and the individual are not two independent magnitudes but rather have a common foundation, namely, three-dimensional time."[27] Thus man's autonomy always involves the delicate balance between the individual and the larger whole in which he participates, whether it be the natural world, the social reality, or the historical process. In all instances the individual man is both the product and the potential creator.

What Kosik's view achieves is a reconciliation within Marxism of man's freedom and autonomy as an individual with his essential participation in the collectivity. It also preserves the value of man as an integrated, self-fulfilling being in the present so that while not denying the future goal of a more perfect man in a more perfect society, it does not reduce present human value to a means and a mere step toward a future ideal in which alone man is integrally realized.

The most creative innovations of Marxist theory and practice have occurred in Yugoslavia which declared its independence of the political and ideological hegemony of Soviet Russia in 1948 at the height of the Stalinist era. In pursuing its own national road to communism, it has drastically altered the traditional blueprint for the structure of an evolving communist society while at the same time it has demonstrated as viable a plurality of approaches within the Marxist camp. Contrary to the Soviet pattern of a highly centralized and paternalistic directing of the entire society from above under the dominance of the party elite, the Yugoslavs have been working toward a democratic or self-management socialism. They have been highly critical of the "statism" they perceive in the Soviet mode and of the rise of a new ruling class, largely identified with the party membership. They do not disdain the label of "revisionists" as they seek experimentally to achieve a society which they are convinced better realizes the core ideals of Marxist humanism. The party as well as the state are subordinated to the goal of placing the means of production directly and as soon as possible in the hands of the workers themselves on a local level. This reinterpretation in practice of Marxist theory in response to the distinctive demands of their largely agricultural society has been explained and supported by a number of gifted original thinkers.

One of the most gifted and original of those thinkers is Gajo Petrovic (1927-   ). Having studied in Great Britain and the United States as well as in Russia, he has constructively reconsidered the thought of Marx and the Marxist tradition. In the process he has reinterpreted the Marxist conception of man and such basic concepts as praxis and alienation. For him, man is the being that exists through and as praxis and, as the being of praxis, he is the being of freedom. The fact that man is not always and everywhere free does not refute the thesis that he is the being of freedom. It merely confirms that "contemporary man alienates himself from his human essence, from what he as man can and ought to be."[28]

Man is the being who freely creates, or better, should freely create himself and his world by his praxis, that is, by his social productive activity. His freedom, however, is an achievement of his being as individual and social. It is possible to have a free man in an unfree society, or an unfree man in a free society; or, in other terms, an unalienated man in an alienating society, or an alienated man in a de-alienated society. "There can be no free society without free persons, or any free person outside a social community."[29]

Man is not merely an economic animal any more than he is merely a biological animal. These only represent stages in his emergence from lower nature. He interprets Marx, therefore, in depicting man as dependent in his being on the economic modes of production as a portrait of man in the class society, which is a transitory phase to be superseded by the classless society. In every phase, man is subject to the possibility of unfreedom, to possible alienating factors, even in the classless society. No society can give man freedom.

Society can be so organized as to enable and encourage the development of free personalities, but freedom cannot be given as a gift to or forced upon anyone. An individual becomes a free person only through his own free activity.[30]

In these words, Petrovic rejects the Marxist thesis that the communist stage of the evolution of society will guarantee man's freedom and his immunity from self-alienation. "It is possible," he writes elsewhere,

to create a basically nonalienated society that would stimulate the development of nonalienated, really human individuals, but it is not possible to create a society that would produce only nonalienated, free, creative individuals and that would exclude every possibility of anybody's being self-alienated.[31]

Human self-alienation will not be abolished then in some future utopian society, communist or otherwise; much less has it been attained substantially in any present actual socialist society. The reason is that alienation or its absence is "a characterization of the ontologico-anthropological nature of the man or society in question."[32] Man alienates himself not merely from his activity or its products, but from his very essence, from what he as man can and ought to be: namely, "a practical, hence free, universal, creative and self-creative social being."[33] As self-creative, man's essence is never finished in any stage of history or social development. Therefore, it is not possible to wipe out alienation once and for all. The failure to achieve freedom is always a possibility in any future situation.

C.   MAO TSE-TUNG: THE 'SINOCIZING' OF MARXISM

The thought of one man directly influences the lives of one-fifth of the human race, the population of mainland China. *Quotations from Chairman Mao Tse-tung* is literally the bible that guides the daily conduct of hundreds of millions of our fellow human beings. Its precepts and directives in the form of aphorisms are memorized, meditated upon and applied scrupulously to the most momentous and the most minute events in the lives of the Chinese people. The importance of China to our world and its future has motivated the government of the United States to foster a rapprochement between the two countries in the interest of pure realism and to acknowledge the significance of Mao and his thought in the formation of our world and its future. The Church's Sacred Congregation for the Evangelization of Peoples has declared that, despite its advocacy of atheism, Maoist teaching affirms human values and that "Christian reflections" are present in his thought.

What is Maoism, this 'Sinocized' version of Marxism-Leninism? What are its sources? What are its tenets? What is its appeal that it can be the creed and code for so many?

Mao Tse-tung was born on December 26, 1893 in Hunan province. Since he did not leave his native province until he was twenty-five, its traditions and special character were significant influences on his formation. Thus it is important to know that its strongest philosophical tradition was a pragmatist interpretation of Confucianism, especially as reflected in the writings of its great thinker, Wang Fu-chih (1619-1692). Contrary to the dominant conviction elsewhere that wisdom is to be found in a return to the past, Wang taught that human nature is malleable and that political and social structures are subject to historical evolution. Wedded to the pragmatist emphasis on the essential role of action in bringing thought to fruition, it fostered an attitude of openness to the possibility of reform, even through revolutionary means, in a larger society that was typically static and archaic. These Hunanese traits are keys to an understanding of Maoist thought.

Mao's revolutionary ardor was fanned by the writings of the insurgents who eventually toppled the Manchu imperial dynasty in 1911 under the leadership of Dr. Sun Yat Sen. But it was not given ideological substance until 1920 when his conversion to Marxism-Leninism was initiated. There began a mental fusion of the Confucian belief in the goodness of human nature, especially as expounded in the thought of the great Mencius (Meng-tse), Wang's theory of characteristic Hunanese impatience with academic theory and his commentators. These ingredients fermented in the mind of a person of shrewd insight into his fellow-man and of characteristic Hunanese impatience with academic theory or of any thought that did not lead to progressive change.

Though he became an official of the Communist Party, Mao felt a stronger identity with the peasant masses whence he had sprung. This tension between loyalties to the Party and to the masses was to continue throughout his career and be resolved by his fundamental confidence in the wisdom of the people. In this he was to depart from the precedent of Lenin, who had himself left behind the original blue-print for revolution of Marx by placing the initiative in the hands of an elite, namely, the Communist party. Mao's own anti-elitism was to reach its shattering climax in the Cultural Revolution that began in the summer of 1966, which attempted to unite the masses under the leadership of the army and the students against the old-line party officials and their followers.

Mao led the effort to 'sinocize' Marxism-Leninism precisely by turning away from the Russian policy of a proletarian revolution under the hegemony of the Party towards "the mass line," that is, a revolution in which the leaders derive their inspiration and their identity from the masses. In the Chinese model, the masses are the peasants rather than the comparatively few urban proletarians.

The Cultural Revolution was the testing ground as well as the decisive expression and vindication of Mao's fundamental philosophy. It was a logical historical step in the gradual socialization and eventual communization of the Chinese people. But it was also an implementation of the Maoist philosophy of man.

The Chinese revolution must advance in three stages toward the final condition of total communism: the new democratic, the socialist and the communist. The first stage was initiated in the 1911 democratic revolution of Dr. Sun Yat Sen directed towards eradication of imperialism and feudalism. The continuation of this in the 'new democratic' revolution transferred the leadership from the bourgeoisie to the working class. After the victory over Chiang Kai-Shek and his Kuomintang army in 1949, the socialist phase began. In this post-war rebuilding period, the help of the bourgeois intellectuals was welcomed, but the socializing of the economic base of national life was carried through. This was accomplished by the establishment of communes in the countryside which were to become the centers of economic and social life, intended to draw the talent from the cities into the rural areas and by the same stroke to eliminate all distinctions between workers, peasants, intellectuals and soldiers. This obliterating of all class distinctions is a goal to be realized in a future not to be expected over-night.

The socialization of the economic base by centering all life, economic, social and cultural, in the communes requires the transformation of the superstructure of cultural institutions which tend to reflect the previous stage of economic development. A 'cultural revolution' is required to eliminate the vestiges of bourgeois and the intellectuals' control of cultural forms and to place cultural leadership and creativity in the hands of the worker-peasant masses. Thus the people themselves, whose thinking and leadership are elicited by a vast intensive education effort, will be encouraged and enabled to decide the kind of world they wish to build.

Mao believes perhaps even more strongly than Marx that the purpose of philosophy is not merely to understand the world but to change it. In pursuing this belief, the stress moves rather decisively from the objective ground to the subjective ground of historical change. Although in peace as in war, men must operate within the limits presented by objective factors, it is their conscious activity and determined wills that will most effectually achieve the desired goals. Mao is convinced that this attitude is consistent with a dialectical as against a purely mechanical materialism, namely, in terms of the reaction of consciousness on the material base by which it has been initially determined.

Thus Mao believes strongly in man and in the mass of men, and in their capacity to determine their own history. Since philosophy must arise as a reflection on the class struggle for production, only those who are engaged in these struggles have the right and the capacity to do philosophy. The masses have the practice, the intellectuals have only the empty theory. Therefore the intellectuals must leave their universities and work in the communes and the working masses must be educated in the theory that will enable them to reflect and to formulate the programs and policies by which they will be responsible for building their future.

Of course Mao believes that his philosophy is the infallible guide and content of this educational program and the myth of his infallibility has been strenuously cultivated. For that reason hundreds of millions of copies of his *Quotations* have been printed and placed in the hands of the student masses. In the Cultural Revolution, the standard "little red books" containing his *Quotations* was the chief and most effective weapon employed by the soldiers of the army and the brash youthful members of the Red Guard. In the long run, the myth of Mao with its inherent limitedness could undo the grandiose ambitions of its chief architect. But the nobility of his desires and ideas cannot be denied.

Mao is determined that the Chinese Revolution will be permanent and that single-minded commitment to its proximate and long-range objectives will never be allowed to flag. This calls for ruthless extermination of anti-socialist attitudes and repudiation of those who maintain them, even in the highest places. It also demands an unceasing campaign to instruct the masses in socialist theory, as found in Mao's writings, in order to equip them to put socialism into practice and to further the revolution towards its goals of total communism.

Mao and his commentators urge the people to align their thinking with that of Mao and yet to do so creatively. This creates a tension between spontaneity and preoccupation with maintaining orthodoxy and it exposes a flaw at the heart of Mao's version of Marxist humanism. For he believes strongly in the potential greatness of Man: in human capacity to overcome every obstacle to his progress, in the worth of man's moral grandeur above material possessions or achievements, in the power of his conscious will to fashion a new world and, in the process, a new stage of human nature. To a considerable degree these ideas approximate a secular version of the New Creation which Christ came to effectuate. Yet in the encompassing of these admirable objectives, Mao and his worshipful followers do not hesitate to practice cruelty, and at times exhibit contemptuous disregard for freedom and human dignity.

D. MARXIST AGGIORNAMENTO: BLOCH AND GARAUDY

In the developing Marxist-Christian dialogue, two men have played key roles on the Marxist side: Roger Garaudy and Ernst Bloch. The former has donated as much by his practical initiative in pushing the dialogue and maintaining its momentum as by his contribution to its substance. The latter has remained aloof from active involvement, but has undoubtedly done more than any other Marxist to create a fresh context in which a constructive exchange can take place. In fact, his thought has become both a stimulus to and an ingredient of the contemporary movement of the theology of hope. With a considerable portion of his major writings undergoing translation into English, it is scarcely rash to predict that his philosophy will soon exercise as large an influence on American thought as any of the great European thinkers of this century, for it incorporates attitudes and themes that are closer to the perennial American spirit than most of those recently imported.

Ernst Bloch (1885-   ) is an atheist who has been accused, much to his chagrin, of being a theologian. Of all atheists, he is the one who has made the most strenuous efforts to incorporate the values of religion into a Godless vision of man. He follows Feuerbach in defining the question of God as the question of man. With Marx he sees religion as at once the expression of man's alienation and a powerful protest against it. His originality is displayed in the painstaking scholarship and the profound sympathy with which he portrays the positive role religion, and in particular Christianity, has fulfilled in man's historical evolution. He has devoted himself to the enrichment of Marxism by incorporating within it the revolutionary Messianism of the Judaeo-Christian revelation. In consequence he has been repudiated by orthodox Marxists as a "revisionist" who would adulterate scientific Marxism with mystical and irrationalist ingredients.

Bloch's constructive critique of religion and theism is prosecuted within the broad context of his fundamental philosophy. In the formation of that philosophy, Marx has of course played the dominant role, but his interpretation of Marxism has underscored the influence of Hegel as well as the factor of the irrational in all human thinking. His erudition is immense and his own thought has been fertilized not only by the principal philosophical currents, but also by his expansive acquaintance with the arts and literature, the human and social sciences, history and theology.

His first major work was on "the spirit of Utopia." (*Geist Der Utopie*[33a], first published in Munich, 1918; recently published in a revised edition: Frankfurt am Main: Suhrkamp, 1964.) It was primarily a work in aesthetics, in particular on the philosophy of music, but it pointed in the direction he was later to pursue: what may be called the "utopian" dimension of reality. For in music man is led to encounter himself at the deepest level and to question himself. But the encounter and the question are concealed in a darkness, the obscure realm of the "not yet conscious." It was a presage of his later preoccupation with the irrational and unconscious life of man from whose depths his irrepressible aspirations form themselves to issue forth in daydreams and the myriad imaginative structures which his hope has assumed, especially as they are projected and consequently catalogued in the history of religions.

Until he was driven from Germany in 1933 as a refugee from Nazism, he was working out his personal version of Marxism. He eventually came to the United States and during his stay here (1938-1949) he produced several writings, including his master work, *The Principle of Hope*.[34] Returning to teach at the University of Leipzig in East Germany, he fell into disfavor with the Communist regime with his proposals for the revision of Marxism. In 1951, he left East Germany and accepted a teaching position at the University of Tübingen, where the thought of this often exiled octogenarian has achieved new renown and influence, not the least in Christian theological circles.

The human quest for Utopia is not only essentially distinctive of man, for man is "the one who hopes," it is also revelatory of the character of reality itself. Hope is the subjective counterpart of the objective constitution of being as that which is essentially "not yet." When challenged by a friend to epitomize his thought in a single statement, Bloch replied: "S is not yet P." As he had already intimated in his early work on the spirit of Utopia, man is ever being moved to confront and to question himself. His present predicament is invariably one of alienation from himself and from nature which he aspires to overcome by humanizing nature and naturalizing himself. The drive toward this goal is pursued in hope as a destiny ever yet to be fulfilled. Until that destiny is achieved man is still living in his prehistory.

Bloch's philosophy of hope is founded, therefore, both in his phenomenology of human subjectivity and in his ontology, each disclosing a reality that is unfinished, processive, future-oriented, and perpetually straining towards a utopian condition of completeness. His inquiry into man has explored both his conscious and his unconscious life in order to account for the hope that constitutes his very humanity. He has done so in continual dialogue with the psychoanalysts, especially Freud, with whom he has often been in basic disagreement. Thus he identifies man's primary instinct in hunger, the instinct of self-preservation, rather than in the libido and death instinct, or the drive for power. He rejects all of these theories somewhat arbitrarily as partial analyses conditioned by the bourgeois culture in which they emerged. His fundamental objection is that they all refer to the human past rather than the future.

Hunger is understood not merely as a biological drive, but as "a transcendental appetite which expresses the radical openness of man's being, the ground of his orientation, and the intentionality of his consciousness."[35] In his ontological analysis of the implications of hunger, he says he sees hunger rooted in the "Not" (*Nicht*) which he distinguishes from "Nothing" (*Nichts*). "Nothing" is related to actual being as an opposition that is hostile. The "Not" is related to actuality or actual things as a lack or a not-having rooted in a subject which has but is wanting. It is not, therefore, opposed to actuality, but rather open and eagerly awaiting the actualization of what is not yet. Thus hunger implies the incompleteness and openness of man's being towards a future of promise in which he can have hope. Anxiety and fear can also enter as negative effects, which hinder man's freedom and forward movement. It is hope that opens and expands man's freedom toward the promise of the future.

Bloch finds in man's dreams the mirror of his hopes and his anticipations of a better future. As a good Marxist revolutionary, Bloch rejects the orientation to the past of Freudian psychoanalysis with its concentration on night-dreams. His opposition is more than doctrinaire, however, for he uncovers in daydreams not merely another form of night-dreams, but a freer and fuller engagement of man's consciousness more directly related to the real world and its transformation. Whereas night-dreams are symbolic re-capitulations of the individual's past, daydreams are antici-pations of a better future, not merely for the individual, but for the sake of others as well.

The daydream is directed not to the satisfaction of hallucinatory wishes, but to the actual fulfillment in the future of what is not yet, but really worthy of human desires. Its object is often obscure, if not undefinable. But the day-dream and its counterparts in literature and the arts disclose a fundamental orientation of man's subjectivity toward the future with its possibilities which are not yet realized but which can spark his hope and his revolutionary zeal to change the world so that such goals can be brought closer to reali-zation.

Bloch thus reinterprets the contents of man's uncon-sciousness and their implications. For Freud, the present unconsciousness, most fully actualized in night-dreams, rep-resents repressed material from the past which is no longer conscious. For Bloch, human unconsciousness both of the past and of the present, most authentically expressed in daydreams, projects the hopes for the future which is not yet actual and, for the individual, not yet conscious.

> This "not-yet-conscious" is therefore the psychic birthplace of the future, of the new. The "not-yet-conscious" is the psychic re-presenta-tion of that which has not-yet-come-to-be in an age and its world, in the "Front" of the world.[36]

Man's fundamental posture of hope has its objective correlate and ground in a processive, open-ended ontology of the "not-yet." Bloch is a convinced dialectical materialist. It is matter that is the ultimate mother of the New from whose womb the future is born. Matter, therefore, is not conceived of as inert or merely mechanistically, but rather as the creative, life-giving subject of all change and progress, spiritual as well as material. It is in constant process toward the future, the "not-yet," from the unfinished present. It is the future as the yet-to-be that powers the process, felt in the present as the "Not," the hunger arising from the want of what is not-yet but can be, or at least can be aspired to.

The "Front" is the temporal point at which the future is breaking through. Since time is constitutive of being, the not-yet is truly novel, the "New" (*Novum*), that which has never really been. Thus man is always on the way (*unterwegs*), travelling through time in a world that beckons him with its infinite potentialities to transcend every present in a project toward a future that is never certain, but always possible. Bloch does not hesitate to call the future that draws man in his hopes his "homeland," but it is utopian because it is in no sense positively real or in any sense already determined or assured. It has, however, been described and illustrated in man's literature and art and religion, above all, in the eschatological imagery of Judaism and Christianity.

In the philosophy of religion, the Marxist Bloch goes far beyond Marx's characterization of religion as man's protest against alienation. For him the history of man's religion has been the history of man's rising hopes, a history which atheism continues as a "meta-religion" that at last recognizes the gods as no more than the projections of the hopes of man. He sees this process as already occurring within those religions as the focus moves from the divinities they worship to their human founders. This is a phase of man's rebellion against the gods personified in the mythical figure of Prometheus, so strongly extolled by Marx himself.

Bloch identifies Moses as the first genuine Promethean rebel against God. For having led his people in a successful uprising against the forces of tyranny, Moses contends with Yahweh, the God of the Promised Land, and in effect challenges Him to stand by His promises. Job continues the same revolutionary tradition of protest and demand. Its logical culmination is in the figure of Jesus, the human religious founder who usurps the divine prerogatives. His authentic identity as a rebel involuntarily executed for his subversive career is covered over by the mythologizing of his death into a freely willed redemptive sacrifice. In fact, he is the final Promethean hero who installs man in the place of the transcendent deity.

"Where there is Hope, there is religion," says Bloch. For religion has always enacted man's desire to overcome his divided, alienated condition in a state of wholeness and reconciliation. It has never accepted his present unresolved state as the norm, but always projected that norm into a beyond, whose presentiment in the depths of man is the numinous presence that is the ground of his hope. The nature religions refer this numinous presence to a static source in a closed complete universe. Mosaic religion translated it into a temporal and historical process straining ever forward toward a future of promise. This goal is envisaged as a Kingdom of fulfillment, which supplants God Who serves only as a concretized projection toward which man directs his hope.

Christ incarnates this Kingdom of promise in His own human identity and ministry, in Whom the future reconciliation of men with one another and of man with himself and with nature is anticipated and prefigured. This Kingdom in its realization lies beyond history, but as the vision of what is not-yet but always beckoning from beyond the horizon, it has served as the ground of man's hope and in some form will always so serve. Bloch believes that atheism must assimilate this Messianic dream and give it actuality in a post-religious form that focuses man's hopes on an earthly rather than a heavenly future.

Roger Garaudy (1913-) must be cited as the Marxist who has most conscientiously promoted and engaged in the Christian-Marxist dialogue. He has frankly acknowledged the indebtedness of Marxism to the Christian view of man. In seeking to assimilate the insights of that view within his own resolutely atheist perspective, he has concretely illustrated the conditions within which such an encounter can be pursued to mutual advantage. He has seriously attempted to disengage what he judges to be the essential truths of Christianity from their culturally conditioned expression in the history of the Church, and he has been as unsparing in his criticism of the latter as he has been candid in incorporating the former in what he believes to be the superior synthesis of the Marxist world view.

According to Garaudy, Christianity replaced the Greek understanding of man as a part of a completed cosmos whose rational order and man's share in it could be thoroughly known and predicted. Christians believed rather in a world created out of the free initiative of divine love in which man participates as a co-creator responding to God's personal call constantly to transcend his present state and that of the world towards an absolute future beyond nature and history. This faith disclosed man to himself as a free subject no longer contained within a closed order, but open instead to a future of wholly novel possibilities. It sacrificed the rationality of the world order and its promise of man's control of nature to the demands of a free, creative subject whose self-transcendence pointed beyond man and his world to a supernatural goal. Christian faith has also enriched human self-understanding with a higher concept of love than the Greek ideal of Eros or love for love's own sake. By the incarnation of God as man, man as the other was given an absolute divine value and love of the other became an authentic form of the love of God. Thereby a merely aesthetic ideal was replaced by the moral ideal of man's creative service in love of his fellow-man.

Having conceded these contributions to the growth of man's knowledge and appreciation of himself, Garaudy then proceeds to point to their shortcomings as well as their greater potentialities in a Marxist humanism. For man, as Christian faith has shown, is indeed a free, self-creating subject not confined to the patterns of a closed cosmos. Though belonging to nature, he has emerged from nature in a continuing process of self-transcendence whereby he humanizes nature in the creation of culture through his work. Christians have mistakenly interpreted this human self-transcendence as directed beyond nature to an other-worldly Being Who is its source and its end. This has transformed the constitutive process of man's self-creation into a process of self-alienation. Transcendence and creation are properly human attributes and not the properties of Another Being men call God.

The grandeur of religion, and in particular of Christianity, Garaudy asserts, is in the questions it raises as it meditates on man's finiteness in the face of death, on his relation to the infinite toward which he strives in the movement of his transcendence. Its fundamental error has been, in the order of knowledge, its attempt to furnish dogmatic answers to those questions. Its corresponding error in the order of action has been to transform man's exigency for infinite progress and self-creation, which is inevitably terminated and thereby frustrated for the individual by death, into a promise and a positive Presence which death cannot negate. Although he rejects the Christian interpretation of man's transcendence, he respects the right of his Christian interlocutor to live by and in his belief and urges his fellow-Marxists to look behind what he calls the religious myth for the genuine human aspiration that brought it to birth.

Thus Garaudy has formulated the challenge of Marxist Humanism for the Christian believer in its most pointed and concrete terms. Man is indeed the free conscious being who constitutes himself in his personal subjectivity by the process of his self-transcendence in interchange with other human subjects in a world which they create by their collaborative efforts pointed toward the future and its hopes. Thus far Marxists and Christians agree. It is in the implications of man's self-transcendence that they part company.

For the Marxist, the infinite is absence and exigency, while for the Christian, it is promise and presence. There is thus indicated an indisputable divergence between the Promethean conception of freedom as creation, and the Christian conception of freedom as grace and assent. For a Christian, transcendence is the act of God who comes toward him and summons him. For a Marxist, it is a dimension of man's activity which goes out beyond itself towards its far-off being. This far-off being . . . is a human future . . . open on the infinite, . . . the only transcendence which is known to us as atheists. If we want to give it a name, the name will not be that of God, for it is impossible to conceive of a God who is always in process of making himself, in process of being born. The most beautiful and exalted name which can be given to this exigency is the name of man.[37]

Secular Humanism

The most influential and pervasive alternative to Christian faith in the Anglo-American world which we inhabit is neither Existentialism nor Marxism, but Secular Humanism. It is of course not limited to the English speaking peoples, but may be said to permeate the intellectual atmosphere of the western world and to enter as an ingredient in the minds of those who are more properly numbered among the other two groups. Yet it is typical of the Anglo-American countries somewhat as Existentialism is more congenial to certain countries on the continent and Marxism is dominant behind the iron curtain.

Secular Humanism is a rather broad term but it is used here to denote the world-view and life-attitude of those, especially in our country, who have turned away from Christianity and any commitment to a transcendent God as the source of the meaning of their lives. To some extent, we have already described the process by which they have become the "cognitive majority" in our culture. Many of them, perhaps most, have not done so by a deliberate decision, but more by default, succumbing to the dominant social trend in a post-Christian age. As a result, the factors that compose their mentality are extremely varied and, except for sociological surveys that have deliberately searched them out, only mediately available as they are reflected in literature, the arts, and the communication media, especially on the more popular level.

Common to all its diverse forms is the assumption that the progress of the sciences has rendered Christian faith and any sort of belief in a transcendent God, or what is more likely to be called the supernatural, obsolete and meaningless for man "come of age." As a consequence, the more direct access to the mind of the Secular Humanist is through the writings of those men who have reflectively articulated this modern faith and whose thematic formulation of it is perhaps most appropriately entitled Scientific Humanism.

Scientific Humanism represents the most deliberate effort to apply the scientific method to the elaboration of a new world-view and of a human faith acceptable to modern man. Tracing its antecedents to the Enlightenment and the attempt to construct a natural religion and morality, its greater impetus stems from Darwin and the synoptic view of man as a constituent of an evolving universe. Its basic element is naturalism: the philosophical conviction that the natural universe is self-sufficient and self-explanatory. Excluded is any need to appeal to a cause, explanation, or destiny which transcends the order of nature. Man's own existence in its origins and finality is totally encompassed within this same order. The dynamics of evolution, wholly immanent to the world process, suffice to account for all the phenomena of experience in their unity as in their diversity and change, as well as to provide the total setting for the human drama. Scientific Humanism as a human faith claims its superiority over traditional religious faiths as the consequence of its fidelity to the scientific method: its freedom from dogmatic commitments and openness to the widest range of human possibilities whose acceptance is subject only to the test of experience rather than to the prior restriction of doctrinal positions. Thus man's destiny is placed entirely in his own hands and is limited only by the range of his creative imagination and the ever-widening potentialities of his evolving nature.

Man's piety, that is, his devout acceptance of his rapidly developing role as the intelligent agent of his own evolution and that of his natural environment, provides the spiritual substance of a truly modern and thoroughly elevating faith. Although many Scientific Humanists eschew any conscious effort to fill the vacuum left by the demise of the traditional religions, the most significant expressions of this new faith have been proposed as authentic religious, though non-theistic, alternatives to Christianity and other forms of traditional religious beliefs. Prominent among these one must mention the proposals of John Dewey and Julian Huxley.

A. JOHN DEWEY: A DEMOCRATIC FAITH

John Dewey's formal treatment of the religious theme came

somewhat late in his long career (1859-1952) with the publication of *A Common Faith* (1934). In his earlier years, he had developed his own version of naturalism in dialectic with his original Hegelian philosophical convictions and his somewhat foreshortened perspective of the Christian view of man and nature. He repudiated the dualism which he found in each that sets man apart from and over against nature in terms of the antithesis of absolute and relative, eternal-spiritual and worldly-temporal, transcendent and immanent.[38] However, his attitude, especially toward Christianity, was one of reconstruction rather than rejection. Accordingly he attempted to distill the essential Christian truth from its culturally relative forms congealed in institutionalized doctrine. He enunciated this naturalistically as man's unity with nature of which he is the organ and expression.

> As such organ, he participates in truth, and through the completeness of his access to ultimate truth, is free, there being no essential barriers to his action either in his relation to the world or in his relations to his fellow men.[39]

For Dewey, the supreme human values were epitomized in science and democracy as the two principles which assured man's free openness to nature and its possibilities and to his fellow-man with whom he shared those possibilities as a common destiny. His notion of the essential Christian idea was a transcription of this faith into religious categories that remained within naturalistic bounds.

Dewey brought these convictions and the implications for religion of his more developed philosophical position to a mature expression in his Yale Terry Lectures published as *A Common Faith*.[40] They represent nothing original or even stirring, yet they are a consistent development of the life-long trend of his thought and a clear statement of a naturalistic humanism being offered to serve the religious needs of modern man. In a broader perspective than before, he attempts to rescue the religious quality from its anachronistic inherence in the traditional religions. The latter are lumped together as so many forms of supernaturalism invariably involving the necessity of faith in a Supernatural Being and in human immortality beyond the power of nature. Belief in so-called "higher powers" which supposedly control the destiny of man has been culturally conditioned in the past, even in the judgment of contemporary religionists. Dewey wants to press this admission home and apply it even to the present state of religion.

Dewey distinguishes *religion* taken as a noun substantive which is collective rather than general as denoting a disparate collection of religions, from *religious* taken adjectivally. The former is defined as a "special body of beliefs and practices, having some kind of institutional organization," whereas the latter "does not denote anything that can exist by itself or that can be organized into a particular and distinctive form of existence. It denotes attitudes that may be taken toward every object and every proposed end or ideal."[41] Historically, religions have tended to encumber the ideal factors that may be called religious with a load of beliefs and practices that are not intrinsic to them or relevant, and thereby they prevent "the religious quality of experience from coming to consciousness and finding the expressions that are appropriate to present conditions, intellectual and moral."[42]

Dewey denies that there is any distinctive religious experience as to content. The quality of being religious may belong to any experience inasmuch as it is characterized by the better adjustment to life and its conditions. It depends upon the imagination and its ability to project ideals in function of which the person can achieve greater self-integration amidst the flux of his experiences and greater integration with his fellow-men and with the whole of the universe. Religious faith can accordingly be defined "as the unification of the self through allegiance to inclusive ideal aims, which imagination presents to us and to which the human will responds as worthy of controlling our desires and choices."[43]

The fatal error of traditional religions has been to convert these ideal ends into constituents of the actual existing world. Thus, a

. . . faith that something should be in existence as far as lies in our power is changed into the intellectual belief that it is already in existence. When physical existence does not bear out this assertion, the physical is subtly changed into the metaphysical. In this way, moral faith has been inextricably tied with intellectual beliefs about the supernatural.[44]

The contemporary crisis in religious faith, in his opinion, stems from a growing scepticism about intellectual beliefs regarding the connection of man and the world with a supernatural order due to the growth of our knowledge of man and his world which does not support such beliefs. The resulting discrediting of religious values does not have to follow since they are not inherently bound to their traditional supernatural context.

An appeal to the scientific method as against the authoritarian doctrinal method customarily employed in religious questions would liberate the religious quality of human experience from its outmoded encumbrances of supernaturalism. Thereby we would be free to recognize that the traditional objects of religious faith are symbolic of the reality of ends which are capable of moving us toward a more integrated life rather than actually existing themselves in some realm of being.

The term "God" itself would seem to refer not to a particular Being, but rather to "the unity of all ideal ends arousing us to desire and actions. . . . The values to which one is supremely devoted, as far as these ends, through imagination, take on unity."[45] The separation of these ideals from the claim to their actual existence emancipates them from corrosive doubts concerning the reality of the supernatural. At the same time it releases man from enervating dependence upon a Being outside the order of nature for the proper human task of improving the quality of his life in the only way in which it is realistically achieved: namely, by the use of intelligence and imagination to generate ideals from goods and values actually realized on a natural basis in human experience. Thus their validity will not depend on their prior complete embodiment in some supernatural region but rather by their projection from possibilities rooted in what is already promised in human capacities for change.

Dewey sees the need for a religious dimension to human life and even for faith in the divine in our distracted age.

Man requires the acknowledgment of a reality greater than himself,

> the sense of a connection, . . . in the way of both dependence and support, with the enveloping world that the imagination feels is a universe. Use of the words "God" and "divine" protect man from a sense of isolation and from consequent despair and defiance.[46]

B. JULIAN HUXLEY: SCIENTIFIC HUMANISM

Julian Huxley (1887-   ), grandson of Thomas Huxley, famed Victorian protagonist of Darwinism, has carried forward the family tradition as the fervent evangelizer of Humanist faith which invokes all the hope and inspiration of man's evolutionary promise. As a renowned biologist who has been honored for his distinguished productions in the field of popular scientific writing, he brings impressive talents to his chosen vocation of preaching a new secular religion for man in a scientific age.

Like Dewey, Huxley believes that religion is a purely human creation whose essential function must be liberated from outmoded and inhibiting historical accretions. In the past, religion developed in the direction of identifying the sacred with a personal god or gods, but that is not essential to religion, as is illustrated in Buddhism which, according to Huxley, is in its simpler forms atheistic (a disputable statement in view of the subtle nuances of its negative theology) and in the reverence and awe directed to the impersonal spiritual force, which is called "Mana" in some primitive religions.

Religion arose as a feeling of the sacred which springs from a fundamental capacity of man as normal as his capacity for anger, sympathy, or terror. It is not necessarily connected with any specific object, but with a type of situation which can be altered with experience and education.

> The history of religions is the history of the gradual change in the situations which, with increase of experience and changed conditions of life, are felt as sacred . . . Regarded as progress, the history of religion is a history of the purging of the religious emotion itself from baser elements such as fear, and of the substitution of ever larger, nobler, and more rational objects and situations on and in which the religious sentiment may spend itself.[47]

Thus in attempting to order his feelings rationally, man first personified the powers revered, then gradually unified them until they were fused into one God. In morality, as man became more confident of his ability to control nature, holiness was thought less a matter of ritual or propitiation and more a matter of personal righteousness. The general conclusion, in any event, is that religion is a normal activity of man subject to change, for better or worse, as any human function is.

In Huxley's view, the chief obstacle to change of man's religion for the better is the tenacious belief in God as "an external, personal, supernatural, spiritual being."[48] What is needed is a naturalistic reduction of God in terms of recognizing Him as a creation of the human soul which tends to organize matter and life in ever wider and deeper visions of unity motivated by man's expanding spiritual and intellectual aspirations. Thus faith in God and His relations to man is not the consequence of divine revelation, but the product of one stage at which man organized his spiritual experience in a new way, just as human genius has accounted for new insights into scientific truth and the apprehension and expression of beauty. The personification of the object of man's feelings for the sacred was an understandable form of his emerging awareness of the unity of his experience which emphasized the congeniality and interpenetration of his own personal being with the reality of the universe around him. As his knowledge of that universe and of his role in it progressed, the explanatory and supportive function of God has receded until it is recognized as totally expendable. What remains is not a spiritual vacuum, but the permanent facts of human existence like birth and death, such facts of his spiritual life as the desire for righteousness and the peace of communion, the reality and the potency of human ideals, and the encompassing being of the natural and living universe in which man is immersed. The residual religious reality includes all of these

. . . in their aspects of relatedness to human destiny . . . as held together, against the cosmic background, by a spirit of awe or reverence . . . It includes them in their sacred aspect, or at least in association with an outlook which is reverent and finds holiness in reality.[49]

Huxley assumes then that religion plays an integral role in human existence as it pursues its evolutionary path. Briefly, it serves as a social organ whose function it is to adjust man to his destiny, "that is to say, his position and role in the universe, and how he is to maintain that position and fulfill that role." All societies develop religions in the sense that they develop "organs for orientating their ideas and emotions and for constructing attitudes of mind and patterns of belief and behavior in relation to their conception of their destiny."[50]

The scientific and technological revolution has drastically changed man's position and role in the universe. He has been installed as the sole agent and managing director of his own evolution and that of the part of the universe under his ever-expanding control. Thus he has displaced the deity whom he himself had in imagination projected as the ruler of a universe which he could not yet control and before which he cringed in fear and awe. What is called for now is a religion which will serve as the social organ that can effectually function to adjust man to this profoundly altered conception of his own destiny.

Huxley calls the religion which would fulfill the needs of contemporary man: Evolutionary Humanism. Like Dewey's proposal, it is professedly naturalistic, anti-dualist, and, in its essential message, cast in the evolutionary framework. It is intended to fit man to confront and fulfill his destiny in the dramatically new role of the agent of evolution. For this is the first epoch of the earth's history in which the evolutionary process has come to self-consciousness in man who has recently arrived at a scientific understanding of its history, its scope, and its implications.

To Huxley's mind, the entire cosmos is involved in a single developing process of self-creation. It has proceeded on the three levels of the cosmic or inorganic, the biological, and the psycho-social, each later stage, whether between or in the major levels, evolving from the earlier within this total process of self-transformation. Hitherto the major advances known to us on earth have been on the biological level, operating according to the criteria of natural selection for the production of novel forms. Out of these, dominant types emerged to mark definitive stages of progress, displacing prior, less efficient, dominant groups.

Progress has not been universal. Many evolving species have ended in blind alleys, in arrested stages of development or in reversion to less developed stages. What has become clear, at least for our section of the universe, is that biological evolution in terms of natural selection has reached the end of the road. It would appear that further evolution is concentrated along the single pathway of man's psycho-social or cultural transformation. However, rather than being a limitation, it is a breakthrough of boundless potentialities.

Man's uniqueness among the evolving forms of life stems from his singular development of brain and mind which exhibits itself in his capacity for conceptual thought and symbolic communication. Derivative from this are the development of a cumulative tradition and the progressive improvement of tools and machinery.[51] Unlike other types, man has developed the broadest range of variability while remaining a single biological species. It is in this single species that the future of evolution lies, no longer as a function of natural selection, but by a process of self-direction whereby man becomes the agent of the evolutionary process. The success of this new cultural or psycho-social phase of evolution depends on the efficacy with which man maintains the conditions of maximum individual fulfillment within a society capable of ever-fresh evolutionary growth.

Paramount in the achievement of this task is the construction of a religious system which will both release and empower man for its fulfillment. Rather than occasion conflict with science, it will employ the knowledge of science to clarify man's destiny. It will integrate that knowledge with man's affective resources to create beliefs and attitudes apt to foster moral decisions and actions suited to man's cosmic role.

Huxley's optimism is tempered by a candid acknowledgment of the evil in individual men and society along with the good. This poses the need of understanding and controlling the forces of human nature as well as of external nature, of recognizing man himself as his own most formidable adversary. The scientific spirit and method which have gradually extended man's comprehension and control of physical nature can eventually yield the wisdom he needs to control his inner forces and direct them constructively. Essential for this is a religious vision of man which participates in the virtues of the scientific spirit and applies the fruits of the scientific method in guiding man's evolutionary task. Such a vision is provided by Evolutionary Humanism, which will, he is convinced, eventually be as universally accepted as the science from which it draws its understanding of man and his world.

C. GERHARD SZCZESNY: THE FUTURE OF UNBELIEF

The proposing of humanism as a world-view and life-attitude to replace the traditional religions, usually denominated as forms of supernaturalism, is never absent from the intentions of secular humanists, at least by implication. This is as true of those who formally deny any further validity to the notion of a specifically religious function or attitude in man as of those who, like Dewey and Huxley, explicitly affirm such a function and offer their version of Scientific Humanism as its most promising application at the present stage of man's history. For in effect the rejection of theism and the affirmation of humanity and its perfectibility as the supreme value and goal for mankind represent a form of faith-option, regardless of the specific context in which it is proposed. One of the striking facts about the writings of the great majority of those who can with some justification be called secular or scientific humanists is the similarity of their fundamental positions in spite of the diversity of their backgrounds and declared intentions. Whether it be a native American like Corliss Lamont, a native German like Gerhard Szczesny, or a naturalized emigre from Germany like Erich Fromm or Walter Kaufmann, the basic message is the same. Among those who advocate the humanist creed without claiming to introduce it explicitly as a contemporary form of religious faith, one of the most forthright and militant is Gerhard Szczesny (1918-   ). His controversial work, *The Future of Unbelief,* is at once a forceful defense of the right not to be a Christian believer and an eloquent assertion of humanism as a superior option to Christian faith for the enlightened post-modern. What he offers in the name of "unbelief" is a *"Weltanschauung,"* a "world-view," which corresponds to "the common human need for a comprehensive interpretation of all existence, within reason's grasp and beyond it," which is arrived at intuitively as well as rationally.[52]

We are entering a post-modern period because we are passing beyond the time when even the modern rivals to the traditional religious faiths were dominated by the traditional religious problematic, and the *ersatz* religions which were thrown up to fill the ideological and moral vacuum left by the collapse of the traditional faiths have demonstrated their impotency. We have even lived through the period of reaction when many succumbed to the temptation to rescue the lost values by a return to traditional religion, that is, to Christianity. Presumably we are in a more hopeful position of those who can totally free themselves of nostalgia for the past that cannot be restored and build for the future afresh from wholly new beginnings. This inevitable transition which has been occurring largely in western man's unconsciousness must be given a conscious and explicit expression.

First of all, we must honestly admit that all forms of religion have been determined by their geographical and historical origins. Szczesny attempts to support this thesis by appealing to the Qumran documents to account for the rise of peculiar Christian views and rites. His somewhat personal and at least questionable use of this material underlines a methodological deficiency in his work: namely, his inclination to generalize abruptly from ambiguous historical sequences to laws of human behavior. In any event, the Christian faith triumphed in Europe in spite of its alien origin and antipathy to the indigenous European mentality. For the native European religions at least reflected the western man's congeniality with the natural world around him and his proclivity to understand himself in terms of his objective experience of that world. Christianity, with its Asiatic origins, proceeded to interpret the universe and man's role within it by extrapolating from man's contemplation of his inner self. Either starting point can lead, and in fact has led, to anthropomorphic interpretations of reality.

According to Szczesny, the Christian faith issued in an irremediable dualism which established an unbridgeable gap between man's natural universe and its divine ground. This in turn led to a chasm within man between spirit and body, between nature and super-nature, and between his self and his world, which has beset European thought ever since and has eventuated in existentialist despair before the absurdity of man's existence in an alien universe· The incompatibility of the Christian other-worldly dualism with the deep-rooted this-worldly and objective mentality of western man has inexorably erupted in the contemporary crisis of Christian faith. That Szczesny has overlooked the quite opposite dynamism of the Christian doctrine of the Incarnation in contrast to the typical Asiatic religions is a sample of his selective approach to the total mass of available data.

Ours is the first truly post-religious age because with the imminent achievement of a genuine world-community, we are freed from the determinism that produces religious perspectives from particular geographical and cultural milieux. At last man can construct a world-view (*Weltanschauung*) that is really universal, unrestricted to specific mentalities, and—thanks to science—based on an objective estimate of man's experience.

The current malaise of western man is due, therefore, at least in part, to the insoluble conflict that has arisen between allegedly revealed truths and those to which he is led by reason and the scientific method: in other words, between his beliefs and his experience. The aftermath of the dualism, which he has in fact repudiated, is a truncated world bereft of its grounds and therefore interpreted by fragmented explanations elevated to ultimate truths. He has been diverted from the recognition of the immanence of the world-ground and therefore a universal explanation based on the oneness of man with his world and the encompassing universe of being, which would restore the unity of his experience and his beliefs.

In consequence he has resorted to an escape into fact. He has placed his confidence in the purely horizontal dimension of empirically demonstrable knowledge both of the objective world of nature and the world of his own subjectivity. In fact, the patent absurdities of Christian faith and its metaphysics have engendered the overreaction on the part of those who have apostatized from them of believing that eventually the whole universe of being will be brought within the range of available fact and the comprehension of human reason and science. Based on this pretentious assumption, a number of *ersatz* religions and pseudo-ideologies have arisen which claim to be founded on fact but which are actually absolutized projections of the purely relative state of man's knowledge at the moment of their origins.

As a matter of fact, man's knowledge will always be relative and tentative, never absolute and comprehensive and there will always be an area of unsolved questions and a depth-dimension of reality which will never cease to elude man's efforts to capture it rationally. This is the vertical dimension of reality which was formerly the dimension of religious faith and which must now be acknowledged as the encompassing boundaries within which our post-modern *Weltanschauung* is to evolve.

We are still in the period of the *ersatz* religions which divide into "objective" and "subjective" as they stress the environment or the individual's inner life. Each is the totalization of a partial view and

> . . . both types, each according to the limitations of its perspective,
> ignore the question of man's position in the cosmos . . . (and) behave
> as if there is no world structure reaching out beyond man's world.[53]

Typical of the objective ideologies is Liberalism, the "mother of all sociologisms," from which in diverse ways have sprung communism and democracy and their offspring: Russian collectivism and American conformism. Each is like the other in that both presume with shallow optimism the future rational solution of all man's questions about himself and the world. The preponderantly subjective attitude is the outcry of the isolated ego left over after the demise of the "Wholly-Other." It is reflected in Existentialism which is "a philosophy born of Christian despair, a way of thinking that has retained Christian metapsychology while abandoning Christian metaphysics,"[54] and it is reflected too in literature and the arts as they escape into an arbitrary subjectivism and abandon the project of communicating meaning.

What is needed is a universal anthropology which recognizes all the powers of man and yet their limits within the universe of being which he inhabits. Beyond both a mere empiricism of facts and the rootless speculations of idealistic reason is the unitary power of empirical reason and creative imagination by which man in his freedom transcends the merely factual and actual. By so doing, man constructs beliefs by which he anticipates the future and achieves "out of our fragmentary knowledge, some intimations of reality as a whole".[55] Yet man will never comprehend the whole since the questions of absolute origins and destinies, of the meaning of man's existence and presence in the world, indicate the horizons beyond the reach of our reason grounded in space-time experience. These horizons in principle will always remain regardless of the extension of our understanding. Still reason's awareness of its own limitedness is itself a proof of a range of being that exceeds its reach.

Although this metaphysical reality transcends the physical universe of our experience and science, it is not an "other-worldly" realm, but entirely immanent as the depths of our empirical world and selves. "The metaphysical is the core, root and source of the physical, and the physical the sole means of approach to the metaphysical."[56] What we are constantly assured of is their ultimate unity as the metaphysical reveals itself to the expanding penetration of our knowledge of the physical. The cosmos is consistently disclosed as a universal continuum in ceaseless process of evolution.

Humanity is a purely natural event and the evolution of man with his intelligence was a story of successful survival and dominance that could have ended in failure. The arrival and departure of a multiplicity of religions and moralities are a part of that story in its earlier stages. At present we are engaged in devising a system of moral values based on man's nature to replace the collapsed religion-based ethics.

Szczesny suggests that man possesses a humanizing impulse, a native tendency to realize a generic idea of what it is to be human. The motivating power of this inclination is the need for prestige, a kind of vanity which drives a man to seek to realize in himself the best images of humanity available to him. A society "becomes truly human when it succeeds in linking social prestige with individual human accomplishment."[57] The only really effective morality for contemporary man is one that recognizes the immanence of the moral imperative to man's own natural inclinations and which does not appeal to a transcendent or heteronomous authority. Man's humanizing of himself and his world will always remain unfinished, but the important truth is that he acknowledge that its continuing achievement is entirely in his own hands.

Szczesny charges Christianity with burdening men with an impossible ideal, focussed on another world and renunciatory of this, which has engendered the widespread anomaly of "an enormously sensitive conscience accompanied by underdeveloped moral behavior in the practical sphere."[58] This involves a truncated image of man as a statically conceived ego over against a static God who can only be approached in submission and by doing violence to man's own nature. On the contrary, man's self, like reality generally, is multiform and richly differentiated. It is considerably more extensive than the limits of ego-consciousness, and in constant process, which is historically and socially conditioned. Fortified with this understanding of himself as organically one with the evolving world continuum and still specifically different as human, he can work out his destiny realistically and yet modestly, acknowledging his greatness and his limitations.

D. SECULAR HUMANISM: COMMON THEMES

The three secular humanists whom we have studied are reliably representative, at least in the major trends of their

thought, of the considerably larger group of leading expo-
nents of this outlook. One could expect the common strands
of their expositions to be woven through the reflections of
most of those who share their fundamental perspective.
Those strands are rather clearly discernible. There is first of
all the universal repugnance to what they label supernaturalism or dualism, namely, the existence of a transcendent God or divine principle or any order above or beyond
or other than that of this natural universe itself upon which
the order of nature is dependent or to which it is subordinate
either for its existence and order, its value or its finality. It is
assumed that man has matured beyond that stage when,
overawed by the menacing immensity of nature, he projected gods behind the scenes who could furnish a feeling
of security as well as meaningfulness to his fragile existence.
Science has naturalized our understanding of even the most
awesome events of nature. Technology has placed within
man's grasp the ability to control them. The theory of
evolution has provided the comprehensive scheme of explanation within which man can adequately account, without
recourse to discredited supernatural agencies, for his own
entire story from its beginnings included within that of his
whole world.

Humanism insists that man has emerged in his total
being from the evolving potentialities of this universe and,
at this stage of evolution, represents its highest achievement.
Endowed with creative intelligence and some measure of
freedom, he is accountable to no one greater than himself
for the success or failure of his efforts to fulfill the destiny
he infers to be his own. In view of his increasing mastery
of his inner and outer environment, it appears ever more
clearly that his destiny is actively to direct the further
evolution of himself and his world. This is of course the
shared destiny of all mankind and involves the shared
responsibility and participation of all. In ascertaining his
goals, estimating his values, confronting his problems, and
making moral judgments about his decisions and actions,
man should appeal no further than his this-worldly-experi-
ence and his own reason as it is most effectively employed in
the use of the scientific method.

This implies that man's judgment stands above all goals and standards. None of them is immune from his critical review, all are provisional, subject to the constant test of experience and liable to even the most radical revision. Absolute only is man's right to subject all systems and viewpoints to the norm of serving his individual and collective well-being, and of enhancing his capacity to achieve a better life in the future. Only this attitude corresponds to the unfinished condition of the universe and its human inhabitants whose future man must be free to plan and form without hindrance from any limitations except those that physical and human nature impose upon him.

Thus the only transcendence which secular humanists recognize is immanent to the universe. It is shared between man, who in his capacity for self-transcendence is the current agent of the world's own evolutionary capacity of self-creation, and the universe itself whose measureless depths and magnitude encompass man and ultimately elude his powers to comprehend or control it.

Notes and references

[1] Edmund Husserl, **Ideas: General Introduction to Pure Phenomenology,** trans. by W. R. Boyce Gibson. (New York: Macmillan, 1958), pp. 110-111.

[2] Quentin Lauer, "Introduction: Structure of the Ideal," in Edmund Husserl. **Phenomenology and the Crisis of Philosophy,** trans. by Quentin Lauer, (New York: Harper and Row, 1965), p. 62.

[3] Pierre Thevenaz, **What is Phenomenology?** (Chicago: Quadrangle Books, 1962), p. 51.

[4] Ibid., p. 50.

[5] The controversy among commentators of Husserl revolves around the issue whether his thought is correctly understood as involving, or at least open to, an existentialist interpretation (perhaps even an empiricist, realistic one) or whether it can only be authentically interpreted as a transcendental idealism. Concerned in the conflict of opinion is the extent and radicality of the phenomenological reduction. Husserl is credited with proposing three forms of reduction, in various places: "1) The phenomenological reduction, in the strict sense, which is also called the 'bracketing of being'. 2) The reduction of the cultural world to the world of our immediate experience (Lebenswelt). 3) The transcendental reduction which is to lead us from the phenomenal worldly 'I' to transcendental subjectivity." Joseph J. Kockelmans, editor, **Phenomenology: The Philosophy of Edmund Husserl and its Interpretation** (Garden City N.Y.: Doubleday, 1967), p. 31. The first and third meanings are proper to an interpretation that favors a strict transcendental

idealism, which would allow the second meaning as well. The existentialist interpretation embraces the second meaning and tends to omit the first and third for various reasons (cf. **Ibid.**, pp. 186-193). We accept the historical fact that Husserl's thought and his phenomenological method have received an influential existentialist interpretation and we leave the controversy over its legitimacy to the professional commentators (cf. also **Ibid.**, pp. 242 ff.).

6 Cf. Lauer, in Husserl's **Phenomenology and the Crisis of Philosophy,** note 30, p. 166.

7 William Richardson, "Heidegger and God," **Thought,** 40 (Spring 1965) pp. 35-36.

8 William Richardson, **Heidegger: Through Phenomenology to Thought** (The Hague: M. Nijhoff, 1963), p. 86.

9 The distinction between an earlier Heidegger represented mainly by **Sein und Zeit** and his works published before 1947 or even 1945, and a later Heidegger expressed in his writings after those dates has not been stressed in this brief exposition. Heidegger himself insists on the inner continuity of the two periods. Cf. Martin Heidegger in "Preface" to W. Richardson's, **Heidegger: Through Phenomenology to Thought,** pp. viii-xxiii. Despite his **Kehre** or "reversal", his understanding of man was always proposed in the ontological setting whether it was man as the revealer of Being or Being as unveiling itself to man; it was never merely an anthropology on the ontic level.

10 Under the pressure of criticism from Merleau-Ponty and on further reflection, Sartre was to modify his position on freedom as offered in **Being and Nothingness.** "I still believe that individual freedom is total, ontologically speaking, but on the other hand I am more and more convinced that this freedom is conditioned and limited by circumstances." Jean-Paul Sartre, quoted in Wilfred Desan, **The Tragic Finale: An Essay on the Philosophy of Jean-Paul Sartre** (New York: Harper and Bros., 1960), p. xvi.

11 Jean-Paul Sartre, **Being and Nothingness,** trans. by Hazel E. Barnes. (New York: Philosophical Library, 1956), p. 615. Also, Alfred Stern, **Sartre: His Philosophy and Existential Psychoanalysis** (New York: Dell Publishing Co., 1967), pp. 178-181.

12 Wilfred Desan, **The Marxism of Jean-Paul Sartre** (Garden City, N.Y.: Doubleday Anchor, 1966), pp. 286-288.

13 Maurice Merleau-Ponty, **Les Aventures de la Dialectique** (Paris: Gallimard, 1953).

14 Desan, **The Marxism of Jean-Paul Sartre,** p. 287.

15 Maurice Merleau-Ponty, **In Praise of Philosophy,** trans. by John Wild and James M. Edie (Evanston, Ill: Northwestern University Press, 1963), p. 43. Merleau-Ponty appears to be thinking of God's causality in terms of "the unilateral and deterministic influence a thing of nature exercises on the being of another thing of nature. And precisely because he has that idea in mind, he is able to reject God as 'cause', for it is evident that a **subject** cannot be caused by a natural force in a natural process. That is also the reason why (he) rejects all 'explanations' of the subject . . . In (his) view 'explanatory' theology uses the same concept of cause as physical science." William A. Luijpen, **Phenomenology and Atheism** (Pittsburgh: Duquesne University Press, 1964), p. 301. To conceive of God's causality instead in terms of the creative causality of love between subjects would not stifle subjectivity or contingency, but rather elicit and enhance them.

16 Maurice Merleau-Ponty, **The Visible and the Invisible; followed by working notes,** edited by Claude Lefort, trans. by Alfonso Lingis (Evanston, Ill.: Northwestern University Press, 1968).

17 Maurice Merleau-Ponty, "Eye and Mind," in **The Primacy of Perception and Other Essays,** edited by James M. Edie, trans. by C. Dalley. (Evanston, Ill.: Northwestern University Press, 1964), pp. 159-190.

18 Merleau-Ponty, **The Visible and the Invisible: followed by Working Notes,** p. 248. The work note is from May, 1960.

19 Ibid.

20 Richard T. De George, **The New Marxism** (New York: Pegasus, 1968), p. 57. I wish to acknowledge my indebtedness to this work, especially for the current Soviet view of man.

21 Leszek Kolakowski, **Toward a Marxist Humanism: Essays on the Left Today,** trans. by Jane Z. Peel (New York: Grove Press, 1969), pp. 67-83.

22 Adam Schaff, "A Philosophy of Man" in **Existentialism Versus Marxism** edited by George Novack (New York: Dell Publishing Co., 1966), p. 301.

23 Adam Schaff, "Marx and Contemporary Humanism," **Diogenes,** 62 (Summer, 1968), pp. 62-75.

24 Karel Kosik, "Man and Philosophy" in **Socialist Humanism,** edited by Erich Fromm (Garden City, N.Y.: Doubleday Anchor Books, 1966), p. 166.

25 Ibid., p. 168.

26 Ibid., p. 170-171.

27 Karel Kosik, "The Individual and History" in **Marx and the Western World,** edited by Nicholas Lobkowicz (Notre Dame, Ind.: University Press, 1967), p. 195.

28 Gajo Petrovic. "Man and Freedom" in **Socialist Humanism,** edited by Erich Fromm (Garden City, N.Y.: Doubleday, 1966), p. 273.

29 Ibid., p. 276.

30 Ibid.

31 Gajo Petrovic, "The Philosophical and Sociological Relevance of Marx's Concept of Alienation" in **Marx and the Western World,** edited by Nicholas Lobkowicz, p. 142.

32 Ibid., p. 144.

33 Gajo Petrovic, **Marx in the Mid-Twentieth Century** (Garden City, N.Y.: Doubleday Anchor Books, 1967), p. 112.

33a **Geist der Utopie,** cf. p. 79.

34 Ernst Bloch, **Das Prinzip Hoffnung,** two volumes (Frankfurt am Main: Suhrkamp, 1953, 1959).

35 Francis P. Fiorenza, "Dialectical Theology and Hope, III" in **The Heythrop Journal,** X (January, 1969), p. 37. I wish to acknowledge my indebtedness to Fiorenza's presentation of Bloch's thought in his extensive article which appeared in **The Heythrop Journal** IX (April, 1968), pp. 143-163; IX (October, 1968), pp. 384-399; and X (January, 1969), pp. 29-42.

36 Fiorenza, **The Heythrop Journal,** X (January, 1969), p. 42.

37 Roger Garaudy, **From Anathema to Dialogue,** trans. by Luke O'Neill (New York: Herder and Herder, 1966), pp. 92, 94-95.

38 Cf. James Collins, "The Genesis of Dewey's Naturalism" in **John Dewey: His Thought and Influence,** edited by John Blewett, S.J. (New York: Fordham University Press, 1960), pp. 1-32, esp. 8 & 14.

39 John Dewey, "Green's Theory of the Moral Motive" in **The Philo-**

sophical Review, 1 (1892), p. 610; cited in James Collins, "The Genesis of Dewey's Naturalism," p. 15.

[40] John Dewey, A Common Faith (New Haven, Ct.: Yale University Press, 1934).

[41] Ibid., pp. 9-10.

[42] Ibid., p. 9.

[43] Ibid., p. 33.

[44] Ibid., pp. 21-22.

[45] Ibid., p. 42.

[46] Ibid., p. 53.

[47] Julian Huxley, Religion Without Revelation (New York: New American Library, 1957), pp. 21-22.

[48] Ibid., p. 24.

[49] Ibid., p. 30.

[50] Ibid., p. 181.

[51] Julian Huxley, "The Uniqueness of Man," in Man in the Modern World (New York: New American Library, 1948), pp. 7-28.

[52] Gerhard Szczesny, The Future of Unbelief, trans. by Edward B. Garside (New York: George Braziller, 1961), pp. 16-17.

[53] Ibid., p. 93.

[54] Ibid., p. 114.

[55] Ibid., p. 134.

[56] Ibid., p. 143.

[57] Ibid., p. 190.

[58] Ibid., p. 197.

Blackham, H. J. *Humanism*. Baltimore: Pelican, 1968.
Bloch, Ernst. *A Philosophy of the Future*. Tr. John Cumming. New York: Herder & Herder, 1970.
Bloch, Ernst. *Atheism in Christianity*. Tr. J. T. Swann. New York: Herder & Herder, 1972.
Bloch, Ernst. *Das Prinzip Hoffnung*. 2 vols. Frankfurt am Main: Suhrkamp, 1959.
Bloch, Ernst. *Geist der Utopie*. 1st ed., München, 1918. 2nd revised ed., Berlin, 1923; Frankfurt am Main: Suhrkamp, 1964.
Bloch, Ernst. *Man on His Own*. Tr. E. B. Ashton. New York: Herder & Herder, 1970.
Bloch, Ernst. *On Karl Marx*. Tr. John Maxwell. New York: Herder & Herder, 1971.

De George, Richard T. *Patterns of Soviet Thought*. Ann Arbor, Mich.: University of Michigan Press, 1970.
De George, Richard T. *The New Marxism*. New York: Pegasus, 1968.
Desan, Wilfrid. *The Marxism of Jean Paul Sartre*. Garden City, N.Y.: Doubleday, 1966.
Desan, Wilfrid. *The Tragic Finale*. New York: Harper, 1960.
Dewey, John. *A Common Faith*. New Haven: Yale University Press, 1969.

Fann. K. T. "Philosophy in Chinese Cultural Revolution," *International Philosophical Quarterly* 9 (1969) pp. 449-59.
Fiorenza, Francis P. "Dialectical Theology and Hope," *The Heythrop Journal* 9 (1968) pp. 143-63, 384-99; 10 (1969) pp. 26-42.

Garaudy, Roger. *From Anathema to Dialogue*. Tr. Luke O'Neill. New York: Herder & Herder, 1966
Garaudy, Roger. *Marxism in the Twentieth Century*. Tr. René Hague. New York: Charles Scribner's Sons, 1970.
Great Lives Observed: Mao. Ed. Jerome Ch'en. Englewood Cliffs, N.J.: Prentice-Hall, 1969.
Green, Ronald W. "Ernst Bloch's Revision of Atheism," *The Journal of Religion* 49 (1969) pp. 128-35.

Heidegger, Martin. *An Introduction to Metaphysics*. Tr. Ralph Mannheim. Garden City, N.Y.: Doubleday, 1961.
Heidegger, Martin. *Being and Time*. Tr. J. MacQuarrie and E. Robinson. New York: Harper & Row, 1962.
Heidegger, Martin. *Kant and the Problem of Metaphysics*. Tr. James S. Churchill. Bloomington, Ind.: Indiana University Press, 1962.
Humanist Anthropology. Ed. Margaret Knight. London: Pemberton, 1961.

Humanist Frame, The. Ed. Julian Huxley. London: Allen & Unwin, 1961.
Humanist Outlook, The. Ed. A. J. Ayer. London: Pemberton, 1968.
Husserl, Edmund. *Cartesian Meditations.* Tr. Dorion Cairns. The Hague: Martin Nijhoff, 1969.
Husserl Edmund. *Ideas: General Introduction to Pure Phenomenology.* Tr. W. R. Boyce-Gibson. New York: Macmillan, 1958.
Huxley, Julian. *Religion Without Revelation.* New York: Mentor, 1957.

John Dewey: His Thought and Influence. Ed. John Blewett, S.J. New York: Fordham University Press, 1960.

Kolakowski, Leszek. *Toward A Marxist Humanism.* Tr. Jane Zielonko Peel. New York: Grove, 1968.
Kwant, Remy C. *From Phenomenology to Metaphysics.* An inquiry into the last period of Merleau-Ponty's life. Pittsburgh: Duquesne University Press, 1966.
Kwant, Remy C. *The Phenomenological Philosophy of Merleau-Ponty.* Pittsburgh: Duquesne University Press, 1963.

Lauer, Quentin. *Phenomenology: its genesis and prospect.* New York: Harper & Row, 1965.
Luijpen, William A. *Phenomenology and Atheism.* Pittsburgh: Duquesne University Press, 1964.

Mao Tse-Tung: an Anthology of His Writings. Ed. Anne Fremantle. New York: Mentor, 1962.
Mao Tse-Tung on Revolution and War. Ed. M. Rejai. Garden City, N.Y.: Doubleday, 1970.
Marcuse, Herbert. *An Essay on Liberation.* Boston: Beacon, 1969.
Marcuse, Herbert. *One-Dimensional Man: Studies in the Ideology of Advanced Industrial Society.* Boston: Beacon, 1966.
Marx and the Western World. Ed. N. Lobkowicz. Notre Dame, Ind.: University of Notre Dame Press, 1967.
Marxism, Communism and Western Society. A Comparative Encyclopedia in 8 volumes. Ed. C. D. Kernig. New York: Herder & Herder, vols. I-IV, 1972.
Merleau-Ponty, M. *In Praise of Philosophy.* Tr. J. Wild and J. M. Edie. Evanston, Ill.: Northwestern University Press, 1963.
Merleau-Ponty, M. *Phenomenology of Perception.* Tr. C. Smith. New York: Humanities, 1962.
Merleau-Ponty, The Essential Writings of Maurice, Ed. Alden L. Fisher. New York: Harcourt, Brace and World, 1969.
Merleau-Ponty, M. *The Primacy of Perception and Other Essays.* Ed. J. M. Edie. Evanston, Ill.: Northwestern University Press, 1964.
Merleau-Ponty, M. *Signs.* Tr. R. C. McCleary. Evanston, Ill.: Northwestern University Press, 1964.
Merleau-Ponty, M. *The Structure of Behavior.* Tr. Alden L. Fisher. Boston: Beacon, 1963.
Merleau-Ponty, M. *The Visible and the Invisible.* Ed. C. Lefort. Tr. A. Lingis. Evanston, Ill.: Northwestern University Press, 1968.

Objections to Humanism. Ed. H. J. Blackham. London: Constable, 1963.

Petrovic, Gajo. *Marx in the Mid-Twentieth Century.* Garden City, N.Y.: Doubleday, 1967.
Phenomenology: The Philosophy of Edmund Husserl and its Interpretation. Ed. Joseph J. Kockelmans. Garden City, N.Y.: Doubleday, 1967.

Quotations from Chairman Mao Tse-Tung. Ed. Stuart R. Schram. New York: Bantam Books, 1972.

Richardson, William, S.J. "Heidegger and the Problem of God," *Thought* 40 (1965) pp. 130-40.
Richardson, William, S.J. "Heidegger and Theology," *Theological Studies* 26 (1965) pp. 86-100.
Richardson, William, S.J. *Heidegger: Through Phenomenology to Thought.* The Hague: Martin Nijhoff, 1963.

Sartre, Jean Paul. *Being and Nothingness.* Tr. Hazel E. Barnes. New York: Philosophical Library, 1956.
Sartre, J. P. *Critique de la Raison Dialectique, précédé de Question de Méthode.* Paris: Gallimard, 1960.
Sartre, J. P. *Existentialism.* Tr. B. Brechtman. New York: Philosophical Library, 1947.
Schaff, Adam. *A Philosophy of Man.* New York: Dell, 1968.
Schillebeeckx, Edward, O.P. *God and Man.* New York: Sheed & Ward, 1969, esp. Section 3, "Non-religious Humanism and the Search for God," pp. 41-84.
Schilling, S. Paul. *God in an Age of Atheism.* Nashville: Abingdon, 1969.
Schram, Stuart R. *Political Leaders of the Twentieth Century: Mao Tse-Tung.* Baltimore: Penguin, 1972.
Spiegelberg, Herbert. *The Phenomenological Movement: A Historical Introduction.* 2 vols. The Hague: M. Nijhoff, 1960.

Szczesny, Gerhard. *The Future of Unbelief.* Tr. Edward B. Garside. New York: G. Braziller, 1961.

Thevenaz, Pierre. *What is Phenomenology?* Ed. James M. Edie. Chicago: Quadrangle, 1962.

Wetter, Gustave A. *Dialectical Materialism:* a historical and systematic survey of philosophy in the Soviet Union. Tr. Peter Heath. New York: Praeger, 1959.

Toward a Christian
Anthropology (I)

*In the preceding chapter we examined in resumé represen-
tative versions of the three major humanisms which are
proposed to contemporary western man as atheistic or
non-theistic alternatives to Christian faith. In doing
so our aim, as Christian believers, was to enter as sympa-
thetically as we could into the minds and attitudes of those
who profess these faiths that we might be able later to
confront them in honest and realistic dialogue. Our present
task is to construct a Christian anthropology or understanding of man in the light of Christian faith which is
truly contemporary, that is, at once true to the image of
man proposed in Christian revelation and professed in the
faith of the Church and yet coherent with what the man
of today experiences and understands himself to be. To
the degree that we shall succeed in that purpose, we shall
be prepared to engage meaningfully and fruitfully in the
dialogue with other believers which is the context within
which we intend to pursue the apologetic goal of this work.
In this chapter we shall study the anthropologies of three
Christian thinkers. Today there is of course a numerous
company of thinkers in the various Christian traditions,
philosophers and theologians, whose views of man, often
influential and justly famed, could have been enlisted in
our cause. From so many a selection has to be made,
especially since our objective is not to survey the field,*

but rather to equip ourselves, within the reasonable limits that a work of this scope dictates, with the components of a truly contemporary Christian anthropology. Our choice has focused on three men who happen to be both French and Catholic. Neither attribute was essential, although it was imperative that the selection be limited to those who are both Christian and western in their outlook.

The three men are Gabriel Marcel, Maurice Blondel, and Teilhard de Chardin. It is hoped that the contributions they will make toward the building of a view of man, infused with a sincere Christian faith, which can be readily recognized by modern men as coinciding with their understandings of themselves, will vindicate their selection from so large a number.

Gabriel Marcel belongs, despite some disclaimers, to the existentialist camp. As a pioneer of the existentialist mode of thought, he has been critical of some, especially of Sartre, yet even his criticism has been creative and has helped to clarify his own position as a Christian theist in contrast with theirs. Martin Buber and Marcel have exercised an enormous influence on theology, psychology, and literature and almost every area where their personalism has helped to illuminate and nurture the understanding of the unique value of individual human beings within the human community.

Maurice Blondel is not yet well known to the English-speaking world. However, his presence has been felt, though unrecognized, in the thought of many better known thinkers, especially theologians, for whom his philosophy has been formative. This was especially true of those theologians whose influence was most potent in the Second Vatican Council. Blondel's principal writings are undergoing translation into English, and, even at this relatively late date, they can be expected to have a strong and crucial impact on American thinkers, and especially on American Catholic theologians. It is not, however, merely on the chance that his thought may soon become *à la mode*, but rather because of its intrinsic character as the authentically Christian vision of a prophetic mind whose insights are more congenial and suggestive to our generation than his own.

The inclusion of Teilhard de Chardin in this company hardly requires a justifying explanation. All of the reasons for doing so will only have become apparent at the conclusion of this volume. In the immediate context, it will suffice to note that his heroic forecast of the future of man and of this world is perhaps the only one proposed by a Christian that has attracted the respectful approval of Marxists and Scientific Humanists alike, and the enthusiastic discipleship of countless persons of every persuasion who perceive in his vision a truly contemporary, scientifically-based faith which they can embrace.

GABRIEL MARCEL: *Existentialist Theism*

Gabriel Marcel (1889-1973), a convert to Catholicism, who has been called a Christian Existentialist, prefers the term Neo-Socratic, which expresses his aversion to metaphysical system-building, his inclination towards tentative explorations of basic human themes presented in almost conversational style. Perhaps the most informative label that has been suggested would be "Reflective Empiricist."[1] For Marcel strives to be a philosopher of the concrete who begins from and never permits himself to stray from the concrete wholeness of existential experience. For him, philosophy is experience transmuted into thought, experience elevated by reflection to self-awareness, self-apprehension.

Human consciousness can and does exist on three levels which are reminiscent of but hardly identical with the Hegelian dialectical stages of immediacy, mediacy, and mediated or reflective immediacy. These are the stages of existence, objectivity, and being. The first is that of immediate experience; the second, the mode proper to science and logical thought, withdraws from the concrete wholeness of experience towards abstraction and logical systematization which are inevitable but are purchased at the price of the subject's disengagement from the unity of experience of which he is originally a participant. Being is indefinable and ultimately identified with the Absolute Thou, the ground of the community of beings, intimations of Whom we gain from the modes of inter-personal relationships.

The search for Being is the proper and exclusive enterprise of philosophy which seeks by reflection to recover the original integrity of existence in its foundations in the mystery of Being. This search does not yield its quarry to the objective methods of science or the techniques of abstract logic but to the more oblique, sinuous, and informal methods of philosophical meditation and reflection.

The primary datum of existence is the originating experience of "my body." It is this primitive experience from which all other experiences flow which gives density to my consciousnss of my own existence, and which provides the point of reference for all other assertions of existence. I experience my body, neither as the instrument of my self nor the term of any relation to it. On the other hand, the body and self are neither identified nor distinguished, for these are descriptions relevant only to objects. If I abstract from the feeling of my body as mine, I can think of it and deal with it as an object among other objects, but that is precisely to depart from what I experience. My body is so intimately one with my self that I must identify my body with my feeling of myself and of everything else that is other than myself. In other words my being is precisely an incarnate existence.

My consciousness of myself is grounded in my awareness of what is not self. I know myself knowing the other. My body which is myself incarnate and the root of all my feeling is the root of my feeling and consciousness of the other. My body is my link to what is not myself. It is my body's openness to and receptivity for others that is the condition for my own self-feeling and self-consciousness. Thus the other, affecting and affected by my body, elicits my active feeling as body-subject and, in its deepest resonances, my experience of him as the other subject, as Thou, elicits my subjectivity as an I in the awareness rooted in my body of our common participation in being.

My body allows me to contact the persons incarnate in other bodies through actions, gestures, and speech. This contact is not something merely passive since my very incarnate being as body is openness to others in view of the community of our participation in being.

When we have clearly understood that feeling is not reducible to undergoing although it is still a receiving, we will be able to discover the presence of an active element in feeling, something like a power of taking upon oneself, or better, of opening oneself to.[2]

Since my body is my incarnate self inserted into and in continuity with the world including other incarnate selves, there is no need of, as it were, getting out of myself to contact objects exterior to myself in a world outside. Rather, I am already constituted by my body as a living, feeling presence in immediate contact with the world.

By my body I am able to participate in the embodied existence of others and they correspondingly are able to enter into and share mine. This reciprocal openness to the incarnate existence of the other in mutual feeling is the root of intersubjectivity which begins with what Marcel describes as the "welcoming" character of feeling. Because I am my body and the other is his, I do not have to establish communication with him through or over barriers that separate our consciousnesses from each other. Instead we encounter each other as persons through bodily communion expressed through gestures, actions, and interactions, and it is as personal selves who are other that we enter into and are welcomed into each other's existence. Thus my existence like his is a co-existence (*co-esse*). By mutual bodily feeling and sensation, we actively share in each other's existence and we recognize that each of us is constituted in himself both by himself and the other without either of us losing his identity as other.

My being is a being-in-the-world-with-others. It is a being-in-the-world because I am an embodied existence. It is a being-with-others in the world because they and I are subject-bodies able to encounter each other directly as incarnate persons. My fullest and clearest consciousness of myself, therefore, is not of an isolated ego, but rather of shared existence with others. In fact, I experience my own personal existence the more deeply I share it with another. This is shown inversely when I tend to think of the other as though absent, as a *he*, and treat him accordingly on this more external and superficial level. In such a shallow meeting, I am aware of myself in a similar merely external way, as though I were someone else meeting a third party. Instead, when I truly open myself to this person and communicate with him not as a "he" but as a "thou," then we have formed a "we-community." I discover the more open I am to him as a "thou," the more open I am to myself, the more deeply I am revealed to myself. In the shared existence of the "we," the "I" and the "thou" mutually constitute each other.

To be open to the other is thus constitutive of the structure of human existence. I am myself because of and to the degree that I share existence, incarnate existence, with others. Marcel calls this structure *disponibilité*, which means "availability" but in his mind is more active and signifies the habitual inclination of welcoming the other into one's own interiority. It is

> an attitude demanded by the fact that the self's subjectivity is constituted by an alter-ego which founds its relations with others, so that it is true to say that it is a **we**—the self and the other—who create the I.[3]

The ontological role played by *disponibilité* highlights a fundamental theme of his metaphysics, the centrality of "thing," culturally understood, would appear to be in opposition to freedom, at least on the ontological level. For Marcel whose concrete philosophy takes its departure from the primitive data of intersubjective participation in incarnate existence, metaphysics is definable as "the logic of freedom."[4] In his mind,

> . . . progress in philosophy consists in the sum of successive steps whereby freedom, aware of itself as a simple capacity of affirmation and denial, incarnates itself, or, if one likes, becomes a real power of conferring a content on itself so as to discover and acknowledge itself for what it is.[5]

Marcel believes that we are identified with our freedom.[6] Since we are constituted in our personal being by our communion or mutual participation in that being with others, our ontological density, the depth of our participation in being is dependent on our openness to others and their openness to us. Such a relationship is not one of objective causality, but rather of summons and response which proceed from the free initiative of personal subjects that are reciprocally creative. The incessant challenge to this ontological responsibility is the temptation to treat the other freedom. A philosophy of being which equates being with or oneself as an object and thereby to debase the relationship by which we are mutually constituted. We are able and therefore free to succumb to this temptation because by virtue of primary reflection, typical of scientific and abstract thinking, we analyze wholes into parts, relationships into terms viewed as isolated. We transform ourselves from engaged participants into detached observers. It is only by secondary reflection, proper to philosophy, that we maintain original unity and wholeness, now more deeply comprehended, or reconstitute them when they have been lost and thereby recover our original authentic condition of involvement and participation.[7] "This reflection of the second degree of philosophical reflection," says Marcel,

> exists only for and by means of freedom; nothing external to me can force me to exercise it in this respect; the very notion of constraint in this context is devoid of content . . . Hence we can confirm the fact that our freedom is implied in the awareness of our participation in the universe.[8]

Freedom is not a problem. It is a mystery, a facet of the mystery of Being. The distinction between problem and mystery Marcel regards as a presupposition of his entire philosophical thought.

> A problem is something met with which bars my passage. It is before me in its entirety. A mystery, on the other hand, is something in which I find myself caught up, and whose essence is therefore not to be before me in its entirety. It is as though in this province the distinction between **in me** and **before me** loses its meaning . . . It is a proper character of problems, moreover, to be reduced to detail. Mystery on the other hand is something that cannot be reduced to detail.[9]

The mysterious and the ontological are identical, he insists, because we are "caught up" in every question of Being, whether it be freedom, my incarnate existence, or intersubjectivity. Each of these is a mystery because its positing and its solution "encroaches on its own immanent conditions of possibility."[10] Thus freedom is a ground of the very thought that tries to conceive it. The one who questions his own incarnate existence or co-existence with others is not addressing a problem which he stands over against as a detached observer, but he faces it from within as a participant of the Being which he questions.

Marcel bemoans the growing ineptitude of man in the technocratic society for the reflection that recognizes and acknowledges mystery and the transcendent dimension of human existence. He is either preoccupied with the end of actively organizing and controlling his world in accordance with the objective categories of science and the impersonal functions of his technology or he is passively accepting the stunted identity of merely functional roles and applying objectifying categories to his understanding of himself and his relations with others. Thereby he has lost the sensitivity to the wholeness of Being in which he participates and the presence of others as his sharers in a common destiny in which all are rooted and find the source of their hope. Man is alienated because he has lost the sense of mystery, of the encompassing Being in which we all commune.

In losing his power of reflection by which the wholeness of being is recovered and recollected, man has forgotten how to comprehend his own experience in its concreteness and its integrity. For his experience, as we have seen, is never his exclusively, but rather a shared experience with others in a we-community wherein each member-self is constituted in a process of creative mutuality. My experience of myself reveals me as drawn beyond myself in the course of my self-realization, rather than driven inwardly and away from others. I am compelled to seek my fulfillment in the fullness of being which overflows me and which discloses itself in the community of others with whom I share it in ceaseless interchange. In other words, it is the other who mediates being to the self.

Man feels the urgent need to ask himself: "Who am I?" Reflecting upon his self-experience in search of the answer, he is forced to look always beyond himself, to the other and to the fullness of being which he mediates and reveals. Man therefore must transcend himself to fulfill himself. But, Marcel insists, the exigence for transcendence is not the summons to transcend experience, to leave experience behind, "for beyond all experience, there is nothing," but rather to refine and deepen our understanding of our experience by the light of a purer, more discerning reflection.[11]

Marcel designates as "presence" the ontological dynamic

of intersubjectivity, the potency of the other and the self to mediate being for each other, to disclose in the process by which they mutually elicit and constitute each other the Being from which each issues as its common source. In an analysis reminiscent of Heidegger's understanding of truth as unconcealment or the self-revelation of being to man as the shepherd of being, he speaks of truth as the process of the revelation of being as the ground of the incarnate existents who share the intersubjective relation. For by virtue of this relation, the subject recognizes within the very experience his own finiteness and the other's, insofar as both are mutually dependent and limited. Further, he discovers in their mutual openness and interdependence the wider and deeper process of being in which they participate and which transcends them and any other finite participant in the community of beings.

The need or exigence for transcendence that powers the subject's drive for self-realization in the inter-subjective relation within which he confers being on the other as well as receiving being from him inevitably leads beyond each "other" to the "Other" whose englobing Presence intimates itself in every finite presence. This intimation is not the product of objective reasoning, but the recovering and re-collecting by secondary reflection of the transcending unity of immediate experience within the intersubjective relation. Marcel refuses resolutely to objectify this Being in a move which would be a betrayal of its mystery, of its encompassing wholeness in which the subject who inquires is also comprehended. By the same token he rejects a pantheistic interpretation which is a similar betrayal because it attempts to conceive Being as the ideal object conclusively enclosed within thought and achieved by the mind and, in that sense, subject to it. Being cannot be the object of experience or thought because it is Being which encompasses and grounds each of them. It is not by the objectifying methods of science, or rational speculation, but by the meditative reflection on the basic dynamics of human relations and their exigencies that the transcending truth of Being will be revealed, not as an Object, but as a Presence.

If it is so, the concrete approaches to the ontological mystery should not be sought in the scale of logical thought, the objective reference of which gives rise to a prior question. They should rather be sought in the elucidation of certain data which are spiritual in their right, such as fidelity, hope and love, where we see man at grips with the temptations of denial, introversion, and hard-heartedness.[12]

It is in those acts which are essentially expressive of our intersubjective existence that the Presence which grounds our communion in being will be disclosed. Since such acts are indeed free, they can proclaim a refusal as well as an assent to the Presence and therefore to our being which is His gift. Therefore, refusal is a perennial temptation and a testimony to the personal as well as the free character of this founding relationship.

The transcendent source and ground intimated by the exigence for transcendence emerging within the interpersonal relation is Himself personal, the Absolute Thou. The need for fullness of being points to Him beyond each finite Thou with whom I seek a relation of total engagement, of completely reciprocal fidelity, whose power to create ourselves is unconditioned. This hope is bound to inevitable frustration between finite, changeable subjects. Ultimately we place the other or ourselves in question; the "Thou" and the "I" are viewed from without and become merely an object.

The "I-Thou" relation is thus subject to many causes of discord. It is rare that I can succeed in seeing the other fully and only as "Thou" and not sometimes and somehow as "he." I am open to misunderstanding him, of creating an idea to which I offer my fidelity, only to have further experience uncover its inauthenticity. The love that the "Thou" has for me and which gives me personal significance is still a limited love which never reaches the depth of the self I know myself to be. I am keenly aware that my love for him fails in the same respect. Moreover, it is subject to the ebb and flow of time that constitutes our incarnate existences. In sum, we are incapable of the fidelity to which we aspire, that "active perpetuation of presence" by virtue of which the I and the Thou are created in a continual rhythm of invocation and response.[13] Thus the absolute fidelity for which each feels the need as the process of his self-creation within the "I-Thou" relation points beyond the finite other to the

Absolute Other Whose unconditional fidelity is not only its guarantee but the source of its meaning.

For Marcel, hope and love are equally eloquent and forceful intimations of transcendence at the heart of common human experiences. Hope confronts what is hopeless by human calculations and refuses to despair. If it is authentic, it is not reducible to wishful thinking or shallow optimism, but it is rather openness to a creative power that transcends the limits of objective probabilities. What is significant is not what is hoped for, but the One Who is the source of the hope. His Presence is freely accepted in a communion which is interior to the one who hopes and is the pledge which is proof against the calculations of those who are exterior to that communion.

Love, like hope, is creative of its object in the sense that love creates the lover as well as the beloved. It likewise transcends the objective judgments of those who are exterior to the love relation and posits the beloved in a realm that is beyond explanation and reduction. "It affirms the value of its object beyond the merely relative and contingent order of merit and demerit."[14] Thus the lover does not judge the beloved or try to justify his love with reasons, except those that are interior to the love itself. Thus to the love is attributed an absolute value and the beloved is thought of as participating in God and thus situated in an order that transcends all judgment. Accordingly love addresses itself to the eternal and in effect says to the beloved: "Thou at least shall not die." The more one loves, the more one sees the beloved as authentic Being, that is, as participating in a presence that cannot fail. Thus, although the Thou who is the object of love and the I who is its subject may partake of all the deficiencies of finite beings, the love that is the intense form of their communion invariably points beyond to the One Who envelopes them with a presence that is unconditioned and indefectible.

Fundamental to Marcel's ontological perspective is his conviction that being cannot be severed from value which he sees as the compelling implication of the exigence for being. This means that knowledge cannot be separated from love and therefore that the proper attitude with which to approach the mystery of Being is one of faith, which is affective or love knowledge, and humility. Otherwise we are in danger of objectifying Being and reducing it to a mere problem. It is this danger which he feels is not avoided in the traditional methods of proving the existence of God which do not take into account the spiritual condition of the one to whom the proofs are directed. What results is that they are least effectual with those who are in most need of them.

For Marcel, therefore, the ontological exigency which points beyond the revealing situations of I-Thou communion, such as fidelity, hope, and love, to the Absolute Thou as their ground does not amount to a logical demonstration of God's existence. It is rather a form of existential faith, and like any authentic faith, it is compenetrated by hope as well as love and it presupposes a radical humility. For it is an approach, not to an Object available to logical reasoning, but to a Thou, an Absolute Subject, Who is not accessible to objectivizing thought.

Therefore, God is approached not from effect to cause, but through the mystery of His Presence, which is welcomed and enjoyed as only a personal presence can be and not apprehended like an object or thing. A presence must be invoked or evoked rather than made the term of a rational inquiry. And so the Absolute Thou is known through a loving communion which presumes not so much an intellectual appreciation of His divine attributes as a volitional attitude of humility and adoration most appropriately expressed in prayer.

The faith that is in question here, Marcel insists, is not a determinate religious faith, and in particular the Catholic faith which he professes. It is rather a faith whose significance is determined completely within a metaphysical and spiritual economy in which, however, he is not compelled to abstract from the data provided by the existing religions. Such faith does not consist in *believing that* something is true, but rather always in

. . . belief in a **thou**, that is, in a reality, whether personal or suprapersonal, which is able to be invoked, and which is, as it were, situated beyond any judgment referring to an objective datum.[15]

There is always the temptation to make this faith the object of a primary reflection, to sever it from my believing relation with the Other and to treat it as something which I have or possess. Torn thus from its personal moorings, it can become alien and problematic. Even in the face of the objections of unbelief, faith as the content of a secondary reflection must remain rooted in an "I" personally related to a "Thou" Who is believed in as the source of his Being. In that situation, the believer can exercise his reflection

> . . . as the trial which will enable him to purify his faith, that is, to progress from a certainty which he is always tempted to look on as a possession, to a certainty that **he is a testimony**.[16]

The witness is not exterior to the One to Whom he bears witness, but rather in a living interrelationship. As long as he remains open to this Presence and permeable to His light, his faith may be limited by the insufficiency of his commitment. But it cannot be wrested from him as an object possessed to which he precariously clings since it is, even if often obscurely, identified with the being he attests to as his own.

Faith, as personal commitment to Another, is essentially free. I can freely choose to follow the path of transcendence with fidelity, to invoke the Absolute Thou in prayer, and to dispose myself for His gifts of grace, or not. I can decide between humility before God or pride which rejects Him. Humility is a form of creative receptivity inasmuch as it acknowledges man's dependence on God in an attitude of welcoming openness to the Author of his being. Thus it is a mode of being the opposite of Promethean pride. It is the admission of one's own nothingness, not in a masochistic gesture of self-debasement, but in the liberating recognition of one's own being as a gift of an infinite creative generosity. Everything is a grace, not least of which is the freedom with which we respond affirmatively or negatively to the Divine Giver.

The Christian who philosophizes does so in an historical context in which he is aware of a positive act of Self-Revelation by God to man in His redeeming Word made flesh in human history in the man, Jesus Christ. This may be a datum bearing on his concrete existence, but he may not employ it in his philosophical inquiry into Being. Yet that inquiry does in fact discover Being to be grounded in the creative Presence of an Absolute Thou, whose grace and revealing word every finite existent is. The gift of His own Person as His Word to man in an ultimate gesture of communion is a free initiative which can neither be anticipated nor demanded. Yet it is a possibility to which man is open as a final extravagance of the Absolute Thou with Whom he conducts a creative dialogue in which he recognizes that his very existence as a participant is a divine gift.

MAURICE BLONDEL: *Philosopher of Action*

Maurice Blondel (1861-1949) is one of the most intriguing and, especially but not exclusively from the viewpoint of a Catholic, one of the most prophetic thinkers that the past century has produced. Within the limited interests of this chapter it is notable that he is acknowledged by both Marcel and Teilhard as a major influence in the formation of their own thought. He was the practitioner of a phenomenological method and a philosopher in the existentialist mode *avant la lettre*, before either of those terms and their present reference had become current. William James, the giant of American Pragmatism, having read Blondel's own copy of *L'Action* (1893) in the absence of printed copies, wrote enthusiastically, "At present you belong for me to the race of absolutely original, probably prophetic thinkers with whom one feels that one must some day settle one's accounts."[17] He was looked upon with suspicion by his French colleagues in philosophy as a disguised apologete for Catholic faith and yet his *L'Action* scarcely escaped being put on the Index of Prohibited Books. Nevertheless he lived to see his principal works receive an official accolade from the French philosophical fraternity and his life-work a warm eulogy from Pius XII over the signature of Monsignor Montini, later Paul VI.

Blondel's philosophical career can be divided into three periods. The first commences on June 7, 1893 with the defense of his doctrinal dissertation at the Sorbonne, *L'Action*[18] and includes his "Letter on Apologetics," which first appeared (1896) in the *Annales de Philosophie Chrétienne,* a journal which he later purchased and revived, and "History and Dogma," which appeared in the periodical *La Quinzaine* in 1904.[19]

There followed a long period (1896-1927) during which he taught philosophy at the university in Aix-en-Province but produced no major writings. He was engaged in clarifying and defending the relation of philosophy and faith against his fellow-philosophers who accused him of compromising the autonomy of philosophy and against the Catholic theologians who charged him with compromising the supernatural character of faith. In the process he was deepening and broadening his vision, a process that would bear its fruits during his third and last period, 1927-1949, when, forced by blindness to retire from teaching, he dictated and published his famous trilogy on thought, being, and action. To this was added *La Philosophie et l'Éspirit Chrétien* which, though never finished by its author, still constituted the completion of the meaning of the whole enterprise.

> Yes or no, has human life a meaning and has man a destiny? . . . The problem is inevitable; man resolves it inevitably; and this solution, right or wrong, voluntary at the same time that it is necessary, each one carries out in his actions. That is why one must study action.[20]

These words from the introduction to *L'Action* set the stage not only for his inaugural work, but to a large extent for his life's work in philosophy. Blondel thus raised the perennial problem of moral philosophy, but it inevitably led him to confront the broad range of philosophical problems. Rapidly dissatisfied with this earliest attempt, he formed the intention of facing the basic problem in the widest possible context, an intention that was finally fulfilled in his trilogy.

Blondel's earliest motivation was apologetic, but he quickly became convinced that the most forceful vindication of the Catholic faith, which he held so dearly, was by a rigorous adherence to the demands and limitations of genuine philosophical method. This most exacting project led him in the constant search to unite the integrity and freedom of life with the logical necessity of reason. In this ambition and the conviction of its rightness, he was of course at odds with Marcel and other existentialist thinkers who would regard such a project as an attempt to square a circle. Whether he succeeded, one must judge from his results.

Blondel then was a Christian philosopher, and no less either for being the other. The tension between these two poles of his life was the mainspring of his thinking. From the beginning it provided his philosophy with a compelling urgency because it led inexorably to a total commitment on the part of the person who followed him. It also set him into instant and unqualified antagonism to the dominant trend of western philosophy of his own time and the century that preceded him which held as beyond dispute the irreconcilable opposition between Christianity and philosophy, between theism and humanism. In that sense he was an anomaly to his contemporaries who were not able to dismiss him in the face of his allegiance to the exigencies of authentic philosophy.

To his mind, philosophy had to concern itself with the ultimate destiny of man which, as a Christian, he firmly believed was truly "supernatural." The very word was anathema! His very personal integrity itself demanded that he determine whether, by philosophical means alone, he could establish that man, by the very dynamism of his nature, aspires to a fulfillment which nature itself cannot provide, which philosophy, confined to the immanence of nature, could propose only as a hypothesis. But would that hypothesis be inevitable, if one were faithful to the demands of the real?

L'Action (1893)

He chose as his starting point what was humanly most real, total, and concrete: *action*. For him it involved all man's activity, including his thought, but always in the context of the complete person, the *agent-in-action*. This very choice, at one stroke, placed him beyond rationalism and voluntarism and any of their modern tributaries, for it pointed beyond intellect and will and any single human power to their unitary source in man's originating power to act.

Blondel gave his dissertation on action the sub-title: "A Critique of Life and a Science of Practice." It indicates the method which the object as well as the aim of his inquiry dictated. Its first movement is a regressive analysis which seeks to determine the necessary conditions for the possibility and fact of action, and having traced the necessary stages of its development, it provides a science of action. This double movement of reduction and deduction constitutes a dialectic which recognizes a distinction or lack of identity between reflection and what is reflected upon, between actuality and thought—in other words, between the living action and our conception of it which is never able to do more than approach by stages its integral reality. Like Hegel, to whom he is often compared, he proposed a dialectic as a logic of the concrete. For both, life is bigger than the logic of abstract thought, but logic is as large as life because there is a logic of life and reason. For Blondel, it was the logic of action within which the activity of reason was only one species.

Is action a necessary datum and therefore an adequate starting point for his philosophy? Yes, because we cannot not act. Even to refuse to act is to act. We are thrust into existence and into the inevitability of acting, whereby our destiny is determined. Even suicide, which would terminate that existence, is an act and fraught with destiny.

The dilettant aspires to complete detachment, to avoid committing himself in action. Yet, as we have seen, even his refusal is an action and it is also an attitude toward life and its meaning. The pessimist who in effect chooses nothingness, the negation of a meaningful life, still chooses, wills, and therefore acts. Thus I cannot not act, I cannot not will, and concretely to will is always to will something. Moreover, I do not will just anything. There is an order to which my willing to act is impelled, and in the mature will this order is definable as the striving for the ever fuller life. Accordingly Blondel applies his regressive analysis to try to uncover the necessary order that the mature will to act follows as it strains for fulfillment. Thereby will be made explicit, if it is successful, the destiny written into the dynamism from which his will to act springs.

Blondel has already uncovered in the dilettante and the pessimist a discrepancy between the conscious will to act or not to act in specific ways and a deeper implicit will or dynamism of action from which the free conscious will would deviate but cannot escape. In pursuing his inquiry, he examines various attitudes which attempt to confine human action within certain limits or to define human existence from a particular perspective. In each instance the would-be limits are surpassed and there always emerges a disproportion between the object willed and the more profound inner force which radically moves us to act. Thus he is led to distinguish the will as free, the conscious source of our deliberate acts, which he calls the *willed-will* (*la volonté voulu*), from the will as necessary, the *willing-will* (*la volonté voulante*), the primordial determinism which is the constituting source of all our actions.

The goal of his dialectical inquiry in *L'Action* is to disclose the series of ends or necessary conditions through which the will to act is compelled to pass as it reaches for human fulfillment. This is revealed negatively in the various attitudes and philosophical positions which betray their limits as they are successively over-reached, and positively in the various levels of human action that man is necessitated to traverse as he strains to realize himself.

Gradually it becomes more apparent that what each person is driven towards in his actions is to will freely and consciously for himself what his primordial will moves him towards, to bring his *willed-will* in conformity with his *willing-will,* to consent to his own being and thus become freely what he is necessarily, or is at least in the process of being determined to become, on the deepest level of his being. In fact, he is free to consent to his being or not at each stage of his development which thus offers itself as an option rather than as an inexorable necessity. But he will not go without penalty for refusing to choose the way that leads to truth and life. For truth is indeed the conformity of mind with life, an adequation between freedom and necessity, between what we freely will and what is necessarily willed by the innermost will. This is the immanent norm whose contents are made explicit by the reflective analysis of life's developing stages and formulated in the science of action. To discover this truth, since man is free to deviate from it, requires a personal asceticism as well as a rigorous method to discover what is necessary and inevitable in the midst of what appears most free.

In his positive analysis, Blondel exposes the various levels and spheres of human action in a sequence which is seen to be necessary and indispensable for human development. Simultaneously each is recognized as incomplete and needing to be surpassed inasmuch as one cannot realize himself fully by remaining at any of them, for an inner urge and dissatisfaction always drives him further. The primary level of action is that of sensation, since it is the most elementary datum or object to be willed. It is rapidly surpassed in the early recognition of the need to organize its disorderly data into some system. At its highest level, this drive expresses itself in science which seeks methodically to organize the diversity of phenomena into an objective system. But from the viewpoint of the agent seeking fulfillment in action, science points beyond itself as the agent's own construction, as the enterprise of a free subject in the very process of uncovering the enveloping system of objective determinism.

The temptation at this point is to limit the horizons of the quest to the individual subject. But the insufficiency is quickly revealed in the interdependence of human actions, by which individual agents are inevitably engaged in a world of other agents with whom they become inextricably and ever more deeply involved. Individual action necessarily becomes social action, and the individual's inner needs and urgings move him toward the most intimate union with others, that of love. This gives rise to the family and the objectivizing of mutual love in children.

The same urges and determinisms of human actions point beyond the family to the society of a nation and humanity itself as the entire family of men with whom we share the same drives and aspirations, the same will. Finally we recognize that mankind is situated within a universe of reality, a totality which is the horizon of man's finiteness but which man can appropriate by his mind and will, preeminently in a metaphysics or philosophy of being and in a morality or philosophy of action by which he strives to give meaning and direction to his life.

The dynamism in this whole surging movement is seen to be the need for man to go outside and beyond himself for his own completion, to transcend himself in order to realize himself, and this precisely in a response to a drive that arises from the most intimate depths of his own interiority. In turn each stage of his campaign for self-realization proves inadequate, the freely willed acts on each level are still unequal to the ceaseless drive that springs from the immanent source of all his actions, the *willing-will*. The outcome of Blondel's analysis is that this disproportion does not cease on the metaphysical level where man understands himself and orientates his actions within the perspective of the Whole of Being. His innermost desire drives him even beyond that horizon to transcend anything and everything that is finite. Thus infinity is recognized at least negatively as an exigency at the very source of man's power to act which gives it an impetus and momentum that nothing finite can definitively obstruct or satisfy. This infinity, which is transcendent to everything human (and, to use Bultmann's phrase, of this eon), is the primary necessity and determinism discovered at the heart of man's immanence, of his contingency and freedom. Its discovery is not the conclusion of a speculative argument from contingency, but rather the unveiling of a transcendent factor in the immanence of actual human action.

The final temptation is to superstition, that is, to turn something finite into the infinite, or, in other terms, to absorb the infinite into some accessible finite object. This is exemplified in every instance of the absolutizing of the relative, whether science, art, man himself or those instances of philosophies which reduce God to man's conception of Him. The intrinsic contradiction of this strategem is eventually uncovered when the finite reality beneath the appearance of infinity fails to satisfy the infinite aspirations of the primordial will. This is the last futile effort on man's part to match his willed actions to the limitless exigencies at the root of those actions within the domain of nature, that is, within the horizon of ends available to the intrinsic resources of human action.

> From all these attempts results this doubly compelling conclusion: it is impossible not to recognize the insufficiency of the whole natural order and not to feel a further need; (at the same time) it is impossible to find within oneself that with which to satisfy this religious need. **It is necessary and yet it is impracticable.** There you have, to put it baldly, the conclusions of the determinism of human action.[21]

Thus the outcome of Blondel's analysis of the dialectics of human action is that the necessary condition for its fulfillment is beyond its reach, that what we will necessarily as the goal of our actions decisively exceeds the range of the actions which we can will. This insufficiency is seen to belong to the human condition itself. It provokes interim crises whenever man's will to act and to transcend his present state is frustrated by obstacles that cannot be presently overcome or faults whose consequences cannot be undone. Death seems to be the final defeat· Yet it is the very indestructibility of the will from which actions spring which underline the frustrations as contrary to its indomitable desires. Man cannot evade the necessity of willing himself, of bringing his willed acts in conformity with the profound finality from which they spring, and yet it is beyond his power finally to bring about their coincidence. What will be the issue of this conflict?

> It is this conflict that explains why there must be present in consciousness a new affirmation, and it is the reality of this necessary presence that accounts for our consciousness of the conflict itself. There is a "Unique Necessary." The whole movement of the determinism carries us towards that end, which is at the same time the source from which arises that very determinism whose whole purpose is to lead us back to itself.[22]

I must affirm the Divine Transcendent as the end of the dynamism of all my actions which is also immanently present as the Source of those actions. For Blondel, the identity of the end and the source of action and its ideal norm, which man himself can in principle never achieve on his own, is required to explain how he can act at all. For the whole magnificent dialectic of his actions from their primitive beginnings to their highest attainments in the pursuit of infinity played out on the stage of the universe itself points to an identity of action and wisdom which man never realizes but which coming from outside him is intimately present to him from his very first act. Whatever one may judge of this analysis as a proof of God's existence, it does stress the immanence of God in every human action as an exigence of action itself, including the action whereby His presence is given an explicit affirmation.

Once the existence of the transcendent end of man's action has been affirmed, the logical possibility arises of a transcendent fulfillment of those actions. For the philosopher this can be no more than a hypothesis, even though a necessary one. For it involves an initiative on the part of the Transcendent, of God, which would be truly *supernatural* and entirely gratuitous.[23] Philosophy can affirm the transcendent inasmuch as it is discerned in the immanence of human existence, for example, in the insufficiency of human action except as rooted in a transcendent source. On the other hand, the supernatural is not discernible in the immanence of human existence, for its initiative, free and gratuitous on God's part, is not implied or required by the existence of the Transcendent knowable in the conditions of man's action and existence. Yet the hypothesis of the supernatural is a necessary one for philosophy and for every man who is at least implicitly aware of it, since it posits the final solution of the enigma of human action and its natural insufficiency. It confronts man with an imperative option: to choose between alternatives that define the meaning and destiny of man.

> Yes or no: would (man) will to live, even to the point of dying for it, so to speak, by consenting to be supplanted by God? Or will he pretend to suffice of himself without Him, profiting by His necessary presence without making it voluntary, borrowing from Him the power to get by without Him, and willing infinitely without willing the infinite.[24]

To choose the arrogance of self-sufficiency is ultimately self-destructive because it denies the very dynamism of his power to act. Man can only fully live and achieve the fulfilling of his life of action by opening his own will to the will of Another, by opening himself to an action other than his own.

The idea of the supernatural, which is indeterminate as

it is conceived in the philosophical hypothesis and is as such available to the reason of men at large, is rendered determinate by the historic religions and especially in historic Christianity. Thus the philosopher who can only consider the supernatural as a possibility, a hypothesis or ideal construction of his own mind, is confronted in man's religions and most specifically in Christianity with the claim of its actual occurrence.

The Christian claim is that God has exercised a free and gratuitous initiative by communicating Himself to man in Jesus Christ and that this salvific intervention continues in human history in the teaching, actions, and practices of His Church. The philosopher can accept these as historical data available to any man and with them to confront the exigencies of human action, the aspirations of man for a fulfillment which seems inaccessible to merely human and natural resources. Do the Christian dogmas and practices, which are presented as coming from beyond the merely natural and human, so determine the possibility of the supernatural that we discover in them the reflection of our real needs and the longed-for response to the profound aspirations which the dialectic of human actions has uncovered?

Regarding them merely as hypotheses, Blondel attempts to show that the logic of Christian truth and practice concretely realized in Christian revelation and faith, salvation and the sacramental economy, is fundamentally identical with the internal logic of human action as it has dialectically unfolded and revealed its finality. This is not an assertion of the truth of Christianity, an action and commitment that can only proceed from itself. Philosophy can only invite a man to make such a commitment and to verify in his own living action the truth of Christianity as that fulfillment of human aspirations that can only originate as a free initiative of the divine Transcendent.

The final option which philosophy offers but which can only be embraced in faith is actually only the last in a series of options that emerge at various stages of the evolving dialectic of human actions. The philosophy of action is a science or logic of practice. "It is not so much reflection *on* action as reflection *of* action on itself."[25] It requires a philosopher to participate experimentally in action, testing and directing it from within. This demands a commitment and engagement on his part which involves his freedom as well as his intelligence. This conjunction of his freedom of decision with a necessity recognized by reason need not jeopardize or compromise either. It is in this context that truth can be defined as the conformity of freedom and necessity. The necessary determinism of the *willing-will* disclosed in the dialectic of action does not necessitate the *willed-will* to submit to its norms and therefore leaves scope for a free decision between both options. But the refusal to consent to its exigencies does not prevent them from making their demands at the deeper levels of one's being-for-action. What we have then is a logic of action, which is a logic because it traces an order of rational necessity, but which proposes this order as a series of norms that must be acknowledged and consented to freely. It is therefore a logic of freedom, which constitutes "an interior norm that is always present and which is ratified in one way or another by an option that is as free as it is inevitable."[26]

Blondel could not affirm the actuality of divine revelation or the truth of Christianity as the authentic determinate form of that revelation as the conclusion of his philosophical analysis of human action and its finality. Philosophy could raise the question, propose a divine revelation as a necessary hypothesis, and examine Christianity in the light of the inner logic of the intentionality of human action as a concretization of such a hypothesis. But it was faith alone that could embrace the Christian option as its fulfilling truth. Quite consistently, however, with his philosophy which required a free commitment to the options offered by the unfolding determinism of human action, he did not hesitate to risk at the very conclusion of his work a profession of his Christian faith as an afterword, an action beyond philosophy that was yet the final personal option which constituted its crowning fulfillment.

The Trilogy: His Mature System

Not unexpectedly, Blondel's treatment of the super-

natural as a properly philosophical theme met resolute resistance from his largely rationalist confreres who accused
him of compromising the autonomy of philosophy and of
its method which was restricted to the immanent bounds
and conditions of human consciousness. His appointment
to a teaching position was delayed for two years and finally,
in 1896, he received a permanent post on the *Faculté des
Lettres* at Aix-en-Provence, where he remained until 1927.

Both as a response to his philosophical critics as well
as a clarification of his view of the apologetic task in the face
of Catholic misunderstanding, he wrote his "Letter on
Apologetics," which appeared in six installments in the
Annales de Philosophie Chrétienne, January to July, 1896.
In it he attempted to expose the philosophical inadequacy of
earlier apologetic procedures while vindicating his own as
an effective apologetics which was at the same time a legitimate and authentic exercise of philosophy.

His simultaneous solution of both issues, the apologetic
and the philosophical, was offered in his method of immanence. It is actually the method of *L'Action* made explicit
in its application to apologetics. For his analysis of action
had revealed the constant and necessary reciprocity of immanence and transcendence, of autonomy and heteronomy,
insofar as man realized himself only at the cost of transcending himself.

This purely philosophical inquiry into the dialectic of
human action eventually arrives at the discovery of its own
incompleteness, of the necessity of invoking the supernatural
as an hypothesis to complete the story of man's striving for
fulfillment which philosophy is unable to finish because the
source of the fullness is beyond human reach or demand.
Thus

> . . . both faith and reason teach that the supernatural must be
> humanly inaccessible. What faith imposes upon us as a reality, reason
> conceives as necessary but impracticable for us. The one declares
> to be gratuitously given what the other can only postulate inevitably,
> so that they coincide not by overlapping but because one is empty
> and the other full . . .
> The method of immanence, then, can consist in nothing else than
> in trying to equate, in our own consciousness, what we appear to
> think and to will and to do with what we do and will and think in
> actual fact—so that behind factitious negations and ends which are

not genuinely willed may be discovered our innermost affirmations and the implacable needs which they imply.[27]

Blondel's use of the method of immanence in apologetics provoked the criticism of many Catholic theologians who accused him of naturalizing the supernatural and denying the gratuitousness of the order of grace. Certain statements in the "Letter" lent themselves to misinterpretation by their ambiguity or imprecision. That the opposite was his intention Blondel insisted in numerous replies. Eventually he allowed the controversy to lapse by withdrawing from it. He became convinced that his most powerful rejoinder would be a more comprehensive development of his thought in which the controversial aspects of *L'Action* and the "Letter" would appear more balanced as parts of a larger whole.

In spite of the near blindness that compelled him to retire from teaching in 1927. Blondel produced his voluminous Trilogy for publication between 1934 and 1937: *La Pensée, L'Être et les êtres,* and his second *L'Action.* His earlier work had been a phenomenology of action. This was a full-fledged metaphysics which carried forward the intention of his original thought within a much broader design. He was to call it a " 'unitary trinitarianism'—a trinity of thoughts, of beings, and of actions, issuing from unity and striving to rediscover it."[28] However, by a deliberate decision, he restricted the Trilogy to the bounds of the more usual philosophical terrain and postponed his confrontation of philosophy and Christianity until he wrote a fourth part: *La Philosophie et l'Éspirit Chrétien,* whose two volumes were published in 1944 and 1946. This work which he was to call "the indispensable coping and keystone of the building"[29] which the Trilogy composed, was the essential completion of his fundamental plan and therefore constitutes a Tetralogy.

Between the early *L'Action* (1893) and the Trilogy, there is a fundamental continuity within the enlarged perspective whereby the living logic of action is seen both as a paradigm and an instance of a broader logic involving thought and being as well as action. He betrays the perduring influence of the German Idealists, Fichte, Schelling, and Hegel, whose thought he had carefully assimilated, in his insistence that it is only within the Whole and always with reference to the Absolute that the dialectical integration of the diverse realms of reality are seen as intelligible. However, throughout his vast enterprise, he never deviated from contact with the real to which action was always his key, that action which served as the intermediary between thought and being.

In *La Pensée*, he is characteristically concerned not with the epistemological question of the objective reference of thought, but with thought as action. He traces its development, not in itself as an isolated entity or process, but as a facet of the cosmic process from its obscure beginnings through its evolution in the organism, mind, and consciousness. Thought reveals a structure of a duality of facets which reproduce the universal pattern of unity in diversity. Thought grasped as a reflection of the cosmic process is seen as an effort towards unification in the presence of multiplicity and change.

Each of these facets is realized in a form of thought. Abstract or notional thought, which he calls *noetic*, is unifying, universal, rational, relational. Concrete or real thought, which he calls *pneumatic*, is concerned with the singular, the unique, the ineffable. These two functions are at once distinct and united in a dialectical tension.

The tension is ceaselessly sustained by their unabating inadequation, by their irreducibility, and it gives rise to dialectic which is recognized as another example of the dynamism which we have already seen as operating in human action. For it is perceived that thought in driving toward the unity of the concrete real which it knows in its diversity and change, a unity which is ever and only abstractly conceived, is doomed never to achieve their reconciliation by its own immanent resources. Thought, like action, is impelled to seek the actualization of its own interior finality beyond itself in a Transcendent Thought which is, in its ultimate form, unity in diversity, concretely realized. At this point the inevitable option presents itself: whether human thought is to content itself with organizing the diversity of its world by recourse to the unity of Absolute Thought possessed merely as object of its own conception, as "Thought Thought" (*Pensée Pensée*), or whether it will open itself to be possessed by Him Who, though Transcendent, would freely give Himself in the personal union of faith as the ultimate principle of man's thought, as "Thinking Thought" (*Pensée Pensante*). Thus the drama of man whose absolute fulfillment is unachievable on his own and relies on his openness to the free initiative and self-gift of the Divine Transcendent is played out on the stage of human thought.

Thought points beyond itself to being. For if thought is of being, it is not itself the whole of being. The philosophy of thought calls for and is complemented by a philosophy of being, presented by Blondel in *L'Être et les êtres*. Its title indicated its principal objective, that of reconciling Absolute Being with contingent beings. Our experience reveals a vast array of existents: matter, organisms, persons, society, and the universe itself, recognized reflectively as constituting a hierarchy or orderly heterogeneity of beings by virtue of a spontaneous idea of Being which conceptualizes a sense of being, a conviction of a real and pervasive presence. This provokes the affirmation of Absolute Being because we are aware that no one being nor the whole universe of beings exhausts being, that they rather point beyond themselves so that being is only equal to itself in terms of the affirmation of Absolute Being. Thus, as in *La Pensée*, we are confronted with an inadequation at the heart of man's immanence which requires an appeal to the Transcendent intimately present to that immanence as the source of its intelligibility.

But what reality can be attributed to contingent beings which require an Absolute Being, wholly self-sufficient and necessarily existing, to account for their own being? The solution lies in resisting any notion of their opposition or exteriority and in affirming their consonance in an interior unity. Man and the universe are incomplete and always open to further development. They are in a constant process of becoming towards complete realization which is animated by a Power that is the creative source of the design by which, as well as the destiny toward which, they are proceeding. The intrinsic plan of this process amounts to a concrete logic of beings which is constitutive as well as normative of their development. This concrete logic is called the "ontological normative" by Blondel. Somewhat like that of Hegel, it expresses the understanding that, in the concrete, beings in opposition do not cancel out one another, as in abstract logic governed by the rule of contradiction, but rather that they compose a system of contending forces, which are related by mutual implication. In this ontological logic, we are brought to a heightened awareness of the ultimate unity of being and thought.

In the last section of his work, Blondel delineates this logic in the cosmic function of matter. Matter is, in a certain sense, the mother as well as the companion of all contingent beings. It is the measure of their contingency, that by which they are divided from one another as well as that by which they are united in terms of their participation in the universe of beings (a theme reminiscent of Marcel or rather anticipatory of him). Matter is the seed out of which higher being germinates, for matter is capable of vitalization and thus the evolving chain of being is propelled towards its goal: life is capable of being spiritualized, and spirit is capable of aspiring to union with the Absolute. Thus the whole universe, pervaded by matter, achieves its goal in spirit; that is, its destiny is one with that of matter, the living, spiritual being that man is. As always, it offers itself as an option which man can embrace or reject. But as an offer to freedom, it is still the expression of normative logic according to which the universe of beings achieves its self-fulfillment by aspiring to the Transcendent Absolute present in the depths of its own immanence.

The final option in which both the philosophy of thought and that of being culminate points to action as its necessary implementation. At the same time action clearly emerges as the mediator between thought and being, the bond that links the ideal and the real orders. Thus Blondel's intention to give his philosophy of action a more balanced role in a more comprehensive setting was being realized.

L'Action (1937) appeared in two volumes. It was not the mere reworking of the earlier thesis, but a largely new work. Its first volume poses the problem of human action in terms of the metaphysical problem of the relation of secondary causes to Pure Action (*le Pur Agir*). It is the transposition of the problem of *L'Être et les êtres,* the relation of contingent and Absolute Being, to the realm of action: that of the relation of secondary causes to the First Cause. It is resolved by an appreciation of the growth of action as causal from a condition of greater passivity on the physical and biological level (*actus hominis et naturae*) to that of greatest activity on the spiritual level (*actus humani*). Even on the highest level of spirit, activity is mixed with passivity. Thus it recapitulates and reaffirms the conditions of action on the levels that precede it, while it acknowledges its own insufficiency. It thus opens the whole sequence of secondary causes which it culminates to affirming its dependence on a First Cause that is Pure Action and the creative source of all action that is less than wholly self-originating.

The second volume leaves the metaphysical study of the essence of action for the consideration of action as it is exercised in living practice. It is to a great extent a retouching of the thesis of 1893, omitting its final sections on the concrete content of Christianity, the link between knowledge and action, and the consonance between the doctrines and practice of Christianity and the inner logic of action. It is more significant for its rounding out of the Trilogy and its unifying themes than for any new development of his general philosophy of action.

In the Trilogy, Blondel elaborated a metaphysical exploration of the fundamental conditions of the created order. In the course of it, he was able to affirm the identity of the concrete logic disclosed by a metaphysics of contingent being with that already uncovered by a phenomenology of human action. He was still intent upon a science of action, to keep knowledge wedded to action and to life. His analysis confirmed his intention by revealing action to be the essential link between thought and being, between science and practice. In thought and in being, as in action, we confront a duality seeking a unity that always escapes us. This universal condition of irreducible inadequation points to the universal truth that everything natural and human is incomplete in itself and must be open to the transcendent to receive as a gift the fulfillment which it is unable to achieve on its own.

Blondel wrote the two volumes of *La Philosophie et l'Ésprit Chrétien* to complete the project which the Trilogy had left unfinished; in his own words to provide

the explanation and the justification of the conclusions which were rather disconcertingly left in suspense where the Trilogy left off: namely, with an incapacity to achieve fulfillment, a nostalgia for knowledge or a beatitude inaccessible to our restless seeking, even to our thought, our apprehension.[30]

He had deliberately omitted the confrontation of philosophy and Christianity with which he had concluded the first *L'Action.*

In his own mind, it was a specifically philosophical work, even though unprecedented, and constituted a philosophy of religion, more especially a philosophy of Catholic Christianity. In it he accosted the imperious but inefficacious aspirations which evoke the hypothesis of a divine revelation with the Christian fact specified in Catholic dogma, sacraments, and practices as the concrete actualization of that hypothesis. What he set out to show was the inner integrity of Catholic faith and its coherence with the human exigencies serially disclosed in the unfolding project of the Trilogy. His aim was to arrange the encounter of the rational and moral intiatives of human nature with man's supernatural vocation. This he went about doing by formulating the philosophical enigmas occasioned by the ultimate insufficiency of those intiatives and confronting them with the Christian mysteries in which the enigmas are resolved by the gratuitous novelties of a transcendent initiative.

There is a correspondence between the enigmas of the philosophers and the mysteries of the Christian faith which Blondel compares to the relation between the baptism conferred by John and the redemptive baptism of the Spirit imparted by Christ for which it served as a preparation as well as an impetus. The philosopher does not merely prepare the way for the mysteries, but raises and provokes the problems concerning man's destiny which he himself cannot resolve. The solutions constituted by the mysteries, incomprehensible and inaccessible to the philosopher's reason, are yet seen in their correspondence to the immanent exigencies which the philosopher has disclosed and in their surpassing power to bring them to an unpredictable felicitous fulfillment. Thus a "symbiosis" prevails between philosophy and the Christian spirit, which is both normal and salutary since it preserves their essential autonomy while it acknowledges their integrating roles in posing and resolving the problems of human destiny.

Blondel never got to write the planned third volume of *La Philosophie et l'Éspirit Chrétien* which would have brought this Tetralogy to a final completion. It was quite appropriate that he should not have done so. His thought constituted a system that was meticulously ordered and yet perpetually open in the recognition of its own essential insufficiency and its insatiable urge to surpass natural and human limitations.

PIERRE TEILHARD DE CHARDIN: *Convergent Evolution*

To one who encounters it for the first time, the convergence of the life-projects of Maurice Blondel and Pierre Teilhard de Chardin (1881-1955) can come as a startling discovery. From the very beginning of his mature life until its end, each man devoted himself very deliberately to developing a truly effective Christian apologetics for his contemporary world. Consequently each addressed himself to unbelievers as well as to his fellow believers and in trying to carry out his intentions with scrupulous honesty often earned the antagonism of both camps. Happily, Teilhard, like Blondel, was to receive strong acceptance from all sides, but, ironically, it would be only after his death that he would attain the status of a cult among his fellow Catholics.

Blondel had already approached his full stature and the maturity of his thought, when the young Jesuit was commencing his career, drawing considerable inspiration from the older man's achievements and their implications. Through a mutual friend, Father Auguste Valensin, S.J., a fellow novice of Teilhard and a pupil of Blondel, they entered into an indirect correspondence regarding some of Teilhard's earlier writings which Blondel agreed to read and comment upon. It was the beginning of a life-long acquaintance.

Their letters reveal the congeniality of their personalities, the fundamental likeness of their world outlooks, and yet the equally emphatic difference which their highly original minds compelled them to acknowledge. Even at this early stage, the younger man was already in firm possession of what were to be his controlling insights.[31] There was an obvious difference in their chosen fields, Blondel being a philosopher, Teilhard a scientist. Yet each combined unparalleled competence and indisputable integrity in his science with his passionate desire to pursue his professional path to that point where, he was convinced, it would converge with the truth he already ardently possessed by his Christian faith.

The extraordinary union of the scientist and the mystic which we find in Teilhard was inherited from his parents: the former from his father, an amateur naturalist, and the latter from his mother's strong and simple Catholic faith. The fusion of these two strains readied him for his unique vocation and ignited him with the burning conviction that would see it through. His reading of Bergson's *Creative Evolution* crowned his growing belief in the unity of the universe as an evolving system growing out of matter to the consciousness of spirit in man. His profound faith in the Incarnation would lead him to focus the cosmic process of evolution on the God-man, Jesus Christ, as its culmination and its driving impetus.

As it had done for Blondel, his Christian faith would serve to provide the unifying vision for his scientific synthesis. Like his philosophical predecessor, however, he would be meticulous, at least in intention, in striving to preserve the autonomy of each: his scientific methodology and his supernatural faith. Both men shared the conviction that the most effective apologetics could be shaped only by the most rigorous adherence to the methodological canons of the sciences they practiced.

It should not be misleading then to state that Teilhard's apologetics was constituted mainly by his scientific work and the theories he built upon it. Accordingly it ought to come as no surprise to learn that one of the most useful synopses of his life-work may be found in a small apologetic essay "How I believe."[32]

Teilhard's scientific specializations were in paleontology and geology, although his voracious curiosity wandered into every other area of inquiry that was at all associated with them. His internationally recognized competence in his special fields earned him a participation in numerous expeditions to Asia, Africa, and the two Americas over a period extending from 1923 until the year of his death, 1955. It was during an expedition in China, the country where he attained his greatest renown as a field-scientist, that he wrote a letter dated 23 September, 1934, outlining his plan for the requested apologetic opuscule.

> I have sketched out a draft of an essay that M. B. de S. [Footnote: "Mgr Bruno de Solages, rector of the Institut Catholique in Toulouse."] has been asking me for for a long time. I am calling it 'Comment je crois' ('Why and How'). [. . .] Thinking this out forces me to analyse and synthesize my own self more fully. I am determined to persevere until I have finished it and with all the sincerity that I can achieve [. . .] I am studying the successive developments of an adherence which, proceeding from faith to faith, rejoins the Christian current (or phylum) by convergence: faith in the world, faith in the spirit in the world, faith in the immortality of the spirit in the world, faith in the growing personality of the world. I feel that I have a better grasp than I had a year ago of concepts which enable me really to have confidence in the thesis.[33]

In his forward to the essay, he disclaims any attempt to propose a theory of general apologetics. It merely describes "the developments of a personal experience" which comprise the reasons for his faith as a Christian. Yet he believes that it has a more comprehensive relevance since "man is essentially the same in all of us, . . . [sharing] a common substratum of aspirations and illumination." Moreover, in terms of his own fundamental thesis: " 'It is through that which is most incommunicably personal in us that we make contact with the universal."[34]

His Faith in the World

The problem which beset his mind all through his life was that of the relationship between the God of his Christian faith and the world, whose mysteries intrigued him and which he dedicated himself to unraveling. For him it was not a theoretical problem, but a very practical one which involved his deepest feelings: how to reconcile two loves and two faiths which seemed so antagonistic. Before the end, he was convinced that he had resolved their antagonism, at least for himself.

> By upbringing and intellectual training, I belong to the "children of heaven"; but by temperament, and by my professional studies, I am a "child of the earth" . . . I have allowed [these] two apparently conflicting influences full freedom to react upon one another deep within me. And now, at the end of that operation, after thirty years devoted to the pursuit of interior unity, I have the feeling that a synthesis has been effected naturally between the two currents that claim my allegiance. The one has not destroyed, but has reinforced, the other. Today I believe probably more profoundly than ever in God, and certainly more than ever in the world.[35]

In his apologetic essay, Teilhard retraces the steps by which those two faiths and loves came together into an interior unity. It is at once a spiritual autobiography and a resumé of his life's work. Somewhat like the stages of Blondel's own dialectic of action, it represents a series of options, which nevertheless represent the responses to a determinism which expresses the irreversible inner logic of the evolutionary process itself. As for Blondel, it begins with a regressive descent to a fundamental datum, which is for Teilhard a primitive intuition or belief. He then reascends through the successive options or acts of faith toward that over-all view or vision which is found to coincide with the Christian faith.

> If, as a result of some interior revolution, I were to lose in succession my faith in Christ, my faith in a personal God, and my faith in spirit, I feel that I should continue **to believe invincibly in the world**. The world (its value, its infallibility and its goodness)—that, when all is said and done, is the first, the last, and the only thing in which I believe. It is by this faith that I live. And it is to this faith, I feel, that at the moment of death, rising above all doubts, I shall surrender myself.[36]

This startling profession of Teilhard was to be misunderstood by those who failed to enter interiorly into the logic of his method.[37] What he was in effect doing was to evacuate all his beliefs until he reached that initial belief which he shared with the "unbelievers" (the Gentiles) to whom he was addressing himself. It was this common faith in the world, which they and he could accept, from which he would attempt to lead them through the series of inevitable options that followed: faith in spirit, in immortality, in personality, and to the very threshold of faith in the Personal God incarnate in Jesus Christ, the cosmic Omega. By making his starting point "faith in the world," he was not merely embarking on a process of reasoning, but rather identifying himself sincerely with the value-commitment, the life-option of contemporary unbelievers. As a scientist who was at the same time a man of Christian faith, he was also basing his apologetic on grounds that a scientific age could understand and accept.

Faith in the world involves the conviction of a Whole of which we and all other things are elements, and therefore the rejection of pluralism. Teilhard attributes this to a kind of "cosmic sense," the intuition of his constitutive condition of "being in the world." This is not merely the matter of individual temperament, but rather of "an *essential* temperament, in which the structure of our being is as necessarily expressed as it is in the desire to extend one's being to attain unity." For him it provides the assurance of a value of a profoundly felt personal intuition based on an almost universal agreement. Perhaps he was insisting more strongly on the inherent character of a monistic over a pluralistic constitution of human mentality as a reflection of the world's own unity than the evidence warrants. However, it would seem that he was interpreting more correctly the irresistible trend of scientific understanding in this age which, in Julian Huxley's words, "is the first in which any both comprehensive and scientific picture (of man's place and role in nature) has become possible."[38] Man's own new and unique role as the agent of evolution, as envisioned by Teilhard and Huxley, is the most significant factor in the cumulative evidence for such an interpretation.

Teilhard was seeking to construct a scientific phenomenology, that is, a super-science of scientific description of the whole phenomenon of man and his world, which at once surpasses and comprehends the description of the individual sciences. The possibility of such an enterprise had entered within man's purview, as Huxley observes, for the first time in our century by virtue of the developing coincidence of the diverse sciences themselves within recent times. Such an effort, Teilhard insists in the preface to *The Phenomenon of Man,* is neither philosophy nor theology, although all such human studies are "bound to converge as they draw nearer to the whole."[39] However, to comprehend the whole phenomenon, it must include its "within" as well as its "without," its psychic interiority as well as its physical exteriority, its immanent meaning as well as its external appearances.

Faith in the world implies faith in spirit. For man has learned more and more cogently during the past century and a half that "the unity of the world is by nature dynamic or evolutive."[40] The first interpreters of evolution were largely materialists who reduced everything to matter as the universal antecedent from which it emerged. But such a mechanistic science could assimilate everything except its own subject, man, and his unique capacity for thought. On the other hand, when even his uniqueness is accepted as an organic element of the evolving whole, one's understanding of the evolutionary process undergoes a drastic conversion. Rather than an anomaly, man becomes the key.

> We must not allow ourselves to be initimidated by the accusation of anthropocentrism. We are told that it is childish vanity for man to solve the problem of the world in terms of himself. But is it not a scientific truth that in the field of our experience there is no thought but man's thought? Is it our fault that we coincide with the central axis of things? Could it, morever, be otherwise since we are endowed with intelligence?[41]

If man is accepted as the key to the evolutionary process, then two important implications are also affirmed. The basis of evolution is not matter but spirit, or rather the evolution of matter is towards and for spirit. Moreover, the history of the earth, which has been the arena and the matrix for human evolution, is seen as the key to the evolution of the universe. Teilhard believes that he can assert the latter as true despite the incomplete and ever-developing and revisable character of our scientific knowledge, for what he has uncovered are the laws which govern evolution in any instance, no matter how much richer our knowledge of that process has yet to become.

Teilhard has in effect opted for the priority of the future over the past, of goals over antecedents, as the only rational way to account for the greater emerging from the lesser, a universal phenomenon of evolution to which the cumulative data of the sciences attest. Accordingly, spirit is not so much understood as a product of matter as matter is seen as spirit or consciousness in an earlier stage.

> By the spirit I mean "the spirit of synthesis and sublimation," in which is painfully concentrated, through endless attempts and setbacks, the power of unity scattered throughout the universal multiple: **spirit which is born within, and as a function of, matter.**[42]

In all events, spirit and matter are not antagonistic, but rather integral and coherent elements of the unified world process, a process which, he firmly believes, is directed toward the growth of spiritual consciousness as the absolute condition of its unity and existence.

The evolving career of the earth has traversed the stages of development toward spiritual consciousness which must typify, at least analogously, any such progress. The three stages are those of inorganic matter, life, and mind. Even at present, each of these constitutes a sphere of our planet: respectively the geosphere, the biosphere, and the noosphere. The emergence of each of the succeeding stages, life and mind, constituted a breakthrough out of its predecessor, a radical discontinuity within the still more profound continuity of this organically single process.

Teilhard generalizes the mass of data bearing on evolution into the encompassing law of complexity-consciousness. From the spiral nebulae through the stars formed within them out of which the planets like the earth arise, the trend toward ever more complexly diverse elements and their compounds is discernible. It is in the relatively quiescent environment of the planets that conditions occur which favor increasingly complex chemical combinations. Complexity itself, as Teilhard understands it, is not indicated by the mere number and variety of elements contained in a system. Rather it is an organized heterogeneity.

> We will define the complexity of a thing, if you allow, as the quality a thing possesses of being composed—
> a of a larger number of elements, which are
> b more tightly organized among themselves.
>   In this sense an atom is more complex than an electron, a molecule more complex than an atom, and a living cell more complex than the highest chemical nuclei of which it is composed, the difference depending (on this I insist) not only on the number and diversity of the elements included in each case, but at least as much on the number and correlative variety of the links formed between these elements. It is not, therefore, a matter of **simple** multiplicity but of organized multiplicity; not simple complication but **centrated** complication.[43]

This idea of complexity (more exactly, centro-complexity, says Teilhard) has the advantage of enabling the identification as well as the classification of natural units. The rising scale of natural units also reflects the chronological table of their genesis in time. Moreover, if we assess the relative value of galaxies, stars, and planets, not in terms of their immensity or their own complexity, but in terms of the elements that compose them, there is a complete reversal of values and perspective. Nebulae, despite their size, are most primitive. Stars which originate from them are laboratories for the manufacture of atoms, but cannot produce the larger molecules. It is only in the fortuitous birth of planets from them which remain in their energy field as satellites that the conditions can arise which allow the evolution of matter beyond the atomic series into the more complex molecules and eventually the improbable components of life.

> In the world, nothing could ever burst forth as final across the different thresholds successively traversed by evolution (however critical they be) which has not already existed in an obscure and primordial way.[44]

This principle, which in Teilhard's own words "runs like a refrain" throughout his book, *The Phenomenon of Man*, is his own formulation of the law of continuity. Before life is pre-life, the womb in matter within which life is being formed and prepared as the conditions favoring its bursting forth gather and center themselves. These interior events escape the measuring instruments and observations of scientists which are sensitive only to the external phenomenon, the "without" of things. The latter aspect of the world fabric is characterized by *tangential energy* "which links the elements with all others of the same order (that is to say of the same complexity and the same centricity) as itself in the universe"[45] and which lends itself readily to measurement. This is physical energy in the customary sense.

However, another form of physical energy, *radial energy*, operates in the "psychic" interior of the world-fabric whose elements it draws "towards ever greater complexity and centricity—in other words forwards."[46] Under the impulse of this energy, matter no longer spreads out into diffuse layers, but rather coils in upon itself, centers and concentrates in a process of involution leading to the formation of ever more complex structures. The movement is toward unity that is ever richer and more heterogeneous.

Thus the trend toward entropy which is typical of tangential energy is counter-balanced by a law of interiorizing complexification by virtue of which our world appears as "a universe in process of convolution upon itself, in a solidary mass, from top to bottom, interiorizing itself into an ever-growing complexity."[47] These two forms of energy operate interdependently so that the spiritual or psychic energy increases in radial value in step with the increasing chemical complexity of the elements of which it represents the inner lining and which occurs in conformity with the laws of thermo-dynamics. Thus ever more elaborate molecular combinations were formed on the cooling surface of the earth: an envelope of protein-type compounds forming a sphere of pre-life from which life itself would abruptly emerge and constitute the biosphere, a thin layer of living matter covering the globe. A giant threshold had suddenly been crossed.

The cell, the natural granule of life, must be understood, says Teilhard, in relation to its antecedent, the mega-molecule, within which the conditions of birth were forming themselves. The perceptible and measurable contrast is striking. In the cell we witness the budding of life: "the thrust forward in spontaneity; the luxuriant unleashing of fanciful creations; . . . the unbridled expansion and the leap into the improbable."[48] To external observation the mega-molecule seems lifeless, inert. Yet the transformation cannot be inexplicable. Within the living cell's predecessor, radial energy was coiling the structure in upon itself, developing an interior center which was prone to be a unified source of activity, a living subject acting on a new level. Pre-living matter is also pre-conscious matter, for psychic life, consciousness on a rudimentary level, is first present in the world with the appearance of organized life in the cell. Thus "*critical* change in the intimate arrangement of the elements induces *ipso facto* a change in the *nature* of the state of consciousness of the particles of the universe."[49]

The vitalization of matter, first occurring in the oceans, emerged onto land in primitive vegetable and animal forms. Each advance in the complexity of structure "without" was a sign of progressive interiorization or of developing "consciousness" or of psychic life "within." This psychic evolution occurred most dramatically in the insects with their cervical ganglion and in the vertebrates with their central nervous system and brains. At this point, the cosmic law of complexity had become the biological law of cephalization. The former operated in fairly straightforward fashion: once the particles reached a volume of a million atoms or so with the corresponding complexity of interrelationships among them the impulse of life was ready to spring forth from within. The next momentous mutation was not the product of sheer complexification, but rather of the specialized development of a nervous system which became concentrated in the cephalic regions of the animal body as the most effective instrument of psychic activity. The insects remained arrested in their development, while the vertebrates raced forward as the vanguard of psychic evolution. Among the latter, judged by the yardstick of volume and the arrangement of the nervous system and size of the brain, it was the primates of the mammal branch and finally the anthropoids among the primates that came to occupy the forward frontiers of evolutionary advance.

The most highly developed anthropoids became concentrated in a fairly limited area (from west Africa across southern Asia) and the increased occasion for mutual communication favored and intensified the psychic life of the group's members. The accelerated interaction of inner psychism and outer structure pushed the process of cephalization up to and beyond a new threshold where a radically new level of consciousness was reached, consciousness to the second degree. "For the first time, . . . consciousness . . . coiled back upon itself to become thought."[50] Man arrived on the scene not only with the ability to know, but to know that he knows.

> To an observer unaware of what it signifies, the event might seem to have little importance; but in fact it represents the complete resurgence of terrestrial life upon itself. In reflecting psychically upon itself Life made a new start. In a second turn of the spiral, tighter than the first, it embarked for a second time upon its cycle of multiplication, compression and interiorization.
>
> This is how the thinking layer of the earth as we know it today, the Noosphere, came rapidly into being: . . . a planetary neo-envelope, essentially linked with the biosphere in which it has its roots, yet distinguished from it by an autonomous circulatory, nervous and finally, cerebral system. The Noosphere: a new stage of Life renewed.[51]

Cosmogenesis, the evolution of the world, having given rise to biogenesis, the emergence of life, has now arrived at anthropogenesis, the advent of man. This latest event is therefore an integral part of the unfolding of cosmic evolution and, in man, the world process has become aware of itself. The law of complexity-consciousness has achieved a new level of operation. The process of the folding in and centering of the world fabric upon itself which gave birth to consciousness has crossed another threshold and borne reflection as a new dimension of psychic life. Evolution has entered an entirely new phase. The appearance of a new living species which formally characterized biogenesis would seem to have come to a halt. It is in hominization, the process of human evolution, that the continuing growth of the cosmos is centered.

Teilhard is convinced, as is Julian Huxley, that man is still at the embryonic stage of his own evolution, that the most dramatic potentialities are yet to be realized in his future. As a species man converges, instead of diverging like every other species on earth; as a zoological phylum, he is "laboriously moving towards a *critical point of specia- tion.*"[52] (Teilhard's italics) He offers three reasons why he believes that the human species is the unique vehicle of evolution, carrying it toward new heights.

(a) First, because he represents a species which has **biologically broken through** (into the reflective);
(b) Then, because in him, as a consequence of this emergence, speciation operates at a new stage (the 'cultural');
(c) And finally, because within this new compartment or realm opened to life, the species tends to pass from the aggregate state to the form of centered unity (phenomena of acculturation and con- vergence).[53]

Man, because reflective, has inaugurated a new form of life, a life of the second degree or order. In him biological evolution has taken the form of cultural evolution. Man's speciation or development as a species is in the realm of socialization or disposition to evolve toward a collective consciousness. Culture is the specific life-form taken by evolution of the Noosphere, the latest and highest level of cosmic evolution constituted by the ambience of free and reflective conscious life that now envelopes our globe. "Culture" is defined by Teilhard as a

technico-economico-mental complex, free and individual in its con- stituent elements and at its beginnings, but rapidly becoming supra- individual and more or less autonomous in its developments.[54]

In man, as the psychological effect of reflection, the technico- mental becomes cumulative to a degree never attained by the insects or any other species.

As anthropologists attest, cultures that are brought into contact with one another tend to be modified by their en- counter and eventually to merge. This process of *accultura- tion* has accelerated in recent times due to the rapid progress in communication and modes of transportation so that "the effects of acculturation have unceasingly *knitted themselves together* till they now form a planetary network."[55] (Teil- hard's italics) Moreover, certain dominant groups have ap- peared within this growing cultural continuum among whom the trend is toward a higher order of magnitude, accom- panied by a parallel decrease in the number of cultural centers and increase in the intensification of their power.

Thus, contrary to the dispersing trend of other species, the human species, though extended over the entire planet, tends "to knit itself together materially and psychologically until it forms in the strict biological sense a single superorganism of a definite nature."[56] In man, in fact, we witness the two seemingly contrary inclinations: one towards the "granulation" of the species into isolated individuals on account of the growth in the psychic autonomy of its single members; the other, the bias towards convergence due to the merging of cultures. This latter process of socialization is, for Teilhard and other like-minded thinkers including Huxley, a continuation of the process of cerebralization which appears to have reached its absolute limits of growth on the individual level. With socialization, cerebralization or the development of the base of reflective consciousness becomes collective and thus ascends to a higher level of potential toward a Super- or Ultra-Humanity.

This collectivizing trend will not lead to the soulless unity of the ant hill or to a single communal mind. As a reflective being, man exists, lives for himself as well as for others. He is *personalized,* that is, he acts and reacts as a center of *incommunicable* value. In effect, man has so developed that he

> . . . has become structurally incapable of entering as a stable element into any 'complexity' of a higher order unless its effect would be to preserve or even heighten his state and degree of personality.
> In the case of man, therefore, collectivization, super-socialization, can only mean **super-personalization**; in other words it ultimately means (since only the forces of love have the property of personalizing by uniting) sympathy and **unanimity**.
> It is in the direction and in the form of a single 'heart' that we must look for our picture of super-mankind, rather even than in that of a single brain.[57]

Teilhard's faith in spirit leads him inexorably to faith in the immortality of spirit and to faith in personality. He understands immortality in the broad sense of irreversibility. Since its bursting forth from its seeds in the biosphere, reflective consciousness realized in man has moved ever forward toward convergence. He acknowledges that there appear to be two opposing currents, each equally irreversible: entropy and life. Science has up to now been accustomed to construct the physical world from elements drawn by the laws of chance and great numbers towards an increasing dissipation of interchangeable energies and a state of inorganic diffusion. These are the external phenomena, propelled by tangential energy and subject to the apparently is-reversible physico-chemical drift towards the "most probable" that is called entropy. But there appears to be another fundamental irreversibility running counter to that of entropy towards ever more improbable and more fully organic constructions.

> Side by side with the measurable current of entropy, or running across it, there is another current, impatient of measurement; it is disguised in the material, comes to the surface of the organic, but is more clearly visible in the human. This is the imponderable current of Spirit.[58]

If the current of Spirit represented by mankind is to continue to flow and to drive ahead, the human mass must retain its internal tension, it must not allow the respect and zest and ardor for life to grow less or to cool. Teilhard concedes that for man in his freedom this is a possibility. But he is even more convinced that men, who are still not fully emancipated from their individualism, are yet gradually and irresistibly awakening to their collective future. This provokes in them the ever more insistent demand that the human project not fall back or fail, a demand that amounts to an inner imperative that will not be denied. Individuals who do not experience this inner tension in themselves, he believes, have merely failed to probe to the full depths of their hearts and mind. It is a denial of the constitutive human passion *for being finally and permanently more.* "Man, the more he is man, can give himself only to what he loves; and ultimately he loves only what is indestructible." In sum, if the world is moving toward spirit (as overwhelming evidence indicates it is), then it must be able to provide what is essential to the continuation of that movement. "It must provide *ahead of us an unlimited* horizon."[59] (Teilhard's italics)

Teilhard's faith in personality encounters two opposing currents extrinsic to his own mind. The first is that of the pantheist who sees the universe's ultimate spirit " 'As a vast impersonal force in which our personalities will be engulfed.' "[60] The other current takes the form of the criticism, especially by some of his fellow-Catholics, that his theory of a Super-Humanity arising from the convergence of individual consciousnesses tends to universalize and therefore depersonalize the human subjects involved.

Teilhard rejects both positions. He would charge his critics with accepting the pantheist assumption that totalization or consolidation into the Whole, even when it is identified with spirit, cannot but be impersonal. He traces this conviction to a spatial illusion, inasmuch as we ordinarily experience the universe in terms of diffuse activities and the "personal" with which we are in contact presents itself as an element or monad within the whole. This leads to the impression that the personal is associated exclusively with the particular and that it must decline as total unification is approached.

For Teilhard, on the contrary, the growth of spirit and of spiritual consciousness is in terms of concentration towards a center. This requires looking at the world-fabric, including man, from within rather than from its external, material aspect. Growth of the psychic interior of the cosmos is by convergence toward a center, the point at which all the radii meet. Development in that direction is toward the intensification of consciousnes, of freedom, of what is constitutive of the personal. He calls this the "super-conscious," the "super-personal" because it is on a higher level. Thus he cannot conceive of cosmic evolution, which is precisely the evolution of consciousness of freedom, of what is constitutive of personal entity; it has to be in a Super-Person, in Someone. But my development toward unity with all other persons in the Super-Person will be an enhancement and fulfillment and not an annihilation of my person, of that unique and incommunicable reality that constitutes the center and subject of my consciousness and my freedom.

> The reality in which the universe culminates cannot be developed from a starting-point in ourselves, unless in so doing it preserves us. It must be that in the supreme personality we shall inevitably find ourselves personally immortalized.[61]

For true spiritual union or union in synthesis leads to a unity that does not dissolve the individuals that compose it, but rather differentiates the elements it brings together into a center which strengthens the lower centers within it in its own image uniting them by the gentle, preservative, and enhancing force of love.

Teilhard calls the Super-Personal goal of the entire evolutionary process the *Omega Point.* "This is the hypothesis forced upon us by experience if we extend the lines of the Phenomenon of Man to their natural limit."[62] It is an extrapolation projected into the future which he feels compelled to make as an implication of his entire phenomenological analysis of the evolutionary process. It is the last in the series of imperative options offered in the course of his analysis which many scientists and thinkers who have willingly followed him through all of the preceding steps are unable to accept.

In filling out his description of the Omega, Teilhard is in effect attempting to ground his synoptic inference that the whole cosmic process is finally explained not "from below" but "from above." Its Prime Mover is ahead, not behind, yet so as to be eminently present in every phase of the process it is drawing towards itself.

"The only universe capable of containing the human person," writes Teilhard in concluding his *The Phenomenon of Man,* "is an irreversible 'personalising' universe."[63] It is the transcendent Super-Person Whom he calls Omega Who is the principle of this universe and of its personalizing process.

> By its structure Omega, in its ultimate principle, can only be a **distinct Centre radiating at the core of a system of centres;** a grouping in which personalisation of the All and personalisations of the elements reach their maximum, simultaneously and without merging, under the influence of a supremely autonomous focus of union.[64]

Egoism makes the fatal mistake of confusing individuality with personality. The self is diminished by self-centered divergence from others. We become more ourselves as persons by advancing towards and being united with others; in such manner, however, that our personal centers do not fuse, but grow in an inter-centric union which strengthens the various personal centers by their reciprocal intimacy. This paradoxical reconciling of unity and multiplicity is the unique potency of love.

> Love alone is capable of uniting living beings in such a way as to complete and fulfill them, for it alone takes them and joins them by what is deepest in themselves. This is a fact of daily experience. At what moment do lovers come into the most complete possession of themselves if not when they say they are lost in each other? In truth, does not love every instant achieve all around us, in the couple or the team, the magic feat, the feat reputed to be contradictory, of 'personalising' by totalising? And if that is what it can achieve daily on a small scale, why should it not repeat this one day on world-wide dimensions?[65]

Human love is the "hominized" form of an energy which pervades the whole cosmos. Though so faint as to be imperceptible at the lowest levels, a rudimentary energy of love operating radially in the "within" of even the molecules accounts for their internal propensity to unite. It is this same force of psychic or spiritual attraction already present in the most elementary particles which manifests itself in more elaborate forms on the higher levels inasmuch as on every level it is the trace of "the psychical convergence of the universe upon itself."[66]

Moreover, this energy moves all toward universal unity. We tend to deny the possibility of genuine love that is universal to insist that love diminishes as it becomes more encompassing. Contrary to this, however, is the nostalgia awakened in us by nature, beauty, music, of the expectant awareness of a Great Presence, the resonance to the All which is the keynote of pure poetry and religion. It is the feeling that the universe is ultimately impersonal which inhibits the free growth of a universal love. But the aesthetic and religious experiences and their intimations of such a love point to the reality of a Source and Object of love at the summit and the heart of the universe. The intensifying drive of mankind toward a convergent unity of our race and our world requires that the universe ahead of us personify itself, but that it do so not as a vague promise of the future, but as a present actuality drawing all personal centers to itself as the center of centers, the Omega Point.

To satisfy the conditions which love demands as well as to assure the survival of the cosmic process which it perpetually empowers, the Omega Point must be not only personal and a focus of love but autonomous, actual or

present, immortal or irreversible, and transcendent as well
as wholly immanent. Love dies in contact with the impersonal, the anonymous, and the remote in space and time.
To exercise the supreme energy of love, the Omega must
be intimately personal and supremely present. As the
Center energizing all other centers, he must be autonomous
and distinct from them. Even more, though he is the summit
and goal of the series of emergences in the evolutionary
process, he must be outside and above the series himself
to sustain it unfailingly, to escape entirely the drag of
entropy. "If by its very nature it did not escape from the
time and space which it gathers together, it would not be
Omega."[67]

Thus Teilhard feels that his faith in the world and his
love for it have been vindicated. For it has not led him away
from his religious convictions, but rather towards them. For
it has brought him by a claim of imperative options to the
conviction of a Super-Personal Reality as the goal of cosmic
and human evolution and therefore to the threshold of an
initiative, a message that could come from that Reality.

World Faiths and His Faith

In a final section of *The Phenomenon of Man,* Teilhard
devotes several pages to "the Christian Phenomenon" which
he very deliberately entitles: "Epilogue," to distinguish it
from the main body of his Christian apologetics. In point of
fact, though candidly acknowledging his personal Christian
commitment, he feels he has a right to introduce the Christian Phenomenon as a very pertinent datum among the
other realities of the world available for scientific study.
The existence of the Omega as a necessary postulate to
account for the entire evolutionary process which is personal
in nature and already existent and operative at the very
heart of the Noosphere demands that one determine whether
there is evidence that such a transcendent Reality does actually exist and act. The Christian claim is that He does exist
in the person of Jesus Christ, Who, as the incarnate God,
is He in whom ". . . were created all things in heaven and
on earth . . . All things were created through him and for

him . . . and he holds all things in unity." (Col 1:16-17)

At this point, Teilhard is indeed speaking as a Christian believer, who may feel that he is entitled even as a scientist to address himself to Christianity as an objective fact of our world but who is nevertheless quite conscious of having reversed his perspective and of surveying the universe now "from the top downwards, starting from the peaks to which we are raised by Christianity and religion."[68]

The faith in the "Cosmic, Universal or Super-Christ" which is the heart of his conviction of Christianity as the world faith that is uniquely and eminently compatible with his scientific vision was not a spontaneous belief but one which he only arrived at after much intellectual struggle. He briefly recounts that struggle in the second and concluding section of his apologetic essay, *How I Believe,* "The Confluence of Religions." There he confronts the three major contemporary religious currents to determine which best fulfills the expectations which his faith in the world has provoked within him.

Teilhard repudiates two notions about religion, wholly mistaken to his mind: that religion is a strictly personal matter and that it is a primitive and transitory stage through which mankind had to pass in its infancy. On the contrary, the religious phenomenon is the response to the Universe as such on the part of mankind as it develops towards collective consciousness and its common destiny. It is therefore one of the aspects of "hominization" and represents "an irreversible cosmic magnitude." Rather than being a pre-scientific stage of man's growth to maturity which is to be superseded by science, it is on a course of convergence with science. For as science itself outgrows its own more rudimentary period when analytic investigation predominates and as it advances toward synthesis which both serves and illuminates the approaching superior state of humanity,

. . . it is at once led to foresee and place its stakes on the **future** and on the **all.** And with that it out-distances itself and emerges in terms of **option** and **adoration.**

. . . when we turn towards the summit, towards the **totality** and the **future,** we cannot help engaging in religion.

[For] religion and science are the two conjugated faces or phases of one and the same act of complete knowledge—the only one which can embrace the past and future of evolution so as to contemplate, measure and fulfill them.[69]

Like Blondel before him, Teilhard adopts a method of immanence in seeking and testing the "true religion." What he regards as a decisive evidence in its favor is "the harmony of a higher order which exists between that religion and the individual creed to which the natural evolution of my faith has led me."[70] That creed is his faith in the unity of the world and in the existence and immortality of spirit summed up in the worship of a personal and personalizing center of universal convergence. To discover where that harmony of a higher order is to be found, he plunges into the currents of the great religions that solicit contemporary man's allegiance. To his mind there are three such currents: the Eastern religions, especially Hinduism and Buddhism, the humanist pantheisms, which are atheistic in the usual sense, and Christianity.

The Eastern religions exerted a great attraction for him by their faith in, and overpowering sense of, the ultimate unity of the universe. But eventually it became quite clear to him that they held a conviction of that unity and its relation to its elements diametrically opposed to his own. For the unity of spirit which they proclaimed and to which they aspired reduced matter to an illusion and led to the dissolution of the personal, whereas for him matter is the womb of spirit and its potentialities, and the unifying goal of the universe is supremely personal and personalizing. For them, unity is won by the suppression of the multiple; for him, it is born of the concentration of the many: unity differentiates. Above all, he sought in religious faith a vindication of man's evolving governance of his world and a salvation of his cosmic task. What they fostered in its stead was an attitude of passive renunciation and salvation by escape from any destiny rooted in human history.

Contemporary humanisms represent a new faith for man: the religion of evolution. It was, to all appearances, his own fundamental faith in the world and in man's active role in directing evolutionary progress. He found himself in immediate sympathy and profound agreement. But always he was left in disappointment. For their faiths go so far as to acknowledge spirit as the interior subject and goal of evolution, but they fall short of assenting to its immortality and personality. He was never without admiration for the great souls among his colleagues who embraced such a faith which emboldened them so readily to accept man's responsibility for his world. But he felt stifled by their foreshortened vision of the cosmos and the consequent incompleteness of their commitment to the infinity of man's future.

As the final available alternative, Christianity had to be the faith he, as a representative contemporary man, was looking for. Yet his personal search was not that easily terminated. Although from his earliest years he gave himself and his soul to the Church, the tension within him grew rather than being resolved. For the Gospel the Church gave him seemed to require a loyalty to heaven at the expense of his allegiance to the earth. It spoke of God as the Personal Creator and End of man, of man's freedom, immortality, and heavenly destiny, but it did not seem to believe in human progress or the significance of man's growing responsibility for this world. It spoke of redemption as though it were purely a personal matter rather than a cosmic drama. In sum, it failed to cohere organically with his cosmic faith, even though it offered him in Christ the only one who could fulfill his hopes.

It was when he came to know the Universal Christ that he saw all his desires fulfilled beyond all expectation. The Universal Christ, in his understanding, is "a synthesis of Christ and the universe."[71] It is this Christ Whom he identifies with the Omega Point, the *Pleroma* or fullness toward which all redeemed creation is evolving. He is convinced that one must arrive at such a form of faith who takes the Incarnation seriously. Thus he conceives the Universal Christ as the cosmic center toward which the universe is irreversibly rising as the ultimate term of its convergence. For his mind, it is his understanding of such a cosmic process of evolution which renders the universal role attributed to

Christ by Saint Paul and Saint John intelligible. "By disclosing a world-peak, evolution makes Christ possible, just as Christ, by giving meaning and direction to the world, makes evolution possible."[72] Such arresting statements left Teilhard open to the charge of confusing the natural and supernatural orders, of reducing the Incarnation to a necessary factor in the natural process of evolution and therefore of at least implicitly denying its gratuitousness as an eminently free divine intiative. What he was in effect attempting to underline was the organic unity of the divine plan, that the world is indeed naturally predisposed to its supernatural end, that the truth of the Incarnation, once revealed, is the key to the unity of creation and the privileged point on which the cosmic process focuses and from which it derives its final intelligibility and direction. The Incarnation was not an afterthought to creation, but the very heart of its meaning, its *raison d'être.*

The Church, like Christ Whose Body it is, is understood as playing an organically integrating role in the rising drama of cosmic evolution. It is a supernatural phylum, growing toward an ever wider and deeper synthesis based on love,

> . . . by her influence vivifying and bringing together the spiritual energies of the **Noosphere** in their most sublime form. The Church, as the portion of the world reflexively made Christ, the Church as the principal center of interhuman affinities through supercharity, the Church as the central axis of universal convergence, is the precise point of the encounter between the universe and the Omega Point.[73]

Teilhard finds in the Universal Christ the authentic expression of the Christ of the Gospel, of the God Who inserted Himself into the heart of the cosmic and human drama as the Man, Jesus of Nazareth. In this Cosmic Christ Who is the term of universal evolution, he discovered what his being dreamed of: a personalized universe, whose domination personalized him. His individual faith in the world and his religious faith expressed in a Christianity extended to cosmic dimensions came together in a congenial and fruitful union. He was convinced that the same forces and tendencies that struggled towards eventual harmony within himself were also working at large and that the solution which modern man is seeking would essentially be the same solution he had reached.

I believe that this is so, and it is in this vision that my hopes are fulfilled. A general convergence of religions upon a universal Christ who fundamentally satisfies them all: that seems to me the only possible conversion of the world, and the only form in which a religion of the future can be conceived.[74]

Distinctive Strands and Common Conclusions

The three thinkers whom we have met in this chapter are truly contemporary and Christian. Each confidently roots his thought in an honest probing of human experience as it occurs to a modern man. Though employing different methods, each meticulously follows the exigencies of his method as it is employed in the unfolding interpretation of the empirical data. All of them agree that the progressive steps of their thought involve options which are demanded by the evidence and yet are free human decisions. In each instance, scrupulous fidelity to the canons of the method chosen leads to a view of man consistent with that of Christian faith at the same time that it is reflective of modern man's self-understanding arising from his own experience.

For Marcel, openness to the other is constitutive of the structure of man's embodied existence. Experience reveals that we realize ourselves by going out of ourselves to others in a movement of transcendence toward an Absolute Thou Whose originating Presence is intimated and mediated by every finite presence occurring in human encounter. This "exigence for transcendence" is disclosed not by departing from experience, but rather by a deeper understanding of it in the light of a reflection that recovers its original unity in the Absolute Being Who is its source. It is in such common but radical experiences as hope, love, and fidelity that this human dynamic of self-transcendence, evoked in intersubjective relations and oriented toward its goal and ground in the Absolute Thou, is most clearly revealed and expressed.

For Blondel, the root human need is to consent to his being, to will freely what the deepest spring of his every action, the willing will, would require him to will. There is a perpetual disproportion between the finite reach of his conscious free will and the insatiable urge of its innermost source to breach all finite bounds. This tension provides the restless power of his drive toward self-realization through self-transcendence. At the same time, it reveals the infinity of his end and therefore the inadequacy of his every effort to attain it within human limits. Rather than call man an absurdity, "a useless passion", he opts for his meaningfulness founded in the free but necessary hypothesis of the supernatural: the gratuitous initiative of the Divine Transcendent to give Himself to the one whose very being is a desire for such a gift. Thus Christian Faith is vindicated as the only intelligible solution to the enigma of human existence. For by it we freely acknowledge and consent to the Transcendent Other as the ultimate goal Whose call empowers us to respond from the immanent recesses of our drive to act. Thus the logic of Christian truth and practice is seen to coincide with the logic of human action even though the decision to affirm the truth of their identity is ever a free, if imperative, decision for man.

Teilhard shares with Marcel and Blondel the Christian vision of man, but his angle of approach is to show its congruity with the scientific view of man as an integral, if crowning, element in an evolving cosmos. He does so by leading his scientifically-minded contemporaries from their common faith in the world through a series of options, each of which is based on converging scientific evidence. However, as he moves from this initial universal faith, through faith in spirit, in immortality, in personality, towards faith in the Omega as the goal of cosmic evolution realized concretely in Christ, his options involve wider trajectories from the commonly accepted data and therefore freer and more responsible decisions on the part of those who would follow him. The power of his reasoning issues from his scientifically grounded conviction that man is the key to the evolutionary process and therefore he is led to the priority of spirit over matter as the premise of its explanation.

Man has become the agent of evolution and its point of self-awareness, as it advances now on the cultural level of converging consciousness. Thus Teilhard situates man's drive toward self-transcendence not only in a social but in a cosmic context. For in him, cosmic evolution has become the evolution of spirit which is progressing rapidly toward unity in a Super-Person (the Omega Point, the Cosmic Christ) Who is its Absolute Future drawing man, and through him all creation, to Himself. Because love is the energy of this process, convergence and unity will not suppress individual autonomy, but rather intensify and perfect it. The Christ Who draws all to Himself is both eminently immanent and eminently transcendent. Thus Teilhard sees not the incompatibility of the Christian and the scientific evolutionary views of man and the world, but their inevitable unification. For it is only in the Cosmic Christ that the gathering momentum and rising convergence of the evolutionary process, indicated by a synthetic view of the scientific data, can be accounted for with utmost intelligibility. Thus his Christian faith and his faith in the world cannot only coexist. They disclose themselves to be distinct but harmonious perspectives on the same underlying reality.

Notes and references

1 Gabriel Marcel, **Creative Fidelity,** trans. by Robert Rosthal (New York: Noonday Press, 1964), p. x, translator's introduction.

2 **Ibid.,** pp. 28-29.

3 Rudolf J. Gerber, "Marcel and the Being of the Other" in **Review of Existential Psychology and Psychiatry,** Vol. VI (Fall, 1966), p. 188.

4 Marcel, **Creative Fidelity,** p. 26.

5 **Ibid.**

6 **Ibid.,** p. 55.

7 Gabriel Marcel, **The Mystery of Being** Vol. I, trans. by G. S. Fraser (Chicago: Regnery Co. Gateway Editions, 1960), especially chapter V.

8 Marcel, **Creative Fidelity,** p. 23.

9 Gabriel Marcel, **Being and Having,** trans. by Katherine Farrer (Westminster: Dacre Press, 1949), pp. 100-101.

10 Marcel, **Creative Fidelity,** p. 69.

11 Marcel, **The Mystery of Being,** Vol. I, p. 59. Cf. also all of chapter III.

12 Marcel, **Being and Having,** p. 119.

13 Gabriel Marcel, **The Philosophy of Existence,** trans. by Manya Harari (New York: Philosophical Library, 1949), p. 22.

14 Gabriel Marcel, **Metaphysical Journal,** trans. by Bernard Wall (Chicago: Regnery Co. Gateway edition, 1952), p. 63.

[15] Marcel, **Creative Fidelity**, p. 169.

[16] Marcel, **The Mystery of Being**, Vol. II, trans. by René Hague, p. viii.

[17] Frederick J. D. Scott, "William James and Maurice Blondel," **The New Scholasticism** XXXII (January, 1958), p. 43.

[18] Maurice Blondel, **L'Action: Essai d'une Critique de la Vie et d'une Science de la Pratique** (Paris: Presses Universitaires de France, 1950).

[19] Maurice Blondel, **The Letter on Apologetics, and History and Dogma**, trans. by Alexander Dru and Illtyd Trethowan (New York: Holt, Rinehart and Winston, 1964).

[20] Blondel, **L'Action**, introduction.

[21] **Ibid.**, p. 319.

[22] **Ibid.**, p. 339.

[23] Blondel defines the supernatural as ". . . that which, proceeding from a gratuitous condescension of God, elevates the intelligent creature to a state that could not be the natural state of any creature, to a state which could not be realized or merited or even expressly conceived by any natural power." Maurice Blondel, "Le Surnaturel" in **Vocabulaire de la Philosophie**, edited by A. Lalande (Paris: Presses Universitaires de France, 1947), p. 1053.

[24] Blondel, **L'Action**, pp. 354-355.

[25] Henri Bouillard, "The Thought of Maurice Blondel: A Synoptic Vision" in **International Philosophical Quarterly** Vol. III (September, 1963). p. 397.

[26] **Ibid.**, p. 396.

[27] Blondel, "The Letter on Apologetics", in **The Letter on Apologetics, and History and Dogma**, pp. 160 and 157.

[28] Jean Lacroix, **Maurice Blondel: An Introduction to the Man and His Philosophy**, trans. by John C. Guinness (New York: Sheed and Ward, 1968), p. 67.

[29] Maurice Blondel, "Deux Notes Inedites sur la Trilogie et L'Esprit Chétien" in **Archives de Philosophie** XXIV (January to March, 1961), p. 119.

[30] **Ibid.**, pp. 119-120. **La Philosophie et l'Espirit Chrétien**, two volumes, (Paris: Presses Universitaires de France 1944, 1946).

[31] Cf. Pierre Teilhard de Chardin and Maurice Blondel, **Correspondence** trans. by William Whitman with notes and commentary by Henri de Lubac, S.J. (New York: Herder and Herder, 1967).

[32] Pierre Teilhard de Chardin, **How I Believe**, trans, by René Hague. (New York: Harper & Row, 1969).

[33] Pierre Teilhard de Chardin, **Letters from a Traveller**, trans. by René Hague, **et al.** (New York: Harper & Row, 1962), p. 205 Ellipses with brackets are in the text.

[34] Teilhard, **How I Believe**, pp. 11 and 12.

[35] **Ibid.**, pp. 10-11.

[36] **Ibid.**, pp. 19-20.

[37] Henri de Lubac, **Teilhard de Chardin: The Man and His Meaning**, trans. by René Hague (New York: The New American Library, 1967), pp. 132ff.

[38] Julian Huxley, **New Bottles for New Wine** (New York: Harper & Row, 1957), p. 41.

[39] Pierre Teilhard de Chardin, **The Phenomenon of Man**, trans. by Bernard Wall (New York: Harper & Brothers, 1959), p. 30.

[40] Teilhard, **How I Believe**, p. 28.

41 Ibid., p. 32, footnote.
42 Ibid., pp. 34-35.
43 Pierre Teilhard de Chardin, "Life and the Planets" in **The Future of Man**, trans. by Norman Denny (New York: Harper & Row, 1964), p. 105.
44 Teilhard, **The Phenomenon of Man**, p. 71.
45 Ibid., p. 65.
46 Ibid.
47Pierre Teilhard de Chardin, **Le Groupe zoologique humain** (Paris: Albin Michel, 1956), p. 34. Quoted in Piet Smulders, **The Design of Teilhard de Chardin**, trans. by Arthur Gibson (Westminster, Md.: Newman Press, 1967), p. 36.
48 Teilhard, **The Phenomenon of Man**, p. 89.
49 Ibid.
50 Teilhard, "From the Pre-Human to the Ultra-Human: the Phases of a Living Planet" in **The Future of Man**, p. 293.
51 Ibid.
52 Teilhard, "The End of the Species," ibid., p. 302.
53 Pierre Teilhard de Chardin, "Hominization and Speciation" in **The Vision of the Past**, trans. by J. M. Cohen (New York: Harper & Row, 1966), p. 260.
54 Ibid., p. 262.
55 Ibid., p. 264.
56 Ibid., p. 265.
57 Pierre Teilhard de Chardin, "Super-Humanity, Super-Christ, Super-Charity" in **Science and Christ**, trans. by René Hague (New York: Harper & Row, 1968), p. 160.
58 Teilhard, "The Phenomenon of Man" in **Science and Christ**, p. 95.
59 Teilhard, **How I Believe**, pp. 43-45.
60 Ibid., p. 48.
61 Ibid., p. 53.
62 Teilhard, "Super-Humanity, Super-Christ, Super-Charity" in **Science and Christ**, p. 163.
63 Teilhard, **The Phenomenon of Man**, p. 290.
64 Ibid., p. 262.
65 Ibid., p. 265.
66 Ibid.
67 Ibid., p. 270.
68 Teilhard, "Super-Humanity, Super-Christ, Super-Charity" in **Science and Christ**, p. 164.
69 Teilhard, **The Phenomenon of Man**, pp. 284-285.
70 Teilhard, **How I Believe**, p. 64.
71 Ibid., p. 77.
72 Ibid., p. 80.
73 Pierre Teilhard de Chardin, "Comment je vois"," note 24. Quoted in Claude Tresmontant, **Pierre Teilhard de Chardin: His Thought**, trans. by Salvator Attanasio (Baltimore Md.: Helicon Press, 1959), p. 77.
74 Teilhard, **How I Believe**, p. 85.

Blondel, Maurice. *Correspondence: Blondel-Teilhard de Chardin.* Ed. Henri de Lubac. Tr. William Whitman. New York: Herder & Herder, 1967.
Blondel, M. *L'Action* (1893). Paris: Presses Universitaires de France, 1950.
Blondel, M. *L'Action.* 2 vols. Paris: Alcan, 1936, 1937; P.U.F., 1949.

Blondel, M. *L'Être et les êtres.* Paris: Alcan, 1935.
Blondel, M. *Exigences Philosophiques de Christianisme.* Paris: P.U.F., 1950.
Blondel, M. *The Letter on Apologetics* and *History and Dogma.* Tr. Alexander Dru and Illthyd Trethowan. New York: Holt, Rinehart and Winston, 1964.
Blondel, M. *La Pensée.* 2 vols. Paris: Alcan, 1934; P.U.F., 1948-1954.
Blondel, M. *La Philosophie et L'Éspirit Chrétien.* 2 vols. P.U.F., 1944, 1946.
Bouillard, Henri. *Blondel and Christianity.* Tr. James M. Somerville. Washington, D.C.: Corpus Books, 1969.
Bouillard, Henri. "The thought of Maurice Blondel: a synoptic vision," *International Philosophical Quarterly* 3 (1963) pp. 392-402.

Cuenot, Claude. *Science and Faith in Teilhard de Chardin.* Comment by Roger Garaudy. Tr. Noel Lindsay. London: Garnstone Press, 1967.
Cuenot, Claude. *Teilhard de Chardin.* Ed. René Hague. Tr. Vincent Colimore. Baltimore: Helicon, 1965.

Duméry, Henry. *Blondel et la Religion.* Paris: P.U.F., 1954.
Duméry, Henry. *La Philosophie de L'Action.* Paris: Aubier, 1948.
Duméry, Henry. *Raison et Religion dans la Philosophie de l'Action.* Paris: Éditions du Seuil, 1963.
Dupré, Louis. "Blondel's Religious Philosophy," *The New Scholasticism* 32 (1966) pp. 3-22.

Faricy, Robert L. S.J. *Teilhard de Chardin's Theology of the Christian in the World.* New York: Sheed & Ward, 1967.

Gallagher, Kenneth. *The Philosophy of Gabriel Marcel.* New York: Fordham University Press, 1962.
Gerber, Rudolph J. "Marcel and the Being of the 'Other'," *Review of Existential Psychology and Psychiatry* 6 (1966) pp. 179-95.

Lacroix, Jean. *Maurice Blondel: An Introduction to the Man and His Philosophy.* Tr. J. C. Guiness. New York: Sheed & Ward, 1968.
Lubac, Henri de. *Teilhard de Chardin: the Man and His Meaning.* Tr. René Hague. New York: Mentor, 1967.
Lubac, Henri de. *The Religion of Teilhard de Chardin.* Tr. René Hague New York: Desclée, 1967.

Marcel, Gabriel. *Being and Having.* Tr. Katherine Farrer. Westminster: Dacre, 1949.
Marcel, Gabriel. *Creative Fidelity.* Tr. Robert Rosthal. New York: Farrer & Strauss, 1964.
Marcel, Gabriel. *Homo Viator.* Introduction to a Metaphysic of Hope. Tr. Emma Craufurd. New York: Harper, 1962.
Marcel, Gabriel. *Man Against Mass Society.* Tr. G. S. Fraser. Chicago: Regnery, 1962.
Marcel, Gabriel. *Metaphysical Journal.* Tr. Bernard Wall. Chicago: Regnery, 1952.
Mracel, Gabriel. *The Mystery of Being.* 2 vols. Vol. I: *Reflection and Mystery.* Tr. G. S. Fraser. Vol. II: *Faith and Reality.* Tr. René Hague. New York: Regnery, 1951, 1960.
Marcel, Gabriel. *The Philosophy of Existence.* Tr. Manya Harari. New York: Philosophical Library, 1949.
Marcel, Gabriel. *Presence and Immortality.* Tr. M. A. Machado. Revised by H. J. Koren. Pittsburgh: Duquesne University Press, 1967.
Marcel, Gabriel. *Problematic Man.* Tr. Brian Thompson. New York: Herder & Herder, 1967.
Miceli, Vincent P., S.J. *Ascent to Being: G. Marcel's Philosophy of Communion.* New York: Desclée, 1965.
Mooney, Christopher F., S.J. "Blondel and Teilhard de Chardin," *Thought* 37 (1962) pp. 543-63.
Mooney, Christopher F., S.J. *Teilhard de Chardin and the Mystery of Christ.* New York: Harper & Row, 1966.

O'Malley, John B. *The Fellowship of Being: An Essay on the Concept of Person in the Philosophy of G. Marcel.* The Hague: M. Nijhoff, 1966.

Poncelet, Albert. "The Christian Philosophy of Maurice Blondel," *International Philosophical Quarterly* 5 (1965) pp. 564-93.

Smulders, Piet. *The Design of Teilhard de Chardin.* Translation from the French edition by Arthur Gibson. Westminster, Md.: Newman, 1967.
Somerville, James M., S.J. *Total Commitment: Blondel's Action.* Washington, D.C.: Corpus Books, 1968.

Teilhard de Chardin, Pierre. *Activation of Energy.* Tr. René Hague. New York: Harcourt Brace Jovanovich, 1971.
Teilhard de Chardin, P. *The Appearance of Man.* Tr. J. M. Cohen. New York: Harper & Row, 1965.
Teilhard de Chardin, P. *Building the Earth.* Tr. N. Lindsay. New York: Avon, 1969.
Teilhard de Chardin, P. *Christianity and Evolution.* Tr. René Hague. New York: Harcourt Brace Jovanovich, 1971.

Teilhard de Chardin, P. *The Divine Milieu.* New York: Harper & Row, 1960.

Teilhard de Chardin, P. *The Future of Man.* Tr. N. Denny. New York: Harper & Row, 1964.

Teilhard de Chardin, P. *How I Believe.* Tr. R. Hague. New York: Harper & Row, 1969. Also in *Christianity and Evolution,* pp. 96-132.

Teilhard de Chardin, P. *Human Energy.* Tr. J. M. Cohen. New York: Harcourt Brace Jovanovich, 1969.

Teilhard de Chardin, P. *Let Me Explain.* Texts selected and arranged by Jean-Pierre Demoulin. Tr. R. Hague and others. New York: Harper & Row, 1970.

Teilhard de Chardin, P. *Letters from a Traveller.* Tr. R. Hague and others. New York: Harper & Row, 1962.

Teilhard de Chardin, P. *The Making of a Mind.* Tr. R. Hague. New York: Harper & Row, 1965.

Teilhard de Chardin, P. *The Phenomenon of Man.* Tr. Bernard Wall. New York: Harper, 1959.

Teilhard de Chardin, P. *Science and Christ.* Tr. R. Hague, New York: Harper & Row, 1968.

Teilhard de Chardin, P. *The Vision of the Past.* Tr. J. M. Cohen. New York: Harper & Row, 1966.

Teilhard de Chardin, P. *Writings in Time of War.* Tr. R. Hague. New York: Harper & Row, 1968.

Tresmontant, Claude. *Teilhard de Chardin. His Thought.* Tr. S. Attanasio. Baltimore: Helicon, 1959.

Wildiers, N. M. *An Introduction to Teilhard de Chardin.* Tr. H. Hoskins. New York: Harper & Row, 1968.

Toward a Christian Anthropology (II)

Transcendental Thomism: Movement and Method

The three Christian thinkers who occupied our attention
in the last chapter do not belong to the main stream
of the Catholic philosophical tradition. Though strongly
loyal in their Catholic faith commitment, their very
contemporaneousness seems to have involved their refusal to enter into that central current of Catholic philosophy usually identified with Scholasticism. This very
aloofness accounts somewhat for their widespread acceptance. It also affords an enriching pluralism within the
community of the Catholic thought-world.
The effort to achieve genuine contemporaneousness
within the central Catholic tradition has been proceeding along at least since the beginnings of the Thomistic revival in the final decade of the last century. What
appears at present to be the most radical and effective
of these attempts is the movement known as Transcendental Thomism. It is more properly called a movement than a school since it lacks the measure of
homogeneity that the latter label would imply. Yet
despite the differing backgrounds and approaches of
its practitioners, there is a unity of attitude and method
that underlies their disparateness.
The adjective, "Transcendental," refers specifically to
the method employed in common by these men. The term

itself is Kantian. Said Kant: "I call all knowledge transcendental which is occupied not so much with objects, as with our manner of knowing objects, so far as this is meant to be possible a priori."[1]

Kant called his the Critical Philosophy. It represented the most radical recognition of the role of the subject in man's knowledge of himself, his world and his God. It was provoked by the impasse created by the object-oriented philosophies that preceded him. He sought to break the impasse by inquiring into the conditions of the knowing subject that make objective knowledge possible.

Transcendental Thomism is post-critical in the broader sense that it not only accepts the legitimacy of the Kantian project, but it takes a positive rather than a defensive attitude toward the later philosophical developments that stem from Kant. Among these it is especially influenced by the German Idealists, by Blondel, Husserl and Heidegger, at least as it has evolved on the European continent.

This positive evaluation of modern philosophy involves accepting the so-called "turn to the subject" that typifies post-Kantian thought. More fundamentally it implies the willingness to acquiesce in the cultural shift, that is the transformation of modern man's self-understanding, which Lonergan analyzes as the transition from a classicist to a historical consciousness. At this stage of his evolution, man has come to realize quite explicitly that neither he nor his world are completed in any sense. On the contrary, man is precisely that being whose existence is an on-going project whereby he continually constitutes himself as a subject in a community of creative inter-action with other human subjects who share a common history. Man's subjectivity is not only elicited in inter-personal relations, but also in his transactions with his world whose evolution toward an ever-open future he learns more and more to control. In this increasingly active and manipulative relation with his environment, he affirms his own unique status as self-conscious and self-possessed subject over against the cosmos of which he would be the master as the object of his intelligence and will.

JOSEPH MARÉCHAL: *Forerunner*

The pioneer of Transcendental Thomism is undoubtedly Joseph Maréchal (1878-1944), who taught the sciences and philosophy at the Jesuit scholasticate in Louvain, Belgium, during most of his academic career. It was he who determined to confront Thomistic realism with the full force of Kant's critique.[2] He did so by applying the transcendental method of Kant to the question of the possibility of metaphysical knowledge. He eluded the German philosopher's agnostic conclusions by avoiding the limitations of his static conception of human knowing. In this seminal work for Transcendental Thomists, Maréchal quite brilliantly vindicated the possibility of a realistic metaphysics while using the very method Kant had employed in denying such a possibility. The telling difference was not therefore in the method but in the conception of knowledge to which the method was applied.

For Maréchal as for Kant, knowing occurs essentially in the judgment. In the Kantian view, a truly objective judgment is confined to the bounds of sense experience, the phenomenal order, and consists in a synthesizing of sense data according to the categories or a priori forms of understanding. As a consequence, all metaphysical assertions, which in principle claim to exceed the order of phenomena, are reduced to a merely logical or regulative function and denied any objective theoretical value as knowledge.

Maréchal charges Kant with a fatally incomplete understanding of the judging function. The fault occurs because Kant, operating out of a rationalist bias, conceives knowledge as a mere relating of the data of experience to the conceptual unity of thought. He is preoccupied with the content of the judgment and overlooks the implications of judgment as an activity, as the act of affirmation. But once judgment as an act of affirmation is taken into account, it is seen to involve the objectifying function of relating its content to the absolute order of reality, that is, to the order of that which is in itself.

In recognizing the crucial role of knowing or judging

as an action or performance as well as in the way he exploits this insight, Maréchal is clearly indebted to the influence of Blondel. For the philosopher of Aix, as we have seen, it is the dynamism of action that insures as it discloses the unity of thought and being. The force that impels the human knower ever forward is the discrepancy between the thought or concept and the act. More is implied in the act than can ever be expressed in the concept and so the knower drives ahead to achieve a fuller adequation between them. This Blondelian dialectic is in contrast with that of Hegel which, relying on the truncated Kantian notion of judgment, must account for the dynamic of knowledge wholly within the unity of thought by an entirely immanent dialectic of concept with concept.

For Blondel, the dynamism of action, including the action of thought, is explained by the immanent presence at the source of human action of an appetite for the Transcendent, the Infinite, the Absolute. Maréchal founds his metaphysical realism on a similar dynamism which operates in the act of judgment. For he agrees with Kant that intuition occurs only on the sense level, since any intellectual intuition, that is, any immanent possession of the object intelligibly apprehended as object, would demand that man in knowing create or produce the object of his knowledge. It is not then in the order of cause and effect, which would apply to creating or producing, that the relation of intelligent subject and intelligible object is to be explained, but in the order of finality or goal-oriented action.

Maréchal distinguishes in the formal structure of the judgment, 1) its synthetic form which unifies its terms or material elements and relates them ultimately to the absolute unity of thought, and 2) the objective form of the judgment or the affirmation. It is the judgment as affirmation or assent which operates in the domain of finality, of movement toward an end, as Maréchal explains in commenting on the theory of St. Thomas. For Aquinas, intellectual assent can be a free or an unfree act. In the former case, it is preceding by virtue of the finality of the will which determines the assent in conscious response to the good discerned in performing such an act. In the unfree assent, where the intellect is responding to the adequate presentation of its proper object, viz., the true, whether immediately or mediately through reasoning, it is still proceeding in terms of finality. This time it is the finality of the pre-conscious "natural appetite" which, in the Thomistic view, is at the source in man's rational nature of his intellectual drive towards the true. Indeed it is at the source of every striving of his rational powers, including the will, toward Absolute Being which as the unlimited true and good is his only adequate end. Each affirmation, whether a free or unfree assent, is a movement towards the absolute as its goal, proceeding from this radical appetite of his rational nature. But each affirmation constitutes only a partial achievement of this final goal, an incomplete satisfaction of the root appetite. For that reason, having proceeded from an antecedent finality which it partially realizes, it gives rise to a consequent finality, or perhaps better, to a new determinate stage of the impetus towards Being from which it had itself arisen.

The objectivity of our knowledge is thus realized in the affirmation. The prior stages of knowledge, including abstraction and conceptualization, culminating in the synthetic phase of judgment, yield the form by which the object is understood. Kant's static notion of knowledge had stopped at this point and had attempted to account for objectivity within these limits. But for Maréchal, the intellect is not a static function, but an activity ever moving toward a goal. Thus each form is being continually surpassed as it had previously constituted a limited goal aimed at in the process by which its predecessor had been surpassed. As an end to be attained in the incessant movement of transcending towards Absolute Being, the determinate form is objectivated, that is, set up or acknowledged as an object over against the subject to which it is opposed as an end is opposed to a tendency. This opposition will be implicit at first and rendered explicit only by an act of reflection.

"Is this not precisely the mechanism of the affirmation?" asks Maréchal. "Is it not on account of it that affirmation necessarily 'objectivates?' Considered as a moment in the intellect's ascent towards the final possession of the absolute 'truth,' which is the spirit's 'good,' it implicitly (*exercite*) projects the particular data in the perspective of this ultimate End, and by so doing objectivates them before the subject."[3]

It is then by the act of affirmation (or negation) that the synthesized form of the object is set over against the subject as an object in itself, whose reality in itself is thereby acknowledged and asserted (or denied). His relating of the form to the real order occurs by virtue of the intellect's drive towards the Absolute Reality realized in partial stages with each affirmation. By being projected on a trajectory towards this final goal, its reality as a partial stage towards that goal and therefore as an object in itself other than the affirming subject is revealed against the horizon of the Absolute Real. In effect, the affirming function of judgment relates the matter being judged to the final end of all activity, including pre-eminently the activity of judging itself.

In his major work, Maréchal believes that he has overthrown Kant's phenomenalism and thus vindicated a realistic metaphysics "by showing, by means of Kant's method, that the phenomenal object is absolutely impossible unless it is contained in a knowledge, which transcends the phenomenal level."[4] We cannot know the phenomenal as phenomenal, he is saying, except in terms of an affirmation that exceeds the limits of the phenomenal, that attains to and thereby establishes a context of the trans-phenomenal within which the phenomenal can be distinguished as such. In terms of the transcendental method, this implies an uncovering of the a priori condition of human knowing that accounts for such a possibility, viz., the immanence of Absolute Being as the final goal of the dynamism of affirmation and therefore as the principle of the objectivity of man's knowledge.

God, the Absolute Being, is therefore present to human knowing from the beginning, though only implicitly. Affirmation is thus "a transcendental anticipation," a ceaseless striving for the explicit knowledge of God which would be ideally realized in an immediate personal intuition. This essential relation of our knowledge of every other object to

Absolute Being can be made gradually more explicit by reflection and is expressly thematized in arguments for God's existence.

As St. Thomas puts it: "All knowing beings *implicitly* know God in *everything they know*. For as nothing is desirable but through some resemblance with the first goodness, so nothing is knowable but through some resemblance with the first truth."[5] (Maréchal's italics) Thus Maréchal makes his own the Thomistic thesis that man has a natural desire to see God. Each affirmation, centered on a limited finite object, is yet a partial anticipation of the eventual full knowledge of God, perfectly realized in intuitive vision. Yet, as he insisted, this goal is truly supernatural and not the theoretical foundation of our natural knowledge. "As far as the foundation of my epistemological theory goes, it is necessary that I show merely that absolute being is naturally striven after in every noetic activity as the ultimate *objective* goal and that this remains true whether we transfer our ultimate subjective goal into a direct vision of God or into the analogical knowledge of him."[6] With this qualification, it would not be an exaggeration to say that for Maréchal man not only *has*, but in a very real sense *is* a natural desire for the vision of God. Since man is engaged always in an anticipatory movement towards God as the goal, at least implicit, of every act of his knowing, we can also say more appropriately that man does not possess the Absolute in his knowing as that he is possessed by the Absolute as the end which validates each affirmation as a further step toward being totally possessed by Him.

KARL RAHNER: *Philosophical Foundations*

Maréchal's transcendental version of Thomism met with severe criticism from Thomists of a more traditional orientation. In spite of this not unexpected opposition many Catholic thinkers began to practice the transcendental method under his inspiration and after his example.[7] Karl Rahner (1904-   ), perhaps the most renowned contemporary Catholic theologian, is also the most effective exponent of the transcendental method in theology. Like most of the other Transcendental Thomists, his theologizing was preceded by an intensive philosophical initiation into the thought of St. Thomas in confrontation with modern philosophy.

A. SPIRIT IN THE WORLD: METAPHYSICS OF KNOWLEDGE

In his case the dominant modern figure is that of Heidegger whose lectures he attended at Freiburg. His doctoral dissertation in philosophy, *Geist in Welt* (*Spirit in the World*),[8] a reinterpretation of Aquinas' metaphysics of knowledge, betrays the influence of Heidegger. But it is Maréchal at least in the transcendental style that he introduced into Catholic thinking, whose influence is powerfully sensed in this highly original work. Its sequel, *Hörer des Wortes* (Hearers of the Word),[9] extends its implications into the philosophy of religion and fundamental theology. Both of these books are indispensable for understanding Rahner's later theological writings inasmuch as his theological method and vision grew organically out of their soil.

Rahner enters modern thought through the thought of St. Thomas because he is convinced that Aquinas was the first of the modern thinkers. Modern thought is characterized by "the turn to the subject," the recognition of the uniqueness of the human subjectivity and its constitutive influence on all that we know. Descartes is credited with initiating this trend and Kant with bringing it to irreversible dominance. Rahner, with the other Transcendental Thomists, sees it already anticipated in St. Thomas, implicitly perhaps but unmistakably. For documentation, he points to the doctoral dissertation of Johannes B. Metz, achieved under his aegis, which discerns in certain key themes of Aquinas' thought a fundamentally anthropocentric orientation underlying the cosmocentric categories inherited from the Greeks with which he was compelled to express it.[10]

As a Christian St. Thomas had undergone a radical personal conversion to the Gospel within his own life. At the same time he submitted himself to the Catholic tradition which had infused a whole culture with the fruits of conversion to the Gospel on the part of numerous generations. When he enlisted the philosophy of Aristotle to perform with scientific rigor the task of reflecting on his own life of faith and that of the Church, he inevitably transformed his chosen instrument by the use to which he put it.

Thus, for example, he converted Aristotle's "act" into "*esse*," not merely as a progress from a metaphysical account of change and stability to one of existence as the underlying problem, but even more by virtue of a deeper grasp of his own subjectivity as a Christian for whom everything, including existence, is a gracious divine gift and therefore contingent. In this he was assisted by the example of St. Augustine, who had bequeathed to later generations of Christians his own penetrating self-analyses and disclosures of human subjectivity and of the inner dynamisms of the man of faith. Aquinas had no alternative but to employ the object-oriented categories of Aristotle's cosmocentric outlook, but as a Christian theologian whose genius opened new horizons for a reflective appropriation of the meaning of the Gospel and especially of the Incarnation, he knew well that man was not to be understood through the world, but the world through man. Therefore the implicit world view which had to be expressed in such categories was itself anthropocentric.

Rahner began his dissertation at Freiburg on the Thomistic metaphysics of knowledge while regularly attending the lectures of Heidegger. He was convinced that he was being unfaithful to neither, when he saw as an authentic transcription of Thomas' intentions the Heideggerian insistence that Being is truly disclosed only in and through *Dasein*, the being that man is. For Heidegger, the primordial situation of man is "being-in-the-world." For Rahner, studying Aquinas' metaphysics of knowledge, "How, according to Thomas, human knowing can be spirit in the world, is the question which is the concern of this work."[11] "By spirit I mean a power which reaches out beyond the world and knows the metaphysical. World is the name of the reality which is accessible to the immediate experience of man."[12] Thus in the very title of his work, Rahner implies two of the great issues of metaphysics: How is man being-in-the-world? How does man come to know Being which is itself transcendent as well as immanent to the world of his experience? He sees the heart of Thomas' answer to those questions in his doctrine of "the conversion of the intellect to the phantasm."

For Thomas, human knowing occurs wholly within the material world of our experience and yet it is not confined to that world. The proper object of our sense-dependent intellect is the quiddity or essence of a material substance and yet it is able to rise from that beginning, immersed in the world of space and time, to the knowledge of God, the infinite and eternal, to the boundless reaches of metaphysics. Rahner approaches the thought of Thomas with his transcendental method and asks: what are the a priori conditions which explain the possibility of metaphysics for such a human knower? It is the same Kantian question, but Rahner, like Maréchal, is able to give a Thomistic answer that is realistic and yet critical in the modern manner.

The question of the possibility of metaphysics is itself the metaphysical question, the question of Being. It is, in Rahner's judgment, the absolutely first question, that which is presupposed by every other. On reflection it is recognized as the question of man himself as the one who is alone able to put the question and seek its answer. Moreover, it is discovered to be implied in every act of man's knowing and therefore as the pre-condition of human experience, understanding and judgment. In this light, metaphysics is seen to be not the discovery of something previously unknown, but as he would put it succinctly in his later work, "the methodical, reflective knowledge of that which one has always known."[13] "In metaphysics the understanding which man as such already has of himself is articulated and hence brought to itself. Metaphysics is the conceptually formulated understanding of that prior understanding which man as man *is*."[14] Thus the question of metaphysics involves that of the metaphysics of human knowing which is in effect the question of the being of man.

Man questions and he questions necessarily. The ground of his being as a questioner is the questionableness of Being. "What is the Being of that which is?" That is the primordial question which turns upon itself and places in question not only the object of inquiry, but the questioner, his question itself, and indeed absolutely everything. "In actually asking the metaphysical question man becomes aware of what he is in the ground of his essence: he who must ask about being."[15] *Man exists as the question about being.*

This points to the paradox of man and his knowing. At the very beginning man is already at the goal, since from the start he is already asking about being in its totality. Yet by the fact that he raises the question and is indeed always raising it, he acknowledges that he himself is finite and not the goal he seeks. And from the beginning, his question has disclosed the horizon within which his life quest will always afterward have to take place. Metaphysics merely makes explicit what is implicit from the very start.

In the beginning the question of being is an emptiness to be filled. "What then is the existent with which man always and necessarily already is, and at which point he is called into the presence of being in its totality? It is the things of the world, he himself with his corporeality and with all that belongs to the realm and to the environment of this corporeal life."[16] Human knowledge in its unity comprises knowledge of an existent in the world in its here and now and the knowledge of being in its totality. This is equivalent to saying that human knowing comprises respectively sensibility and thought which are always concretely one inasmuch as each is at once itself and yet different from the other precisely because of its unity with the other.

Since being is questionable in its totality, it is knowable in principle before the empty notion of being is filled out by particular experiences of the beings of the world. It is, in Thomas' terms, the formal object of the intellect, the horizon with which man approaches everything to be known and within which alone he is able to experience, understand and judge everything as existent. The implications of this for Rahner are profound. For Thomas being and knowing exist in an original unity. Knowing does not come upon *that which is* as a subsequent relation, through a contact of the intellect with the intelligible thing. As he expresses it: "the intellect and the intelligible in act are one."[17] Being and knowing are the same, says Rahner, and in terms reminiscent of Heidegger he states his well-known metaphysical position: "Knowing is the being-present-to-self of being and this being-present-to-self (*Beisichsein*) is the being of the existent. Therefore the beingness, the intensity of being of the being of an existent is determined for Thomas by the *reditio super seipsum*, the *intensity* of being is determined by the degree of possibility of being able to be present to itself."[18]

Knowing cannot be understood merely as the relationship of a knower to an object different from him, as intentionality. Rather it must first and fundamentally be understood in the light of the fact that being is of itself knowing and being known, it is being-present-to-self.[19] Being is therefore "the one ground which lets knowing and being-known spring out of itself as its own characteristics, and thus grounds the intrinsic possibility of an antecedent, essential, intrinsic relation of both of them to each other."[20] This is Rahner's interpretation of *"Ens et verum convertuntur,"* the transcendental intelligibility of being. In summary:

> Knowing is understood as the subjectivity of being itself, as the being-present-to-self of being. Being itself is already the original, unifying unity of being and knowing, is ontological: and every actual unity of being and knowing in the actualization of knowledge is only raising to a higher power that transcendental synthesis which being is 'in itself.' . . . the principle that being is being-present-to-self and that thus the known is always the being of the knower must be taken seriously.[21]

It is in the light of this understanding of being that Rahner defines spirit and matter, sensibility and intellect, and their operations and relations.

B. SPIRIT AND MATTER, INTELLECT AND SENSE

As the antecedent and original unity of knowing and known, being is essentially indefinable, prior to and presumed by definability. Being is and always remains questionable for man and he exercises his very being in continually pursuing the question. In asking about being he is already with being, but he is never with being in its totality except by anticipation and so questions always remain. His being is finite, it is never absolutely present to itself. To the degree that it is not, he is a compound of non-being. Thus is indicated the analogy of being as it is understood here: viz., the intensity of an existent's presence-to-self, knowledge or subjectivity, is the measure of its intensity of being. God is absolute presence-to-self, identity of knower and known, not questionable to Himself. At the opposite end is prime matter which is not at all present-to-self, since it is not for itself but entirely for another.

Since knowledge is the being-present-to-self of being and matter is that which is entirely for another, knowability and matter are related in an inverse proportion. The less related to matter a being is, the more is it able to be present-to-self. For Thomas, immateriality is the condition for actual knowing and knowability. The degree of a being's immateriality is the measure of its being-able-to-be-present-to-self, therefore, of its knowing and its being.

> Thus for the Thomistic metaphysics of knowledge the problem does not lie in bridging the gap between knowing and object by a 'bridge' of some kind: such a 'gap' is merely a pseudo-problem. Rather the problem is how the known, which is identical with the knower, can stand over against the knower as other, and how there can be a knowledge which receives another as such. It is not a question of 'bridging' a gap, but of understanding how the gap is possible at all.[22]

This problem of a receptive knowing is in effect the problem of man himself. For he "invariably finds himself already with the other of the world, hence . . . the other as such is his proper object, . . . his being-present-to-self is thus a being-with-the-other."[23]

This is the problem Rahner sets himself in his inaugural work. *How is receptive knowing possible?* It is the question of the being of man because it is asking what are the intrinsic conditions which explain an existent whose being-present-to-self is being-with-the-other, who comes to know himself by virtue of knowing-the-other. His solution illustrates his transcendental method inasmuch as it describes man's actual being as a knower and then attempts to establish the conditions which account for the possibility of such a being (reduction): in a second step, it shows how the actual human condition flows from its a priori conditions (deduction). Throughout the process, he is vindicating his fundamental metaphysical conviction that Being is being-present-to-self, that knowing is the subjectivity of being, and therefore that Being is a constitutive factor in every instance and level of knowing.

Man's being is in the world, the material, corporeal, sensible world. But it is man who is in the world, not an animal: that is, the one who incessantly questions Being. What are the conditions which explain man's knowing presence-to-self in the world that yet reaches always beyond the confines of the world?

Man participates in the material world as himself material in his body. As material, he is not present-to-self, but rather existent for another. To that degree, he is passive to the material other, his being is wholly potentiality for the being of the other. He is acted upon by the other. But his body is not pure prime matter, sheer potentiality. It is informed by spirit, it partakes of immateriality. Therefore its powers of sensibility are actively receptive. Man as sensible subject actively performs as his own act the act of the other that is taking place in his material self. This is what is meant by intuition: the act of the object which takes place in the subject-as-material becomes the act of the subject inasmuch as the subject performs it as his own act. There is identity of subject and object in the act, and at this point the subject is not able to distinguish itself from the object. Rahner agrees with Kant that for man intuition occurs only on this level of sense. But as against Kant, for Rahner intuition does not produce the identity, but only recognizes it as already present.

Our experience assures us that man is always driving towards the realization of his being, towards greater presence to himself in a process of increasing self-appropriation by return to self (*reditio super seipsum*). Identity with the other by sense intuition is only the price and condition for such a return and differentiation of self from the other in the opposing movement of objectivation. This occurs on the level of intellectual thought in the two stages of *abstraction*, which presupposes the power known as Agent Intellect, and *conversion to the phantasm*, which presupposes the power known as Possible Intellect.

The capacity to become present-to-self is in direct

proportion to the immateriality of a being, to its being 'spirit.' This capacity itself is called thought or intellect. "It is first through thought that the undifferentiated unity of sensibility and sensible object which is had in sensation, of subject and object, really becomes the subject who in his self-possessed existence has a world over against himself; it is first through thought that human experience of an objective world becomes possible."[24]

Abstraction is the first stage of thought as a process of return to self in a differentiation of self from its unity with the object in sense intuition. This stage is expressed in the formation of a universal concept which refers to but is other than the individual object of sense. It is something known about the object, a form derived from the object but predicable not only of it, but of an unlimited multitude of similar objects. Thus it is the result of an *excessus* (to use Thomas' term), of a transcending movement of going beyond the sensed individual. Simultaneously it is a return to self inasmuch as it is setting the object off from the self which as subject of the abstraction is moving beyond the object as intuited.

This movement of return to self as opposed to or as over-against-another is completed in the synthesis of judgment where truth (or error) can first occur as a valid (or invalid) estimate of the other as *in itself*. In any event, man's being present to himself is grounded in his standing-over-against-a-world, and the combination of these two defines the uniqueness of human thought. They also designate in their unison the two facets of intellectual operation, called by Thomas the Agent and the Possible Intellect.

Rahner reinterprets Aquinas' theory of the Agent Intellect as the power of abstraction. It is transcendentally inferred as the a priori condition for the possibility of abstraction. As such, it is not, as it has often been understood, merely a counterpart of sense perception, that is, a power to impress on the Possible Intellect a spiritual image of what has been intuited sensibly. Instead it is the capacity to know the sensibly intuited precisely *as limited,* and thus as embracing the ever further possibilities which constitute the universality of thought. How does the Agent Intellect operate as the a priori condition of the possibility of abstraction? Inasmuch as it involves a priori grasp or pre-apprehension (*Vorgriff*) of the field of possibilities within which the individual sensible form is apprehended as a concrete limitation of these possibilities able to be multiplied within the field.

In effect, this *Vorgriff* apprehends a priori a horizon within which the limited and finite character of the sensible individual appears. Since it is in essence a condition of the very possibility of objective knowledge attained in human thought, this pre-apprehension does not itself attain to an object. It is itself non-objective, unthematic and pre-reflective inasmuch as it is always providing the context within which objective, thematic and reflective knowing is taking place.

How broad is the horizon apprehended by this *Vorgriff*? Is it that of the imagination of infinite space and time, or is it the absolutely unlimited horizon of Being which transcends space and time? Rahner concludes with Thomas that it must be *Esse*, that is, the ultimate act of anything and everything *as what is in itself*. It is therefore infinite in an absolute sense and not limited to the relative infinity of the spatio-temporal dimensions of matter. This absolute *Esse* is then ground or principle or act of all that is in itself. It is not yet recognized as God. For that recognition further reflection explicitated in proofs of His existence is required. However, one can say that the reality of God as that of absolute *Esse* is implicitly, i·e., non-objectively, unthematically and pre-reflectively, co-affirmed in every affirmation by virtue of the infinite scope of the pre-apprehension within which it occurs. Thus Rahner interprets the meaning of St. Thomas' statement: "Every knower implicitly knows God in every act of knowing."[25]

The ordering of man's knowledge as pre-apprehensive to what is absolutely infinite defines man as spirit, but as finite spirit. He is *spirit* because he finds himself situated before being in its infinite totality. He experiences his own movement toward absolute *Esse* in a transcending process that surpasses every limit to his knowing and that leaves him open to being in its totality. Yet he is *finite* spirit because he cannot comprehend this infinite *Esse* as the object of his knowing, but can only know it non-objectively and unthematically in the unlimited scope of his pre-apprehension, in the boundless horizon of his unrestricted desire to know. It is this *Vorgriff* or *excessus* to absolute *Esse* that essentially and sufficiently defines man's Agent Intellect as the power of abstraction and the light which illumines the content of the phantasm or sensibly known. It accomplishes this not by transposing it into an intellectual content, but by disclosing the sensible content as being universal, that is, as the possible form of a multiplicity of individuals projected against the horizon of infinite *Esse*.

For Rahner, therefore, sense and intellectual knowledge are not two levels of knowing occurring in sequence and each concerned with its own peculiar content. Rather they are correlative operations in which the sensed object grasped in the immediacy of intuition is then mediated, that is, grasped in its otherness from the subject in the spiritual operation that is at once a return to the self in abstraction and a standing over-against-another (viz., the object) in the conversion to the phantasm. In fact, "conversion to the phantasm" is the term that can designate the complete human act in its sense and intellectual components inasmuch as it defines its fulfillment.

By abstraction the Agent Intellect makes objective knowledge possible by setting the particular datum of sense intuition in the horizon of absolute *Esse* and disclosing its otherness from the totality of other possibilities which constitutes its universality. Simultaneously the subject as spirit is freed for its native movement of return to self to the degree that its otherness from the phantasm or sensed datum is rendered discernible. The full realization of this otherness or objectivity and the simultaneous rendering the subject present to self is only achieved in the complete act of knowledge. For only then does the subject in actuated self-presence affirm as objective its conceptual understanding of the particular sensed datum arrived at in the light of its pre-apprehension of infinite *Esse*. The performance of objective knowledge which culminates in the affirmation is attributed to the power known as Possible Intellect.

Man is spirit precisely to the degree that he is present to self. But he is a finite spirit who is not always wholly actually present to self, but must rather grow towards full self-realization. He is spirit in matter, in the world, and it is by virtue of his material involvement in the world that man grows in presence to self. He must realize himself through sensibility by turning to the world, becoming identified with it in intuition, and then in a movement of transcendence, grasping it in its objectivity and otherness as he is coming into fuller presence to and possession of himself.

This drive towards transcendence is ceaselessly actuated by the pre-apprehension of absolute *Esse* which constitutes his Active Intellect as the a priori with which he confronts his world and himself within a horizon that always surpasses both. Thus man realizes himself as a being-in-the world by the power of a movement that continually strives to surpass it towards the Absolute Being Which is its ground. He becomes himself and can return to himself only by first giving himself to the finite other, to his world. He must therefore commit himself to the world in order to be himself. Yet in the whole process he is actually seeking God Who is present non-objectively, unthematically, in every affirmation in which the world and self are thematized. "Thus man encounters himself when he finds himself in the world and when he asks about God; and when he asks about his essence, he always finds himself already in the world and on the way to God."[26]

Metaphysics attempts to thematize this fundamental human situation which appears so ambivalent. From one point of view, man is irretrievably involved in this world and the transcendent direction of his life project towards the Absolute seems to serve only to make possible his fuller experience and involvement in the world and his correlative personal growth as a being of this world. But the process of transcendence which constitutes his being as spirit in the world places him beyond the world in an insistent movement that expresses his essential discontent with anyone or anything less than the divine Absolute. We can never shake ourselves of the necessity to confront our world and ourselves with the question of Being and therefore to question both to their absolute ground.

> Thus every venture into the world shows itself to be borne by the ultimate desire of the spirit for absolute being; every entrance into sensibility, into the world and its destiny, shows itself to be only the coming to be of a spirit which is striving towards the absolute. Thus man is the mid-point suspended between the world and God, between time and eternity, and this boundary line is the point of his definition and his destiny.[27]

Rahner approached man exclusively from the viewpoint of the metaphysics of knowledge in his *Spirit in the World*. It was a rich beginning for his life-work as a theologian during which he would exploit the many fascinating and useful pathways that would emanate from it. But it yielded an incomplete portrait of man since it almost completely overlooked man's freedom and affective life. These would achieve greater prominence in his subsequent work in the philosophy of religion, *Hearers of the Word*, which would require the more full-bodied portrait of man as openness to God's Self-Gift of love in a history of salvation. Before we follow him in this more mature development of his Christian anthropology, we shall first consult the thought of another transcendental Thomist who was at once a follower and critic of Rahner.

EMERICH CORETH: *Metaphysics of the Question*

Emerich Coreth has been a professor of philosophy at Innsbruck in Austria where Rahner began his teaching career in theology. Though influenced by Rahner and revealing striking similarities in his thought, he has pursued his own independent way. He has developed a transcendentally grounded metaphysics much further in a fully rounded systematic explanation of the principal metaphysical problems. He has also challenged Rahner's starting point of the question of Being as not being critical enough. For before the question involving any content, including Being, is the question itself as a performance. The question of questioning itself is the absolute, presuppositionless and self-validating starting point for metaphysics and any human knowledge.

For Coreth as for Rahner, metaphysics is the reflective possession of the validating ground of all human knowledge. It is the science that must be absolutely self-validating since it furnishes the grounds for the validity of all other sciences as ways of man's knowing.[28] Its starting point must be such that no one can deny it without at the same time affirming it. In effect, the starting point must involve those conditions for the possibility of man's knowing at all which are presupposed and implicitly co-affirmed even in the judgment which denies its possibility. The method which uncovers those conditions, as we have been seeing, is the transcendental method, which Coreth has brought to a new high point of refinement.

What act of knowledge should constitute the starting point of metaphysics? Maréchal had used the affirmation, Rahner, the question of Being. Each of these, says Coreth, has a definite content whose validity must be taken for granted. On the contrary, it must be subject to unreserved questioning. There is one cognitive activity which by its very nature takes nothing for granted: the question itself. For even to challenge it, we have to appeal to it to issue the challenge, and thus we are back at the same starting point.

The question is unique also in that it supplies its own method for the inquiry. Other starting points assume their content and their method. The question assumes neither, but rather establishes both. It supplies the content, viz., the question itself, and the method, viz., questioning as a transcendental procedure. Man's nature is thus revealed in the primordial movement that is the source of all his knowledge: man "the questioner, the inquirer, the wonderer, who discovers being more in the act of questioning than in any definite content of the mind, because being always extends beyond any knowledge, and man knows it as thus extending beyond anything he knows."[29]

There is a double movement in the transcendental method which is most clearly operative in the dynamic of the question: *reduction,* which proceeds from an act to the conditions of its possibility, and *deduction,* which moves from these conditions to the essential structures of the act.

Reduction, usually the more prominent feature of the method, is a process of return from what is explicitly or thematically known to that which is implicitly or unthematically co-known in the act in question, and thus to what is pre-known as a condition of the act. Deduction reverses this process by inferring the act, its nature, possibility and necessity, from their conditions disclosed by the reduction.

Every question involves a mixture of knowledge and ignorance. There is not only the knowledge already achieved before the particular question arises. There is the knowledge of something unknown, yet to be known, which provokes the question itself and which is therefore intrinsic to the questioning act. This knowing of one's own ignorance not only generates the question but also gives it a direction, thus anticipating in a kind of pre-knowledge what is not yet explicitly known.

This pre-knowledge is not itself explicit or thematized. If it were, the question would not be necessary; it would already be answered. It is rather present implicitly, presupposed, and enters into the very act of the question insofar as it is unthematically co-affirmed in the very performance of that act. It constitutes the horizon of the question since it furnishes the field within which the question emerges and is defined.

The dynamic of the question is thus seen to involve a continual dialectic between concept and act that is characteristic of all knowing. It obtains between "the conceptualized, explicit, thematic content of our knowledge and the unthematic, pre-reflexive, implicit knowledge that is co-affirmed with the act of knowing itself."[30] The latter can be called *lived or exercised knowledge* because it is implied in the very performance of the act of knowledge itself. In every act of knowing or inquiring, therefore, more is known than is thematized or made explicit by the content of the act or question. As Blondel showed at great length in his *L'Action,* this discrepancy between *thought thought* and *thinking thought,* between what is conceptualized and what is yet anticipated and driving the knowing act ever onward, is the underlying dynamic of the human knowing process. As Coreth observes, "reflex explicit knowledge is always surpassed by implicit exercised knowledge."[31] What is only implicit in exercised knowledge can be made explicit through the mediation of reflection, but it is never exhausted in the process. The richness of the act always exceeds the capacity of the concept to express it.

The process is one of *mediated immediacy*, to use Hegel's term. Each new concept or explicitation must be mediated, that is, brought by reflection out of the immediate lived knowledge implied in the act itself. Inasmuch as the starting point chosen is the question about questioning itself, it is from the performance of questioning and its implications that the concepts and insights are to be derived that will constitute an emerging thematic metaphysics. In the process the two moments of the transcendental method, reduction and deduction, will move in continual interaction.[32]

Coreth commences his metaphysics with the question of its starting point. But it is evident that prior to any starting point comes the question about it. Thus the question about the starting point becomes the question about the question, which is alone the first, self-validating and unquestionable starting point. For any challenge to it becomes itself the question about the question, so that any denial of its possibility involves an implicit contradiction.

What is beyond doubt is the act or performance of questioning, not its content. For any content can be called into doubt, whereas the act of questioning is confirmed by the very question which calls it into doubt. Like any cognitive act, questioning is conscious and aware of itself, at least implicitly and non-thematically. What must be uncovered and explored by the transcendental method is this implicit, unthematic awareness that is involved in every act of questioning and what is implicitly affirmed in it. Coreth applies his dialectic of mediating reflection to the questioning operation.

Because the fact of the possibility of the question is beyond doubt, the inquiry is turned rather upon the conditions of that possibility. *How* is the very act of questioning possible? That which is uncovered as the condition without which the question as such cannot be explained is the presence of a concomitant knowing that is unthematic, not yet formulated in concepts. This condition is not an *ontic* condition, that is, one "whose existence is presupposed by the act, but which does not enter into the act as one of its constitutive elements and is not co-affirmed in the act. Hence it cannot be derived or deduced from the act."[33] Neither is it a *logical* condition, that is, one whose *knowledge* is presupposed by the act, not as a condition of its possibility, but of the validity of its content. Rather it is a *transcendental* condition, that is, a condition of the very possibility of the act which enters into the constitution of the act inasmuch as it is unthematically co-affirmed in the question.

Thus the question about the question becomes the question about the transcendental conditions of its possibility. In terms of the dialectic of act and content, the act of questioning and what is unthematically co-affirmed in it must be explicitated and given a conceptual content. While this explicit knowledge must be continually nourished on the lived knowledge of the act itself, it will recognize that it will never succeed in fully expressing it.

In terms of the double movement of transcendental method, reduction and deduction, it is seen that both interact in a mutual process that moves the inquiry forward. Reductively, the act is questioned for its conditions of possibility. This uncovers the unthematic, preconceptual knowledge co-affirmed in the act which must be itself thematized. What is revealed is the structure of knowing ignorance; that is, what is questioned is known in order for it to be open to question; but it is not fully known, for otherwise it would not be possible to ask a question about it. Deductively, the actual structure of the questioning act is explained in terms of a pre-knowledge of what is questioned whose very inadequacy provokes and compels the explicit question itself.

Every determinate question, including the question of the starting point of metaphysics, involves such co-knowledge which precedes the question and enters into it in some way. Some co-knowledge is merely *modifying*, that is, it merely modifies or affects the meaning of the question for the one asking it, but it is not a condition of its very possibility as a constitutive element. What we have been speaking about is *constitutive co-knowledge,* which is a condition of the very possibility of the particular question. It is co-known in the question, though unthematically, and co-affirmed as so known. Thus it is able to be derived reductively from the content of the determinate question.

What is sought, however, is something more fundamental: namely, the conditions of the possibility of any question insofar as it is a question. It will not be conditioned on any specific content, either as known or as yet to be known. Rather it will concern the sheer movement of the question beyond what is known into the unknown, the pre-knowledge or inquiring anticipation of the as-yet-unknown. Hence it is a question neither of a constitutive or modifying co-knowledge insofar as each of these anticipates something of the content of the object of a *particular* question. What is required as the condition of the question *as such* is a pure pre-knowledge, a pure transcending of what is already known and an anticipation of what is not yet known. This does not establish the limited and partial horizon of particular questions which are conditioned by the questioner's own past experience. It is instead a total and all-encompassing horizon of all questioning and knowing which is purely a priori and within which the limited empirical horizons of particular questions are situated as in their context. Thus we can ask particular questions because we have the ability to question as such, and not the other way around.

What is the horizon or direction of the pure anticipation which constitutes the question as question? It is not a particular or limited direction as arising from a previous well-determined knowledge or content which directs the anticipation. This applies to the co-knowledge that is a condition of the possibility of every single question. For the question as question, it is the full range of everything that may be inquired about: in other words, the totality of the questionable, the questionable as such. The question as such is made possible by a pre-knowledge or pure anticipation of the questionable as such.

The questionable as such is without limits. For if there

were limits, we could question them and thereby surpass them. Therefore, the questionable as such is simply everything: not everything in particular, but rather in its unity. What the question seeks to know is what everything is. The questionable as such, that is the condition of the question as such, is the totality of being in its unity; that is, Being itself. It is not the sum of all previously known beings, but rather the anticipation of all beings in their unity, in the act of being (*esse*) by which all *are*. Thus the condition of the possibility of questioning is the unthematic anticipation or pre-knowledge of the act of being by virtue of which the totality of beings constitutes a unity. As anticipatory, it is not the product of an induction, but rather the previous horizon within which every individual question or particular act of knowledge takes place.

Man is a ceaseless inquirer because he is a metaphysical animal. He is endlessly asking questions. He is the questioning being, because the horizon of his consciousness is the totality of being which is unthematically preapprehended and co-affirmed in every question and every act of knowing, continually summoning him beyond every frontier of his current knowledge. Moreover, it is being *in itself* that is the goal of every question, not merely being in relation to us, being for us. Our questions want to know how and what things really are *in themselves*. This is even true of the affirmation that we only know things as they *appear* to us. For implied in this explicit affirmation is the unthematized co-affirmation that it is absolutely so that things are only as they appear to us; in other words, that such is the situation *in itself*. Hence the horizon of our questioning is being in itself, as absolute or unconditioned.[34]

This absolute being is not yet God known explicitly, but rather being (*esse*) in general. The distinction within being must be made between finite and infinite being. The procedure will not be to argue from finite beings as conditioned and contingent to infinite being as unconditioned and necessary, since we cannot know the conditioned and contingent as such except against the horizon of the unconditioned and necessary. "We start by establishing the unconditioned and absolute nature of being as a whole, which is presupposed and co-affirmed in every question, as a condition of its possibility."[35] Man as subject recognizes his own finiteness in his continually limited efficacy in reaching the unconditioned and unlimited being that is the goal of his ceaseless questioning, and he recognizes by contrast his own conditioned nature alongside that of the other beings of his experience. Thereby he is able to distinguish from himself and them the unconditioned Absolute Being Which is their ground and is able to vindicate his right to affirm Its existence.

Every being, *insofar as it is,* is itself necessarily and cannot not be or be something else. This necessity is conditioned (*"insofar as it is"*) and implies a ground or foundation in the unconditioned necessity of being as such which *absolutely* cannot not be. Within the affirmation of the unconditioned necessity of being as such, the absolute being of God is co-affirmed but unthematically. It is only made explicit when we realize that no finite being, as limited and conditioned, can be absolute being or being itself. Rather the existence of the totality of finite beings, whose necessity is relative, inescapably implies the reality of that Being Whose necessity is absolute, Who is Being Itself.

We come to an explicit knowledge of God through the mediation of the finite beings of the world of our experience which we constantly transcend by dint of our unthematic pre-knowledge of the absolute and necessary character of being. Already implied is the knowledge of the Absolute Being, but it is only able to be thematized and made explicit when we come to realize that the beings of our world,

in their multiplicity, relativity, and finiteness, are not themselves the being which is necessary and necessarily always already affirmed but presuppose this being beyond themselves. Thus it is only through the mediation of the finite beings of experience that we discover that the necessity of being is distinct from them as the absolutely other, as absolute Being. Nevertheless, it follows from all this that the knowledge of God does not really represent a passage of our mind to something hitherto wholly unknown, but only an explicitation and development of our knowledge of the necessity of Being.[36]

In this manner and also by appealing to the principles of causality and finality, we do not demonstrate the existence of God so much as we vindicate our right to affirm his existence as necessarily implied in every act of knowing and indeed in every act in which the transcending human spirit comes to further self-realization in its transactions with the beings of its world.[37]

As the horizon within which all knowledge of objects takes place, the Absolute Being is the necessary condition for objective knowledge. It cannot itself be apprehended as another object of knowledge. It is rather the goal toward which the finite human spirit is always necessarily transcending. For in every act of knowing, it is co-known and co-affirmed as the true itself and in every act of will it is co-intended as the good itself.

This does not mean that we cannot know God or make assertions about Him with a positive even though only analogous content. The human spirit, although finite, has an infinite capacity for knowing Being as the unlimited goal of its transcending. In its own limitless reach reflectively appropriated, it is able to intend the pure perfections of Infinite Being which it can never grasp in an achieved understanding. "That is why (man) really knows God, although he can never enclose him in a concept or a definition. Whatever he *conceives* about God is hopelessly inadequate, yet what he basically *means* or *intends* through his concepts comes up to some extent, dynamically not statically, to what the Absolute really is."[38]

The Absolute Being we intend is the Personal God and not an impersonal principle. For He is the ultimate ground as well as the absolute fullness of the powers of our spiritual life: the knowledge, will, love and freedom that constitute our personhood. For philosophy left to itself, this Infinite Person can be known only as the receding horizon of the ceaseless process of transcendence which comprises our life-project. But as Person, He is able, if He so wills, to come toward man in a free initiative of self-communication and engage man in a loving dialogue that annuls the infinite distance which separates them.

KARL RAHNER: Hearers of the Word *and Later Writings*

Rahner's writing of *Hearers of the Word,* the sequel to *Spirit in the World,* represented a shift in perspective: from a metaphysics of knowledge to a philosophy of religion, or as was seen more clearly afterward, a fundamental theology. Each yielded its anthropology or understanding of man, the later building on and fulfilling the implications of the earlier in a new context. The first portrayed man as spirit-in-the-world, who transcends ceaselessly toward Absolute Being with Whom he is, unobjectively, from the beginning. Thus there is provided the dynamism of his life-project in which he comes to greater self-possession by being with and inter-acting with the beings of his world. The second saw man not merely as transcendence to the Absolute Being as the horizon of his worldly life and activities, but as a potential 'hearer of the Word,' as a possible sharer of a common history with the Absolute Mystery, should God in His freedom come out of His silence to reveal Himself to man in a saving dialogue.

At the conclusion of *Spirit in the World,* Rahner acknowledges the theological thrust of the thought of St. Thomas whose metaphysics of knowledge he had just interpreted. He believes that he has uncovered there an understanding of man as openness to God's Self-Revelation and therefore to theological understanding of man himself. For man was disclosed as the unique one whose very being in the world involves the habitual knowledge of the Presence of God, Who is yet hidden from him and therefore ultimately Absolute Mystery. Man's being is thus essentially orientation to the possibility of an initiative of Self-Gift on the part of the Absolute Mystery, which would yet be free and un-owed to man, since his own existence would still be meaningful in its absence.[39]

Man's being-in-this-world is as an incarnate spirit for whom God is the Known Unknown and the necessary horizon against which he works out his destiny as a being of this world, unreservedly committed to it at the same time that he is irresistibly driven to transcend beyond it. This is an understanding of man that is thoroughly Christian without needing to claim or avow the label. For it is, at least in potency, the portrait of that Man in Whom God relinquished His remote Silence and committed Himself to this world as His definitive Word of revelation. In *Hearers of the Word,* Rahner draws out the further implications of his Christian Anthropology on which his developing theological vision would be nourished as a coherent synthesis in which Christ would be the meeting place of God and man, Christology the unity of Theology and Anthropology.

A. MAN BEFORE GOD AND HIS POSSIBLE REVELATION

Man constitutes himself as he constitutes his world. In the same action by which he goes out to-be-with-others in his knowing, he returns to himself. This movement of complete return to self (*reditio completa in seipsum*) is his very subjectivity and is the distinctive attribute of spirit. This double movement of being-with-others to be-with-himself is characteristic of all human actions as specifically human. Its structure in judgment as the completive act of knowing is most evident. Especially manifest there is its effect of constituting man in his subjectivity and self-subsistence over against the objective other which he gradually organizes into his world. However, it is also realized in its structure and effect in the other activities which typify man as a free, affective, willing, social, historical being.

This double movement is the root of man's freedom. Because he returns completely to himself in his judgments and thus grows in the self-subsistence by which he differentiates himself from the other and becomes independent of it, he is enabled to act freely upon it. But this effect is heightened in man's willing. Willing and knowing interpenetrate in the concrete unity of single human actions, but they are clearly distinguishable as realizing opposing inclinations in the subject-object dialectic.

Each realizes an identity of the human subject and his object which presupposes their difference. If the act of their identity is posited in the subject: that is, if the object is posited and affirmed not as in itself, but is acknowledged in its otherness precisely as in the subject, it is an act of knowing. If the act of their identity is posited in the object: that is, if the subject posits itself in the object as it is in itself as the goal of the subject's striving, then it is an act of willing. This latter is a more radical return of the subject upon itself, of being-with self. This ever-deepening self-possession is human freedom in its primary form, and it is the ground of freedom of choice. For it is only insofar as the human subject possesses himself and can thus dispose of himself that he is able to commit himself to this or that individual good against the horizon of Absolute Being as Good Itself.

Willing accordingly actuates the same basic structure and dynamic of human action as knowing does. The latter performs the two-fold functions of being-with-the-other and being-with-the-self in striving to fulfill its appetite for Absolute Being as Absolute Truth, pre-known unthematically as the condition of every judgment. Willing performs the same double function insofar as the subject can desire and strive for an individual good only because he unthematically co-intends Absolute Being as the Absolute Good. For Absolute Being as the Good is the ultimate goal of every act of willing an individual good upon which it confers its value and desirability. Thus the dynamism of transcending towards the horizon of Absolute Being as the spring of every human encounter with finite being operates in willing as well as in knowing, and through the will in every specifically human activity.

In pursuing the objectives of *Hearers of the Word,* Rahner probed man's being with his transcendental analysis until he uncovered the basic ontological unity from which his activities flow and diverge. What he sought was to determine the transcendental conditions of being in general and of man's finite existence for the possibility of a revelation from God and of its being heard by man.[40]

By virtue of the pre-knowledge of Absolute Being, man transcends toward the Infinite, but known negatively as the absence of limitation rather than in its positive meaning. Thus God remains veiled to man in the positive content of His Infinity, although the negative pre-apprehension of infinity as the exclusion of all limitation provides the necessary condition for the objective knowledge of finite being in its specific limitedness. Therefore, man's factual spiritual nature as transcendence towards Infinite Being does not supersede an act of divine Self-Revelation nor is it the equivalent of it. Rather it leaves an opening in man for such a possibility. Moreover, although man may have a natural desire for an immediate vision of God as the ultimate fulfillment of the infinite aspiration of his transcendence, such a fruition cannot be required, since even in its absence the dynamism of the human spirit remains meaningful as the condition for the possibility of an objective knowledge of finite existents and of man's own self-subsistence. Consequently, from man's side it is seen that a revelation by God to man would be a free act of self-disclosure.

The natural possession of the beatific vision of God as man's due end is excluded also by the fact that being for him is both intelligible and unintelligible. Even though he is from the beginning with being as a whole by anticipation, being always remains problematic and questionable for him. It is never wholly self-luminous. Yet if the beatific vision were his natural end, it would mean that the immediate self-luminosity or intelligibility of being would be available to him as the immediate cause of his own self-fulfillment.

Why then must man affirm the luminosity or knowable presence to self of being, when for him it remains always questionable as well as luminous, unintelligible as well as intelligible? The answer is that man is compelled both to continue to question being and to affirm its knowability as the condition for his taking possession of his own existence. He must affirm both his right to question being and its luminosity with the same necessity with which he must unceasingly affirm his own unique existence.

Man's existence is contingent and finite. In his experience of his own limited being, he becomes aware that being itself is not at his disposal. Yet he must affirm his own being, contingent as it is, with necessity, the same necessity with which he must co-affirm the luminosity of being as the horizon of his own existence. This necessity with which he must affirm his own contingent being is unconditional, absolute, undeniable.

What is the peculiar principle or source that accounts for this concurrence of contingency and necessity? It is *will*: not as an irrational force, but as an inner factor of knowledge itself. Thus man, in experiencing the necessity with which he must affirm his own contingent or non-necessary existence as limited being within the horizon of Absolute Being, experiences himself as the product of will. In the unconditional affirming of his own contingent existence, he is affirming himself as one who has been freely and deliberately posited by God. Thus he faces Absolute Being, the horizon of his self-constituting process of transcendence, as a free autonomous power; therefore, as a free person.

Every encounter with a free person requires the deliberate act of self-disclosure of that person for him to be known. Otherwise, the one who is known remains an unknown. Therefore, insofar as man stands always before God as a Free Person, he exists in the presence of One Who can disclose His own Mystery or refrain from doing so. Because man's own self-understanding is that of one whose very existence is grounded in and necessarily related to His Absolute Being, every initiative on God's part is a form of revelation in which man is intimately and inevitably involved. Their relationship thereby constitutes a history in which man stands always before God and the possibility of his incalculable free acts. Accordingly God is known not only as the Absolute Being toward Whom man is always transcending in the finite project of his life in the world, but also as the Free Person Whose actions can go far beyond this possibility as a revelation of Himself.

Whether God chooses to speak or to keep silence, some sort of revelation takes place. For man, as spirit, stands before the Divine Spirit known to be free and thus able to speak or be silent. Either is a revelation as a freely chosen course. For "whoever stands as one free person before another forthwith discloses himself. He discloses himself precisely as the one who he desires to be in the eyes of the other, either the hidden or the revealed."[41] In this sense, revelation necessarily occurs and is always addressed to man. By the same token, man is always essentially the listener for a possible revelation, that is, for "a possible speech from God that breaks his silence and discloses his depths to the finite spirit."[42]

To pursue his analysis of man as potential hearer of God's Word, Rahner returns to his thesis asserting will to be an inner factor of knowledge.[43] He employs it in trying to reconcile the contingency of human existence (which must necessarily be affirmed by man) with the luminosity of being in general. His effort will be to show how freedom and comprehensibility are related, not by an inverse, but by a direct proportion.

We have just seen how the contingent being of man is comprehended and necessarily affirmed insofar as it is grounded in the absolute being of God Who posits it nevertheless by a free intention or act of will. "How are we to grasp the luminosity of being so as to be able to grasp the free action of God as being itself luminous?"[44] Knowledge is the more perfect to the degree that the being to be known is more perfectly present to itself. It is "a *coming to oneself*, a *being present to oneself*, within oneself."[45] The free act is that act which belongs to the deepest meaning of the being subsisting in itself and which most of all exists in the being in which it originates. Thus one can comprehend that a free act is at once luminous in all its depths to the free self but obscure and hidden from any other being who is external to it. It can become luminous and comprehensible to another being than the agent only if he enters into it through the unitive and identifying force of love. By a kind of sympathy, the other makes the act his own and enters into it as if it proceeded from his own personal depth.

"And so," concludes Rahner, "the finite has its foundation or reason in the free luminous act of God. This free act which is present to itself is *love*. For love is the self-luminous act of movement towards a person in his underived uniqueness. . . . The finite contingent thing is illumined in the free love of God for himself and therein for his freely delimited work. . . . In its ultimate essence, knowledge is but the bright radiance of love."[46] In His love for Himself, God freely loves as the power which at once posits and lovingly comprehends the finite. Thereby the finite is elevated into the light of being, participates in the self-presence of being, by a kind of creative sympathy or infusion of divine love. Thus God's free act of creative love is not in conflict with the luminosity of being, but rather constitutes luminosity as it engenders being.

As a consequence, man's transcendence toward Absolute Being, the Absolute Person, involves not only knowledge but love. In its process, man not only affirms his own existence, but takes a deliberate attitude toward himself in a reaching out of his finite love towards God. This love of God is not something added to the knowledge which constitutes man as spirit, but is actually its deepest factor as condition and cause. Thus man stands as potential hearer of God's Word by an attitude toward himself that embraces an attitude toward God. Knowledge and love constitute together the basic disposition of the single human existence.

Just as absolute being pre-apprehended non-objectively as intelligible or true provides the necessary condition for the objective knowledge of finite things, so absolute being pre-known non-objectively as good is the necessary condition for comprehending some finite good, and as co-intended in every will-act confers goodness or desirability on each finite object of will. In each instance, the knowing spirit at once grasps the finitude of the individual object or particular good and its own freedom as a subject confronting it.

Man is free with respect to particular goods because he is necessarily oriented to the absolute good pre-known and co-intended non-objectively as the condition of his freedom. Ultimately it is the love of God which constitutes man in this dynamic structure and thus at once grounds the condition of man's freedom and furnishes its unavoidable context. But man must ratify this right order of the good rooted in God's creative love by the use of his freedom relative to particular goods. Each free decision about a particular good is actually a decision about himself and is constitutive of himself and of the standards of his future decisions. Thereby he is forming himself in his freedom either according to the right order of good and thus of the demands of God's love implied in his basic constitution, or he is in effect legislating his own order in contradiction of the true order of love. He is thus becoming either good or evil.

"Man always possesses the God-given order of his love only in unity with the freely delimited order of his love which he has constituted correctly or falsely by his free response to the particular good."[47] Thus man's free decisions are continually affecting the subjectivity within which the knowledge and love of God operate. This means that man's knowledge of God, the most profound truth he can possess, is also the most free, since it is always conditioned on the order (or disorder) of his love concretely determining the subjectivity in which the knowledge arises. As a result, it becomes clear, first of all, that a purifying of our knowledge of God always involves a "conversion," insofar as one's openness to God is in function of his moral self-determination. Secondly, it also implies that a man will tend to worship as God the being to whom his self-determined love orients him.

Our knowledge of God is no less objective or rigorous than any other knowledge because it is free. Rather its freedom is a measure of the depth of its implication in the foundations of man's existence. From that point of view, it is capable of a stricter proof since it is grounded in the necessity of what man is as the subject of every other form of knowledge. By the same token, however, it is made apparent why proofs for the existence of God may be objectively sound and logically correct, and yet remain unconvincing.

B. GOD'S FREEDOM AND MAN'S HISTORY: THE PROBLEM OF REVELATION

In his developing view of man as a potential hearer of God's Word, Rahner concludes that "man is that existent thing who stands in free love before the God of a possible revelation."[48] But a further question imposes itself. Where is man to encounter God's initiative of Self-disclosure, if He has chosen to exercise it?

The very question itself raises problems. Can we hold the divine initiative to anything that we determine *a priori*? We certainly cannot do so with respect to the content of such a revelation, as a modernist philosophy of religion might affirm. We can say that thematic relevation would involve either a direct disclosure of His Self to man in an immediate vision or, in the absence of vision (which is man's current situation), a self-imparting by way of the "word," that is, through a mediating symbol. Finally, we can securely hold that God can reveal to man only what man is able to hear.

To say that God is only able to reveal what man is able to hear does not set prior limitations on possible objects of revelation, in view of the unlimited transcendence of the human spirit and man's absolute openness to being. It asserts, first of all, that it is man as man, that one whose nature is that of a spirit transcending without limit towards absolute being, who would receive the revealing word. Secondly, it reminds us that God's Self-revelation, as a free divine action, while it is not a natural event able to be derived from a preceding cause, would nevertheless be one that occurs within human history.

What is implied in saying that the place of meeting between man and the God Who may reveal Himself is man's transcendence operating within an historical context? The reply requires that we recall that human knowing is a receptive process in which the "return to oneself" that is knowing is only possible for man through a going out to something other than himself as the first object of his knowledge. Moreover, man as embodied spirit is spirit that participates in being-outside-itself inasmuch as it enters into matter and thereby into the world.

By virtue of his material nature, man exists in space and time. As spatial, his form or kind of being is intrinsically repeatable, so that he is essentially one among many, the member of a race. As an individual in time, his possibilities can never be realized except in an indefinite sequence of his inner activity. But his possibilities as human can never be achieved by him as an individual alone, so that his full reality necessarily involves his co-existence in a world of other human persons. With them he shares an existence that is intrinsically historical.

In sum, man's historicity or intrinsically historical nature belongs to him as a free person in company with others like himself. Within a society of free persons who subsist in themselves, he experiences his self-realization in space and time. However, since his freedom originates in his transcendence towards the Absolute Person, he works out his destiny with others in a common history that is ordered, at least non-objectively, towards God as its ultimate horizon.

How does man's historicity affect his openness to the possibility of a free Self-Revelation by God? Can an otherworldly existent reality be made known to man where he is, as the incarnate spirit whose absolute transcendence is essentially linked to his historicity? Can an existent being, which in itself does not appear sensibly, be apprehended by a way of knowing that is essentially linked to sensible appearance? More specifically stated in Thomistic terms, does man have the obediential capacity (*potentia obedientialis*) to be a hearer of God's Self-disclosing Word?

In responding to the question, Rahner attempts to explain how it is possible that any existent, even one exceeding the realm of sense appearance as the natural limit of human knowing, can nevertheless be definable within those limits. Such a definition has to be by way of negation, that is, by denying of the other-worldly existent the essential limitations of this-worldly existents. A definition of this kind need not be purely negative. By virtue of the inner drive of man's knowing towards the Absolute Being of God, such concepts tend to grow positively from within as approaching the absolute positivity of the divine Being. This tendency is of course restrained within the limits of the original definition by negation and derives its content always by reference to the sphere of sense appearance from which it is projected by way of analogy.

This position does not claim that man can *naturally* know a supramundane or other-worldly reality in its actual existence or even in its intrinsic possibility. Man cannot experience or intuit, that is, apprehend by his receptive mode of knowing, any existent but one of this world of sensible appearance. But should such an existent being be intimated to man, he is capable of understanding or defining it, or receiving it into his finite spirit through the word. By 'word' in this context, Rahner means not merely a representative symbol of some kind, but specifically the *conceptual* symbol of the human mind directly applied to the entity in question. Such a human word spoken by God can reveal the existence and inner possibility of an other-worldly existent inasmuch as it can define such things by reference to the sphere of sensible appearance through the way of negation and of an analogy developing within the unlimited reach of man's transcendence.

A divine revelation to man is possible therefore inasmuch as the transcendent truths it would communicate can be expressed specifically, though by negation, in the 'word' as an occurrence immanent to man's history. Such a revealing act, should it occur, can be called 'historical' on God's part inasmuch as it is the unique action of a free person exercising an unpredictable initiative towards another free person. What of its historicity on man's side? As entering man's individual existence, the revealing word can appear only at a special point in human history. This point may occur in the history of each individual or only in the history of special individuals. It is sufficient that it be an event of a determinate time and place within the total history of mankind.

Man is required to listen for God's free revelation within his own history because his transcendent openness to God and His possible revelation operates in a subjectivity which must always be turned to the world of sensible appearance and therefore towards history: his own history as integral with that of his world, his race. Since the revelation is free on God's part, He may choose to remain silent, not to disclose Himself in man's words. But even His silence is a revelation of a kind, since it is an attitude freely assumed by the Divine Person toward the finite persons who are attentive listeners for His possible spoken communication.

At the terminus of his inquiry, Rahner is able to define man as

> the one who listens in his history for the word of the free God. Only thus is he what he must be. Metaphysical anthropology has thus reached its conclusion when it has comprehended itself as the metaphysics of a **potentia obedientialis** for the revelation of the supernatural God.[49]

In his later writings, Rahner was gradually to achieve

a more organic, nuanced and comprehensive formulation of the theological implications of his philosophical anthropology. John Baptist Metz incorporated many of these developments along with his own personal contributions into his approved revision of the original text of *Hearers of the Word*.[50] Of special interest was the deepening insight into the nature of revelation as a transcendental grace existentially affecting every man within the universal economy of salvation. In this wider context, his former understanding of revelation would appear as a special categorical thematizing of the saving grace of God's Self-communication constituting man's being and consciousness in a supernatural order of adoptive sonship. These ramifications would emerge initially in his reflections on the problem of the relationship of nature and grace and more fully in the evolution of his Christology.

From Philosophy to Theology: The Problem of Nature and Grace

Philosophy of religion has shown itself to involve a metaphysical anthropology as an essential inner moment. As the rational interpretation of the existential bond between God and man, it must concern itself with God and man. It does so in a philosophy of being, an ontology which is equivalent to a metaphysical anthropology because it is in man as spirit that being comes to itself in knowledge and Absolute Being is uncovered as its ultimate ground. This in turn is recognized to be a fundamental theological anthropology inasmuch as the nature of man disclosed by the metaphysical inquiry is that of an existent person who necessarily stands in freedom before the God of a possible revelation and therefore in readiness for faith and for theology as its reflective understanding.

Philosophy and the Fundamental Theology that employs it in its prolegomena to theology can take us no further than this: man is openness to the possibility of God's Self-Gift and Self-Revelation. The commitment of Christian Faith is required for the firm assertion to be made that, as a matter of fact, this possibility has been realized and therefore that man as an obediential potency for God's Self-Revelation has actually been fulfilled. At this point metaphysical anthropology has explicitly become theological anthropology.

Rahner's theological investigations grew organically out of the fundamental perspective that he achieved in his inquiries into the metaphysics of knowledge and the philosophy of religion. By the same token, the anthropological orientation of his philosophical researches was sustained in his developing theological system. Early in his theologizing, he had to face the problem of the relations of nature and grace. His solution, foreshadowed in his previous thinking, was to play a preponderant role in the formation of his integral theological outlook.

Like Blondel before him and like many contemporary Catholic theologians, Rahner reacted against the interpretation of the relations of nature and grace which had come to be regarded as the traditional one in Catholic theology. The distinction between nature and grace was not really given clear formulation until the time of St. Thomas, one of the first Christian thinkers to stress the autonomy of reason and the 'natural' order of creation within the comprehension of reason over against faith and the supernatural order of God's inner life and His redemptive dealings with man, especially in Christ, which can be known only by His revelation. The supernatural character of grace and of the other salvific gifts was not adverted to in official Church teaching until the 14th century.[51] The distinction has been appealed to primarily to vindicate the gratuitousness of redemption and of incorporation into the divine life through Christ over and beyond the gratuitousness of creation.

Cajetan, Renaissance commentator on St. Thomas' writings, had already introduced into the stream of Catholic theology the idea of 'pure nature' with the hypothetical possibility of a purely natural end for man. This device for explaining the distinction of the orders and the gratuitousness of the supernatural came into greater prominence under the impetus of the Bainist and Jansenist controversies and the polemic against the rationalism of the 17th and 18th centuries.

In responding to the challenges of rationalism,

Catholic apologists unfortunately appropriated some of the rationalist premises, including that of restricting human consciousness to its purely natural elements. Nothing that entered into or affected human consciousness, in this view, could be supernatural or the result of grace. As a consequence, the influence of grace on man was purely entitative, non-conscious. The ensuing portrait of grace was of a factor that had no direct impact on man's conscious existence. Its actuality could only be known obliquely as the object of a verbal revelation accepted on faith. Therefore, it appeared to be more and more extrinsic and unrelated to man's conscious life and enterprises.

The notion of 'pure nature' as it has been employed theologically in recent centuries has been criticized for being 'extrinsicist.' The latter term, at least in its present usage, should probably be attributed to Blondel. It has been used by contemporary Catholic theologians, especially by Rahner. As they remind us, the idea of 'pure nature' is, after all, a purely speculative construct that has never had any existence. It is, moreover, the product of a brand of metaphysics which claimed the patronage of St. Thomas while departing from his authentic thought. For it conceived human nature as a self-enclosed system, since it was modelled on a concept of nature derived from sub-human creation, rather than the open spiritual nature of man emphasized by Aquinas. As a consequence, the supernatural is conceived as adding only an extrinsic layer or supplement to a nature already complete in itself.

The assumption is that everything we know directly of ourselves is of the natural order and that we only know of the impact of grace on us indirectly through our faith assent to its verbal revelation. Thus grace appears, as Rahner observes, to be merely a superstructure imposed on nature by a free divine decree so that their relationship is scarcely conceived as more intimate than that of co-factors between which there is freedom from contradiction. What he challenges is the premise that one can know precisely what human nature is and how far it extends. For like most of his contemporaries, Rahner rejects an abstractly speculative approach to man in favor of the more concrete existential one of historical man factually called to grace from the beginning of his history.[52]

He begins therefore from the existential fact that man has always been in grace or fallen from it. Man in the supernatural order of grace, that is, man the beneficiary of God's free Self-Gift, is the concrete given fact. The knowledge of 'human nature' as such can only be derived by abstracting from engraced man those elements of him which are not constituted by the Self-Gift of God. These constitute for him the residual concept (*Restbegriff*) of 'nature.' Thus grace is not something added to nature; rather nature is something distilled from the total reality that is engraced man.

This concept of nature is consequently a theological notion which can only be arrived at by the reflection on himself of a man of Christian faith. He alone is in a position to distinguish the natural from the supernatural dimension of human existence. The consciousness of a person who does not apply this theological reflection, whether it be because he lacks explicit Christian faith or because he is a Christian believer who is not engaged in such a reflection, is in every instance under the influence of the offer of grace and therefore a unity compenetrated with supernatural and natural factors.

We can never be sure by a mere appeal to experience that we can precisely distinguish the natural from the supernatural elements within us. Human nature as such has always existed in a supernatural economy and therefore must be considered as an inner moment of the order of grace, rather than the easily discernible foundation to which grace has been added and consequently able to be subtracted by our reflective knowledge. For grace as the call to divine sonship cannot touch man only extrinsically, but must be acknowledged as a "new creation," affecting us in our inmost being and therefore in every aspect of our life and action.

Rahner developed his position on nature and grace not only as a reaction to the 'extinsicist' thesis, but also in controversy with that of the so-called *"Nouvelle Théologie,"* which had arisen in the 1930's and 1940's especially among French theologians as a similar reaction against 'extrinsicism.' This group, most prominent of whom was Henri de Lubac, was greatly influenced by Blondel and Maréchal among modern thinkers, but appealed in a special way to the patristic tradition and particularly to St. Augustine. Their approach like that of Rahner was to historical existential man, therefore to man called from creation to divine sonship and existing in an order of grace. They made capital, as Maréchal had done before them, of the Thomistic thesis of man's natural desire for the beatific vision. In the process they rejected the notion of 'pure nature' and its corollary of a hypothetical natural end for man.

Father de Lubac himself insisted on the gratuitousness of the supernatural order and conceded the theoretical possibility of God's creating a human being not destined for the beatific vision in some other created order. However, he rejected completely the notion of pure nature for man, since man is not a thing of nature, as we know nature in the present universe. "*L'homme n'est pas chose naturelle.*" ("Man is not a natural thing.") For him, man as a spiritual being has a natural desire to see God, that is, to possess Him immediately in the beatific vision, because it is the only possible goal of a spiritual being. Gratuitous though this goal is, its gratuity cannot be interpreted so as to deny that it alone is possible. In fact, the gratuity of this solely possible end, namely, the beatific vision, is the more apparent, according to him, precisely because it is naturally desired as a gift. We do not demand gifts, nor, having a natural desire for it, do we *not* desire this gift.

According to de Lubac, then, man has one and only one end, the vision of God. There is no other end to which a spiritual creature like man can be directed. The fact that God could have *not* called man to this end in another order does not prove that there was another and alternative end to which God might have directed man which the supernatural end has replaced.

The gratuity of grace therefore does not imply that the beatific vision has been substituted by God for what might have been the natural rest of the spiritual creature in the possession of its natural beatitude. It means rather that God has *called* man to his end, that man can reach his end only by being called to it, and that this calling and elevation, being entirely gratuitous, might not have taken place. The alternatives envisaged by de Lubac are not two ends, one natural and the other supernatural, but rather alternatives between achieving the only end in which a spiritual creature can find repose, namely, the beatific vision, or failing that, an endless search for repose and hence no final repose at all.

The fact that God would create that type of being whose finality is precisely to an end that is gratuitous is, says de Lubac, the Christian paradox of man which is overcome only in faith. The Christian is exactly that person who knows in faith that man is the being who is called to an end beyond anything he has a right to or to which his being is proportioned.

In the encyclical, *Humani Generis* (1950), Pius XII, in a defense of the absolute gratuity of the supernatural order, repudiated the opinion of those who, in his words, "corrupt the gratuitousness of the supernatural order when they suppose that God could not create intelligent creatures without ordaining and calling them to the beatific vision."[53] This statement was interpreted at the time as being directed against the position of the *Nouvelle Théologie,* and particularly against de Lubac's thesis expressed in his *Surnaturel* (1945).[54] This eminent French theologian defended himself then and since rather effectively against the charge that his writings were open to this adverse judgment.[55] Others in the same movement were perhaps less balanced in their presentation and as a result less successful in eluding the criticism. In any event, Rahner in the course of his debate with some of them hammered out his own nuanced position which was indeed already implied in his general view of man.

Rahner agrees that God's free gift to man of a supernatural end has from his creation rendered man "everywhere inwardly other in structure than he would be if he did not have this end."[56] The divine decree that calls all men to the beatific vision must have a real effect on each man who is so called. God could not will to make men His adopted sons unless there resulted an interior orientation in the depths of them to this actual end that would be a constant goad obliging them either to choose or reject his call. In his mind, to conceive this call as a purely extrinsic, juridical reality, as the earlier theologians did, is to leave an actual historical decree of God without a corresponding historical term. It is this supernatural destiny, freely conferred, that engenders in man an affinity for the end for which he has in fact been made. This affinity touches the very source of man's existence so that man never ceases to be called by God's love, regardless of his response. It is this which Rahner came to call the *supernatural existential,* a resonance of man's very being that results from an unconditioned and positive tendency to the vision of God derived from God's free gift of a vocation to supernatural life. As he himself expresses it,

> man should be able to receive this Love which is God himself; he must have a congeniality for it. He must be able to accept it (and hence grace, the beatific vision) as one who has room and scope, understanding and desire for it. Thus he must have a real 'potency' for it. He must have it **always**. He is indeed someone always addressed and claimed by this Love. For, as he now in fact is, he is created for it; he is thought and called into being so that Love might bestow itself. To this extent this 'potency' is what is inmost and most authentic in him, the center and root of what he is absolutely. He must have it **always**; for even one of the damned, who has turned away from this Love and made himself incapable of receiving this Love, must still be really able to experience this Love (which being scorned now burns like fire) as that to which he is ordained in the ground of his concrete being; he must consequently always remain what he was created as: the burning, longing for God himself in the immediacy of his own three-fold life. The capacity for the God of self-bestowing personal Love is the central and abiding existential of man as he really is.[57]

He explicitly rejects the position attributed to the *Nouvelle Théologie* and condemned by *Humani Generis,* namely, the postulate of an unconditioned disposition to grace and the beatific vision *in man's very nature* which seems to compromise, in his judgment, the undue and gratuitous character of grace. If there is such a disposition to grace in man, he would maintain that it must belong to the *supernatural* order and is thus itself already a gratuitous gift, although pertaining to man's condition prior to the actual gift of grace as the conferring of adoptive sonship. It is, as we have seen him observe, a disposition possessed even by the damned who have definitively rejected the offer of divine sonship and it can be conceived as the dynamism at the root of their pain of loss.

Unlike de Lubac, Rahner does accept the notion of 'pure nature' in a qualified sense insofar as we must postulate a subject or recipient for whom the supernatural existential and grace can be an undue gift. But man (and in this instance it must be the man of Faith) comes to know his nature as what is the remainder in his personal being after the supernatural existential as the potency to receive God's unowed Love has been abstracted. However, since one does not know the full impact of the supernatural existential, one cannot say definitively what this 'pure nature' would be. Consequently, contrary to the claim of the earlier proponents of the 'pure nature' theory, it is not possible to determine its limits with clarity or to define it without ambiguity.

At the conclusion of *Hearers of the Word,* Rahner had defined human nature, that is, man the incarnate spirit, as an obediential capacity or openness to the Self-Gift of God's love in grace. The factual elevation of man to the supernatural order of grace and the achievement of the beatific vision represent the absolute fulfillment of man so conceived. However, even in the absence of this supernatural elevation, that is, of God's Self-disclosure actualized in His Self-Gift to man, man's nature would be meaningful and could pursue a significant autonomous existence in the face of God's silence. For man's nature is that of a spirit in the world, transcending twards God as the horizon of Absolute Being within which he enacts his existence by knowledge, volition and action in reciprocity with other persons and things and he differentiates them objectively from himself at the same time that he comes to fuller self-presence and self-realization. Such a purely 'natural' existence would have an integrity and meaning of its own, even while it would fall far short of that absolute fulfillment to which man as spirit is open. As a consequence, Rahner can say that the disposition of man's nature to grace and to the beatific vision is conditioned on the free intiative of God's Self-Gift, whereas for the practitioners of the *Nouvelle Théologie,* this disposition must be unconditioned.

Although man could have led a meaningful existence in the absence of a supernatural calling, de facto he has never existed in a purely natural creaturely state. From the beginning, his destiny has been to partake of the divine nature, he has been called to be a "son in the Son." In Rahnerian terms, human nature has always been endowed with the "supernatural existential."

For Rahner, this latter theory was a step toward a more organic theological vision beyond the tentative and unfinished stage of his reflections within the somewhat confining context of the relations of nature and grace. It was a move toward a fuller appropriation of the transcendental theology which his transcendental philosophy and its view of man implied and had made possible. For his philosophical anthropology had proposed a view of human existence as essentially related to God, the absolute horizon and goal of man's life in this world with others, before Whom he stands in freedom and love as a potential hearer of His Word and recipient of His Self-Gift. Christian Faith affirms that human nature has always been transformed by the grace of God's Self-Gift and Self-Communication to man. Reflecting on this understanding of man in the light of his faith, the Christian theologian must acknowledge that human nature is indeed the presupposition of grace, that man as creature is the a priori condition constituted by God as the Other to whom He could give Himself in a free gesture of love. Even more, as we shall see, in the light of his Christological reflections, Rahner with others would define man as the a priori condition or created possibility for God's Self-emptying to *become* Another in Jesus Christ in the ultimate act of Self-giving.

Notes and references

1 Immanuel Kant, **Critique of Pure Reason** trans. by F. Max Mueller, second edition, revised (Garden City: Doubleday, 1961), p. 32, n. 7.

2 Cf. especially, Joseph Maréchal, **Le point de depart de la metaphysique** Cahier V. (Louvain: Museum Lessianum, 1926); second edition (Paris: Desclée de Brouwer, 1949).

3 **Ibid.**, second edition pp. 313-314. English translation in **A Maréchal Reader** edited and trans. by Joseph Donceel, S.J. (New York: Herder &

Herder, 1970), p. 152.

⁴ Otto Muck, **The Transcendental Method** trans. by Wm. D. Seiden-sticker (New York: Herder & Herder, 1968), p. 45.

⁵ Maréchal, **A Maréchal Reader,** p. 152. Cf. Aquinas, **De Ver,** 22,2, ad 1.

⁶ Joseph Maréchal, **Mélanges Joseph Maréchal,** I (Paris: Desclée de Brouwer, 1950), p. 336. Cited in Muck, **The Transcendental Method,** p. 103.

⁷ Most of these thinkers were on the contitent of Europe and include such names as André Marc, Joseph de Finance, Auguste Gregorie among the French; Johannes B. Lotz, Karl Rahner, Max Müller, Emerich Coreth, Bertrand Welte, Johannes B. Metz, to choose but a few names among the Germans. Of the Anglo-Americans the greatest and best known is the Canadian Jesuit, Bernard Lonergan. Cf. Otto Muck, **The Transcendental Method,** pp. 205ff.

⁸ Karl Rahner, **Geist in Welt,** (Munchen, Gr.: Kösel Verlag, 1964) **Spirit in the World,** trans. by Wm. Dych, S.J. (New York: Herder & Herder, 1968).

⁹ Karl Rahner, **Hörer des Wortes,** (Munchen, Gr.: Kosel-Verlag, 1963), **Hearers of the Word** trans. by Michael Richards (New York: Herder & Herder, 1969).

¹⁰ Johannes Baptist Metz, **Christliche Anthropozentrik** (Munchen, Gr.: Kosel-Verlag, 1962).

¹¹ Rahner, **Spirit in the World,** p. liii.

¹² **Ibid.**

¹³ Rahner, **Hearers of the Word,** p. 31.

¹⁴ Rahner, **Spirit in the World,** p. 34.

¹⁵ **Ibid.,** pp. 58-59.

¹⁶ **Ibid.,** p. 62.

¹⁷Thomas Aquinas, **In Metaphysicam Aristotelis, Proemium** (Turin: Marietti, 1935), p. 2.

¹⁸ Rahner, **Spirit in the World,** p. 69 with references to **De Ver.,** 1, 9; 10, 9; **Summa Contra Gentiles** IV, 11.

¹⁹ Rahner, **Hearers of the Word,** p. 40. Here Rahner expresses it in more modern terms as the luminosity or self-illumination of being.

²⁰ Rahner, **Spirit in the World,** p. 69.

²¹ **Ibid.,** p. 70.

²² **Ibid.,** p. 75.

²³ **Ibid.,** p. 77.

²⁴ **Ibid.,** p. 118.

²⁵ Thomas Aquinas, **De Ver.,** 22, 1, ad 1.

²⁶ Rahner, **Spirit in the World,** p. 406.

²⁷ **Ibid.,** p. 407.

²⁸ Bernard Lonergan, in his brilliant review of Coreth's work, "Metaphysics as Horizon," which is included as an appendix to its English translation, pp. 199-219, and which was first published in **Gregorianum** 44 (1963) pp. 307-318, agrees that metaphysics equates with the objective pole of the total and basic horizon, but differs in asserting the prior necessity of an inquiry into cognitional theory, since the incarnate inquirer as the subjective pole is open to social and historical conditions which necessitate a distinct critique and a transcendental doctrine of methods previous to the use of metaphysics as one of many methods.

²⁹ Emerich Coreth, **Metaphysics** trans. by J. Donceel (New York: Herder & Herder, 1968) p. 39. This is a revised abbreviated translation

of **Metaphysik**, (Innsbruck: Tyrolia Verlag, 1964).

30 **Ibid.**, p. 40.

31 **Ibid.**

32 "When questioning the question, we go back to that which is presupposed by it and implicitly co-affirmed in it (reduction). Once we have discovered these elements, we can deduce from them the necessary essential structure of the act of questioning. There is a shuttling from fact to necessary conditions, from these conditions to the essential features of the fact." **Ibid.**, p. 41.

33 **Ibid.**, p. 50.

34 "Being as act exists in itself, as a totality, as the ultimate and unconditioned within whose horizon we can inquire about single realities or about all reality. This is always and necessarily presupposed as the condition of every question and is co-affirmed in the very act of questioning. Otherwise, we should not even be able to ask a question." **Ibid.**, p. 65.

35 **Ibid.**, p. 66.

36 **Ibid.**, p. 175.

37 "All demonstrations of God's existence are ultimately based upon the **transcendence of the spirit**. It is only because and insofar as the finite spirit operates in the horizon of being as such, because it possesses an essential relation to the absolute and infinite being, that in every one of its spiritual activities it always already transcends the conditioned towards the unconditioned, the finite towards the infinite. Thus whenever we wish critically to reduce a proof of God's existence to the ultimate conditions of its possibility, we must, by means of transcendental reflection, render thematic the essential transcendence of the human spirit. Or the other way around: Whenever through reflection we make explicit the metaphysically transcendent nature of the human spirit, we have a proof of God's existence —or rather we have **the** proof of God's existence, which is the ground and foundation of all the other demonstrations." **Ibid.**, pp. 180-181.

38 **Ibid.**, p. 183.

39 "In order to hear whether God speaks, we must know that He is; lest His word come to one who already knows, He must be hidden from us; in order to speak to man, His word must encounter us where we already and always are, in an earthly place, at an earthly hour. Insofar as man enters into the world by turning to the phantasm, the revelation of being as such and in it the knowledge of God's existence has already been achieved but even then this God who is beyond the world is always hidden from us. Abstraction is the revelation of being as such which places man before God; conversion is the entrance into the here and now of this finite world, and this makes God the distant Unknown. Abstraction and conversion are the same thing for Thomas: man. If man is understood in this way, he can listen to hear whether God has not perhaps spoken, be-cause he knows that God is; God can speak, because He is the Unknown. And if Christianity is not the ideal of an eternal omnipresent spirit, but is Jesus of Nazareth, then Thomas' metaphysics of knowledge is Christian when it summons man back into the here and now of his finite world, because the Eternal has also entered into his world so that man might find Him, and in Him might find himself anew." Rahner, **Spirit in the World**, p. 408.

40 In writing **Hearers of the Word**, Rahner was still thinking of Revelation as Special Revelation that is thematized in the words and deeds of Salvation History. Later he was to call this, "Special Categorical Revelation" in distinction from "Transcendental Revelation" with which every

human consciousness is graced and whose thematizing ("General Categorical Revelation") is coexistensive with the general history of the race. Cf. the final section of this chapter "From Philosophy to Theology: The Problem of Nature and Grace."

[41] Rahner, **Hearers of the Word,** pp. 92-93.

[42] **Ibid.,** p. 93.

[43] This insistence on the role of will in knowledge (and in the luminosity of being) recalls Maréchal's treatment of the Thomistic doctrine of will as nature or as natural appetite as well as Blondel's emphasis on willing will as the primordial source of action.

[44] Rahner, **Hearers of the Word,** p. 98.

[45] **Ibid.**

[46] **Ibid.,** p. 100.

[47] **Ibid.,** p. 105.

[48] **Ibid.,** p. 108.

[49] **Ibid.,** p. 162.

[50] **Hörer Des Wortes.** Neu bearbeitet von J. B. Metz (Munchen: Kösel Verlag, 1963). Karl Rahner, **Hearers of the Word** trans. by Michael Richards (New York: Herder & Herder, 1969).

[51] Cf. Constitution, "Ad nostrum qui," Council of Vienne, 1312, DS 895; Benedict XII, Constitution, "Benedictus Deus," 1336, DS 1000-1001. It was not given a clear and explicit formulation until the condemnation of the proposition of Baius: "The exaltation of human nature to a participation of the divine nature was due to the integrity of man in his first state and for that reason should be called natural and not supernatural." (St. Pius V, Bull, "ex omnibus afflictionibus," 1567, DS 1911) and of similar errors attributed to Jansen (1653, DS 2001-2005) and Quesnel (1713, DS 2500-2501).

[52] "Actual human nature is **never** 'pure' nature, but nature in a supernatural order, which man (even the unbeliever and the sinner) can never escape from . . . And these 'existential facts' of his concrete (his 'historical') nature are not just accidents of his being beyond his consciousness but make themselves apparent in his experience of himself. He cannot clearly distinguish them by simple reflection (by the light of natural reason) from the natural spirituality of his nature." Karl Rahner, **Nature and Grace** (New York: Sheed and Ward, 1964), p. 135.

[53] Denzinger-Schönmetzer, **Enchiridion Symbolorum,** 3891.

[54] Henri de Lubac, **Surnaturel** (Paris: Aubier, 1945).

[55] Henri de Lubac, **Le Mystère du Surnaturel** (Paris: Aubier, 1965) trans. by Rosemary Sheed, **The Mystery of the Supernatural** (New York: Herder & Herder, 1967).

[56] Karl Rahner, "Concerning the Relationship between Nature and Grace," **Theological Investigations,** I (Baltimore, Helicon Press, 1963), pp. 302-303.

[57] **Ibid.,** pp. 311-312.

Baker, Kenneth, S.J. A *Synopsis of the Transcendental Philosophy of Emerich Coreth and Karl Rahner.* Spokane: Gonzaga University Press, 1965.
Burns, J. P. "The Maréchalian Approach to the Existence of God," *The New Scholasticism* 42 (1968), pp. 72-90.

Carr, Anne. "Theology and Experience in the Thought of Karl Rahner," *The Journal of Religion* 53 (1973), pp. 359-76.
Coreth, Emerich. *Metaphysics.* English edition by Joseph Donceel, with a critique by Bernard J. F. Lonergan. New York: Herder & Herder, 1968.

Donceel, Joseph. *The Philosophy of Karl Rahner.* Albany: Magi, 1969.

Ebert, Hermann. "Man as the Way to God," *Philosophy Today* 10 (1966), pp. 88-106.

Foundations in Theology. Papers from the International Lonergan Congress, 1970. Ed. Philip McShane, S.J. Notre Dame, Ind.: University of Notre Dame Press, 1972.

Gelpi, Donald L. S.J. *Life and Light: A Guide to the Theology of K. Rahner.* New York: Sheed & Ward, 1966.

Language, Truth and Meaning. Second volume, papers from the International Lonergan Congress, 1970. Ed. Philip McShane, S.J. Dublin: Gill and Macmillan, 1972.

Lonergan, Bernard. *Collection.* New York: Herder & Herder, 1967.

Lonergan, Bernard. *Insight.* New York: Philosophical Library; London: Longmans, Green, 1957, 1970.

Lonergan, Bernard. "Insight: Preface to a Discussion," *Proceedings of the American Catholic Philosophical Association* 32 (1958) pp. 71-81; also in *Collection,* pp. 152-63.

Lonergan, Bernard. "Metaphysics as Horizon," *Gregorianum* 44 (1963), pp. 307-18; also in *Cross Currents* 16 (1966), pp. 481-94; in *Collection,* pp. 202-20; and as an appendix in E. Coreth, *Metaphysics,* pp. 199-219.

Lotz, Johannes, B. "Metaphysical and Religious Experience," *Philosophy Today* 2 (1958), pp. 240-49.

Maréchal, Joseph. *Le Point de Depart de la Metaphysique.* Cahier V. Paris: Desclée de Brouwer, 1949.

Marechal Reader, A. Ed. and Tr. Joseph Donceel, S.J. New York: Herder & Herder, 1970.

McCool, Gerald A., S.J. "Philosophy of the Human Person in Karl Rahner's Theology," *Theological Studies* 22 (1961), pp. 537-562.

McCool, Gerald A., S.J. *The Theology of Karl Rahner.* Albany: Magi, 1969.

Moran, Gabriel. *The Present Revelation.* The Search for Religious Foundations. New York: Herder & Herder, 1972.

Muck, Otto. *The Transcendental Method.* Tr. William D. Seidensticker. New York: Herder & Herder, 1968.

Niel, Henri. "The Old and New in Theology: Rahner and Lonergan," *Cross Currents* 16 (1966), pp. 463-82.

Rahner, Karl. *Hearers of the Word.* English translation from German edition revised by J. B. Metz. Tr. Michael Richards. New York: Herder & Herder, 1969.

Rahner, Karl. "Nature and Grace," *Theological Investigations,* IV. Tr. Kevin Smyth. Baltimore: Helicon, 1966, pp. 165-88. Cf. also, "Concerning the Relationship between Nature and Grace," *Theological Investigations,* I. Tr. Cornelius Ernst, O.P. Baltimore: Helicon, 1961, pp. 297-317.

Rahner, Karl. "Philosophy and Philosophising in Theology," *Theological Investigations,* IX. New York: Herder & Herder, 1972, pp. 46-63.

Rahner, Karl. "Philosophy and Theology," *Theological Investigations,* VI. Baltimore: Helicon, 1969, pp. 71-81.

Rahner, Karl. *Spirit in the World.* Tr. William Dych, S.J. New York: Herder & Herder, 1968.

Reichmann, James B. "The Transcendental Method and the Psychogenesis of Being," *The Thomist* 32 (1968), pp. 440-508.

Riesenhüber, Klaus, S.J. "The Anonymous Christian according to Karl Rahner," in Anita Röper, *The Anonymous Christian,* pp. 145-79.

Roberts, Louis. *The Achievement of Karl Rahner.* New York: Herder & Herder, 1967.

Röper, Anita. *The Anonymous Christian.* Tr. Joseph Donceel. New York: Sheed & Ward, 1966.

Shepherd, William C. *Man's Condition: God and the World Process.* New York: Herder & Herder, 1969.

Spirit as Inquiry. Studies in Honor of Bernard Lonergan. Ed. Frederick E. Crowe, S.J. *Continuum* 2 (1961), pp. 308-552.

Tracy, David. *The Achievement of Bernard Lonergan.* New York: Herder & Herder, 1970.

Vorgrimler, H. *Karl Rahner: His Life, Thought and Works.* New York: Paulist, 1966.

A Christian Theological Anthropology

At the very beginning, we announced that we would attempt to justify Christian faith to contemporary men by engaging in dialogue with 'unbelievers,' that is, with men of other than Christian belief, revolving around our contending views of man himself. Acordingly we listened rather attentively to representative expressions of the principal atheistic humanisms and then set about to build a Christian anthropology that would be in at least equal accord with what contemporary men experience and judge themselves to be.

At this point, the view of man that has emerged is more precisely called theistic than strictly Christian. It has proposed a self-understanding of contemporary man that essentially involves God in the very process by which man becomes himself and defines himself, but which does not yet explicitly assert it to be the God of Christian faith. However since this definition includes an openness on man's part to the possibility of God's Self-Revelation in man's history, it can be called at least tentatively a Christian view, since a historical divine revelation is a distinctive doctrine of Christian faith.

What we have achieved is a Christian philosophical anthropology inasmuch as we have been conscious of our Christian commitment in the course of our argumentation without invoking any tenet of Christian faith as a premiss or presupposition of our reasoning.[1] However, to be fully and authentically Christian, an understanding of man cannot stop short of faith itself. It must be more than philosophical. It must be a Christian *theological* anthropology. Only then can the full force of the Christian view of man be brought into confrontation with other anthropologies in the dialogue that is yet to take place.

We believe that we have taken the first decisive step toward the goal of Christian apologetics namely, to show the credibility of Christian faith for contemporary man. For we have exhibited with some cogency that men, as we modern men understand ourselves, are by virtue of our natural capacity for transcendence open to the possible initiative of a free and gracious Self-communication of the Absolute Person we call God. The actual realization of this divine gratuity on man's behalf is precisely what is affirmed by Christian faith and is in fact identified with it. This fundamental accord of contemporary man's self-understanding with what Christian faith affirms him to be is at least a demonstration of the viability and acceptability of that same Christian faith for the men of our age, among whom we would include ourselves as subjects of today's doubts and temptations to unbelief. Therefore, we are entitled at this point to proceed as Christian believers who can appeal without compunction to our Faith and its revealed sources for the further building and enriching of an integral Christian anthropology.

Anthropology is Theology

To be able to adopt the posture of Faith implies that we are now in a position to reflect on what we have hitherto discovered about ourselves in the light of the Christian Revelation. The advantages of this are almost unlimited. For it brings into play the central Christian belief in the Incarnation: the faith affirmation that man is precisely that being Who God became in Jesus Christ. The implications of this doctrine for our self-understanding are mind-shattering.

What we have discovered about ourselves is that we are

by nature potential hearers of God's Self-revealing Word and possible sharers in His Life and Nature. As incarnate spirits, we are always in process of transcending towards Him as the absolute goal and horizon of our this-worldly experience. What we assert in Faith is that this Absolute Being Who is personal has always offered Himself as the unconditional fulfillment of man's transcendence in a relationship of absolute intimacy. But much more is implied in this affirmation. For what we are declaring as Christian believers is first of all, that God created man-in-his-world precisely for this purpose: namely, to have Another to Whom He could give Himself. Even more astonishingly, we profess that God's Self-Gift to all men is founded in the absolute form that that Self-communication took in Jesus Christ Who is the Man God personally became. In Christ, man is understood as God's Other.

Christian philosophical (fundamental theological) anthropology disclosed man to be by his nature transcendentally related to God: relation to God constitutes his very meaning as man. Man cannot be understood integrally except in terms of his relation to God. God enters into his definition. Christian *theological* anthropology, taken in the full and formal sense, reveals man to be God's Other, the One He created to become in Christ and thereby to give Himself to universally in a gratuitous divinizing union. Consequently the God Who enters the definition of man is the One Who has revealed Himself as Three: the Father Who gives Himself in His Son by the power of His Spirit.

Previously we could say that ontology is anthropology because Being comes to itself and is for-itself only in man, in his self-knowledge and self-possession. Simultaneously we were able to state that anthropology is philosophical theology, because the being man can only be understood in terms of his transcendental relationship to God as the absolute goal and meaning of his existence.

Now in the light of our faith in the Incarnation, we are able to proclaim that anthropology is Christian Theology through the mediation of Christology. For the absolute norm of what man is is Jesus Christ, and every other man must be understood in relation to Him. But what man is in Jesus Christ is God's Other, the One whom God created to become, emptying Himself into His creation in a total act of self-giving. Every other man is defined by derivation from this unique instance as the recipient of God's Self-Gift definitively imparted in the incarnate Son of God.

Christ's humanity is the perfect revelation or Self-expression of God. It is also the norm and standard of what it is to be man in every other instance. It is not only true, therefore, that Christology is the essential key to theology and the foundation of a total anthropology. It is also true that in Christ man can only be understood in his relation to the Triune God and therefore that an adequate anthropology cannot be other than a Christian Theology. For that reason, we can say that Anthropology is Theology.[2]

As Rahner points out, our theological understandings of God and man are not only inter-related from the point of view of content, but also from the angle of knowledge itself. For theology, like philosophy, is transcendental insofar as it acknowledges the primary and central role of man as the knowing subject and asks about its object from the perspective of the necessary conditions in the subject that make it possible for it to be known. In inquiring into God, therefore, or into any part or aspect of creation *sub ratione Deitatis* (as related to God), the theologian must ascertain the conditions of man as knower which account a priori for the possibility of making cognitive statements about God or creation as God-related. As a consequence, whether it concerns God or the universe in whole or in part, a theological statement must involve man as a necessary condition of its possibility and its validity.

This does not deny the a posteriori character of the content of Faith and of theology as a reflection on the Faith, derived as it must ultimately be from the revealed sources and their authoritative proclamation in the Church. Rather it asserts that a truly reflective, systematic, self-possessed understanding of the data of Faith must involve a transcendental inquiry into the a priori conditions that ground the possibility of such an understanding. This inevitably implicates man in his self-understanding as the engraced subject of Faith and recipient of God's Self-communication.

For just as man cannot be understood except in his transcending relation to God as the absolute horizon of his existence, it is equally true that God cannot be understood except as the unlimited goal of man's transcendence. Thus once again theology, the human study in Faith of God's Self-Revelation, must be anthropological, just as an anthropology that fully accounts for man in his concrete existence must be theological.

Christ, the Norm of Man

Christ is the ultimate fulfillment of human nature as the obediential potency for the Self-Gift and Self-Revelation of God. He is that man in whom the transcendence toward the Absolute Mystery, God, achieves its ultimate possibility: personal unity with God. It is in the light of His humanity that our own humanity is to be understood and evaluated. If that be so, then in order to understand man in terms of the Christian Revelation it is important that we try to understand that humanity which is precisely Christ's own.

Too often we tend to think abstractly of Christ's human nature as that instance of humanity which was de facto assumed by God the Son. Concealed in this approach is the supposition that His humanity somehow enjoys an identity of its own which is subsumed by the Logos as a sort of addition to His own divine identity and which could have quite readily been replaced by another. The Hypostatic Union is thereby understood, it would seem, as largely an extrinsic relation between two entities.

On the contrary, granted that we accept and quite deliberately maintain the freedom of Creation and of the Incarnation itself on God's part, we must seek the underlying intrinsic unity within this actual order He has brought into being. For what God has given existence to as other than Himself is a disclosure of Himself to a greater or lesser degree. It is a projection on the screen of creation of His own Self, that is, His own inner life, in finite created forms. Most conspicuously it will manifest in the relative terms of His creation the absolute unity in absolute diversity of His own Trinitarian Life.

In his reflections on the dogma of the Incarnation, Karl Rahner takes as a point of departure the formula of the Council of Chalcedon: one person in two natures. He seeks to rethink its implications in the new context of his transcendental theology without compromising or losing its essential meaning. His effort is to avoid 'extrinsicism' here as in the relations of nature and grace. Therefore he rejects any understanding of the Hypostatic Union as the uniting of two entities able at least to be conceived as previously apart. Similarly he refuses any version of the Union which is merely factual and admitting no further explanation than its actual occurrence.

No, the distinction of Christ's concrete humanity from His Divinity as the Logos must be grounded in its very unity with the Logos. The unity with the Son as divine is precisely that which constitutes Him in His humanity, and therefore as other than divine. In sum, the unity of the Hypostatic Union is the ground of its diversity. The Second Person, the Logos, who pre-exists the Incarnation, remains 'immutable' in Himself, but He comes to be in what he constitutes as the 'Other' which is united with Him and diverse from Him. Christ's Humanity exists precisely as the 'Other' of His Divinity.

For Rahner, the Hypostatic Union is one instance of the symbolic character of all reality, including the divine reality itself. He proposes this thesis in a *theology* of Symbol: a theology, because it draws upon Revelation, especially that of the Trinity.[3] He offers a theory of *real symbol*: that is, an understanding of symbol that is ontological and not merely logical or semantic. To be symbolic is of the very structure of the real.

"All beings are by their nature symbolic, because they necessarily 'express' themselves in order to attain their own nature."[4] The function of symbolizing essentially implies a plurality or otherness by which one entity or facet of being can be representative or expressive of another. What is sought is the primordial way in which one reality can represent or express another.

We start from the affirmation that all being is multiple, that is, a plural unity. This is evident of finite being, whose very finiteness appears in its composite character, its lack of absolute simplicity and self-identity. From the source of Faith, we know this to be true of God too, Who is One in Three. This leads one to think that plural unity is not restricted to finite being, but is rather a transcendental attribute of being as such.

The multiple aspects of a being must have an inner agreement precisely because of the underlying unity. Since the many cannot of itself produce or account for the one in its unity, it follows that the many comes from the unity as original. In fact, the one gives rise to the many in order to fulfill its very unity, as is supremely true of the Blessed Trinity. Thus we can say that every being, according to its degree, forms that which is distinct from itself and yet one with itself, precisely to fulfill itself. Every being as such possesses a plurality as intrinsic to its unity.

"A being expresses itself because it must realize itself through a plurality in unity."[5] This is evident in knowledge where the subject comes to itself in self-knowledge by positing within itself an object distinct from itself, and in love where the subject achieves self-possession by going out of itself to the 'other.' Being *is* actually to the degree that it is for-itself, that it comes to itself or is present to itself. Therefore being is symbolic insofar as it comes to itself by means of 'expression' or symbol which mediates its self-presence.

This symbolic character of being accounts not only for *self*-knowledge, but also for knowledge of one by another. For that plurality in unity which makes a being knowable for itself is also the ground of its knowability by others. The 'otherness' by which it expresses itself to itself is also that by which it expresses itself for others. We may then in summary define symbol (*real symbol*) as "the self-realization of a being in the other, which is constitutive of its essence."[6]

Rahner feels that any theology to be complete must be a theology of the symbol. This is especially true of a theology of the Logos, both in relation to the Trinity and to the Incarnation, for the Logos is the Supreme Symbol. He is the 'Word' of the Father, generated within the Godhead as the image and expression of the Father. The Father is

Himself precisely as He generates this Other, this image, Who is of the same essence, and therefore absolutely one with Him and yet the Other in Whom He possesses Himself as Father. Because the Word is the real-symbolic expression of the Father within the Trinity, Rahner is convinced, against St. Augustine and with the theological tradition that preceded him, that of the Three Persons only the Son could become incarnate as the created saving Self-Revelation of God.

The implications of a theology of the symbol are dramatically realized in the doctrine of the Incarnation. Rahner seeks further illumination concerning our faith in the Incarnation by reflecting on the creedal statement: "The Word of God became man."[7] Thus he incidentally carries forward the project of a theological anthropology derived from Christological insights.

How do we understand 'man' as the one who the Word of God became? Man is, first of all, 'mystery' in his essence. This is not a mere figure of speech. Rather it is the recognition that man, who by his very nature is perpetual transcendence toward the Absolute Mystery Who is God, is himself 'mystery' by participation in the Divine Mystery with Whom he is essentially related. The term 'mystery' does not refer to that which is not yet known or understood, but presumably will be. It is rather, in its absolute sense, the Incomprehensible, which is always already present as the horizon or context of all understanding that makes it possible for everything else to be understood. As expressed earlier, God, the Absolute Being, is the co-known non-objective condition of our objective knowledge of all beings.

What is the meaning of man in the context of the Incarnation? It is to be that being whose nature it is to transcend towards the Divine Mystery, "that which fulfills itself and finds itself by perpetually disappearing into the incomprehensible."[8] Man is thus understood as the one who *is* insofar as he gives up himself, and the most perfectly realized instance of man so understood was that One who belonged so little to Himself that He became personally one with the Divine Mystery. The Incarnation of God the Son brings into being the supreme realization of humanity because man's nature as reference to the Absolute Mystery attains its ultimate fulfillment when it is assumed by God as *His own reality.*

"The Word of God *became* man." How can we say such a thing, especially when we uphold as a fundamental theological doctrine that God is unchangeable? And yet we are constrained to affirm with equal emphasis that the life, death and resurrection of Jesus happened to the Person who is God the Son and constitute a history for Him.

Rahner tries to reconcile the two members of the dilemma and it leads him to radically intriguing conclusions. "If we face squarely the fact of the Incarnation, which our faith testifies to be the fundamental dogma of Christianity, we must simply say: God can become something, he who is unchangeable in himself can *himself* become subject to change *in something else.*"[9]

He accepts the term "becomes" at its full face value. Accordingly he rejects an understanding of the Incarnation as the assuming by God of a created nature which is thereby presupposed as already constituted, at least by a logical priority, in order for it to be assumed. God's humanity must rather be the result, that which eventuates from His "becoming." Rahner explains its possibility in terms of God's Self-emptying. He Who is not only the fullness of being, but subsistent love and freedom, can freely, out of love, will to fill the emptiness by giving Himself into another. Thereby He becomes another, Who is constituted as distinct from Himself as His Own. He remains in Himself unchanged, and yet He changes *in the Other* He has become.[10]

For Rahner, this becoming of God realized in the Incarnation is primal with reference to Creation which is a more derivative relation of God to what is other. For in Creation, He does not become that which He constitutes in otherness. However, it is possible that He create a being, whose nature is open to the possibility of becoming God's Other, of being His self-utterance into the emptiness of what is not Himself. We other men who are not Christ are such creatures of God, and yet it is our nature which the Word of God became and made His own in the one individual man, Jesus Christ.

We can say then that the Humanity of Jesus Christ comes to be inasmuch as the Word of God empties Himself to become Another. The Word of God is the eternal self-utterance or Symbol of the Father in the immanence of the Trinity. Because God expresses Himself when He empties Himself, the humanity of Jesus Christ is the Symbol or Self-utterance of the Word of God into our history and our world of space and time.

Jesus Christ is the only man who is the Self-utterance of God. We other human beings are not. Yet it is our human nature that God the Son became; it is our reality that He made His own as the vehicle of His Self-communication. Thereby He made our history His own, our life His own, and He posited at their core the saving grace of His own Self-giving Life mediated through the One among us Who is His own unique Other.

In retrospect we can say, realizing that the Incarnation is at the heart of our history, man is that 'other' God created to become. What is prior to the creation of man and therefore to creation itself is God's free loving will to empty Himself, to become what is not God. The Humanity of Christ is the outcome of that will and derivatively, the whole of creation. But since what God becomes when He empties Himself in Self-utterance is man, humanity itself shares in that definition which belongs in a unique way to Christ: Man is God's Other. The finite mystery of man is founded in the infinite mystery of God. Mediated by Christology, Anthropology is recognized as the correlate of Theology.

Man In The Light of Christ His Norm

How do we men who are not Christ understand ourselves in the light of Christ? How does the fact, that one who shares our nature is the One Who God became as His Other, affect our existence, our destiny?

To affirm that Christ is the norm of man is to say that the identity of Christ, Who and what He is, enters intrinsically into the meaning of man, into his self-understanding. Because human existence is understood as a historical project in which the individual as subject comes to increasing self-actualization as he grows in self-knowledge and in conscious self-possession in community with others in the world, the impact of the Incarnate Word on his self-understanding must be a conscious one and affect the awareness he habitually has of himself. Indeed the intensity of this transformed awareness will be proportionate to the depth of his preoccupation with his personal destiny, the seriousness with which he has asked: Why am I? and, if he is a professed Christian, the caliber of his faith in God revealed in Christ as the One in Whom his destiny is grounded.[11]

In our study of man that culminated in a fundamental theological anthropology, we discovered that human nature can be defined as an obediential potency for God's Self-Revelation. This inquiry 'from below,' that is, on the basis of man's experience and reflective understanding of his concrete existence without explicit recourse to revealed sources, had showed man to be essentially a spirit-in-the-world who constitutes himself in his spiritual activities of knowledge, self-disposition and love, transacted with the other beings of his world in a constant transcending thrust toward the Absolute Mystery of Being. This ultimate ground of his own personhood and freedom was recognized as Himself personal and free Who could, if He so wished, initiate a history with man, that is, enter into an interpersonal dialogue with man which would be constituted by His initiative of Self-communication. For man this would be a purely gratuitous gift, a grace.

In our formal theological anthropology, our inquiry 'from above,' we have begun with the affirmation of faith that God has in truth always exercised this initiative toward man. In consequence man has never concretely existed except in an order of grace. He has since his beginnings been the addressee of God's unceasing Self-communication and therefore His unfailing loving summons to share His life. He has from his genesis always been inwardly transformed by a 'supernatural existential' which orients him, infinitely beyond the reach of his natural transcendence, to the God Who offers Himself to man in absolute intimacy. In Christ Whom we know and accept by faith, we have already arrived by anticipation at the summit of this theological anthropology, of this understanding of man as engaged in a constant divinizing encounter with God. Man is the being who is capable of God (*capax Dei*), and Christ is the highest possible actualization of this capacity.

Because God willed to be Other in His incarnate Word, the created universe was destined to be the environment within which man would be the heart and focus of its meaning and its purpose. For man was to be the subject who could be engaged freely in a dialogue of love by God. Created reality, with man at its center, is the condition of the Incarnation. At the same time, it must be said that Creation is for and on account of the Incarnation as the creation of God's Other in the humanity of Christ.

As we discussed earlier, there is an analogy of being with man as its key in as much as Being comes to itself in man and the rest of creation *is* in man and for man. There is also an analogy in the supernatural order of being in which all creation participates through man. The order of nature is for the order of grace, and through man it is open to God's saving Self-communication. Thus the lower order exists for the higher, Creation for the Incarnation, by virtue of which created reality centered in man is saved. God imparts Himself to man-in-and-of-his-world through Christ in Whom He not only utters Himself into creation, but accepts His creation as His own, once and for all.

This perpetual giving of Himself to man saves him by drawing him into the Divine Life "as son in the Son." Factually, it has always had to be a healing as well as an elevating process. Salvation has had to be a redemption, because man has always been a sinner, prone to reject God's incessant call to live His life as His son by adoption. And so God the Son had to enter our history as a suffering Redeemer.

He assumed our sinful condition as His own in order to redirect it toward the loving Father. He became the Head of Creation and the Lord of History, not by the mere taking up of our flesh and history in the Incarnation, but by the anguish and contradiction of transforming our rebellious No into the obedient Yes of His suffering and dying.

Therein He lived humanly, in our place and our time, the eternal fidelity with which he expresses, accepts and reciprocates the Self-gift of the Father. And we are called upon to subject ourselves to Him as our norm and exemplar by following His way of the cross, dying with Him that we might rise with Him.

Salvation: God's Revelation and Man's Faith

This is good and it is acceptable to God our Savior, who desires all men to be saved and to come to the knowledge of the truth. For there is one God, and there is one mediator between God and men, the man Christ Jesus, who gave himself as a ransom for all. I Tm 2:3-6.

God's will to save encompasses all men of every age from the creation of man to the Parousia. He calls everyone to partake of His own life who shares the humanity into which His Son emptied Himself and in which He "gave himself as a ransom for all."

When the Creator willed to become the creature, He thereby defined Man as the possibility for His emptying Himself of His own divine status that there might be Another to whom He could give Himself in love. In himself, therefore, man is openness to the possibility of God's Self-gift, a possibility that is most fully realized in the Incarnation where the union between God and man is *hypostatic*: that is, God and man are one in the Person of the Son. For the rest of mankind, the Self-gift is a grace by which men are enabled to participate in that Sonship by adoption through incorporation into the divine life which the man, Jesus Christ, possesses in its fullness.

The theology of salvation has a necessary correlate and complement in the theology of revelation and faith. When God gives Himself, He expresses and communicates Himself. God's Deed and His Word are one. His Word is His Deed; that is, His revelation of His will to save man is efficacious of that will, it is one with the actual accomplishment of salvation. Revelation is really the cognitive side of salvation, the Word that effects salvation, pre-eminently in Him Who is that Word in person, His Son made incarnate in man's flesh. Faith is man's free response, made possible by God's own gift, to the Father's free and gratuitous invitation to become His son in Christ.

The grace of salvation comes to man whose very existence is a *conscious* process of self-appropriation powered by his transcending drive toward the Divine Mystery. As a result, the 'supernatural existential' and its actualization by the offer of saving grace, which elevates man to the level of divine life, must have an impact on that conscious process by which man constitutes himself in his being and activities. In effect, the grace of salvation, which is God's gift of His own life to man, affects the consciousness of every human being and has done so since the beginning in view of God's universal will to save. Since it affects the consciousness of all, it implies that every man is the recipient of God's revelation and therefore of the gift of faith as man's God-given ability to respond to this revelation, at least as a constant offer. The inevitable question of course is: how can God's revelation be said to affect the consciousness of all men, when there are so many who are not apparently conscious of it?

The answer is found in the understanding of man and his consciousness which was developed in the previous chapter. For there we discovered that the Absolute Divine Being Who is the goal of man's transcending activities is not a direct object of his knowledge and love. He is rather the perspective or horizon which is co-known as the necessary condition of every act of knowing, loving, freedom. It is this perspective or horizon which constitutes the conscious subjectivity with which man approaches every act of the human spirit that is affected and transformed by the gift of God's grace. It is the impact of grace on this subjective perspective of man which constitutes God's Self-gift and Self-revelation as constantly and perpetually impinging on and affecting the human self who knows, loves, makes decisions and acts in freedom. Faith is the God-given power bestowed on each man to respond out of his freedom to this impact of God on his conscious life, either affirmatively or negatively.

Karl Rahner calls this pre-reflective, pre-conceptual, non-objectified and merely implicit divine communication which always affects the consciousness of every man—*Transcendental Revelation*, for it represents the gracious supernatural actualization of man's transcendental openness to the Divine Mystery and God's possible Self-revelation. Since every man is impelled to thematize, that is, to try to understand, conceptualize, make judgments and decisions about his experience, this merely implicit revelation must inevitably be given some explicit formulation by every man both as an individual and as a member of a community. The history of man's religions is constituted of the various attempts, some more successful than others, to thematize or give explicit expression to this divine factor in human consciousness. But it is not only in formally religious modes, but in every mode, religious, non-religious and even anti-religious, in which man seeks to express his understanding of himself, his destiny, the meaning of his life and death, of existence itself, that this Transcendental Revelation and the faith corresponding to it are being thematized and given some symbolic or conceptual form. Rahner names every effort to give thematic expression to graced consciousness,

Categorical Revelation.

Man's consciousness and self-understanding are never composed of purely human and natural elements alone. They are always pervaded by the permanent presence of God. When man confronts himself in his most intimate depths, he is already enveloped in the co-presence of Him Who gives Himself in absolute nearness and calls each individual to a life of loving dialogue with Himself. Man's living of this dialogue with God, whether recognized as such or not, constitutes his personal history as a strand of the universal history of salvation.

Christ, the Incarnate Word, is the final, conclusive and definitive revelation of God's Saving Will for man. He is the summation of the history of salvation and the anticipation of its victorious outcome. He is therefore the norm of the Transcendental Revelation with which God communicates Himself to every human consciousness and in the light of which every human being understands and interprets himself. His Gospel as the explicit expression of the meaning of His life, death and resurrection is not something extrinsic and foreign to the concrete self-understanding of man. Rather the "expressly Christian revelation becomes the explicit statement of the revelation of grace which man always experiences implicitly in the depths of his being."[12]

A. REVELATION AND THE HISTORY OF SALVATION

Revelation and salvation are two facets of the same process. For salvation is the term used to express the basic truth that God chose to become God-for-us. He willed to create another than Himself whose very essence would be openness to Himself, to whom He could give Himself in an enduring gesture of love. Revelation follows from the nature of what God has brought to pass. In giving Himself to man, He expresses Himself as the initiating Word in a dialogue for which man has been precisely yet gratuitously created to be a partner. The grace by which he is empowered to engage in this divine-human encounter is Faith.

Since all men exist in the economy of salvation, every man is the recipient of what we have called Transcendental Revelation and of the gift of faith corresponding to it. Human self-understanding in every instance occurs within a consciousness that is illuminated and transformed by the light of the Self-disclosure of Him Who is the ground and the goal of human existence. Though always a grace, this divinized dimension of man's consciousness is a supernatural *existential,* that is, a constitutive component of his being-in-the-world. Wherever man is, will be or has been, there is someone living in the tension of God's incessant summons to accept and reciprocate His Self-offering.

Historicity is also an existential of man. It is characteristic of his process of becoming. A man's personal history emerges as the on-going pattern of the project of his self-constitution. Because no man is an island, but is rather a relational being, whose life-project is woven into those of his fellow-men within his community and his world, his own career is part and parcel of the history of the race.

Man's history is a *Salvation* History because the project of his life is that of one called to share God's life, infused with the saving grace of adoptive sonship. Because it is in solidarity with his whole race that he is saved, his personal salvation history is a sub-theme of the general history of man's salvation. Moreover, since revelation is the other side of salvation, their history is also identical.

The history of revelation is the history of man's experience of his dialogue with God, of the Transcendental Revelation by which man's consciousness of himself and his world is transformed into the life of a son within a community of sons unceasingly engaged and challenged by the Father Who is the source and end of his existence. However, as Transcendental, this Revelation is non-objective and still unthematized. It is translated into the warp and woof of human history in the very process by which it is given explicit formulation in signs and symbols, in words and deeds and gestures. Indeed this process comprises the whole of human history because it is the living out of man's understanding of himself. This translation of Transcendental Revelation into the social and cutural expressions that give form to the historical process is called *Categorical* (*or Predicamental*) *Revelation*.

This Categorical Revelation has had two careers, one within the other. The whole history of man's unabating effort to symbolize and interpret the meaning of his existence and his destiny comprises *General Categorical Revelation*. As we have observed, this consists largely of the history of man's religions and philosophies, but actually it must be said to encompass every interpretation of human life, whether professedly religious or not. For inescapably it is interpreting man's self-understanding in response to the ever-present and ever-pressing invitation of the Father, calling us in every juncture of our lives and every value-laden decision to live divinely as His adopted sons.

We can affirm in faith that God has not abandoned any of his sons, but is faithfully active at the very heart of every human consciousness, even where His presence is unrecognized or denied. Accordingly every human effort to confront the fundamental questions of man's existence and destiny is part of the General History of Salvation and Revelation. In conformity with His universal will to save, God has actually used these quite fallible and often grotesque efforts of man to understand Him and to grope towards Him according to that understanding as the very instruments of the grace and sharing in His life by which His saving Will is implemented. "But as God permits human sin . . . and this obscures and corrupts every dimension of human life, individual and social, the history of man's attempts to objectify revelation is not excepted; the attempt is only partially successful and revelation is mingled with error and culpable ignorance."[13]

God chose to enter human history understood as the unceasing effort to express man's self-understanding within the ambience of Transcendental Revelation in order to provide the normative expression of His Self-communication and will to save mankind. This is now called *Special Categorical Revelation.* This constitutes what we have been accustomed to name Salvation History and is a Special History of Revelation. It marks the career of an objectification of revelation guided by God for the sake of the human community, a process of thematizing performed by divinely inspired prophets and therefore one whose purity and authenticity are guaranteed by God's own Spirit. This is Revelation in the strictest sense, a historical dialogue between God and the people He chose especially to be His own, embodied in a covenant and representing a special history within universal history and the general history of religions.

The Judaeo-Christian Revelation, culminating and definitively achieved in Christ, is this divinely inspired thematization of the Transcendental Revelation with which every man is graced. It provides the standard and norm by which other thematization is to be judged. For the completely and finally authentic revelation of God's saving Self-gift to man is His own Word made flesh, Jesus Christ, and Salvation History from Abraham to the Parousia is the divinely governed explicitation of that Incarnate Word of God.

Transcendental Revelation is the Self-communication of God to the graced consciousness of every man and is revelation in its radical sense. Categorical Revelation, most perfectly achieved in Special Categorical Revelation, is the necessary expression of the revelation in the idiom of our history, including its central occurrence in the humanity of Christ, the very core of history as salvific and the primal source of its unfolding meaning.

Most properly and precisely we should say that there is but one revelation inasmuch as God always and everywhere is offering Himself in absolute intimacy to man's supernaturally elevated transcendence, in the face of refusal as well as acceptance. This revelation and its impact on man's conscious being and self-understanding have to be known and made explicit in conceptual formulation and/or symbolic expression and enter in decision, action and event into the fabric of man's on-going history. This historic thematization is itself validated as the true self-understanding of the transcendental experience of God by reference to the Christ-event which is the absolute and definitive unity of God's Self-communication and its historical thematic expression. For in Jesus Christ, the Word Incarnate, we have at once "God himself as communicated, the human acceptance of this communication and the final historical manifestation of this offer and acceptance."[14]

B. FAITH: MAN'S RESPONSE TO GOD'S REVELATION

Transcendental Faith corresponds to Transcendental Revelation. It is the elevation of the transcendence of man's spirit to the capacity of actually hearing God's Self-revealing Word and of accepting in freedom His gracious Self-offering. It is therefore the supernatural transformation of man's subjectivity or a priori perspective on reality by which he is not only intentionally open to the Infinite, but is in fact enveloped by virtue of his 'supernatural existential' and redeeming grace in the life of the Trinity and in its inner eternal dialogue in which we are now able to participate because of Christ.

Transcendental Faith, like Transcendental Revelation, can only be understood in its categorical form. The divine conversation into which we have been drawn must be translated into our idiom: symbols, thoughts, decisions and events, all the ingredients of our ineradicably historical existence. Since Christ is the normative expression of this meeting of man with God, faith as the human side of this encounter must be understood as the response to the Special Categorical Revelation of which He is the last word. The sources of this revelation are Scripture and its authoritative interpretation in the developing understanding and teaching of the Church.

Faith in the Bible and in the Teaching of the Church

Modern scriptural exegesis recognizes that, in both the Old and the New Testaments, faith is man's total response to God Who reveals Himself as the Savior, and this response includes both acceptance of God's message of salvation and confident submission to His word.[15] Besides its cognitive or intellectual character, which is never absent but is not always its most prominent feature, it includes the elements of obedience, trust, hope and personal commitment to God or Christ. In the faith of the Old Testament, the emphasis is on trust and the more volitional aspects, while in the New Testament, there is greater stress on acceptance of the saving message, now decisively achieved and expressed in Christ, while necessarily retaining the more conative components as essential to the central experience of conversion to Christ.[16]

Until the Council of Trent, the Church did not concern itself so much with faith or revelation as processes in themselves as with their content. Even at that council, its treatment of faith occurred in the context of justification and the polemic with the Reformers. While stressing the necessity of faith for justification and therefore of its volitional elements as factors in the human response to the saving Gospel message, it tended to weight the balance in favor of faith as an intellectual assent to the truth of that message as a reaction against the Reformers' insistence on faith as fiducial.

The first Vatican Council echoed Trent but in its own historical context. It had to cope with the rationalism inherited from the Enlightenment even in Catholic thought as well as with the anti-rationalist reactions of the romantics and fideists of its own age. Against the rationalists who declared the autonomy of human reason as judge even of divine truth, the Council Fathers insisted on the necessity of faith beyond reason for the saving knowledge of God requiring man's voluntary obedience to God and His will to redeem man. Against the Fideists and Traditionalists who exaggerated the impotence of reason and necessity of faith, they proclaimed the power of reason, unaided by faith, to know God's existence and attributes as well as the supernatural and gratuitous character of faith, as God's free gift for man's salvation (DS 3008-3020).

The emphasis of Vatican I was on the intellectual dimension of faith as a free assent, illuminated by grace, to the truths revealed by God, whose motive was the authority of Him who reveals them. It was an understandable emphasis in the face of the errors it was intended to combat and, as at Trent, it was balanced by the acknowledgment of the role of non-intellectual factors. Part of the credit for this must be attributed to the theology of faith of St. Thomas on which both councils generously drew. However, the robust intellectualism of Aquinas had been supplanted by a more pallid rationalism especially in the effort to accommodate to the rampant rationalism of the Enlightenment and successive periods. It produced an apologetics that put a greater burden on reason and its capacity to attain certainty than it was able to sustain realistically, especially under the pressure of the newly refined methods of historical criticism. It was responsible for a theological notion of revelation that reduced it to an almost exclusively conceptualized communication of divine truth and a corresponding notion of supernatural faith as an intellectual assent to revealed truths so conceived. It was not an erroneous understanding of revelation or faith, but it was woefully incomplete.

In its Dogmatic Constitution on Divine Revelation (*Dei Verbum*), the Second Vatican Council deliberately returned to scriptural sources for its teaching on revelation and faith. Restored was the emphasis on the inter-personal as well as the social and historical character of revelation and therefore of faith as its response on man's part.

In His goodness and wisdom, God chose to reveal Himself and to make known to us the hidden purpose of His will by which through Christ, the Word made flesh, man has access to the Father in the Holy Spirit and comes to share in the divine nature. Through this revelation, therefore, the invisible God out of the abundance of His love speaks to man as friends and lives among them, so that He may invite and take them into fellowship with Himself. This plan of revelation is realized by deeds and words having an inner unity: the deeds wrought by God in the history of salvation manifest and confirm the teaching and realities signified by the words, while the words proclaim the deeds and clarify the mystery contained in them. By this revelation then, the deepest truth about God and the salvation of man is made clear to us in Christ, who is the Mediator and at the same time the fullness of all revelaion.[17]

Here we clearly recognize the *historical* dimension of revelation as the unfolding history of salvation willed by God Who manifests Himself and His will in "deeds and words having an inner unity," culminating in the saving words and deeds of His incarnate Son. We also see intimated the *social* or *ecclesial* dimension, since it is a people, a community, a Church, whose history is lived under God's saving will. Finally, we witness the *interpersonal* character of revelation as the divine invitation to friendship and intimate fellowship, "out of the abundance of His love." It calls for man's response in faith as a total personal attitude, comprising indeed a free intellectual assent in grace to truths conceptually received in doctrinal form, but included within the fuller human context of a personal commitment in trust, obedience, hope and love. In a word, it is man's engraced encounter with God his Father revealed in the person of Jesus Christ, his saving Lord.[18]

Faith in Contemporary Catholic Theology

One of the more arresting facets of Catholic contributions to the theology of faith in recent years is the frequency with which they take their point of departure from the doctrine of St. Thomas. It is especially true of those who have established the trend to interpret faith personalistically, that is, as a living encounter with God in Christ. This is all the more surprising in view of the oft-repeated charge that he is unduly intellectualistic or rationalistic in his treatment of religious or theological themes. There is a surface plausibility to these censures, but deeper probing often enough gives the lie to their appearance of validity. Thus St. Thomas defines faith or the act of believing as "an act of the intellect assenting to the Divine Truth at the command of the will moved by the grace of God."[19] At first reading it seems like a cold and abstract definition, but its fuller treatment by Aquinas leaves that impression far behind. He insists shortly afterward that faith is lifeless and not a genuine virtue unless it is informed by Charity, that is, unless it is the faith of a person whose will is ordered by the sharing in God's own love, which is the virtue of Charity, toward God as man's Absolute Good and End.[20]

There are two statements of St. Thomas that are given a pivotal and axiomatic significance in the contemporary Catholic theology of faith. The first is fundamental to his epistemology of faith: "The act of the believer does not terminate in a proposition, but in a reality. For just as in science we do not form propositions, except in order to have knowledge about things through their means, so is it in faith."[21] The second statement is this: "Everyone who believes assents to someone's words; and thus, in any form of belief, it seems that it is the person to whose words the assent is given, who is of principal importance, and, as it were, the end; while the individual truths through which one assents to that person are secondary."[22]

The import of both of these statements is clear. The terminus of Christian Faith as an act of believing is not propositions primarily, but the Divine Reality. The propositions are only the means through which that Reality is achieved. Since faith is an acceptance of truths because of the Person who witnesses to them, the truths through which one assents to the Person are subordinate to Him, and the assent to them is dependent on the prior acceptance of the person who is witness.

These observations of St. Thomas are borne out by the contemporary phenomenology of human faith. First of all, it has to be distinguished from its imitations, namely, those states of mind which are often designated as faith, or more likely, belief, but which are really only forms of the impersonal calculation of probabilities. On the contrary, authentic human faith engages one in the depths of his personal freedom in response to the subjectivity, the self of another, a Thou. The free acceptance of the truth of a witnessed assertion is preceded by the free acceptance of the person, the Thou who witnesses, as worthy of truth. In fact, faith-in-an-assertion is nothing else than the 'Yes' we say to a Thou, insofar as this assertion is included as an expression of the concrete personality of the Thou in the 'Yes' we say to the Thou himself.

The force of this becomes clearer

> if we consider more closely the most significant example of faith—the faith which unites people who love each other. If I believe the words of a person whom I love very much, then this person becomes a second 'I.' I take him just as he is and place myself within his 'I.' He has become my 'I'; he takes my place; he becomes my representative. The non-identity which exists between us is surpassed somehow on a higher level. Without ceasing to be myself, I become identical with him, with his total 'I,' with his concrete historical 'I.' That I believe him merely means that I accept and recognize this Thou in its total singularity. This faith is fundamentally nothing else than the cognitive correlative of love. Indeed, love is love in the true sense only insofar as it is coupled with this faith. This cognitive acceptance of the Thou as a concrete whole is the fundamental element of personal faith . . . I say 'yes' to his assertion and accept it because I have said 'yes' to him as a whole . . . The object of the act of faith is therefore primarily the concrete thou, and only secondarily his assertions.[23]

In Divine or Christian Faith, this faith-in-a-Thou is directed to no other than the Divine Reality revealed in Christ. To put it more precisely, it is the Personal Thou of Christ, Who exists as a Person in his divine and human nature, Who is the direct object of supernatural faith. Since, however, the personal Thou of Christ, the deepest center of His Person, is essentially Trinitarian, which means that it can only be properly understood as a relation within the Godhead, then the Father and the Holy Spirit are always and inevitably involved inasmuch as they subsist as relations within the same Godhead. Whoever then says 'Yes' to the Thou of Christ says 'Yes' also to the Father in the Holy Spirit.

Faith is ordered to the vision of God as its beginning in this life. Faith and vision are thus related to each other as imperfect and perfect participations in the knowledge and life proper to God, and by faith a man shares this divine knowledge and life as a purely gratuitous and supernatural gift. Faith is a beginning of this vision of God and a sharing in God's own knowledge of Himself and us, not only because of *what* we accept on faith about Him and us, but especially because of the motive, *why* we accept it. In faith, the object and the motive are one and the same, namely, God Himself as Truth in Person. Thus faith rests on God as uncreated Truth and not on any creature, even though, as we shall observe, the content of our faith is always mediated through men, through creatures. And so in faith, man begins to know God by God's own knowledge of Himself: therefore, it is a personal knowledge which will be consummated in the Beatific Vision. Yet though personal, it is not unmediated. It is seeing "in a mirror dimly," filtered through many intermediaries, attested to by various signs.

God is the Witness Whose Word we accept in faith, yet He speaks to us in diverse ways and behind many disguises. In bearing witness to Himself, He accommodates Himself to our human historical situation. The prime accommodation was the Incarnation itself and it is the paradigm of His Self-communication in all other instances. Thus He speaks His Word in public revelation in the words of men. Yet though He speaks through men, it is He Whose Word we accept.

He spoke to Israel through His prophets. He spoke to the Jews of the first century through Jesus Christ, His Incarnate Son, and then through His Apostles and disciples to an ever expanding circle of men beyond Israel. Until the end of time, He speaks to mankind through the Mystical Christ, His Church. He addresses Himself to us now in word through the Scriptures and preaching of the Church and by giving us Himself, His love and mercy, in the Eucharist and the other sacraments of the Church. He speaks to us, often wordlessly, in prayer and meditation, in the revelatory power of human friendship and love, in the sharing of common human experiences of suffering for a better, more just and meaningful life for all our fellow-men, which is itself a participation in the unending work of bringing all creation within the Redemption He has won for us all.

It is not then in word alone, but in the union of word

and deed or event, that God employs His creation and men in particular as the mediators of His Self-communication. For nature and history become not only the stage but the instrumental agencies of His Revelation, and men its ministers.

The efficacy of this mediating function is accomplished and guaranteed by the Holy Spirit Who inhabits the created organ as well as the human recipient of the divine message. It is therefore by His interior witness that God enables us in faith to recognize His presence and Word in these various forms. For He both invites us to believe and enables us to give our free response of faith by the grace of His Spirit. The New Testament variously describes this gentle operation of the Spirit within us as the mission given Him by Christ: as an interior illumination, opening the heart and enlightening the mind to receive the preached word (Acts 16: 14; cf. 1 Cor 1:10; 2 Cor 4:4-6; Ep 1:17, etc.); as the inner grace by which the Father draws us to His Son (Jn 6:44-46); as a power of understanding by which we acknowledge Him as true (1 Jn 5: 20); as the spirit of sonship by which we are empowered to call God truly our father (Rm 8: 14-17; Gal 4: 5-6).[24]

This interior role of the Holy Spirit in the process of revelation by which God is always offering Himself to us, expressing His faithful will to save us and soliciting our personal commitment to Him in the response of faith, has been the developing theme of the Church's teaching and of the theological tradition stemming from St. Augustine.[25] This tradition, especially as it later passed through the mind of St. Thomas, interpreted the pertinent biblical texts as implying that the presence of God's Spirit in man has an impact in the depths of his consciousness. This expresses itself in an habitual inclination of his spiritual powers toward an intimate communion of knowledge and love with God. Though referred to as an inner Word of God, this enlightening influence of the Spirit is wordless in the sense of being beyond concepts and images. This is in accord with the mission of the Holy Spirit as Our Lord described it in relation to His own. "These things I have spoken to you, while I am still with you. But the Counselor, the Holy Spirit, whom the

Father will send in my name, he will teach you all things, and bring to your remembrance all that I have said to you" (Jn 14:25-26). Christ Himself is the content of the revelation which He Himself mediates. The Spirit is the gracious gift and inner power by which that revelation is to be understood and lived.

St. Thomas refers to this grace as an interior instinct; others, following his lead, as a God-given inclination or connaturality. In other words, God has graced man, who is naturally inclined by his intellect to truth and his will to good, with a supernatural inclination to Himself as Truth and Good in Person. Man's knowing and loving powers are put on the beam toward the Self-revealing God. As a consequence, the man of faith, by virtue of his faith, recognizes that God is giving and manifesting Himself in various outward forms and media: the word of Scripture, the sacramental sign, human friendship and love. These constitute the language in which He addresses Himself to us. By faith we are enabled to discern, acknowledge and respond to the One Who speaks to us in these terms, to assent and surrender to His call so expressed, because we experience in ourselves a resonance, a conformity or connaturality between the revelatory event and our own God-given inclination. Thus the believer, as it were, instinctively (to use Aquinas' term), judges that the Divine Person is addressing him and he is moved to respond. He accepts the truth of what he hears or reads or experiences because he accepts the Person Who thereby speaks to him in love as an offer of friendship and community of life.[26]

St. Thomas contrasts this kind of judgment by inclination or affective knowledge, which is proper to faith and to its extensions in the gifts of the Holy Spirit, especially wisdom, with scientific knowledge (in his wider use of the term, science), which is proper to Theology or *Sacra Doctrina*. This is especially evident in the field of morality, as he points out with a reference to Aristotle (X *Ethics, lectio* 8). One can use the example of differing knowledge or judgments relating to the virtue of chastity. The theologian knows chastity scientifically: that is, he knows *about* chastity. He knows its definition, its distinction from and relation to the other virtues, etc., but he may not be chaste himself. At least he would not be merely because of his scientific knowledge of it. On the other hand, the man who is chaste may not know much *about* chastity, its definition, species, etc., but he knows chastity by the experience of it in himself. He needs only to consult his own habitual inclinations and reactions. It is part of him. It is the way he feels and behaves. It is the orientation and direction of his own desires and appetites. It is the very form his love takes.[27]

In a similar way the man of faith is endowed by God with an inclination and attraction toward Himself by which the believer discerns the presence, the call, the Word of God, by means of the very inclination and attraction divinely infused in His own spiritual powers. Because it is an affective or love-knowledge (faith informed by charity), it is powered and guided by our sharing in the love by which God loves Himself. Consequently, as we grow in charity, we are ever more strongly inclined towards Him wherever His presence is disclosed. When we are confronted with one or another form of His Word or call, we perceive a congeniality, a mutuality, conformity or agreement between the message and our God-given, grace-produced inclination, so that acceptance and self-commitment freely given by us are recognized as the only suitable response. We have here neither a vision of God nor an immediate experience of Him, but rather the living of a tendency or inclination toward Him which is His own gift. Of course, this grace of faith must, like any virtue, be nurtured and developed; or perhaps more appropriately, like any love-union or friendship, it must be lived and cultivated. It may often have its dark moments and periods of dryness and desolation. If neglected, it can even be lost.[28]

The interior and exterior dimensions of revelation and faith as the divine-human encounter are equally indispensable and essential for its occurrence. Without the enlightening grace of the Holy Spirit, a man could not in faith distinguish the Word of God in the words of men or His saving will in the events of his history; neither could he assent to its truth as God's own nor surrender himself to it as his own. On the other hand, unless the message was mediated through word and sacrament, human gesture and historical event, a man could not grasp the saving divine Reality Whom they mediate in a truly human way.

Of the two, it is the interior grace that is primary, indeed primal. For it is the very Divine Mystery Itself, the Self-communication of God in His Spirit touching man to the depths of his being and resounding to the furthest recesses of his consciousness. It is indeed what Rahner calls Transcendental Revelation, the non-objective, pre-conceptual and pre-reflective Self-offering of God. It is the invitation by which God calls each of us to share His life by inclining our spiritual powers of knowing and loving to Himself as the One Who is man's absolute fulfillment as the True and the Good. This is the grace of a living faith informed by Charity.

The external dimension of revelation and faith is secondary but indispensable as the thematizing of the ineffable, the wordless Mystery. This is the Special Categorical Revelation and the faith which corresponds to it, by which the Divine Reality, in which the act of the believer terminates, is mediated in symbol and concept and thus made available to man's understanding and transforming acceptance. This divinely guided thematization of the Divine Mystery encountered in the depths of every human consciousness is itself a dimension of revelation as integral to the full Self-disclosure of God to man. It is absolutely necessary if the Father's call to us to become His sons in Christ by the transforming power of His indwelling Spirit is to be rendered intelligible to us and therefore able to receive our filial response in the life of faith. Its fullest expression, as we have noted, is in the Incarnate Word Who is therefore its absolute norm.

Faith occurs in its primary form as man's personal commitment of himself to God in response to the interior call of His Spirit. In its equally essential but subsidiary form as the acceptance of the message, the assent to the revealing word, man is confronted with the divine invitation expressed in his own idiom and therefore able not only to be understood, but to be responded to intelligently and therefore freely. Concretely, these two forms are dimensions of the one act in reciprocal relationship. The inner form confers life and reality on the outer because it is indeed the encounter with Him Whose Self-revelation is thematically expressed for our benefit in its external and usually verbal form.[29]

C. FAITH AND REVELATION IN THE CHURCH: COMMUNITY OF SALVATION

Faith as the saving encounter with the Self-revealing God is a *personal* activity expressing a fundamental life-attitude. Since God's utterance and gift of Himself includes His Will for us which expresses our individual vocation, our responding gift of self in faith must include our own will and freedom. In other words, it must involve the surrender of ourselves over which we are able to exercise self-possession and the power of self-disposition precisely as the measure of our personal freedom. For God calls us to the profoundest depths of our being. His word summons us to grasp ourselves in our total personal existence and then to commit that entire self to Him. What is being evoked then is not a simple modifying of our attitudes, but a re-orientation of our whole being; a conversion or transformation in Christ which is not a once-for-all decision, but a daily laborious and often painful growth.

Like personal human existence itself, faith as our divinized life of encounter and union with the triune God Who reveals Himself must be mediated in history and community. We have already reflected on this in terms of man's historicity and relational being. For each individual man is saved in solidarity with his whole race, extended in time as well as in space. Each person grows in his humanity by virtue of language and other symbolic forms with which he communicates and shares himself with others in a community that itself grows in a living tradition linking it with its past and future. Translated into the terms of man's fullest self-understanding in faith, we recognize that our growth as those called to be sons of the Father involves us in a community and a shared history to which we belong by virtue of a common language and system of symbolized meanings.

The central symbol is the Word of God Himself in our flesh, for He is the Other Who God Himself became. In Him the history of man's salvation converges and from Him it radiates as the unfolding in time of the restoration of men to the life of God which was effected through Him. In every age and place, the grace of salvation is the grace of Christ. By the will of the Father which He expresses, that grace is made actual for each successive age and place in the human community which is His Church. It is His embodiment in our history.

This saving grace of Christ, which expresses itself in the daily encounter of the man of faith confronting the Self-revealing God, is therefore not only profoundly personal, but with equal necessity *ecclesial* and *historical* as well. This is most patent in the case of the formal Christian believer. His saving encounter in faith with the living God not only touches him personally to the core of his being, but occurs to him precisely as a member of the community of faith that is the Church. As a believer, he participates in the Church's life of faith which traces its beginnings to the faith and testimony of the Apostles and which is vivified and guaranteed by the indwelling Spirit of Truth promised and sent by Christ until the end of time. Therefore, his faith response, though individual to him, proceeding from his personal center as a free rational being elevated to the divine level of action by the power of the Spirit Who inhabits him individually, if it is to be recognizably genuine, must correspond to and be subject to the faith of the Church which is alone divinely guaranteed. The objective norm of the authenticity of this faith is the Apostolic witness, embodied in the primitive Church principally in the New Testament, but made present to us in the continuing and developing witness of the faith and teaching of the Church today. And so the individual Christian's faith is not only his personally, but is also ecclesial and historical, because it belongs to him precisely as a member of the Church in the present moment of its historical pilgrimage from Pentecost to the Parousia.

How can we say that revelation is taking place right now and will continue to do so until the Second Coming? Was not revelation closed with the end of the Apostolic age, that is, with the completion of the canonical Apostolic writings of the New Testament? Yes, it was, in this sense. Jesus Christ is the fullness of divine revelation, for in the Word made flesh, the Father accomplished the complete giving of Himself to man and the perfect achievement of His saving will. Revelation is the cognitive side of redemption and the redemptive revelation was consummated on the cross and is perfectly perpetuated in the glorified Christ. However, we have traditionally distinguished objective and subjective redemption: that is, the redemption of mankind definitively achieved in Christ and, on the other hand, the free and contingent subjective appropriation of that which constitutes the personal salvation history of each individual.

In a similar way, we can distinguish the fullness of redemptive revelation, realized in Christ, transmitted through the normative testimony of the Apostles and preserved and preached in each age by the Church which is constantly developing in its understanding and corporate realization of the saving mystery of Christ. On the other hand, we can distinguish the subjective process by which the individual Christian as a member of the Church, the community of faith, appropriates that revelation for himself and thus enters salvation history in the present stage of the Church's deepening consciousness of the mystery of redemption. Nothing can be added to the absolute fullness of the revelation of our salvation incarnate in Christ and contained, at least in germ, in the apostolic testimony. But the Church itself will never cease in the Spirit to develop in her understanding of that definitive Word of revelation, and the Christians of each generation who constitute the Church will in faith receive that revelation as an ever-renewed invitation of the Father to those whom He would make His sons in Christ.

Faith and revelation, then, as essential moments in the process of salvation, that is, of God's saving Self-communication to man, are ineradicably ecclesial and historical.

The Church of Christ is a necessary and constitutive factor in the salvation of mankind. Its history, as that of the Body of Christ on earth, is the central and governing force within the universal history of salvation and revelation. This is true not only because man is by nature a social and historical being or because it is explicitly revealed as the positive will of God, although the latter is its best guarantee. It is true also because the saving grace of Christ, which is offered without exception to every man, is by its nature ecclesial and has an inner orientation to the Church which is essentially a historical phenomenon.

"Outside the Church there is no salvation"(*Extra ecclesiam nulla salus*). This statement has had unfortunate connotations in its dramatic history and perhaps it is best left to die quietly in our ecumenical age. Yet if it is properly understood, its validity can still be maintained. For it respects a fundamental truth about the economy of salvation, namely, its incarnational or sacramental character.

God chose to become Another in our flesh and in our created space and time. Thereby he established the dynamic of creation within the economy of salvation. For every man, as creation come to itself, was destined to be another to Whom God could give Himself and whom He could draw within the community of His own Triune life as a member of its created counterpart within the community of man. That community of man has its ultimate source and goal in the eternal community of the Trinity made historically tangible and available in Christ and now in His Church. All men are always and everywhere being invited to live in that divine family as sons in the intimacy of their consciousness by virtue of God's redeeming transcendental Self-revelation. The thrust of this private and inarticulate experience is in every instance towards its social and historical expression in religious and other institutions. But the divinely sanctioned norm of the authenticity of these institutions is Jesus Christ, God's Word incarnate, and the Church which He established to be the permanent historically visible presence of his saving grace. The inner dynamism of every human effort to give socio-cultural and historical expression to this unifying experience, by which all are called to be

God's family, is oriented toward the Church as Christ's own historical embodiment as human community and sacrament of His salvation for mankind.[30]

Man, Christ and the Church

Christian Faith claims to tell man what he is now and in every age. As making explicit the transcendental revelation by which God communicates Himself to each human being and summons him to realize his true self by responding to the divine call, Christianity posits itself as the absolute religion, that is, as the truth about man, his meaning and destiny, to which his self-understanding in any age must conform, if it is to be authentic. This implies that every human being must be a Christian, if he is to be truly human.

The whole thrust of our philosophical anthropology was to show that every man is a theist, even in spite of himself, because his very nature and concrete existence as man is a transcendental relationship to God as the goal of his being, as the necessary though non-objective condition of his knowledge and of all his spiritual activities by which he prosecutes his life-project. Even the very act by which he explicitly denies the existence of God is an implicit affirmation of His reality insofar as it is unintelligible without Him as its unconditional horizon and ultimate originating source.

Christian theological anthropology has shown that this God-oriented understanding of human existence must be given the fuller interpretation of a filial participation in the life of the Triune God. For, in the light of Christian faith, we are able to assert that the obediential potency for God's Self-communication which man's nature discloses itself to be, is and has always from the beginning been actualized by virtue of the redeeming Incarnation of the Son of God. To be man is to be a member of that species God created to become in Jesus Christ and thereby it is to be constituted as Another to whom He could give and thus reveal Himself, His Trinitarian life, in a relation of adoptive sonship.

The Christian Revelation is an infallible explicit account, because divinely inspired and guaranteed, of the meaning of human existence. It is the authenticated articulation of the mystery which every man confronts in his own developing conscious life. Who and what am I? Why am I? What is the context in which the ambiguities, perplexities and unresolved problems of human existence can be brought together and which founds the hope of their eventual solution? It is in essence the revelation of the infinite answer that God is to the infinite question that Man is.

Because the key to the answer is Jesus Christ and what His coming has done and is still doing through the Church He founded to make of human history a history of salvation, the whole thrust of Christian theological anthropology has been to show that every man is a Christian, even in spite of himself. To use Rahner's terminology, every human being is, or is called to be a Christian, at least anonymously.

A. THE ANONYMOUS CHRISTIAN

The theory of the "Anonymous Christian" is an application of the theological anthropology we have been developing. More directly, it is an effort to face the problem of the salvation of mankind in a world that is, to all appearance, preponderantly non-Christian. This issue has become ever more urgent in modern times as Christians and their Church have become more aware of the immensity of the earth's population and of the relative ineffectiveness of its evangelization.

God wills that all men be saved (1 Tm 2:4) and that they be saved through Christ alone Who is historically present to men through His Church which embodies His saving grace for each generation. On the other hand, most men are not Christians. They have either never heard of Christ and His Church, or, if they have, they have never had them adequately preached and manifested to them. How are such men brought into the saving dialogue of faith with the Father Who has revealed and given Himself to man through His incarnate Son? How are they related to

Christ their Savior through His Church, the medium of His earthly availability?

In the past, theologians have proposed such solutions as Baptism of desire (*in voto*) or of an implicit intention to be a member of the Church (*votum ecclesiae*). These were obviously an advance over the earlier conviction that membership in the Church was, presuming one's cooperation in grace, a sign of election for salvation out of the general *massa damnata*. However, they appeared to be *ad hoc* solutions or a kind of theological afterthought, especially as it became more and more evident that professed Christians were such a slight minority of the human race and threatening to become ever more so with the passage of time.

What was sought was a more organic theory, one that was more intrinsic to our experience of the human situation, more coherent with our growing self-understanding. The theory of the "Anonymous Christian", which is associated especially with the name of Karl Rahner but which in substance is implied in the proposals of Schillebeeckx, Alfaro and others, is an effort to achieve a more systematic and plausible explanation, one which required a re-thinking of the theology of grace, salvation, faith, revelation, and of the Church in its nature and its mission.

The Church itself gave increased impetus to this development in the documents of Vatican II, especially in the Constitution on the Church, *Lumen Gentium*. In contrast to the encyclical, *Mystici Corporis*,[31] which identified the Church of Christ, His Mystical Body, with the corporate identity of the Roman Catholic Church comprising all those who fulfilled the canonical conditions of its membership, the Constitution not only acknowledged the ecclesial character of the non-Catholic Christian communities, but also admitted various degrees of relationship to the Church and inclusion within the economy of salvation.[32] Thus even atheists: " those, who without blame on their part, have not yet arrived at an explicit knowledge of God, but who strive to live a good life" are not denied grace or "the help necessary for salvation."

Being a professed Christian demands that a person acknowledge in faith that he is redeemed by Christ by living that faith as a member of the Church through which he is incorporated into Christ and participates in His saving grace. Being an 'anonymous Christian' implies that a person, to whom Christianity has never been effectively presented and who may in fact though in good faith explicitly reject Christ and His Church, so orders his decisions and the fundamental orientation of his life that he in effect has implicitly chosen Christ in the values by which he lives and has related himself to the Church as the visible community of those for whom He is "the way, the truth and the life."

How is it possible to be a Christian without knowing it? to be saved by faith in Christ despite ignorance or even rejection of His unique identity and mission? to be vitally associated with His Church without the faintest desire to belong to it? In attempting to cope with those questions, the theory of the "Anonymous Christian" invokes most of the themes of Christian anthropology which we have traced.

If God truly wills that all men be saved, then it must be assumed that He offers everyone the means for fulfilling the conditions of salvation. This requires, by the very nature of the case, that every human being be given the power to respond by an act of personal faith to God's revelation and gift of His own life to man mediated for us through Jesus Christ. The grace of salvation is a general term which can be used to cover the whole divine-human encounter, and by its very meaning it refers to the gratuitous or gift character of the relationship in its totality.

Salvific grace is both divinizing and healing or forgiving, but the former aspect is primary. God's bestowal of His own life is wholly unearned and infinitely beyond the meriting of anyone who is not God. Factually His Self-communication comes upon a creature who is a sinner, one who habitually tends to reject His saving will and who thereby renders himself doubly undeserving: as a sinner as well as by virtue of being a creature. But even if man were not a sinner, the gift of God's Life would be an entirely unearned grace. In the present economy in which salvation comes as redemptive of sinful man through the merits of Christ, every grace of God for man is a grace of Christ. Though it is not a certain teaching of the Church, it would seem to be the stronger opinion among contemporary theologians that even if man had not sinned, every grace of God would be a grace of Christ. It undoubtedly follows from the theological anthropology that has been proposed here, one of whose presuppositions has been that creation was on account of the Incarnation and that man is that Other whom God created to become and to give Himself to in love and community of life.

Grace, in its widest sense as co-terminous with the supernatural, must be, first of all, 'prevenient,' that is, it must capacitate man the creature (a fortiori, man who is also the sinner) for receiving and freely accepting the divine life. Rahner, as we have seen, postulates the 'supernatural existential' as a gracious constitutive factor of human existence whereby man's nature as the obediential potency or 'opening upwards' for sharing the infinite life of God is actualized. His natural transcendence toward the Absolute Mystery is always in fact transformed into an unconditional receptivity for the grace of God's Life. But grace is also prevenient inasmuch as it enables a man who is elevated in being and potency by virtue of his 'supernatural existential' to act out of his freedom in response to God's free offer of a shared divine life.

Grace is *uncreated* as the very life of God Who offers Himself to man. It seems that grace must also be *created* as terminating in the finite being of man by way of a created participation in the uncreated life of God. The more precise understanding of the relation of grace as created and uncreated is a matter of divergent interpretation among Catholic theologians. All agree, however, that justification, the initiating event of salvation, constitutes man as a "new creation" by divinizing him intrinsically in his own being and not by a mere juridical or extrinsic imputation to him of Christ's redeeming merits. This created grace of man's inner transformation is best understood, it would seem, as contingent upon uncreated grace as the gift itself of God's own life and accordingly as a constant factor of man's relationship with God rather than as an occasional and intermittent divine intervention.[33]

Grace as God's Self-communication to man empowers and disposes him to confront himself in the unfaltering immediacy of God's loving presence. As we have already considered, this constitutes a Transcendental Revelation, a transformation of the horizon of his subjectivity, of the field or context within which he is constantly coming to consciousness of himself. The very reality of God, Father, Son and Spirit, is co-present and co-known in every conscious human act and event. It is the Absolute Mystery into which man is always entering in every effort to comprehend himself and his world. It is the content and ultimate structure of every attempt to thematize the mystery of man and his life, including his religions and philosophies. It is the truth and the life definitively disclosed in Christ and explicitated in the Scripture and the teaching of the Church.

Every man is endowed with divine faith as the gracious power to respond to God's revelation as the constant invitation to live God's life as his own. This ceaseless call resounds non-objectively in his consciousness. He gives his life its form as a response in faith to God's call more by the decisions and actions in which he orients his freedom and constitutes his life and its direction than by the formal words and gestures in which he may seek to express his understanding of them. He may deny God and His Christ in words and yet affirm them by his life. For when he accepts himself within a meaning and a destiny that transcend himself and human boundaries, when his actions and decisions point beyond himself to others as the source of their value, he is in effect affirming the Absolute Other as his End and the reason for his self-acceptance. For the reality of God is rooted more deeply in his consciousness than the images and concepts with which he tries to articulate it.

The human being who implicitly affirms the reality of God as the supreme value by which he lives is thereby also committing himself in faith to Jesus Christ. For He is not only the final utterance of the Triune God into our creation and our history, He is the norm of humanity. In the Incarnation of God the Son we have the highest actualization of the grace by which God enables and summons man to find his utmost fulfillment by surrendering himself into the infinite divine mystery. In accepting himself as he really is, man is professing his loving faith and trust in Him in Whom the Father has definitively accepted the whole of His creation.

God's entrance into our history in Jesus Christ in order to make of it a history of salvation foreordained the Church as the visible evidence, the sacrament of His commitment to man. It is intended to be the community of all men redeemed in Christ, but as an historical phenomenon, it is subject to limitations of time and place and the vagaries of free and often perverse human wills. The Church is an eschatological community in the sense that it embodies in the midst of each generation the irrevocable will of God for the salvation of mankind achieved once and for all in Christ. But it is a pilgrim Church comprising a minority of sinful mankind who are graced with an explicit faith in man's redemption by Christ and who are thereby elected to the corresponding responsibility to proclaim, celebrate and witness to this Good News before their fellow-men.

The Church is not the exclusive society of the saved, whether it be conceived in traditional Catholic terms as a visible organization or in traditional Protestant terms as the invisible choir of the elect. The truth is that the whole human race belongs to the community of the saved in the sense that all men are offered the grace of faith to accept freely the Father's call to be His sons in Christ. Rather the Church is the Body of Christ in the world. It is the sacrament or visible historical sign of His triumphant redeeming grace. As a sacrament, it effects what it signifies. By embodying Christ's redeeming grace, it renders that grace available effectually wherever it is present and operative in the hearts of men and in their history. It follows that anyone who professes faith in Christ and thus opens himself to the saving grace of Christ, even without formal awareness and therefore anonymously, does so through the Church which incarnates Christ in his world and makes His grace effectively present in his history.

The Church preaches the Gospel to those who are already caught up in the mystery of God and in the salvation of man that He has accomplished through Christ. Though they are not able to call Him by His Name, they have already been offered and perhaps have accepted the justifying grace of Christ and an implicit faith in his saving power. Yet the existence of this 'Anonymous Christianity' does not rob the Church's mission of its urgency. For the Church must not only continue to exist as the sacrament of the glorified Christ and His saving grace which enables that grace to be effectively and corporeally present among men. It is also the vanguard of that People of God which is intended to encompass the entire race and to acknowledge, worship and glorify as their God the One Who has brought them into an everlasting covenant with Himself by the blood of His Son.

That Christianity should still exist anywhere in an anonymous condition can only be regarded as an unsatisfactory and provisional state of the relationship of God and His People. The whole dynamic of human history is towards the fullest and most explicit realization of the wondrous vocation to which the Father has called and never ceases to call our race. The successful outcome of this movement is assured by the Paschal victory of Christ and will be definitively achieved in the post-historical event of His Second Coming. But as in the whole economy of salvation, God approaches men through other men and solicits their response in freedom. Therefore the implementation of this divine plan within history waits upon the evangelizing effort of His Church and the uncoerced wills of those to whom the Gospel is preached. For it is still true of the full and formal realization of that plan for man's salvation that saving faith comes by hearing and men will not be able to hear God's inviting word of love unless the Gospel be preached to them (Rm 10:12-17). In the final analysis, if men are to be truly self-actualized as those called to be sons of God as their Father, the living of this identity must be raised above the level of an implicit unrecognized status into the light of a fully conscious and articulated life-project. Only then will men be able to become themselves completely.

B. CHRISTIANITY AND THE NON-CHRISTIAN RELIGIONS IN THE HISTORY OF SALVATION

The theory of the 'Anonymous Christian' is an attempt by Catholic theologians to explain in a manner that is consistent with faith and experience how non-Christians *as individuals* are included within the divine economy of salvation deriving essentially from Christ through His Church. That non-Christians as individuals are so included is clearly the teaching of the Catholic Church, a teaching that was unequivocally restated in various documents of the Second Vatican Council.[34] However, beyond this relatively settled question, there is a further issue that is considerably less resolved: what role, if any, is played in that salvation by the non-Christian religions within which those individuals live out their lives and from which they accept their religious beliefs?

The non-Christian religions which we have in mind are the so-called 'world religions': Hinduism, Buddhism, Jainism, Shintoism, Moslemism, Confucianism, and Taoism. However, the interpretation will be broad enough to comprehend all man's religions, including Animism and the more primitive faiths of Africa, Asia and Oceania and analogously, the quasi-religions such as Communism, Socialism, Secular Humanism and other world views that fulfill the function of a religion for their devotees. Modern Judaism is a special case, but it is encompassed within the broad sweep of the final position, even though it is recognized that further special qualifications would have to be introduced.

There is no developed theology of religions. It is only in our age of religious pluralism, recognized as a universal phenomenon which promises to be an enduring one, that the need of such a theology has impressed itself with inevitable urgency. Besides the developed theology of salvation as it applies to non-Christians as individuals and as a category, there are directions and intimations in Scripture and tradition that provide a starting point for theologizing on this subject.

The scriptural directions are largely couched in the judgments found there on the pagan peoples and the world which surrounded Israel and the early Church. The Old Testament attitude toward paganism is largely negative in tone, but not exclusively so. This largely condemnatory attitude toward its pagan ambience is understandable and can even be seen as providential in view of the need of preserving this small and weak people in its fidelity to monotheism and its relatively high moral code.

The absolute claims of Israel to a unique divine revelation have been rejected by such commentators on religious and cultural history as Arnold Toynbee because of its particularism and "exclusive-mindedness." He and others regard it as arrogance and pure pride to believe that the Absolute Being would restrict His message to such a small portion of the human race, and he extends the same judgment to Christianity inasmuch as its claims are derived from Israel and are equally absolute, though representing such a minority of the human family.[35] Such strictures are not totally unjustified, but they do seem to misunderstand the point of Salvation History and of the incarnational principle which operates therein. For Israel is the vessel of election not for its own benefit, but precisely to serve the entire race from within the human family. In His inscrutable and mysterious designs, God has chosen to save man through man, and preeminently through The Man, Who is His only begotten Son incarnate. Man's situation is ineradicably historical; that is, he lives out his existence in the particularities and limits of space and time. The election of Israel, like the election of the One born of Mary, is an inescapable consequence of this divine accommodation to man's historicity as the freely chosen, self-limiting context within which God has elected to extend His call to man to share His own life as sons.

As Hans Küng reminds us,[36] there were two streams of tradition in the Old Testament out of which, despite the weight of national particularism, there began to develop gradually and with greater clarity a more open, universalist view of pagan peoples.

The *prophetical* tradition is self-critical of Israel and its evolving trend through the great prophets culminating in the Deutero-Isaiah is toward the universal participation of all nations in the eschatological salvation to be wrought through the servant of Yahweh. The *priestly* tradition is, if anything, more openly universalist, for it portrays the salvific vocation of Israel against the background of God's creation and of His universal dominion over it. Its account of Israel begins not with the first Jew, but with the first man. It is man himself who is called to share God's life, who falls and who shares in the promise of redemption. Before the covenant with Abraham there is recounted the prior covenant with Noah, which is a universal and everlasting cosmic alliance "with every living creature on earth" (Gn 9:9-17). The covenant with Abraham is with a particular portion of the human family, but the promise was that in Abraham "all the peoples of the earth would be blessed." (Gn 12:3; 28:14). In other words, a total reading of the Old Testament reveals that there is indeed a strong condemnation of the sin, error and darkness of paganism, but only insofar as it represents man's rejection of God's saving will. Since God is the God of all men and peoples, the negative judgment is also a call to conversion and to participation in the fruits of the coming Messianic age.

Our Lord limited His preaching to His own people and forbade His disciples to preach to any but those of the house of Israel during His own lifetime (Mt 15:24; 10:5ff). Yet He promises that many will come from the east and the west and sit with the patriarchs in His Kingdom, but the children of the Kingdom will be cast outside. The Son of Man is Savior of all men, and He will judge all men, not on the basis of their origin, but according to their practice of love of neighbor (Mt 25:31-46).

The early Church had to go through a similar process of discovering its universal mission somewhat like the old Israel. St. Paul of course played the major role in this discovery. He deals with paganism most directly in the first two chapters of Romans. There the pagans are held accountable for their errors about God and their sinfulness because they could have known God revealed in His creation and they could know His will as it is reflected in their own conscience. But God is no respecter of persons, and the Jews within the Law and the Greeks outside the Law are equally subject to divine wrath, just as each shall receive the reward of glory, honor and peace for his goodness. There is then a revelation of God to the pagans outside the special revelation to Israel. Moreover, all men, Jew and pagan alike, are under the same rule of sin and are in the same need of justification through Jesus Christ (Rm 3:9-31). Paul's discourse on the Areopagus in Athens is of great significance. After noting their religiousness and in particular their altar to the 'unknown God,' he remarks: "What therefore you worship as unknown, this I proclaim to you." Their religion is indeed conceived in darkness, for which they should repent, yet it does embody their groping after the God Who had not left them alone, but disclosed His presence in His creation. For He is near to every human being since in Him "we live and move and have our being." Thus even before Paul came to preach to them they were not removed from God as they groped after Him in their own religious modes (cf. Acts, 17).

We can say then by way of concluding the biblical testimony that all men, including the pagans, are encompassed by the divine plan of redemption, for the God of saving grace is the God of all men. Thus even outside of Israel and its special salvation history and before the preaching of the Christian gospel, men have encountered the saving God, in however obscure and perverted a manner, in their own religious environments. For, as St. Paul emphasizes: "God desires all men to be saved and to come to the knowledge of the truth. For there is one God and there is one mediator between God and men, the man Christ Jesus, who gave himself as a ransom for all" (1 Tm 2:4-6).

Modern Christian theology has tended to take two stances toward the non-Christian religions. The one is especially associated in recent time with the dialectical theology of Karl Barth; the other, that of the "theology of fulfillment," is an expression of the dominant Catholic tradition. The Barthian posture, applied to missiology by his follower, Hendrik Kraemer, is strongly based on biblical sources and the negative judgment pronounced there on the pagan cults.[37] Barth contrasts religion, which in every instance is a futile attempt on the part of man to reach God by his own finite, sinful and therefore doomed efforts, with Revelation, identified with Christianity and its roots in the Old Testament. This is the initiative of God's Word and grace that can alone lift man out of his helpless condition of sin and corruption and make possible a saving history of dialogue with God in and through Christ. As a consequence, Christianity is in a unique and exclusive position as the only bearer of God's saving Word to man. All others as religions are man-made counterfeits and to be rejected as signs of man's rebellion against God.[38]

The alternative position is that of the "theology of fulfillment," which in accord with the Catholic theology of sin and redemption that regards nature as wounded, but not essentially corrupted by sin, interprets Christianity as the fulfillment of the non-Christian religions which are regarded as pre-Christian and preparatory phases in the economy of redemption. Their defectiveness is not so much as signs of man's rebellion against God, although that element is not overlooked. It consists rather in their incompleteness, their tentativeness and fragmentary character as anticipations destined to yield to the fullness of Christianity at the providential moment, and in the danger that men will not recognize that moment or will choose not to acknowledge the purely preparatory role of these other faiths. This position reflects the predominant viewpoint of the early Fathers, who, with some exceptions, regarded man as 'anima naturaliter Christiana', and looked for signs or intimations of revelation and Christian truth in the teachings and practices of their pagan neighbors and in their traditions. This is found in such early Christian writers as Justin Martyr, in those of the Alexandrian school and even in St. Augustine.[39] The data of the history of religions suggests this same thesis, namely, that even the most idolatrous of them can be understood as so many forms of waiting for Christ, that is, for the Incarnation.[40]

More recent theologians have attempted to achieve a synthesis that moves beyond both of these positions, since each is regarded as to some extent an extreme that does not take into full account all the data of Scripture or of Tradition. Obviously the dialectical position takes full account both of Scripture's negative judgment on the pagan religions and the long traditions of the Church, Catholic as well as Protestant, which interpreted the mandate to preach the Gospel as involving the rejection of other religions in favor of a complete conversion to Christ in His Church. It also recognizes that God's revelation in Christ was a special free action on His part that cannot be achieved by some sort of extension of the so-called 'natural' state of man. Therefore, the revelation of Christ involves both a free initiative on God's part and, on man's part, a free response in the form of a conversion from sinfulness and from the condition of rebelliousness.

On the other hand, the theology of fulfillment recognizes that the many positive elements in the non-Christian religions are not lacking all objective significance for salvation, that God revealed in Christ is truly the Lord of History and that His saving grace is not wholly inoperative in the prayers and faith of those men who, through no fault of their own, are lacking the fullness of His revelation. It also acknowledges those universalist elements that we have briefly discussed in the Old as well as the New Testament. Like many Fathers of the Church, this position claims that all that is good and true and beautiful has the Holy Spirit as its source, wherever it is to be found.

Our own instincts perhaps incline us toward the second position, but like its counterpart, it appears to labor under some difficulties, and it needs to be transcended, if a more satisfactory solution is to be found. Schlette draws the following conclusion concerning both:

> Although both dialectical theology and that of fulfillment in their extreme form contain elements of a theology of the history of salvation, both nevertheless appear to lack a deliberate and unambiguous orien-

tation towards sacred history. Dialectical theology in its radical form implies the denial of the unity of the human race and of its (sacred) history, and the denial of continuity. If the theology of fulfillment, exaggerating continuity, is in too great a hurry to interpret nature as the presupposition of grace, it does not take sufficiently seriously decision, freedom, refusal, catastrophe, the Cross, the overcoming of obstacles and the originality of Christianity.[41]

Schlette suggests that what is lacking and needed for a satisfactory synthesis of both is an adequate theology of redemption and redemptive history. In our theological anthropology and in our treatment of the theory of the 'Anonymous Christian,' which we drew largely from the thought of Karl Rahner, we have already begun to present such a theology.

As we have previously discussed, no man is outside the economy of salvation, whatever his historical, geographical or cultural situation. Wherever there is or has been a man, there is someone who is redeemed in Christ and therefore included somehow within salvation history. Moreover, salvation history is always a revelation history because every human consciousness is transcendentally related to the Self-revealing God whose constant summons is ever receiving a response from men who are graced with some form of faith. The thematizing of this ever-present transcendental revelation translates it into a categorical revelation that is co-extensive with God's offer of saving grace to man and therefore coextensive with the history of the human race. Consequently, we can say that man's salvation history takes place within his profane history since his constant response in freedom of acceptance or refusal of God's saving call occurs in the midst of his ordinary history, in his encounters with other men, with his own tasks, with the world of his everyday life; all this lived out, because he is by nature a social being, in various human communities.

We can speak then of a General Salvation and Revelation History of mankind which is the career of man's efforts from the beginning, in dependence on God's indispensable grace, to objectivize and thematize, in other words, to give expression to his response to God's saving grace impinging on his consciousness. He articulates this response not only in his own conduct, but also in myth and theology, in ritual and liturgy, in his understanding of himself and his world, his origin and his destiny. By and large, then, General Salvation History has taken the form of the history of man's religions.

As that history discloses, however, man's efforts to give expression to his encounter with God in the mystery of his own consciousness have led to startling, often grotesquely varied forms. For God has permitted man's sin as the price of his free personal participation in the encounter. Thus as it does to all dimensions of human life, sin has obscured and corrupted man's efforts to objectify his relations with God and the divine revelation has been mingled with error and even culpable ignorance.

Man's General Salvation History could hardly have been distinguished from his profane history, in which it is embedded, unless God had graced man with a Special Revelation and therefore a Special Salvation History which has gradually brought man's obscure encounter with God's saving grace and call to fullest self-consciousness and effectiveness. For this Special History marks the career of an objectification of transcendental revelation especially guided by God for the sake of the human community, a process of thematizing performed by divinely inspired prophets whose purity and authenticity are guaranteed by God. But it was in God's Incarnate Word and conclusively in the Paschal Event that the final thematic and objective word was spoken and God's Self-gift to man and man's incorporation into divine sonship achieved an eschatological finality. In other words, the final form of God's saving will for man has been revealed in the Christ-Event. All future objectivizations of revelation must be judged by and subjected to the norm of this Event as it is embodied and perpetually made present among men in the Church which has both received and must proclaim this absolute revelation until Christ returns in glory.

Salvation history is always at the heart of profane history as the source of its profound meaning and the religious dimension of history is man's unceasing effort to express that meaning, not merely as an immanent product of that history but as the response to a Transcendent presence in its interior depths. Wherever this effort at a religious interpretation strains toward an ever fuller self-understanding, it tends to be joined at various points with the Special Revelation which was given to Israel and which received its climactic definition in the Christ-Event. Rahner believes it quite possible that special revelations other than that of the Old Testament could have occurred outside Israel and been given historical expression in other religions as preparatory to the definitive revelation in Christ. Thus the inner tendency of General Salvation History, especially as it is constituted by the history of man's religions, is toward identification with Special Salvation History.

According to Rahner:

> Of course, it remains the privilege of Israel that its tangible and to some extent distinct salvation-history was the immediate historical prelude to the Incarnation of the divine Word, and that this history of Israel alone was interpreted authoritatively by the word of God in Scripture in such a way that it was thereby distinguished from any other profane history (which also always contains religious elements), and that only thus it became the official and special salvation-history in distinction to profane history. Only in Jesus Christ did the divine and the human reach an absolute and indissoluble unity; only in the self-revelation of Jesus is this unity also historically present; only now is this saving history clearly and permanently distinguished from all profane history. Everything, such as the Church, the sacraments and the Scriptures, which follows from this Christ-event and participates in its own way in this unsurpassable finality of the Christ-event, participates also in its distinction from profane history. Here in Christ and in the Church, saving history reaches its clearest and absolutely permanent distinction from profane history and becomes really an unequivocally distinct manifestation within the history of the world, thus bringing the general salvation-history to self-realization and to its historical reality in word and social structures within the history of the world. By this very fact, this distinct salvation-history of an explicitly verbal, social and sacramental kind is also something destined for all men of every future age. It intends to gather into itself the whole general salvation and revelation-history and to present it historically within itself; it strives therefore to coincide with the general salvation and revelation-history and thus also with profane history although it knows quite well that these two can never be fully identified in history but only in the culminating dissolution of history.[42]

What we recognize in faith therefore is a situation in which all men have been gifted with Christ's saving grace by which they have been made participants in a General Salvation History. However, most men have known this ever-present and actual fact of their redemption obscurely and implicitly so that the General Revelation History in which they have shared has been characterized by a merely tentative and incomplete, often erring and misleading self-realization of their redemption, expressed in their religious beliefs and practices. It is in Christ and His Church that this redemption has been definitively achieved and its adequate revelation definitively proclaimed. In relation therefore to all others, Christianity understands itself as the absolute religion, intended for all men, which cannot recognize any other as equally valid. For valid religion is not man's own interpretation of himself, but rather God's action on men and His relationship to them, freely established and freely revealed to them. This relationship of God to man is basically the same for all men since it is founded on the identical redeeming Christ-Event.

It was a conviction of the past that since the coming of Christ, the Church which He founded as His continuing historical presence in the world is *the* exclusively valid religion relating man to God. As a consequence, it was thought that children dying before the age of reason had to be baptized in order to be saved because with the founding of the Church the period had passed when any but the Christian faith had efficacy for salvation. However, in the light of later history and contemporary experience this attitude seems to be an over-simplification which overlooked man's own thoroughly historical existence. Since Christianity itself is rooted in an historical event, it must come to men in a historical way, confronting them with its exacting decision. The question is whether the moment at which the adequately proposed demand for this decision takes place for all men is the same chronological moment, or whether the occurrence of this moment itself has a history and therefore cannot be said to occur simultaneously for all men and cultures. The latter position certainly seems to take into account the historicity of Christianity and the fact that salvation itself has a history.

Rahner therefore goes on to propose the following thesis: "Until the gospel actually enters the historical situation of a certain person, a non-Christian religion contains not only elements of a natural knowledge of God mixed with depravation caused by original sin and human elements, but also supernatural elements of grace. It can therefore be acknowledged to be a legitimate religion, even though in different gradations."[43]

Granted the presence of saving grace outside the membership of the Catholic Church and Christianity itself, the question is whether this grace is made available to non-Christians as individuals precisely through the non-Christian religions themselves as the vehicles of this saving grace. It is proposed that the answer to this question is affirmative. We can infer, for example, that these religions can be positively willed by God as means of salvation, even though they contain elements of error and depravity from the example of the religion of Israel. "For the Old Covenant, understood as a concrete, historical and religious manifestation, contained what is right, willed by God and what is false, erroneous, wrongly developed and depraved."[44]

Moreover, in Israel, except for the office of prophet which was occasional and not always distinguishable from its false imitations, there was no court of appeal available to the conscience of the individual clearly to distinguish the right and true from the wrong and false elements in his own religion. This could be definitively achieved only in the light of the New Covenant. It would seem to follow then that a religion can be a legitimate one even if it is weighted with error and objectively wrong moral elements and is lacking a means of final recourse for its individual members whereby they can clearly and certainly distinguish what is of God from what is corrupt and merely of man.

Consequently if, as it would appear, God can positively will to use a non-Christian religion as a means of saving grace for its members in spite of its errors and aberrations, then it would seem theologically feasible to regard even contemporary non-Christian religions as such 'ways of salvation,' at least until that moment when its members are clearly and inescapably confronted with an adequate and effective manifestation of the Christian Gospel as the eschatologically definitive and therefore absolute form of the presence of Christ's saving grace among men. The decisiveness of this moment would indeed apply to the individual consciences of its members, who would be thus confronted, rather than for the religion itself which does not have a conscience of its own and could still survive as a 'way of salvation' for those of its members who had not yet been so decisively confronted.

This thesis seems especially persuasive in view of the social nature of man, a human trait that is even more conspicuous in those non-western cultures where the Christian Gospel has had its least impact. For man, as we have previously discussed at some length, is a relational being who achieves himself within a community of his fellows as the inevitable context in which he works out his transcendental relationship to God. Moreover, man's religious beliefs and practices have to emerge out of the social and cultural setting within which his life is enacted and acquires its meaning. Otherwise, religion would be condemned to being a purely interior and private affair and to that extent something less than fully human. As a consequence, "if man can always have a positive, saving relationship to God, and if he always had to have it, then he has always had it within *that* religion which in practice was at his disposal by being a factor in his sphere of existence."[45]

It is possible, therefore, for us who are professed Christians to look on our world which is to all appearances so predominantly non-Christian with hope rather than dismay. For we are permitted to interpret this non-Christianity as Christianity of an anonymous kind which has only to be brought "to the explicit consciousness of what already belongs to it as a divine offer or already pertains to it also over and above this as a divine gift of grace accepted unreflectedly and implicitly . . . (If this be so), then the Church will not so much regard herself today as the exclusive community of those who have a claim to salvation but rather as the historically tangible vanguard and the historically and socially constituted explicit expression of what the Christian hopes is present as a hidden reality even outside the visible Church."[46]

The existence of Anonymous Christianity outside the

Church does not render its missionary task any less urgent. By its very essence the Church is mission, to reveal to man what they are called to be through Jesus Christ. For man achieves himself by the gradual transformation of his given nature into the fully conscious, free, self-possessed person. This requires that he realize his identity to the fullest. The most profound truth of this identity is that every man is called to live the divine life humanly as a son of the Father through his Savior, Jesus Christ, Who has made him His brother. Moreover, it is as a member of a People of God that he is to live this universal vocation. There is no more imperative mission in God's and man's world than that of bringing all men to the fullest and most reflectively conscious realization of this sublime destiny.

Ultimately we must realize that the primary mission of the Church is not the salvation of men any more than it was the primary mission of Christ. It is rather the revelation of the glory of the Father, the establishment of His Kingdom or Reign. In this sense the mission of the Church is the extension in history of the mission of Christ and of His Holy Spirit. This is the goal in relation to which the salvation of men is properly only a means. For God became man as His Other in Christ to draw us into His life and to communicate and manifest Himself in the otherness of His creation. Salvation is the mediating implementation of this primary mission.

Through Christ all men are saved in the sense that all are always being called to share His divine life and are engaged in the process of ratifying their redemption by their affirmative response or frustrating its achievement for themselves by their rejection. This salvific process has taken place in the past, and from all indications, will in the future continue to take place anonymously for the great majority of men. From this point of view it would appear that the non-Christian religions are for that vast number that adheres to them in good faith the *ordinary* way of salvation, and membership in the Church with the profession of an explicit Christian faith is the *extraordinary* way. In this perspective the non-Christian religions are seen as integral elements in the history of salvation constituting its general form. On the other hand, the Church constitutes its special form as the revelation within history of its definitive fulfillment already achieved in Jesus Christ. "The Church is . . . the eschatological community called together from the four winds which by its existence in the world is to bear witness to the goal to which the ordinary way of salvation (the religions) lead, and which at the same time demands in the name of God that the extraordinary way should be followed in obedience and humility."[47] Election to the extraordinary way of salvation is not an occasion of self-glorification, but rather for proclaiming, celebrating and giving witness to the glory of God in the service of that greater number of men whom the Father is calling to Himself in the conglomerate of religious forms that comprise the ordinary way of salvation.

This interpretation of the mission of the Church in the light of our historical experience does not deny the purely provisional and preparatory character of the other religions any more than it forecloses the possibility of a fully successful evangelization of the world and enfolding of the whole human family within the Church in the historical future. It is rather the acknowledgment that such an eventuality is not a necessary implication either of what we know from revelation or of what we can understand to be the mission of the Church as the continuation of Christ's own mission.

The Church is the 'manifest presence' of the saving grace of Christ among men, whereas that grace is only 'latently present' in those apparently non-Christian religions which are actually Christian anonymously. However, the latent presence of saving grace, which is the life-source of anonymous Christianity, is dependent on its manifest presence or explicit revelation in Christ's Church. For Christ is in truth the full and definitive revelation of God's saving Self-gift to man as the manifestation of His eternal glory. He is therefore the head of mankind as the Second Adam and the Lord of History from Whom ultimately all human history derives its meaning. The Church of professed Christians was instituted therefore as the visible and effectual sign of His permanent presence among men.[48]

The Church must prosecute its mision with unabating

vigor. It must confront men wherever it can reach them with the full force of the Gospel as the very truth of their existence in order to build up the People of God as the visible earthly Body of Christ, giving glory to the Father in His Name. It may be that the Gospel will never be preached with total effectiveness until the end of time, for it will always be hampered by the sinfulness of those who preach and those to whom they preach. In any event, "what is asked of Christians is faithfulness to their mission. They can leave the determination of visible results to God."[49] For the Church constitutes only the penultimate stage in the history of salvation on the way to the Kingdom. The ultimate stage will be constituted by the event that will mark the end and dissolution of history: the revelation of the victory of Christ in the Parousia when He subjects all things to the Father, "that God may be everything to every one" (2 Cor 15:28).

Notes and references

[1] The Rahnerian view is that philosophy is an inner moment of theology, since reason always operates within a consciousness engraced with at least the unfailing offer of divine revelation and the faith with which to respond to it. Cf. e.g., Karl Rahner, "Philosophy and Theology," **Theology Digest** XII (Summer, 1964), pp. 119-122, trans. from "Philosophie und Theologie" **Kairos** 3-4 (1962), 162-169. In his mind and that of J. B. Metz who revised **Hearers of the Word,** the philosophy of religion which is the area of inquiry into which it would customarily be placed, is seen to be more properly, in the context of this work, a task of a Fundamental Theological Anthropology. For the philosopher of religion in the course of his inquiry has come into formal self-consciousness and self-understanding as a potential hearer of God's Self-revealing Word. "Philosophy, as genuine philosophy, is Christian when, as fundamental-theological anthropology, it loses itself in theology. Indeed, insofar as it is the constitution of man as a listener for a possible revelation from God, it always becomes merged with theology." Rahner, **Hearers of the Word,** p. 175. Later discussion of this issue has refined the discipline involved as "Formal and Fundamental Theology" as distinguished from Fundamental Theology whose primary function is apologetic.

[2] "We see that Christology is at once beginning and end of anthropology, and that for all eternity such an anthropology is really theo-logy. For God himself has become man. The less we merely think of this humanity as something added on to God, and the more we understand it as God's very presence in the world and hence (not, all the same) see it in a true spontaneous vitality and freedom before God, the more intelligible does the abiding mystery of our faith become and also an expression of our very own existence." Karl Rahner, "Current Problems in Christology," **Theological**

Investigations, Vol. I (Baltimore: Helicon Press, 1963), p. 185.

[3] Karl Rahner, "The Theology of the Symbol," **Theological Investigations**, Vol. IV (Baltimore: Helicon, 1966), pp. 221-252.

[4] Ibid., p. 224.

[5] Ibid., p. 229.

[6] Ibid., p. 234.

[7] Karl Rahner, "On the Theology of the Incarnation," **Theological Investigations**, Vol. IV, pp. 105-120.

[8] Ibid., p. 109.

[9] Ibid., p. 113.

[10] Rahner insists that this understanding of the Incarnation in terms of a dialectic of immutability and change is analogous to the dialectic of unity and plurality required for a theology of Trinity.

[11] We shall discuss later the possibility of a Christ-oriented faith, which is conscious, but is not explicitly recognized as such.

[12] Karl Rahner, "Anonymous Christians", **Theological Investigations**, Vol. VI, (Baltimore: Helicon, 1969), p. 394.

[13] Karl Rahner and Herbert Vorgrimler, **Theological Dictionary**, edited by C. Ernst, O.P., trans. by R. Strachan (New York: Herder & Herder, 1965), pp. 411-412.

[14] Karl Rahner, **Sacramentum Mundi**, Vol. V, (New York: Herder & Herder, 1970), p. 349.

[15] Rudolf Schnackenburg, "Biblical Perspectives of Faith", **Toward a Theology of Christian Faith: Readings in Theology**, (New York: P. J. Kenedy and Sons, 1968), p. 37. "In the Bible, faith means a total personal submission to God in humility and trust, in surrender and obedience, in mind and deed."

[16] J. Alfaro, S.J., "The Dual Aspect of Faith: Entrusting Oneself to God and Acceptance of the Christian Message," in **Man as Man and Believer** (New York: Paulist Press, 1967), pp. 53-66, esp. 54-55.

[17] "Constitution on Divine Revelation", (**Dei Verbum**), Ch. 1, 2. **The Documents of Vatican II**, Walter M. Abbott, S.J. editor (New York: America Press, 1966), p. 112.

[18] Ibid., Ch. 1, 5: "The obedience of faith (Rm 16:26; 1 Cor 10:5-6) must be given to God who reveals, an obedience by which man entrusts his whole self freely to God, offering the full submission of intellect and will to God who reveals. (cf. Vatican I, Const. on the Catholic Faith, ch 3, DS 3008) and freely assenting to the truth revealed by Him."

[19] Thomas Aquinas, **S. Th.** II-II, q. 2, a. 9, c.

[20] Ibid., q. 4, a. 3, c. and a. 5, c.

[21] Ibid., q. 1, a. 2, ad 2.

[22] Ibid., q. 11, a. 1, c.

[23] C. Cirne-Lima, **Personal Faith** (New York: Herder & Herder, 1965), pp. 28-30.

[24] Cf. Alfaro, "The Dual Aspect of Faith", p. 59.

[25] "Constitution on Divine Revelation," ibid., p. 114. Cf. also, 2 Cn. of Orange, c. 7, DS 377; Vatican I, Const. on Catholic Faith, c. 3, DS 3010).

[26] Jean Mouroux, **I Believe: the personal structure of faith**, trans. by Michael Turner, (New York: Sheed & Ward, 1959), pp. 19-32 and **passim**.

[27] Thomas Aquinas, **S. Th.** I, q. 1, a. 6, ad 3.

[28] Juan Alfaro, S.J. "Supernaturalitas fidei iuxta S. Thomam," **Gregorianum**, 44 (1963), pp. 501-42, 731-88. Abbreviated English translation,

"The Supernaturality of Faith in St. Thomas", **Theology Digest**, 14, pp. 111-16. Also, **idem, Fides, Spes Caritas, II**, (Rome: Gregorian University Press, 1963), esp. pp. 357-78.

29 Alfaro, "The Dual Aspect of Faith," pp. 60-61.

30 Cf. Karl Rahner, **The Church and the Sacraments**, (New York: Herder & Herder, 1963) and numerous articles including, "Christianity and the non-Christian Religions," **Theological Investigations**, Vol. V, (Baltimore: Helicon: 1966), pp. 115-34; "Dogmatic notes on 'Ecclesiological Piety,'" **Ibid.**, pp. 336-65. Cf. Edward Schillebeeckx, **Christ the Sacrament of the Encounter with God** (New York: Sheed & Ward, 1963). Cf. Richard McBrien, **Do We Need the Church?** (New York: Harper & Row, 1969) and **Church: the Continuing Quest** (Paramus, N.J.: Paulist-Newman, 1970). McBrien does not see the Church as the necessary means of the saving presence of Christ among men. Rather it is the community of those elected from the whole of mankind to preach, serve and give witness to the Kingdom of God to which all men are called. Both points of view stress the relativity of the Church as existing purely to be at the service of the Kingdom, and the plan of God to draw all men into the earthly participation in His eternal Trinitarian Life. The main point of difference is in the acknowledgment of the need for Church as the incarnational reality of the Kingdom to which all men are called in a pilgrimage that is intended to encompass the whole race as a visible community moving toward its eventual fullness of unity as the embodied realization of Christ's final victory.

31 Pius XII, **Mystici Corporis, Acta Apostolicae Sedis** 35 (1943), pp. 193-248; cf. esp. p. 199.

32 "Dogmatic Constitution on the Church", 16, **The Documents of Vatican II**, Walter M. Abbott, S.J. ed., p. 35.

33 The traditional distinction of actual from habitual grace would consequently be so interpreted as to do justice to "the unity and nature of the one grace which divinizes the essence, powers and activity of man. All 'actual' graces refer to the one dynamism for human action of the one divinizing grace as offered (actual grace for justification) or as already accepted (actual grace for merit on the part of the justified person). They are only distinguished from one another by the different degrees of actually vital acceptance of this one grace by man (grace for mere faith, for faith in hope, for love which integrates faith into itself). Karl Rahner, "Grace", **Sacramentum Mundi**, 2, p. 420.

34 Cf. "The Dogmatic Constitution on the Church," #16; "The Pastoral Constitution on the Church in the Modern World," #22, "The Decree on the Church's Missionary Activity," #7; also the "Declaration on Religious Freedom" and the "Declaration on the Relationship of the Church to non-Christian Religions."

35 Arnold Toynbee, **Christianity Among the Religions of the World** (New York: Charles Scribner, 1957), pp. 95ff.

36 Hans Küng, "The World Religions in God's Plan of Salvation," **Christian Revelation and World Religions**, Joseph Neuner, ed., (London: Burns and Oates, 1967), pp. 38-41.

37 Hendrik Kraemer, **The Christian Message in a Non-Christian World** (London: Edinburgh House Press, published for the International Missionary Council, 1938).

38 Karl Barth, **Church Dogmatics**, Vol. I, 2, 17, and Vol. 1. 60, 3 (Edinburgh: T. & T. Clarke, 1956), pp. 280-361.

39 Piet Fransen, "How can non-Christians find Salvation?" in **Chris-**

tian Revelation and World Religions, pp. 81ff. Cf. also the writings of Danielou, Congar and de Lubac in this same volume.

⁴⁰ Mircea Eliade, Patterns in Comparative Religion, (New York: Sheed & Ward, 1958), p. 30.

⁴¹ H. R. Schlette, Towards a Theology of Religions, (New York: Herder & Herder, 1966), p. 38.

⁴² Karl Rahner, "History of the World and Salvation-History," Theological Investigations, Vol. V, p. 109.

⁴³ Karl Rahner, "Is Christianity an 'Absolute Religion?'", in Grace and Freedom (New York: Herder & Herder, 1969), p. 83; cf. also "Christianity and the Non-Christian Religions", Theological Investigations, Vol. V, p. 121.

⁴⁴ "Christianity and the Non-Christian Religions," ibid., p. 126.

⁴⁵ Ibid., p. 128.

⁴⁶ Ibid., p. 133.

⁴⁷ Schlette, Towards a Theology of Religions, p. 90.

⁴⁸ Charles Davis, God's Grace in History (New York: Sheed & Ward, 1966), pp. 89-124.

⁴⁹ Ibid., p. 118.

Alfaro, Juan, S.J. *Fides, Spes, Caritas. Adnotationes in Tractatum de Virtutibus Theologicis.* 3 vols. I, II. Romae: Pontificia Universitas Gregoriana, 1963.

Alfaro, Juan, S.J. "The Dual Aspect of Faith: Entrusting Oneself to God and Acceptance of the Christian Message," *Man as Man and Believer.* New York: Paulist, 1967, pp. 53-66.

Aubert, Roger. *Le Problème de l'Acte de Foi.* Louvain: E. Warny, 1958.

Balthasar, Hans Urs Von. *A Theological Anthropology.* Translated from the German. New York: Sheed & Ward, 1967.

Bulst, Werner, S.J. *Revelation.* Tr. Bruce Vawter, C.M. New York: Sheed & Ward, 1965.

Christian Revelation and World Religions. Ed. Joseph Neuner. London: Burns & Oates, 1967.

Cirne-Lima, Carlos. *Personal Faith.* Tr. G Richard Dimler, S.J. New York: Herder & Herder, 1965.

Constitutio dogmatica, "Dei Filius," de fide catholica. First Vatican Council (1870), 3rd session, c. 3: *De Fide.* DS 3008-3014.

Cuttat, Jacques-Albert. *The Encounter of Religions.* Tr. Pierre de Fontnouvelle with Evis McGrew. New York: Desclée, 1960.

Davis, Charles. *Christ and the World Religions.* London: Hodder & Stoughton, 1970.

Davis, Charles. *God's Grace in History.* New York: Sheed & Ward, 1966.

Dogmatic Constitution on the Church (*Lumen Gentium*) in *The Documents of Vatican II.* Ed. Walter M. Abbott, S.J. New York: Guild Press, 1966, pp. 14-99.

Dogmatic Constitution on Divine Revelation (*Dei Verbum*) in *The Documents of Vatican II,* pp. 111-28, esp. pp. 111-14. Cf.also in the same volume: Declaration on the Relationship of the Church to non-Christian Religions, pp. 660-68; Declaration on Religious Liberty, pp. 675-96; Decree on the Church's Missionary Activity, pp. 584-630; The Pastoral Constitution on the Church in the Modern World (*Gaudium et Spes*), pp. 199-308.

Donceel, Joseph, S.J. "Second Thoughts on the Nature of God," *Thought* 46 (1971), pp. 346-70. Condensed version reprinted as: "Can God never change?", *Theology Digest* 20 (1972), pp. 207-12.

Dulles, Avery, S.J. *The Dimensions of the Church.* Westminster, Md.: Newman, 1967.

Dulles, Avery, S.J. *Revelation Theology.* New York: Herder & Herder, 1969.

Durrwell, F. X. *The Mystery of Christ and the Apostolate.* Tr. Edward Quinn. London and New York: Sheed and Ward, 1972.

Eliade, Mircea. *Patterns in Comparative Religion.* Tr. Rosemary Sheed. New York: Sheed & Ward, 1958.

Faith; Its Nature and Meaning. Papers of the Maynooth Union Summer School, 1970. Ed. Paul Surlis. Dublin: Gill and Macmillan, 1972.

Latourelle, René, S.J. *Theology of Revelation.* Translated from the French. Staten Island, N.Y.: Alba House, 1966.

McBrien, Richard. *Church, the Continuing Quest.* Paramus, N.J.: Newman, 1970.

McBrien, Richard. *Do We Need the Church?* New York: Harper & Row, 1969.

Monden, Louis. *Faith: Can Man Still Believe?* Tr. Joseph Donceel, S.J. New York: Sheed & Ward, 1970.
Moran, Gabriel. *Theology of Revelation.* New York: Herder & Herder, 1966.
Mouroux, Jean. *I Believe: the personal structure of faith,* Tr. Michael Turner. New York: Sheed & Ward, 1959.

Pius XII, Encyclical Letter on the Mystical Body of Christ (*Mystici Corporis,* 1943) DS 3800-3822. English translation. Washington, D.C.: N.C.W.C., 1943.

Rahner, Karl. "Anonymous Christians," *Theological Investigations,* VI. Baltimore: Helicon, 1969, pp. 390-98.
Rahner, Karl. "Atheism and Implicit Christianity," *Theological Investigations,* IX. New York: Herder & Herder, 1972, pp. 145-64.
Rahner, Karl. "The Christian among unbelieving relations," *Theological Investigations,* III. Baltimore: Helicon, 1967, pp. 355-72.
Rahner, Karl. "Christianity and the non-Christian Religions," *Theological Investigations,* V. Baltimore: Helicon, 1966, pp. 115-34.
Rahner, Karl *The Church and the Sacraments.* Tr. W. J. O'Hara. New York: Herder & Herder, 1963.
Rahner, Karl. "Current Problems in Christology," *Theological Investigations,* I. Baltimore: Helicon, 1963, pp. 149-200.
Rahner, Karl, "Dogmatic Notes on Ecclesiological Piety," *Theological Investigations,* V, pp. 336-65.
Rahner, Karl, & Alfaro, Juan. "Faith," *Sacramentum Mundi,* 2. New York: Herder & Herder, 1968, pp. 310-26.
Rahner, K., Berger, K., & Auer, J. "Grace," *Sacramentum Mundi,* 2, pp. 409-24.
Rahner, K. "History of the World and Salvation History," *Theological Investigations,* V, pp. 97-114.
Rahner, Karl. "Is Christianity an 'Absolute Religion'?," in *Grace in Freedom.* Tr. Hilda Graef. New York: Herder & Herder, 1969, pp. 81-86.
Rahner, Karl. "On the Theology of the Incarnation," *Theological Investigations,* IV. Baltimore: Helicon, 1966, pp. 105-20.
Rahner, Karl, and Ratzinger, Joseph. *Revelation and Tradition.* Tr. W. J. O'Hara. New York: Herder & Herder, 1966.
Rahner Karl. "Theology and Anthropology," in *The Word in History.* Ed. T. Patrick Burke. New York: Sheed & Ward, 1966, pp. 1-23.
Rahner, Karl. "Theology of the Symbol," *Theological Investigations,* IV, pp. 221-52.
Rahner, Karl. "What does Vatican II teach about Atheism?," *The Pastoral Approach to Atheism.* Ed. K. Rahner. New York: Paulist, 1967, pp. 7-24.

Schiffers, N., Rahner, K. "Revelation," *Sacramentum Mundi,* 5. New York: Herder & Herder, 1970, pp. 342-55.
Schillebeeckx, Edward, O.P. *Christ the Sacrament of Encounter with God.* New York: Sheed & Ward, 1963.
Schlette, H. R. *Towards a Theology of Religions.* New York: Herder & Herder, 1966.
Schnackenburg, R. "Biblical Perspectives of Faith," *Toward a Theology of Christian Faith.* New York: P. J. Kenedy & Sons, 1968, pp. 36-54.
Stokes, Walter E., S.J. "Is God really related to this world?," *Proceedings of the American Catholic Philosophical Association* 39 (1965), pp. 145-51.

Tillich, Paul. *Christianity and the Encounter of the World Religions.* New York: Columbia University Press, 1963.

Walgrave, Jan H. *Unfolding Revelation. The Nature of Doctrinal Development.* Philadelphia: Westminster, 1972.

/ 6 /

Unbelief:
Transcendental Malaise

*Faith is a transcendental grace. It is the gift offered by
God to every man in the very depths of his consciousness,
inviting him to a life-long dialogue with Himself. It is in
fact the fulfillment of the infinite promise implied in that
human nature whereby as "Spirit in the world," man
constitutes himself in living concert with his fellow-men
as he transcends incessantly toward the Absolute Mystery
which is the goal of his striving.*

*The tragedy is that so many men engage in this divine-
human encounter with little or no formal awareness or
acknowledgment of Who it is who calls them to their destiny.
Yet it is not unrelieved tragedy, since even in their unin-
formed consciences, multitudes are following Christ as
faithful sons of the Father Whose very name they fail to
recognize or, out of misunderstanding, might even re-
pudiate.*

*The more poignant tragedy is the "infidelity of the faith-
ful," "the unbelief of the believer." For in the very same
depths of his conscious being to which God calls by His
gift of faith, there is a fatal flaw, a perverse proneness to
say No! to Him Who is the meaning of his existence. This
is the primal sin in the sense that it is the source and
inner substance of every form that human sinfulness takes.
Yet of course the proneness is not personal sin unless it is
willfully implemented.*

We are sinful redeemed men, at the same time justified and sinners, *simul justus et peccator.* This theme of the Reformation was rejected by the Council of Trent in the strict meaning it had for the Reformers. But it can be given a meaning that Catholics are able to accept. In this ecumenical age, we should even try to find a broader sense that could encompass both Protestant and Catholic understandings. This becomes more possible in the enlarged meaning of Faith that recent Catholic theology has both regained and further developed· For it represents an even broader middle ground which is also occupied by modern Protestant theology as it evolves in its understanding of the traditional Reformation concept of Faith.

"The unbelief of the believer": this is the transcendental malaise. It is coextensive with the universal offer of saving faith to all men, because it stems from a defect in every man to whom that offer is made and by whom it is accepted. Thus unbelief is an attribute, not of some, but of all. It seems to be present more conspicuously in those who outwardly reject Christian faith. Actually genuine unbelief is more discernible in those who outwardly accept Christian faith, for there the deviations from authentic faith stand out in bolder relief. We shall better understand the phenomenon of unbelief in our fellow-man when we begin to understand its occurrence in ourselves. We shall at the same time more fully appreciate that all men without exception are 'believers,' that the dialectic of belief-unbelief is not limited to some of us, but is omnipresent in the human species.

To develop a truly theological understanding of unbelief, it is necessary to treat it not merely psychologically or sociologically, but within the theological dimension of faith itself. Psychology, sociology and philosophy will contribute to this understanding, but always within the comprehension of man which Revelation alone can furnish. It will be an insight into unbelief as intrinsic to the man of faith, the believer. Accordingly, it will be derived from an exploration of the properties of faith which make it vulnerable and open to deviations as well as from a probing of the existential situation of man the believer to uncover the tension that is disclosed in the lived dialectic of belief-unbelief.

Faith and Freedom

The situation of faith is in its deepest reality the confronting of two freedoms, human and divine. It is the high point of man's self-realization as the being who is freedom, whose identity is constantly being invoked in committing himself to the life-project of a son of God. As the freest of human acts, the norm by which the freedom of all others is judged, it is the most personal, fully possessed and sure; and yet at the same time it is the most precarious and least to be taken for granted. For it is shrouded in the mystery of the infinite and finite persons involved.

Faith is not some "thing" that is given to man and held on to as a possession. It is rather a saving relationship of man with God, ever proceeding from and dependent on the initiative of God, even while it is the human individual's most profoundly personal response to that divine call. Like any other inter-personal relationship, it cannot be taken for granted, for that very attitude is not only a menace to its well-being, it is a sign of its deterioration.

Supremely beyond all other relations, man's relation with God is not at his own disposal. Faith is God's gracious free gift to man, not only initially, but always. It comes to him as a summons, ever fresh and new, totally unearned, from the incomprehensible abyss of God's infinite goodness and love. Man's faith can only be a response to this unfailing yet undeserved invitation, fittingly as diffident as it is grateful. As a consequence, he must acknowledge its ultimately precarious and imperilled status, delicately balanced as it is at the meeting point of God's free grace and man's freedom.

Man's freedom is the key to the understanding of faith, and of unbelief as an intrinsic possibility for the believer. Its significance can be stated so broadly because freedom is what man is, it is not merely something man has. Man is constituted by his freedom.

That man is constituted by his freedom is a thesis of contemporary Christian anthropology which we have already explained and defended. For there we recognized that man is that being in this world who uniquely constitutes himself in a process of self-transcendence by which he develops toward greater self-actualization: self-appropriation, -possession, and -disposition. This occurs in a dialectic of interchange with the persons and things of his world, and is transacted within the horizon of the Absolute Mystery of Being. This process of self-actualization, by which the individual participates in a common history with others in the human community, is a growth in freedom because it is a growth in the individual's self-appropriation and therefore in his capacity of self-disposition: to donate himself to or withhold himself from other persons. By his freedom, man is capable not only of a highly personal union of love with other human beings. He is open to its possibility, if given, with that Absolute Other toward Whom he transcends in all his other personal relationships. Faith is the God-given capacity to realize that possibility.

Man's freedom is therefore not merely one of his functions, the operation of one of his faculties. It is rather the measure to which he has effectually 'come to himself,' has realized himself and is able to determine and to commit the self which has thus come to be. All other meanings of 'freedom' are more specific derivations of that fundamental "existential freedom."

Friendship or the love-relationship is the fullest flowering and expression of that freedom, since it is the self-gift to another which freedom enables. The absolute fulfillment of the freedom of man is offered in the gift of Faith whereby man is empowered to share in a mutual self-giving with Him Who is the Absolute Ground and Goal of his existence. This relation calls forth the fullest possible engagement of man's freedom inasmuch as he is challenged to give himself to the One Whose infinite fullness of truth and goodness is the very source and end of his freedom. It is also on this deepest level of his relation with the divine Person that a man constitutes himself in his 'fundamental option' or life-orientation, whether it be done with explicit reference to God or only implicitly.

Because freedom is one with who and what we are, it shares in the mystery of the self. Since the self is always and inescapably the subject of every act by which we would know it, it ultimately eludes our grasp, our comprehension. For that reason we cannot capture it in our reflection and bring it under our full conscious control. All this applies to our freedom and accordingly to our faith, in which our freedom is most fully realized. Consequently we can never be sure of the faith we possess, we can never make it the object of a secure scrutiny. The quality of its motivation, its purity or impurity, its depth or shallowness, though surely not beyond our knowing, will ultimately escape our definitive judgment. What we believe and hope to be true faith, may indeed be unbelief.

This ambiguity of our faith stems from the freedom which is its root in the depths of the subjects we are and constantly become. For faith is freedom in action in the sense that it is the commitment of ourselves to others or to another as the peak exercise and expression of our freedom. Faith, whether human or divine, is first and essentially inter-subjective, involving attitudes of trust, confidence, love, obedience, respect and all those factors that comprise free self-giving and acceptance of the other in inter-personal relations. Therefore it is inevitably immersed in the mystery of the selves engaged, their hiddenness and obscurity for themselves as well as for one another.

The Intellectual Assent of Faith: "Restless Conviction"

Faith has another dimension which is especially emphasized when it is called 'belief.' It is the primarily intellectual dimension. It has to do with what we believe as distinguished from the one we believe in. It is subsidiary to the personal dimension inasmuch as we have faith-in-an-assertion because we have faith-in-a-Thou who makes the assertion. The assertion is invariably some form of self-revelation even when the subject-matter might be quite other, for it will always solicit our acceptance primarily for motives intrinsic to the character of the person who witnesses and not for the reasons intrinsic to the assertion itself.

What is of significance at this point is that freedom and ambiguity suffuse the believer's intellectual assent to the witnessed assertion just as radically as they pervade his personal commitment to its very grounding in his subjectivity. This is clearly seen even in the traditional Catholic theological understanding of faith which stressed the role of intellectual assent, often to the understatement of its other more personalist aspects.

St. Thomas, whose notion of faith is more nuanced and balanced than that of most of his theological successors, still belongs in the intellectualist tradition. He defines the act of Faith as "an act of the intellect assenting to the Divine Truth at the command of the will, moved by the grace of God" (*S. Th.*, II-II, 2, 9, c.). The voluntary assent of faith is not a purely intellectual judgment extrinsically affected by the intervention of the will. It is rather an operation emanating from intellect and will conjointly, for though it is a judgment or assent of intellect, its motivation is the value of assenting to which only the will can respond. In effect, through the will freedom is inserted at the very source of the intellectual assent of faith, and with it the ambivalence and ambiguity which accompany what is radically free. Thus, in spite of his intellectualist leaning, Aquinas maintains the strong role of freedom in faith which arises from the more ancient Christian tradition originating in the scriptures themselves.

He achieves the same result in even more intriguing fashion in a different though related context. It has to do with his analysis of St. Augustine's definition of the act of believing: "to believe is to deliberate in conjunction with assenting" (*credere est cum assensione cogitare*). It represents his rather successful effort to reconcile the strongly affective Augustinian psychology of faith with the rigorously intellectualist Aristotelian theory of science.

St. Thomas wishes to situate faith among the ways of knowing in a manner that respects its uniqueness and, at the same time, Aristotle's criteria of knowing. Thus faith is different from a state of pure doubt or suspended assent, because it involves the making of a judgment. It is distinct from opinion or probable judgment, because its assent is firm and sure. Yet it is not the same as the certain assents of understanding self-evident principles or of demonstrative reasoning, because they are based on evidence which is intrinsic to the propositions asserted to be true, whether known immediately or mediately. The motive for the certain assent of faith is the testimony of the witness which is extrinsic to the proposition accepted as worthy of belief.

Reasoning is accompanied by deliberation which, if the reasoning is demonstrative (able to yield certainty based on necessity), will terminate in the certain assent to the conclusion. The intellect rests, as it were, in the truth of the conclusion seen now to be implied in the previously grasped truth of the premises, and the momentum of its restless inquiry or deliberation is halted in the possession of evident truth. In contrast, the process of inquiry that preceded the certain assent of faith is not put to rest in the achievement of the faith judgment or commitment. For the assent of faith is not the intellectually satisfying result of an immediate understanding of truth or of a demonstrated conclusion whose truth is seen to be interiorly implicated in truths already accepted.

The person who believes gives his firm assent not because he is responding to preponderant evidence which satisfies him intellectually. Rather he is surrendering in his will to the values perceived in the person who witnesses and therefore by his free assent to the statement which that person proposes as the truth. The response to the person who witnesses is a strong total commitment which expresses itself in a firm adherence to his testimony as true. The assent of the intellect has in effect been captured by the will which has succumbed to motives proper to itself. As a consequence, the believer remains intellectually dissatisfied in the absence of adequate intrinsic evidence. Despite the firmness of his adherence to the truth of what he believes, his intellect continues in its restless process of inquiry. Assent and deliberation coexist, and because the intellect has not been satisfied by its own proper motives, its faith assent can even be accompanied by doubts arising from the absence of such evidence. Thus by its very internal dynamic, belief is open to unbelief. In fact, it would appear that the inclination to unbelief is built into its very structure.

St. Thomas' definition and description of the act of

faith are incomplete in the light of the more recent developments in the theology of faith, but it is authentic as far as it goes and quite readily assimilated into the more complete notion. This is evident in the number of contemporary Catholic theologians who have used Aquinas' treatment of faith as the point of departure for their own. More than likely this follows from the fidelity with which he roots his theology in the biblical sources.

The very constancy of his intellectualism leads him to acknowledge the imperfection of faith as a form of knowledge. For though believing or the act of faith is an operation attributed to the intellect, since it is concerned with adherence to the truth, that very adherence or assent is not caused by intellectual perception of the intrinsic evidence of the truth believed. Thomas knows from scripture as well as from his own Christian experience that faith is "the evidence of things not seen" (Heb 11:1). It is precisely an assent to a truth that is not evident. For that reason, as we have considered, it is the freest of all judgments. It is quite uncoerced. In St. Thomas' phraseology, though an act of the intellect, it is "commanded by the will, moved by the grace of God." It is the most profound instance of man determining himself, disposing of himself and surrendering himself in response to the self-gift of Another. For that reason it is able to be the most decisive commitment of himself, body and spirit, intellect and will, and thereby able to give rise to the most certain conviction. Yet it is not free from anxiety and doubt.

The same lack of evidence which allows for the assent of faith to be the freest and most committed also leaves the believer intellectually discontented and vulnerable to the temptation to disbelieve. Human faith is a continual test of our capacity to trust the person we love, a person whom we see and hear as he witnesses to the truth he asks us to accept on his word. Divine or Christian faith is a much severer test, since it challenges us to trust a Person we love Whom we do not see or hear, a Person who is transcendent to every earthly experience and whose witness is communicated to us always through intermediaries whose credentials as His spokesman are often far from compelling in their evidence.

Add to this the strong bias of our culture against faith in the Transcendent which surrounds the Christian believer like an atmosphere and insinuates itself through the pores of his mind and feelings. Confronting the same enigmas and threats, the same enormous evils and inequities as do his unbelieving contemporaries, it is inevitable that he too be beset by uncertainty and anxious doubts: in a word, by the temptation to unbelief. This could be a reason for dark pessimism were this temptation not itself an intrinsic element in the very existence of faith and a condition of its deepening and growth.

Unbelief as an Existential Dimension of Faith

It is possible to pursue even further the question of unbelief as an interior factor within the faith situation. This would involve a theological probing of the existential context of man the believer as that is able to be known from revealed sources.

Is doubt a derogation from the perfection of faith, as it has usually been regarded, or is it not rather an inevitable counterpart to faith? Can it be that doubt plays a necessary role in the dialectical process by which faith lives and grows?

This issue has been faced perhaps most directly by Paul Tillich who deals with it in the context of the Protestant principle of justification by faith.

For Tillich, "faith is the state of being ultimately concerned."[1] Though the content of faith matters infinitely for the life of the believer, it does not matter for the formal definition of faith. A concern claims ultimacy if it "demands the total surrender of him who accepts this claim, and it promises total fulfillment."[2] The content of the demand and promise accepted in the act of faith can be expressed in symbols, none of which is itself ultimate.

Faith is an act of the total personality and includes all the elements of personal life: reason, emotion, and the rest. In the past, attempts have been made to reduce faith to one or another of these elements. The effect is always a distortion.

For faith tends to transcend all of these even while it includes them all. "It is the unity of every element in the centered self."³

What is important in the content of faith is not the name we give it, e.g., 'God,' but the element of the unconditional and ultimate which characterizes the divine or the holy. Whereas man's experiences, feelings and thoughts are conditioned and finite, he is able in a personal central act to understand the meaning of the ultimate, the unconditional, the infinite. He is thus open to faith by which he does not possess the infinite, but is rather possessed by it. Thus faith is a finite act with all the limitations of its finiteness. Yet those limitations are transcended because in his very faith the man of faith is grasped by and turned to the infinite.

Insofar as the believer is turned toward the ultimate, the infinite, his faith is certain. The infinite is as immediate to him as his own self, since it is the self as self-transcending, as grasped by and turned toward the infinite. But insofar as the infinite is received by a finite being and understood in terms of contents that are without this immediate awareness, faith is uncertain and inevitably so. For the contents that express ultimacy are not themselves ultimate any more than they are immediate. Therefore to accept those contents as expressive of what is ultimate, whether one has made a 'god' of power, pleasure, patriotism, or Biblical God, there is always a risk involved and therefore courage in taking the risk. Since one's commitment to something as ultimate is the source of the meaning of one's existence, the risk of failure is the risk of fundamental despair, of meaninglessness. Yet since ultimacy must always be given some concrete expression and content, faith can never be without the element of risk and so must always involve the element of courage to face the ever-present risk of radical failure.

Whereas doubt is incompatible with faith understood as belief that something is true,⁴ it is a necessary element of faith understood as being ultimately concerned. It is part and parcel of the risk of such a faith. This is what Tillich calls "existential doubt." It is neither the methodological doubt of the scientist nor the skeptic's attitude of rejecting every concrete truth. Rather it is the pervasive awareness of the element of insecurity in every existential truth, of the unavoidable risk of failure in any effort to seek ultimate meaning for one's life in a concrete someone or something.

Thus doubt is not a negation of faith. It is an invariable factor in the dynamic of faith. It is the personal awareness of risk in the face of the threat of meaninglessness and is thus needed to evoke the courage with which faith affirms its meaning as an expression of ultimate concern. "Existential doubt and faith are poles of the same reality, the state of ultimate concern."[5] Therefore serious doubt is a confirmation of faith since it demonstrates the definitive seriousness, that is, the ultimacy of the concern.

Following the example of his teacher, Martin Kaehler, Tillich was led to reinterpret the Protestant principle of justification by faith as referring not only to the religious-ethical but also to the religious-intellectual life. "Not only he who is in sin but also he who is in doubt is justified through faith."[6] He who doubts, doubts from faith, faith in the truth. He who does so from an attitude of ultimate concern is justified by his "faith," the divine is present to him, and he is in effect affirming God even in the very act of denying him. Thus it is not in the "work," that is, the concrete content by which the faith is expressed, by which one is justified, but rather in the very faith itself, that is, the attitude of ultimate concern. "Just as you are justified as a *sinner* (though unjust, you are just), so in the status of doubt you are in the status of truth."[7]

Man at Once Sinner and Justified: Protestant and Catholic Interpretations

The Council of Trent rejected the Reformation formula: *simul justus et peccator,* as it was understood then, and Catholics must continue to refuse a Protestant interpretation which conflicts with the fundamental Catholic understanding of justification. However, an attempt to determine if there is a sense that is acceptable to the Catholic theological consciousness may further our understanding of the dialectic of belief and unbelief operating in the existential situation of man the believer. We must at least listen to the Protestant Christian speaking of his experience of justification and be ready to learn from him.

The radical religious insight of the Reformation would seem to be the realization of man's absolute and perpetual dependence on the justifying mercy of God before Whom he stands always as a sinner. No work of his can play any role in effecting his justification. Rather he has been justified purely and exclusively by Christ's redeeming death, as the work of God's wholly gratuitous merciful favor. Thus man knows by faith and is certain that he is indeed saved, yet he knows equally well that in spite of being justified, he is still in himself only a sinner before God. Thus he is "justified and a sinner at the same time."

The Catholic Christian must agree with the Protestant that his redemption is purely the gratuitous work of God in Jesus Christ and that no work of his could contribute to the effectuation of this result. Thus justification is by faith insofar as it is personal acceptance of and commitment to the Savior God Who has received and alone could receive man into His friendship and the sharing of His life. However, what God has wrought in man's history through Jesus Christ is a true "new creation" by which man the sinner has been interiorly transformed into a son of the Father, into a "new man" who has left the "old man" behind.

This divine deed of man's justification is not necessarily reflected in an experience which coincides with it. It will have repercussions in experience, but the decisive and effective factor is the justifying action of God which no human experience or formulation can approximate. Rather Catholic faith attributes to God the glory of genuinely transforming man to the core of his reality from sinner to son, divinizing him, even though his experience may not duplicate the radicality of this renovation.

In truth, the justified man has left behind his status of sinner and rebel and has been interiorly made new. God's justifying grace has vanquished sin in him. He is no longer sinner now that he is justified. That is the objective effect of the deed we must credit to God's saving merciful love.

Is there, however, any sense which a Catholic theologian can assign to the formula: "sinner and justified at the same time"? Yes, it has to do with our subjective awareness and certitude of our personal salvation and our inner state of fidelity to God. Catholic theology clearly distinguishes *justification* from *salvation* in its definitive achievement for each individual toward which we move through our lives "with fear and trembling."

Trent teaches contrary to the Reformers that we cannot be absolutely certain of our own individual salvation. We cannot appropriate ourselves even in faith so completely that we can with assurance assert our present condition as one of the saved. Yet in spite of this we can and must have Christian hope and trust in the unspeakable mercy of God toward us. This strong yet precariously balanced hope yields God the total glory of our salvation which it refuses to compromise by the self-sufficiency, at least in appearance, of one who has absolute assurance that he is numbered now among the saved.

This fact that we cannot be certain that we are definitively saved leaves us always under the suspicion, at very least, that in view of our experience of our own fragility and weakness we may very well be unfaithful to our justified status as sons of the Father, that we are, in a word, sinners. This consequence is applicable to the specific context of the Christian as believer, as the man of faith. Thus just as we cannot be certain that, though justified by God's grace, we may yet be sinners and interiorly unfaithful to our God-given status as His sons, so must we likewise acknowledge that, graced as we are by divine faith, we can and indeed very likely may, in the heart of us, be unfaithful to the commitment with which we have freely responded to God's gracious initiative. We can then rightfully be called both believers and unbelievers, *simul fidelis et infidelis.*

This statement hardly seems startling in the light of our common experience of our own infidelity and proneness to unbelief. The significance of it is not the patent fact that we do fall away from the high demands of our Christian calling. It is rather that, even in the Catholic understanding of justification and faith, that falling away is seen as an inevitable correlate within an existential tension or dialectic: man at once justified and sinner, believer and unbeliever.

Unbelief as a Consequence of Concupiscence

Once again within the Catholic theological setting, this conclusion seems to be confirmed by recent refinements of the notion of 'concupiscence.' Like death, concupiscence can be regarded as a natural fact or as a consequence of original sin. Scripture treats it almost exclusively from the latter aspect: that man is concupiscent is a revelation of his sinful condition, for concupiscence is defined as man's proneness to sin even prior to his exercise of free and responsible decision. Yet concupiscence is clearly not to be identified with formal sin and it is present even in justified man.

Karl Rahner is one of those Catholic theologians who have contributed to the recent discussion of concupiscence. In his treatment of concupiscence, Rahner is faithful to his method. He accepts a distinction between nature and grace in which nature occurs as a moment operating within the larger concrete existential context of grace and attempts first to distill the natural component within the supernatural order and then reintegrate the natural factor within its broader setting. In pursuing this method, he discloses concupiscence as a natural attribute of man. As such it may be defined as "man's spontaneous desire, in so far as it precedes his free decision and resists it." Concupiscence belongs to man as 'nature' as opposed to man as 'person'; that is, it belongs to man's permanent structure insofar as this is the principle and antecedent law of his activity as distinguished from man as self-transcending and free spirit whose task is precisely to appropriate his nature and responsibly direct it toward his transcendent goal in a process that constitutes his personal fulfillment. In this context, concupiscence is bivalent, that is, it is man's capacity for spontaneous desire which both precedes and resists his free decision whether that freedom be oriented toward good or toward evil. In this sense, it cannot be called simply 'evil' or 'disorderly,' but rather would appear to be a natural property of man as a spiritual-material nature and a finite creature. To that extent, it can be called morally neutral.

In the Bible and in Christian tradition, however, concupiscence has usually been thought of as sinful desire and as a consequence of original sin. Though the Church has taught that it is natural (DS 1979 ff), it has also taught it represents a deprivation of what God originally intended for man in the state of original justice. Accordingly Rahner attempts to reintegrate his notion of concupiscence as a natural attribute within man's concrete supernatural situation. For every man is *de facto* endowed with a "supernatural existential", that is, an ontologically objective orientation to God as his supernatural end. Moreover each man habitually is offered the grace needed to pursue this end.

Since this supernatural orientation and habitual offer of grace influence and transform man's consciousness as well as his very being, he is not in a state of pure nature either ontologically or psychologically, in his fundamental condition or in his conscious life. Consequently, man experiences the concupiscent desires within himself no longer as merely neutrally bivalent and as a predictable consequence of his finite creaturely nature. Rather they enter his consciousness as alien and contrary to the supernatural orientation of his concrete nature and its promised fulfillment in the habitual invitation implicated in the conferring of justifying grace. Concupiscence remains in its bivalency, that is, it is still the capacity of spontaneous desire in his 'nature' which is prior to and resistant to the personal exercise of his freedom whether for good or for evil. Thereby it is an ever-present factor, even in his justified nature, obstructing and preventing him from appropriating his nature and thus ever fully succeeding in the process of his self-constitution, whether authentically or inauthentically.[9] In our actual situation in the supernatural order, concupiscence operates more significantly in contradiction to our supernatural orientation and therefore to what we ought to be 'authentically.' Consequently it can clearly be designated as a manifestation and a consequence of that originating condition of human inauthenticity which we call 'original sin.'

What are the implications of this notion of 'concupiscence' for our better understanding of the immanence of unbelief in the believer? Hitherto we have considered first those properties of faith in itself which render it vulnerable to unbelief: its freedom which emerges from the mystery of the persons involved and therefore its fullness of commitment along with its obscurity, its ambiguity, its precariousness. Considered primarily in its intellectual component, especially as St. Thomas interpreted it, we have seen that it is intrinsically a firm assent which coexists inevitably with continued inquiry and deliberation that express the intellectual dissatisfaction of the believer whose assent is a response to values loved rather than to evidence perceived. Thus, in anticipation of Tillich's own proposal, doubt or unbelief, at least as a possibility, is seen to belong intrinsically to the faith of the human believer.

In probing the existential situation of the Christian believer as that is understood by a theological reflection on the revealed sources, we explored the dynamics of faith in the larger context of man as justified. We did so by way of considering the Reformation formula of man, in particular, the Christian man, as being "at once justified and a sinner." A Catholic theological analysis and evaluation rejected this as an expression of the objective effect of God's justification of man, but accepted it in a highly nuanced understanding of the ambiguity and uncertainty of our subjective experience and judgment of our actual fidelity to God's justifying grace.

Our study of recent refinements in the Catholic theology of Concupiscence should have deepened our understanding of the sinner the Christian man of faith experiences himself to be. It more profoundly traces the roots of our infidelity and unbelief beyond the intrinsic properties of faith to the fundamental condition of man into whom faith is received. For even though justified, he is subject to concupiscence, to those eruptions of his rebellious nature which obstruct his free adherence to the truth of his being, his full commitment to that Person Whose ineffable love continually calls forth and reveals that truth which constitutes him in the divine life. There is an ambivalence in the heart of man's being which consistently tends to cloud his faith perception and to divert his power of decision from effectively committing himself to his authentic goal. There is an inertia and an impenetrability indigenous to man which does not permit him by his personal freedom totally to integrate what he finds himself to be into his deeds by which he aspires to become that which he is called to be.[10]

Our faith commitment is not expressed to its depths in a series of individual acts whose only link is their successiveness. Our lives are more of a whole. They articulate themselves in a fundamental option or life stance by virtue of which we habitually direct ourselves towards God or are turned away from him. But this deepest orientation of our person is not easily accessible to our reflection. We can survey and estimate with some success the individual acts of our lives, but we can hardly cast more than a measure of light on the profound source of those acts in the dark mystery of our subjectivity. Our scrutiny is circumscribed by the elusiveness of the self which is always *subject* by the obscurity and ambivalence of the freedom from which our commitments arise, but above all by the deceitful insinuations of our concupiscent desires which can make a shambles of our profoundest commitments; or are they not instead the truer expression of those commitments?

The temptation to unbelief should not too easily be dismissed as only a temptation. We can never be sure of our justified status. In the half-hidden and complex springs of our personal decisions and deeds, what appears as an alluring temptation may indeed be the disclosure of an unbelief already embraced in the recesses of our selves.

This gloomy and forbidding portrait is of course not the last word. That is spoken rather in the accents of the hope that is rooted in the triumphant redeeming love of God revealed for us in Jesus Christ "who was put to death for our tresspasses and raised for our justification" (Rm 4:25). We who have been given faith must live by hope, but always humbly. For though we hope that we are and shall always remain faithful sons of the Father, we cannot cease to fear that we may be something quite different, "as long as the basic roots of our heart continue to bring forth fruit which is not really the fruit of the Spirit."[11] In the specific terms of our problem, we can never boast that we are believers, and not like those others, "the unbelievers." For we can never be able to say for certain that the temptations to disbelieve, to betray our faith-commitment, which are not few, are not so much assaults on the citadel of our faith from the outside, as surfacings of a betrayal that has already taken place within.

We are always merely "on the way." What we strive for in hope, we have not yet become. As justified, we are already in Christ what we are called to become. As concupiscent, free men, we are sinners, who are able at any time to nullify the victory which we are continually being invited to share but which will not be definitively ours until the end. We live always in the tension of righteousness and unrighteousness, of faith and unbelief.

The Unbelief of the Believer

We may conclude this chapter on a note analogous to and interrelated with one of the main themes of the last chapter. There we discussed, in the light of faith as a transcendental grace, that many men who appear to be 'unbelievers,' lacking or perhaps even rejecting Christian faith and the reality of the God Christians worship, may actually be 'anonymous Christians' who in effect have accepted and are responding affirmatively to the divine offer of faith and God's free gift of Himself in the pre-reflective depths of their consciousnesses. Similarly here we can conclude that many of us who seem to be faithful Christian believers may actually be 'unbelievers' because we are in effect disloyal to our apparent Christian commitment at the deeper level of our fundamental option where the process of constituting our real selves is taking place. More likely we are believers, really and not only apparently, whose basic life orientation is still somewhat unresolved and less than decisive. We have still not yet "let ourselves go" towards God, though His Self-gift to us is total and unconditional, for we are too cowardly and small-hearted to surrender ourselves without reservation. Though believers, we are unbelievers still keeping a portion of ourselves to ourselves, lest we lose all. We still do not really believe that it is only at the cost of losing ourselves for Christ's sake that we shall gain ourselves. And so we do not have to look beyond ourselves to find an 'unbeliever.'

Before we approach the dialogue with the so-called 'unbeliever' and hope to do so honestly and with an open mind and heart, it is important that we first undergo this process of self-discovery and self-criticism. Before we dare to confront the unbeliever who is the other, we must first face the full truth of the unbeliever in ourselves. When we are able openly to acknowledge that truth, then we shall be able to engage in an honest dialogue with the other, free of self-righteous distortions or condescension. Having owned up to the greater evil of our own unbelief, we can talk with the humility and candor that will more easily permit the truth to be our motive and our goal, rather than self-justification, domination over others, or some other irrelevant and unworthy objective. In a word, our attitude should be that of the father who wanted his loved son to be healed: "I do believe; help my unbelief" (Mk 9:24).

Notes and references

[1] Paul Tillich, **Dynamics of Faith** (New York: Harper, 1957), p. 1.

[2] **Ibid**

[3] **Ibid.**, p. 8.

[4] On the contrary, cf. the Thomistic account given earlier in the chapter.

[5] Paul Tillich, **The Protestant Era** (Chicago: University of Chicago Press, 1957), p. 22.

[6] **Ibid.**, p. x.

[7] **Ibid.**, p. xi.

[8] Karl Rahner, "The Theological Concept of Concupiscentia", **Theological Investigations**, Vol. I., p. 360.

[9] One's self-constitution is authentic when one's 'fundamental option' is in accord with the constitutive orientation of his being, viz., God as the horizon of Absolute Mystery Who factually has freely come forth from his hiddenness to offer Himself as our supernatural End, elevating us to such a possibility by investing us from the beginning with a supernatural existential.

[10] Karl Rahner, "The Theological Concept of Concupiscentia", p. 375.

11 Karl Rahner, "Justified and Sinner at the Same Time," **Theological Investigations**, VI, (Baltimore: Helicon, 1969), p. 227.

Gibson, Arthur. *The Faith of the Atheist.* New York: Harper & Row, 1968.

Metz, Johannes B. "Freedom as a threshold problem between philosophy and theology," *Philosophy Today* 10 (1966), pp. 264-79.
Metz, Johannes B. "Unbelief as a Theological Problem," *The Church and the World.* New York: Paulist, 1965, pp. 59-77.

Novak, Michael. *A Time to Build.* New York: Macmillan, 1964.
Novak, Michael. *Belief and Unbelief.* New York: Macmillan, 1965.

Pastoral Approach to Atheism, The. Ed. Karl Rahner. New York: Paulist, 1967.

Rahner, Karl. "Justified and Sinner at the Same Time," *Theological Investigations,* VI. Baltimore: Helicon, 1969, pp. 218-30.
Rahner, Karl. "Salvation," *Sacramentum Mundi,* 5. New York: Herder & Herder, 1970, pp.405-9.
Rahner, Karl. "The Theological Concept of Concupiscentia," *Theological Investigations,* I. Baltimore: Helicon, 1961, pp.347-82.
Rahner, Karl. "True Freedom," in *Grace in Freedom.* Tr. Hilda Graef. New York: Herder & Herder, 1969, pp. 203-64.
Richardson, Herbert W. "The Nature of Unbelief," *Continuum* 5 (1967), pp. 106-17.

Tillich, Paul. *Dynamics of Faith.* New York: Harper, 1957.
Tillich, Paul. *The Protestant Era.* Chicago: University of Chicago Press, 1957.

Unhjem, Arne. *Dynamics of Doubt.* A Preface to Tillich. Philadelphia: Fortress, 1966.

Van Riet, Georges. "Unbelief Today: its Christian source," *Louvain Studies* 1 (1967), pp. 143-57.

The Christian-Humanist Dialogue

Prelude to the Dialogue:
The Role of Atheism, Positive and/or Negative

Like unbelief, atheism has always been with us. It seems to be a correlate of theism as unbelief is for faith. Whereas unbelief is a primordial defect in man and serves no positive purpose except to remind us of our common fragility, atheism is not reducible to pure unbelief and has in fact performed a medicinal role in the history of theism. It would be wrong and harmful to overlook the enormous injury that atheism, especially in its organized forms, has done to men, above all in our age. It is not our intention to make that mistake. However, in the spirit of dialogue and the desire to be open to truth wherever it is to be found, we would be doing a disservice to all concerned, including ourselves, to fail to acknowledge the truth which atheism confesses at least implicitly.

Herbert W. Richardson distinguishes various forms of atheism and his distinctions can aid us to make our point. First of all, he divides public from private atheism. The latter is professed by those individuals "who choose to oppose the religious beliefs of a predominantly religious culture."[1] Public atheism, which has become more predominant in our age, is one which pervades an entire culture and is therefore expressive of its prevailing ethos. In searching for the prophetic role of atheism and for the type that fulfills that role, he distinguishes an atheism of concern from an atheism of boredom and an atheism of protest. The first of these is truly prophetic because it antici-pates the future by critically opposing the religious assump-tions of a declining culture, especially as they express them-selves in the conception of God or "holy ultimates" of that culture. This prophetic species of atheism is quite clearly significative of an epoch of cultural transition.

The other two types of atheism are not prophetic be-cause they are in one or another way tributary to the matrix of meaning, what Richardson calls the "intellectus," of the declining culture. The "atheism of boredom" is a symptom of the decay of the traditional "intellectus" rather than a force effecting its demise. The "atheism of protest" is a negation which necessarily lives off the cultural affirmations which it only exists to oppose. Both of these are to some extent constant factors in every cultural situation. They are not transitional because they do not signify the end of an epoch. They are not prophetic because they have nothing to do with bringing the new situation into being.

The "atheism of concern" is of theological significance because it raises new questions and seeks new truths within a new 'intellectus' or cultural matrix of meaning. This inevit-ably compels a reexamination and rethinking of the religious conceptions which express the sacredly ultimate presuppo-sitions on which a culture is based. Hopefully this ought to lead to a more adequate conception of God for the new age.[2]

There is probably no pure example of an "atheism of concern" which is totally free of elements of the other two types. However, it seems clear enough that the atheistic humanisms we have studied are in the main expressions of the intellectual and social forces that have brought about the cultural revolution of our time. For that reason we have had to cope with them in erecting an adequate Christian anthropology for the future and simultaneously an adequate theology or understanding of God. In formulating our theo-logical affirmations, it would be well to be attentive to their 'a-theological' negations.

Does Christian theology make room for atheistic denials within its own process of development? The answer to that question requires a multitude of qualifications, but it cannot be simply negative.

An axiomatic statement of St. Thomas remains as cogent and relevant now as when he first uttered it. "The act of the believer terminates in the reality and not in the proposition."[3] This is the classical statement of theological realism, the traditional Catholic position. As Aquinas goes on to say in the same text, faith resembles scientific knowing in seeking to understand and in affirming the reality for which its concepts and language merely serve as the media or vehicles of expression and communication. The authentic object of Christian faith is the Divine Mystery Who graciously communicates Himself to man. The value of the doctrines by which that faith attempts to express itself is purely relative to the Divine Mystery and those doctrines are in principle perpetually inadequate as the formulation of that Mystery. Like the minds of those who formulate those doctrines and those to whom they are addressed, the doctrines themselves cannot surpass the limitations of the culture and period in which they are proposed.

This does not compromise the divinely guaranteed truth of defined dogmas, which assures their continuity with and fidelity to the revelation. It is rather the inescapable recognition of their inadequacy to the Absolute Mystery which they seek to express and of their consequent developing character. Even more must we acknowledge the inadequate and tentative nature of the teachings of theologians which have not yet matured to the point of meriting definition by the Church.

God is essentially and eternally the Absolute Mystery Who eludes our comprehension and the clear grasp of our understanding. This will remain equally true in the beatific vision as it is true of our present pilgrim state. For God is the infinite abyss into which we are drawn in the process of transcendence by which we are constituted as spirits in the world. By His gratuitous initiative He has come near to us and made us participants in His own life by a saving grace afforded us through the redemptive incarnation of His Son. Yet it is still the infinite and incomprehensible

God Who has approached us in awesome intimacy to draw us into the Absolute Mystery that He is and thus fulfill the utmost possibility of our being by which we perpetually transcend toward Him as the ground and goal of our being.

The essential incomprehensibility of the divine Mystery has been acknowledged by the basic intuitions of all the great religions of man which have dared only to call Him the Nameless, the One Who is beyond all human categories and distinctions. It is the necessary agnosticism of theology proclaimed by St. Thomas: "The supreme knowledge which man has of God is to know that he does not know God, in so far as he knows that what God is surpasses all that we can understand of him" (*De Pot.*, 7, 5).

The strict mysteries (*mysteria stricte dicta*) of Catholic faith, viz., the Blessed Trinity, the Incarnation and the grace and glory in which man shares in the divine life, are so many facets of the single Divine Mystery. They express the inaccessible Reality Which has revealed definitively in Jesus Christ the Will to communicate and give Himself to man in absolute nearness. Their definition by the Church as 'strict mysteries', that is, truths about God which in principle eternally surpass our capacity to understand, is an articulation of the necessarily inscrutable character of the Absolute Mystery Who has disclosed Himself to us in these terms. By the very fact that He is Who He is and that we are other than He, He is and will everlastingly always be for us this Absolute Mystery Who is the source and end of the dynamism by which we can know all things other than Himself with clarity and completeness. But His mysteriousness is not provisional or temporary. It is eternally the incomprehensible ground of our capacity to comprehend all others except Himself.

This essentially 'mysterious' nature of the Divine Reality in Whom our faith terminates implies that in principle every effort to thematize that Reality will be inadequate and will founder in the infinite abyss which it seeks to plumb. This is admitted in the traditional theory of analogy, especially as practiced by St. Thomas, the goal of which is to vindicate human reason's ability to achieve a positive knowledge of God whether by itself or as enlightened by faith. For that positive knowledge based on the similarity founded in the creative causal relation is acquired at the cost of acknowledging the infinite distance or dissimilarity between the Creator and His creature. Therefore the knowledge that is claimed culminating in the *via eminentiae* is arrived at by virtue of a dialectic of affirmation and corresponding negation in which the latter plays the necessary function of a corrective and a purification.

What is being asserted then is not our failure to know God at all in a positive way. For we recognize that He is indeed the pure positivity of being, the One in Whom there is no negativity but Who is in absolute unity and simplicity perfectly identical with Himself. Though finite enfleshed spirits, we have an openness and capacity for the infinite towards Whom we are transcending in every act and effort. The Absolute Mystery of God is the goal and objective toward Whom our every act of knowing is ultimately pointed. Therefore His reality is what our knowing and loving mean and intend, even while our conceptions and thematization of Him are doomed to be eternally inadequate.[4]

The mystics have experienced this frustrating incapacity to express or even to understand the ineffable Mystery into Whose depths they have been swept so powerfully. So Other was the One Whom he encountered than any reality he could categorize that St. John of the Cross felt compelled to call Him "Nothing." This is the response of the mystics in almost all religious traditions. For the meaning-content of our conceptions is drawn from the finite world of our experience. When we attempt to transfer them to the Infinite One, it is as proper for us to say: "He is not," as to say, "He is."

Our congenital tendency, however, is to try endlessly to capture Him within our thoughts, to enlist Him in the service of our schemes. We would master Him rather than accept being mastered by Him. This path leads to, and from the beginning has led to idolatry. For that reason God has always raised up prophets to smash our idols and to recall us to the worship of the true God. But the prophetic word has been needed to interpret the historic event in which the will of God to purge and to summon has been most powerfully present. For the Israel of old it was the destruction of the Temple and the Exile. For us it seems to be in many and varied ways the experience of the 'absence or the death of God,' Whom we tried to reduce to the One Who temporarily filled the gaps in our scientific knowledge or to the projection of our self-directed wishes and needs. Secular prophets, Marx, Nietzsche, Freud et al, have arisen to smash the idol and to recall us to a chastened faith.

The atheisms which have grown up and prospered in the western world, especially Marxist atheism, have actually been anti-theisms that are specifically anti-Christian. Whereas Absolute Atheism neither affirms nor denies God's existence since it finds it inconceivable within its universe of meaning, Relative Atheism or anti-theism is precisely a denial of His existence, especially as He is professed in Christian faith. Thus the Christian God is allowed as a conceivable reality since such an atheism originates within a Christian world of meaning. The forms of western atheism we have considered all offer themselves as 'Humanisms.' The denial of God is thus not their principal thesis; it is rather the affirmation of man. For all of these humanisms, the full-blown reality of man is incompatible with the existence of God as they have come to understand its implications in the light of their experience within a Christian faith context.[5] Thus, as we have discovered, their atheism occurs as the postulate of their humanism.

Conditions of the Dialogue

The angle of approach of this work as an effort at Christian apologetics was announced as one of dialogue. We have attempted to maintain that posture consistently by listening with honesty and openness to the self-explanation of those humanisms which propose themselves as alternative faiths to Christianity for contemporary man. By the same token we have offered those versions of a Christian anthropology which, in our judgment, have furnished the most effective media for proclaiming the Christian message to the men of today. Thereby we have been enabled to enter the dialogue from a position of strength. Actually of course the dialogue has been underway since the very beginning. Now, however, having given all sides the chance for a positive presentation of their positions, we are now ready to engage in the confrontation of those positions in the process and spirit of a dialogue that is hopefully a sincere mutual quest for truth.

In the previous two chapters, we pursued the subjects of faith, or belief, and unbelief as transcendental attitudes and therefore as unexceptionably common to all men. We treated of faith in what we believe to be its only authentic form, namely, Christian faith, whether realized formally or anonymously: the grace of God's Self-Gift to every man as redeemed by Christ, calling upon him to live as the Father's son a life of total self-surrender to the Father after the model of Christ's own life. We explored the role and presence of unbelief in the spiritual depths of those of us who acknowledge ourselves to be Christians, even the most committed, in order to confront and admit this unsavory truth about ourselves. However, we discovered that its source and its dynamism belong to the human condition itself and therefore that it is a transcendental malaise afflicting every human believer.

This approach was not intended to prejudice the dialogue before it even gets underway. Admittedly we have dealt with faith and unbelief in a Christian context. We have in a sense laid claim to all men of good will, whether theists, atheists or what have you, as our anonymous brothers in the Christian faith. Thus we have signalled beforehand how our faith vision enables us to transcend all divergences of formal belief among men and to comprehend them all within the Christian economy. However, we are not trying to win the battle without engaging in the struggle. We are merely "laying all our cards on the table," and now are willing to take our place on terms of uncompromised equality with all who are ready to enter the dialogue with us.

That we Christians believers have recognized that we

are also and inevitably unbelievers has assured that equality by emphasizing our lack of privileged status. We are unqualified to be the judges of anyone else. We are only entitled to approach our fellowmen as brothers and equals and, presuming their like attitude toward us, attempt to discuss the values and disvalues of the faiths which we respectively embrace.

The presupposition is that all of us are believers of some kind, that we are all committed to some meaning of man or at the very least to some attitude regarding the possibility of such a meaning. By the same token, we are all also unbelievers in the sense that we are all open in some degree to being unfaithful to what we profess as our faith commitment. Because we are believers, we have a basis for discussion. Because we are also unbelievers, we can truly dialogue; that is, we can conceive the possibility of untruth in our position and therefore the necessity and even desirability of sincerely discovering and acknowledging whatever truth may be contained in the other position. At the same time we do not reject beforehand the possibility of altering our own position. Consequently we do not enter the dialogue as proselytizers with closed minds. We can be genuinely open to truth as the supreme value that we seek in a common venture with others who have a similar fundamental commitment.

What we have just said does not mean that we are ready to abandon our faith commitment. What we desire is rather a deepening of that commitment. Presumably we are the believers that we are precisely because we are convinced that what we believe is the truth.

However, if we are offered the opportunity to expand and refine the truth that we already possess, we should experience no reluctance to do so, but rather welcome such an offer as pure gift, a grace. This presupposes that we are personally secure in our faith: not denying the fact that we have just admitted, namely, that we are indeed all unbelievers to some degree, but rather having confidence in the faith that is in us despite our personal weaknesses and infidelities. It also presupposes our theoretical and practical acceptance of the possibility of change, at least in the sense of development of the faith we profess. This latter presupposition is integral to the view of Christian faith that we have already proposed, not only on the level of the individual Christian, but also in the faith understanding and commitment of the Church as the total Christian community.

It is clearer than ever since the Second Vatican Council that the Catholic Church understands itself and its faith as 'on the way,' in pilgrimage, engaged in an on-going history of becoming more fully what it already is in the victorious Christ toward Whom it is always moving with faltering steps but with unbounded hope. This growth in faith and trust toward the Parousia takes place within a historical experience which is one of learning by openness to truly new and therefore quite unpredictable insights which are afforded especially by sensitively attending to "the signs of the times." For this process to be one of genuine development it has to make provision for discontinuity and continuity at the same time.[6]

The Dialogue Itself

In order to initiate the dialogue for which we have been preparing ourselves, we have to recall what our explorations have led us to agree upon as the common basis or subject-matter for the discussion as well as its recognized limits. From the beginning it was clear that in an age when not only belief in God's reality but the very meaningfulness of asserting it is questioned, we are left only with the reality of man and his meaning as the basis of discussion. Common to Christian and non-Christian alike is this faith in man, this humanism.

Although this was a promising beginning, we sought for something more specific, an underlying theme that somehow might provide a common strand, a fundamental point of agreement in these various contending anthropologies about which a fruitful conversation could revolve. Accordingly we listened to the self-explanation of the most influential atheistic or non-theistic humanisms and then to a number of spokesmen for a Christian humanism who seemed most faithfully to reflect contemporary man's self-understanding. A number of shared themes emerged, but that which appeared to be the most profound because it seemed to be at the root of all the others was man's capacity for self-transcendence.

It would be needlessly repetitious to review all those presentations, even in summary, to rediscover this commonly accepted truth. It is only necessary to consult again the resumé at the conclusion of each section to refresh our memories and our impressions of its universal presence. The intentionality of human consciousness, man's subjectivity uncovered as a "being-in-'the'-world" and the bearer of its meaning, his historicity as an essentially finite temporal life-project who constitutes himself in a dialectical tension with his fellow-men and his world; therefore his essentially communal nature as well as his role of humanizing his universe, taking over the direction of its evolution, in a process in which he is simultaneously creating himself: these are several of the more significant themes which these anthropologies have underscored. Some of them are more characteristic of one rather than another. However, at the core of every one of these diverse understandings of man is man's self-transcendence as the radical dynamic of which all these themes are so many formulations and by virtue of which the human dimension of being is set off from every other existent form.

Now that we have agreed on a basis of discussion, how shall we initiate and conduct the dialogue itself? What format ought it to take?

Fortunately such dialogues have been occurring with some frequency and substantive issues have been confronted on both sides. A whole new literature has arisen which consists of reports on those meetings that have taken place or which represents in itself the actual process of the dialogue. The most fully evolved of these encounters is that which comprises the Christian-Marxist dialogue especially as it has taken place on the Continent. For that reason it should be the most helpful precedent to follow even though the greater need for us in the United States is the fostering of a Christian-Secular Humanist dialogue in view of the greater influence of that movement in this country. Even though some tentative efforts have been made toward initiating such encounters here, it still remains true that the more developed stage of the dialogue between Christians and Marxists in Europe constitutes a useful model for our purposes and for any other similar undertakings under whatever auspices.

A. THE CHRISTIAN MARXIST DIALOGUE

The Christian-Marxist dialogue on the Continent received its strongest stimulus from the meetings arranged by the *Paulusgesellschaft*, the Society of St. Paul, an organization of German Catholics drawn from various professions dedicated to the discussion of religious and philosophical issues. Encounters between Christian and Marxists thinkers were arranged in Salzburg (1965), Herrenchiemsee (1966) and Marienbad (1967). From the beginning these meetings were officially encouraged by the Church through its Secretariat for Non-Believers, especially through its president, Cardinal Koenig of Vienna. A similar encounter occurred under the auspices of the World Council of Churches in 1966 in Geneva which devoted its attention particularly to the problems of the Third World. Numerous similar dialogues have taken place in Europe, England and the United States, usually in a less official format.

In our earlier treatment of Marxist Humanism, we spoke of the unique contributions made by Ernst Bloch and Roger Garaudy to the substance as well as the very process of the dialogue. Most energetic of all the discussants from the Marxist side is M. Garaudy and it is from his writings that we shall draw to initiate our version of the discussion.

Garaudy, as we have seen (cf. *supra*, pp. 84-85), credits Christianity with uncovering the constitutive dynamic of man's subjectivity, his uniqueness in nature as the self-transcending being who is self-creative in the process whereby he humanizes his world, and finally the supreme form of human love, Agape, whereby men are elevated to the selfless loving service of the other as a form of the absolute love of God Who became incarnate as man in Jesus Christ. However, he finds fault with the interpretation

Christians have placed on these indisputably valuable discoveries about man, in particular, that of human self-transcendence.

Christianity has indeed asked the right questions about man as it meditated on his finiteness measured by the infinity of his aspirations. It has erred in the definitive positive answers it has presumed to provide to those questions.

Historically Marxist Humanism is dependent on Christianity in the sense that its critique of religion, its atheism and therefore its humanism as the positive side of its atheist negation are a protest against Christianity as a historical and cultural fact. This order is reflected somewhat in the dialogue itself, at least to the extent that its initial phases took the form of a Marxist reaction to Christian affirmations. Thus, for example, at Salzburg, and in his more recent writings, Karl Rahner proposed his understanding of the meaning of a Christian Humanism, and Garaudy has couched his rejoinder in terms of an acceptance as well as a critique.

Rahner makes a powerful presentation of Christianity as the religion of God as "the absolute future of man". This truth is the ultimate guarantee of man's freedom, creativity and self-transcendence because in man's consciousness of himself and his world it relativizes all events and movements that are immanent in his history. Because God is the transcendent source and end of man's subjectivity, he is never enclosed wholly within any historical or cultural boundaries. Rather he is free to project himself beyond those limits creatively, realizing their finiteness against the infinite horizon of the Absolute Mystery toward Whom he is always aspiring. This is the most radical humanism because it gives man himself an absolute value since he recognizes in himself an infinity of desire and expectation which is grounded in the reality of the Absolute Being Who incessantly summons man to Himself. Against that horizon man recognizes all systems and movements as 'ideologies,' that is, merely relative viewpoints, which cannot ultimately explain him or satisfy his endless hopes. Similarly he perceives as idolatry every effort to give a final form to the divine End toward Whom he is drawn.

Christianity, however, does not end up in a purely abstract version of man and his finality. It is always bound up in the decidedly concrete humanism that is rooted in the very real person who is Jesus Christ, the human reality of the infinite God. For that reason it is always prepared to offer a concrete understanding of man as an alternative to every other historical concrete humanism. Is it therefore doomed to the same relative role played out on the stage of history by each successive effort to understand man and his destiny? Not if it remains true to its own faith in the trans-historical and trans-cultural value of the One in Whom it rests its faith; that is, if it remains always prepared to question and criticize and surpass every historical and cultural form in which it inevitably is led to clothe its faith.

The consequence of this faith in God as man's Absolute Future is to liberate man from every present moment of his history to be radically open to the creative possibility of his always as yet uncharted and therefore adventurous and challenging future.

Does this eventuate in a humanism that is a-historical? Once again, it should not. For man, as the Christian understands him, is inescapably bound by his incarnate nature to realize himself and his possibilities in the task of humanizing his world of space and time. For that reason, he is never emancipated from the need to choose some humanistic alternative, assimilable to his belief, which his historical and cultural situation enables him to formulate. Thus, as a matter of fact, the Christian is not exempted from the risk of faith that besets every human effort at self-understanding. He is rather very much committed to the common dialogue in which all men strive for the fuller understanding and to the common effort by which all men seek for the richer life which can elicit their loyalty and give promise of the fulfillment of their best hopes.[7]

At Salzburg, Gilbert Mury, a French Marxist, chided the Christian position with lacking the criteria for verifying its assertions about man's absolute fulfillment in God, since they can only be verified by faith itself. On the other hand, the Marxist is more scientific, proposes his solutions as hypotheses which are open to being verified within the process of history itself. He proposes the total humanism of man entirely on his own, no longer dependent on the gods and religion, who completely takes over his own destiny and rejects every dualism, including religion, as an unjust alienation. Mury's own position was to be charged with being unduly rigid and presumptuous with respect to the future and the range of its possibilities for man.[8]

In contrast to the rigidity of Mury's position, Johannes Metz joined Rahner in proposing Christianity as the religion of man's absolute future which does not commit man beforehand to any closed alternative but leaves him always free before the unpredictable choices of the future. Is man so fully the master of his own future? Is his human essence not realized rather in the very openness of his future as something he cannot wholly foreordain? "Isn't every vision of the future of an autonomously perfected humanity bound to be shipwrecked by man himself?"[9]

The latter question particularly raised the specter admitted by the Christian, but overlooked by the Marxist, of the basic flaw in man which is always present as a threat to man's enterprises though not fatalistically. It is a realistic trait of Christian humanism in contrast to the 'optimism' of the Marxist brand, which oddly the Marxists seem never to have confronted directly. This last point illustrates a typical feature of the dialogue which is perhaps almost inevitable: viz., the presence of 'empty spaces' in the dialogue, issues raised by one side that for whatever reason are not explicitly confronted by the other.

Garaudy, at Salzburg and since, has honestly and forcefully attempted to respond to the strong presentations as well as the pointed critiques of Rahner, Metz and other Christian thinkers. We have already given a digest of his cogent rejoinders.[10] He acknowledges readily the Marxists' indebtedness to the Christian's uncovering of man's subjectivity as self-creative and self-transcendent. However, he sees in man's dynamic of transcendence an exigency and an aspiration rather than the intimation, much less the evidence, of a Presence that beckons man toward Itself as man's absolute future. It is the sign of an absence therefore rather than a presence, of an emptiness which it is man's task to fill, rather than a fullness toward which man is called as to his fulfillment. Thus Christianity is right in discerning man's nature as the infinite question, but it is wrong in affirming dogmatically that God is man's infinite answer. It is not only wrong, it is perpetuating the error of which every religion has been guilty in alienating man from his authentic task of self-creation by assigning its ultimate responsibility and execution to One Who is Other than man himself. And so, in a linear descent from Feuerbach himself, he affirms infinity as an adjective of man and not as a substantive existing in itself on which man mistakenly projects the glory which belongs to him alone.

Garaudy accuses Christianity, therefore, of mythologizing human existence, of impatiently and uncritically leaping from the exigency for the infinite in man to the assertion of a transcendent, trans-historical solution to man's infinite questioning. It is mythological because it goes outside history to resolve the human question which is immanent to history. Metz replies by pointing to the 'negative theology,' the iconoclastic, 'myth-breaking' dynamism that is inherent in the biblical faith in God. From the beginning of the account of the biblical revelation, God has disclosed Himself as the God of promise Whose transcendence is not realized a-historically as the one Who is timelessly above man, but as the One Who is ahead of man, his Absolute Future. Thus instead of being the alienating source of man's escape from his historical task, He liberates man for historical initiative. He calls man beyond himself and what are his possibilities at any historic moment into a future which can constitute for man the 'Novum,' the utterly new, that which is truly 'not yet.'[11]

The latter point recalls us momentarily to the contribution of Ernst Bloch. He has attempted the most adequate account of the role of the future in man's development within the Marxist context with his phenomenology of human unconsciousness and his ontology of the 'Novum,' the 'not-yet.' Especially in the latter phase of his thought, he attempts to give the objective ground for the creative imaginings, arising out of his unconscious, by which man projects the shape of his hopes for the future. Where does Bloch situate that objective ground? In matter, "the ultimate mother of the New, from whose womb the future is born . . . the creative life-giving subject of all change and progress, spiritual as well as material."[12] In order to account for the future as utterly novel and new in relation to man, he quite logically feels required to locate its origins in a source other than and beyond man. Matter is immanent to the historical process as its ultimate subject, but it enters the historical dimension through man who is the maker of history. From that point of view it tends toward being the trans-historical principle of the historical process, just as, being other than man and his humanized world as their ultimate source, it tends toward being transcendent to both.

The issue being discussed can be concisely put as follows. The utter novelty of the future for man cannot be due to man himself, even to his latent possibilities, for then it would not be the utterly new in relation to him. It must, therefore, as Bloch recognizes, be accounted for from a source other than man himself. He locates it in matter, a solution that is inescapable for any dialectical materialist, like Garaudy. The recourse to a metaphysical principle, such as matter, is an admission that man's role in creating his world cannot be exercised in total autonomy but rather in dependence on a source that is other and which is able to summon him beyond himself in the process that constitutes his self-transcendence. His ability to transcend himself demands a Transcendent Other.

Quentin Lauer, in his very close and direct published confrontation with Garaudy[13], also tackles his dialogue-partner on his burdening Christianity with being an alienating myth. Lauer asks if science, which Garaudy uses as the norm against which he measures the mythic character of religion, does not itself alienate man and become 'myth' "when it seeks to solve problems outside its province or when it simply classifies them as illegitimate problems."[14] Moreover, it is arbitrary to emphasize man's transcendence and yet to assert that the Christian interpretation of it is "alienation" because it points beyond man in a way that cannot be verified as the purely human can. This merely illustrates the fact that the Marxist has not had the Christian experience of transcendence as grounded in his belief in

God. In point of fact, the Marxist is limiting the explanation of transcendence to the bounds of his own experience and interpretation of it, a limitation which demands its own justification. His promulgation of the total autonomy of man is a postulate and not a demonstrated truth.

The believer is convinced that his transcendence is a response to a divine summons. The Marxist reduction of this conviction to the projection of his subjective need is not a necessary conclusion. For the Christian, it is rather a truly human decision made in the light of his religious experience. It does not alienate him as a man because the transcendent call that elicits his response occurs in the immanent depths of his own subjectivity. For this reason his theology is an anthropology, if indeed a supernatural one, and he can within his own context call transcendence an adjective of man rather than an attribute of God, as long as he does not claim divinity for himself as well. His faith experience cannot be adequately accounted for as solely a felt exigency, a mere phenomenon of his consciousness pointing to an absence and not to the presence of the divine, much as this conclusion may be required by the Marxist's undemonstrated postulate of man's total autonomy.

The divine call to a love relationship in faith is at the same time inevitably a call to a love relationship with one's fellow man. This is another facet of the immanence of the transcendent divine in the human, an intimacy which attained its peak in the Incarnation and is the heart of the Christian Gospel, as Garaudy himself graciously concedes. On this account, the Christian, rather than being alienated from this world, is commanded to realize his divinely grounded transcendence in the loving service of his fellow-man.

Garaudy responds forcefully if not directly to the critique of his Christian interlocutors. Though he has on previous occasions strongly accented the inconsistency of the Church's performance in history with the implications of the lofty function she claims for herself, he chooses to consider instead whether the alienating role he attributes to her as institution is indeed a necessary consequence of the faith she professes. He focusses on two accusations made against the Church by atheistic humanism as acknowledged in the Council's Pastoral Constitution of the Church in the Modern World, viz.: 1) "Religion puts in question the autonomy of man. 2) Eschatological experience is an impediment to the full flowering of man in history."[15]

He has already appealed to Karl Barth's attack on that theological dogmatism by which the theologian pretends to speak for God. There is instead a strict discontinuity between God, the "totally other", and man. This not only protects God against man's pretensions, but it also safeguards man's autonomy and his responsibility for his own history. Then he quotes from his favored Catholic writer, Father Gonzalez Ruiz, who in his *El Christianismo No Es Un Humanismo* stresses God's radical freedom in relation to His creation and the gratuitousness of His presence in the evolution of the world and of man which can only be perceived by an express revelation. This rejects any version of a "God of the gaps" at the same time that it guarantees man's unhindered responsibility for the task of humanizing the cosmos.

Garaudy reminds us that Christianity has not always lived the fulfillment of its biblical faith. For many centuries it succumbed to the dualism of Greek thought and culture and encouraged an attitude of turning away from this world and its problems. At the same time it allied itself with the reactionary forces that resisted and crushed every revolutionary effort to humanize the world and put an end to injustices. It is only in this century that men like Bonhoeffer have recalled us to the commitment to this world which is the form the Bible enjoins for the authentic living of our Christian faith and others like Bultmann and Dewart have attended to the imperative need of dissociating the heart of the gospel message from the transitory forms it assimilates from each culture in which it exists.

Garaudy continues his procedure of pointing to what a Marxist expects of Christianity and in particular of the Catholic Church by uncovering implications of the Christian faith for the service of man with which he can agree but to which the Church has too often given a minimal fidelity or none at all. Thus, for example, whereas Christians in the past have located God's role in human affairs at the edge of man's insufficient knowledge and power, at the risk of having him gradually pushed out of the world as man's knowledge and power increased, the God of the Bible is seen at the heart of man's creativity, "whenever something new is in the process of coming to life."[16] It is as creator that man is most clearly the image of God.

In the past the Church has been untrue to its mission, devoting itself to its own defense rather than the defense of man. What the Marxist would hope is that the Church judge individuals and regimes on their attitudes toward men and their rights rather than on their attitudes toward the Church and its rights. "Why should God always be on the side of 'the establishment' and never on the side of change?"[17] What has become of its prophetic mission, of denouncing evil wherever it is practiced, even by non-communist regimes?

Garaudy attributes this conservative social attitude somewhat to the traditional interpretation of sin which has been almost identified with insubordination or pride. This favored a view of piety as willing acceptance of the established order, however unjust, and impiety or pride as insubordination toward such an order. In this conception there is no room for the Promethean figure of the rebellious hero or the grandeur of a revolutionary movement in behalf of exploited men. What is needed is an understanding of sin which sees it not so much in doing what should not be done (after the example of pride), but in not doing what ought to be done (after the example of cowardice). "In a word, sin is not wishing to be more than a man, it is accepting to be less than a man."[18]

Marxists must charge Christians with neglecting the very lessons about man which they learned from Christianity. This is the advance of the Judaeo-Christian conception of man over the Hellenic: namely, of man who is free not merely because he has a knowledge of necessity, but because he participates in the divine power to create the new and thus overcome all determinisms and necessity. This is a revolutionary message which the Church has inherited and it should be faithful to it by encouraging and not by stifling the desire of men to break with the past. It presupposes that Christians like Marxists will oppose every agency and force that alienates man by depriving him of his subjectivity as a creator and would reduce him to an object and a mere means in the service of production or any exploitative system.

The outcome of Garaudy's dialogue with Lauer as with Rahner, Metz and other Christian thinkers is to agree that both sides acknowledge man to be essentially the transcending creator of himself and his world. It is in the further understanding of human transcendence where the disagreement takes place. Both recognize man as open to an infinite future. For Marxists, the infinity is conceived negatively and resides solely in man's freedom and exigency for endless progress and his capacity of going beyond any present achievement. For Christians, the infinity is affirmed in the Person Who is the promise and the gracious reality that summons man to his Absolute Future. Each conception has its own grandeur. The most constructive attitude for each side is not to hinder man's progress by continuing the refusal to cooperate with those who hold the other interpretation. Rather each should be true to its faith in the possibility of that progress which the other likewise cherishes.

B. THE CHRISTIAN-SECULAR HUMANIST DIALOGUE

The dialogue between Christians and non-Marxist or Secular Humanists is not so advanced as that with the Marxists. Thus far two Catholic-Humanist dialogues have taken place under the joint auspices of the International Humanist and Ethical Union and the Vatican Secretariat for Nonbelievers. There has also been a similar encounter more recently here in the United States. All of them leave the impression of being still quite tentative and exploratory and of seeking the common ground on which the discussions can fruitfully proceed.

In the dialogue with the Marxists, there have often been lengthy and profound philosophical debates due perhaps to the strong metaphysical traditions on both sides. In the Catholic-Humanist encounter, the inclination has been to get down more swiftly to practical moral and social issues.

This may be due at least in part to the proverbially more empirical and less metaphysical orientation of the predominantly Anglo-American principles on the Humanist side as contrasted with the largely continental European composition of the meeting with the Marxists. However, as Paul Kurtz, editor of *The Humanist* and prime mover as well as energetic participant in these meetings, has observed; "The very fact that humanists and Catholics can engage in dialogue is a historic achievement."[19]

As in the previous section, the objective here is to report on those dialogues that have actually taken place and were publicly available up to this writing. It is expected and even hoped that this report will be quickly dated by subsequent meetings that will move the dialogue further and to more fruitful outcomes than have yet been achieved. However, an effort will be made even at this early moment to analyze the progressing situation and to hazard predictions of future directions at least as they seem to be implied in present possibilities.

The ultimate objective of course is to confront these two world-views, Christian and Humanist, to ferret out their shared as well as their opposed positions, and thus be enabled honestly to estimate their relative validity as faiths for modern man. The accounts of officially sponsored meetings that have actually taken place are chiefly intended as methodological devices for achieving our own goal. However, they certainly lend a realistic base for our program of effecting dialogue between the Christian and other contemporary belief-systems.

The two Catholic-Humanist dialogues which will be analyzed and reflected on here are those held in Brussels, October 2-4, 1970 and in New York City, May 5-7, 1972. The Brussels meeting was the second in five years to be convened in Europe under the joint auspices of the International Humanist and Ethical Union and the Vatican Secretariat for Non-believers. The New York encounter occurred under the sponsorship of the American Humanist Association, the American Ethical Union, the (Catholic) Council of Belief and Unbelief and the John LaFarge Institute.[19a] It was the first to take place in North America and, it is hoped, it is the initiation of a series of exchanges between the two groups.

The Brussels conference began with major presentations from single representatives of each side in three rather broad sectors: the common underlying values of humanism, the concept of 'an open society,' and common responsibilities in world policy. The actual dialogue occurred not so much between the presentations as between them and the commentaries that followed as rejoinders of the respective parties.

In the opening paper within the section concerned with "common underlying values of humanism," J. P. van Praag, chairman of the International Humanist and Ethical Union, attempts the define "The Humanist Outlook," on the assumption that 'Humanism' only makes sense when it is clearly set apart from religious creeds and therefore from anything like a 'Christian Humanism.'[20] After citing the 1966 (Paris) statement of the commonly shared views of Ethical Humanists, he seeks to make more precise what specifies 'Humanism' by isolating the mental attitude presupposed by its theory and practice. This fundamental orientation is constituted by a moral conviction based on the strictly 'human.' It relies on man's resources alone to realize what is characteristic of our common humanity. Unlike the religious creedal positions, Humanism not only makes man central, it posits him as the only foundation of his own existence, excluding any recourse to the 'divine.'

Dr. van Praag proposes ten postulates as a distillation of the presuppositions accepted by all modern Humanists, regardless of their subsequent divergences. These are named as: equality, secularity, liberty, fraternity, reason, experience, existence, completeness, contingency and evolution. Of these the one which is most clearly at variance with the Christian outlook is "completeness," as van Praag defines it: "The world is complete and does not imply an upper or outer world. Completeness is not perfection, but means that the world is not thought of as dependent on a creator, nor is there an empty place left vacant by an absent creator."[21]

As J. Gomez Caffarena, S.J., observes, this is hardly

accurate as a presumed counter-position to the Christian belief in a Creator, which it tends to depict in mythologized terms. However, Fr. Caffarena is able to integrate even "completeness" into his humanism as a Christian believer, if it is properly qualified as "completeness of the world *in its order*" rather than completeness in the absolute sense, which is hardly verifiable.[22]

Caffarena rather modestly seeks only admittance into the ranks of those who can be called 'Humanists.' He shares their belief in Man but roots it in the One Whom Jesus called "Father" and St. John "Love." If asked why not simply Man without God, he responds that there is a "plus" in the spiritual dimension of man as the subject of freedom and rights and especially as the participant in interpersonal love. This points to God not merely as the ultimate Ground of Being, but as Love itself, the support of human existence. If this is not a logically necessary implication, it is at least able to be assimilated to an authentically humanistic outlook.

Vincenzo Miano, SDB, the secretary of the Vatican Secretariat for Nonbelievers, is less irenic in his longer reflection on the dialogue as a whole. Among the various historic forms of Humanism, he situates van Praag's among those that can be best described as forms of anthropocentrism. This conception understands man as the measure of being and as the source of his own salvation, values and potentiality for progress, excluding any recourse to superhuman powers. Somewhat more forcefully than Caffarena, he insists on the right of Christians to be called 'Humanists.' It is a matter of different kinds of humanism which uphold common as well as opposed beliefs, not of a distinction between Humanism and other interpretations of man outside its fold, including the Christian version.

Christian Humanism affirms not only the dimension of religious transcendence, but of the biblically-grounded awareness of man's sinfulness and need for salvation through Christ, Who reconciles man to God, to his fellow-man and to himself. A completely autonomous humanism without Christ can avail for a time, but inevitably it comes up against its inherent limits. Man's autonomy is relative, not absolute.

Without God and His Christ, "the riddles of life and death, of guilt and of grief, go unsolved, with the frequent result that men succumb to despair" (*Gaudium et Spes*, #21).

Dr. van Praag had already spoken of his Humanism in the face of the problems of evil, sorrow and death as compared with the great religions. Unlike them, Humanism does not pretend to give final answers to their ultimate questions. In fact, it raises quite different questions. It faces evil, sorrow and death and accepts them as the very fabric of human existence whose temporal and contingent character is not denied or muted by recourse to other-worldly ends or outcomes.

This life is its own goal. The values man himself creates are final. There is no cosmic mind or purpose above or beyond him. In growing community with all men, we must shape our own ends and be the source of our own developing possibilities as a species. These are realized especially in widening freedom of choice and the justice which insures it in their range and in their participation by an ever greater number of world citizens. Thus men themselves confer evolving meaning on a universe originally bereft of it.

Albert Dondeyne, eminent Louvain philosopher, seeks the basic values modern Christians share with non-believers who are ethical humanists. He finds the meeting ground for dialogue in contemporary man's self-understanding as incarnate freedom who creates culture out of nature and thereby founds a world and constitutes his own history. Man humanizes his world through his work and confers meaning on it through the social symbol-making that is his language. Both of these give rise to human solidarity and co-responsibility at the same time that they rise out of them. Thus it becomes apparent that for man, moral reason takes precedence over his scientific and technical reason which is, or ought to be, instrumental to the ethical dimension that is most intimate and interior to his essential meaning. Thus being human is defined as openness and transcendence. Both ethical humanism and the post-Conciliar Church, especially as it has expressed itself in *Gaudium et Spes*, are committed to "the concern to safeguard man's autonomy, creativity and responsibility in the construction of a more human world."[23] This should provide the theme of the dialogue that has commenced.

Msgr. Dondeyne urges each side to seek genuine insight into the actual position of the other without compromising its own. The Christian must acknowledge that an atheistic humanism can be authentic, even if it cannot be integral, and that its proneness to divinize relative values is a temptation to which Christians themselves have succumbed. He calls the non-believer's attention to the Church's recovery of the biblical truth that love of God and love of man are reciprocal and complementary rather than mutually opposed.

The Humanists were surprised at the amount of common ground shared with them by the Catholic participants, and more than one recalled remarking: "The Catholics sound like humanists; the humanists sound like Catholics!"[24] On more sober reflection they recognized that the Catholics they were meeting were perhaps atypical in being more 'progressive' than most of their co-religionists and the officially stated position of their Church. Their prompt response to Msgr. Dondeyne was to reclaim the title of 'integral humanism' for themselves. For in their mind, a total humanism is man-centered, secular or world-oriented, naturalistic and empirical in method rather than reliant on a divine revelation as its ultimate norm. Though Catholics and other Christians can be humanistic, they are prevented from being entirely so by their commitments to the Transcendent and its superiority to the human.[25]

A rather amusing illustration of this counter-argument was provided by the English Humanist, Christopher Macy, who recalled a discussion with the chairman of the Catholic Renewal Movement in Britain. The debate reached an impasse when each declared that the valuable elements in the other's position was a lesser realization of what was wholly verified in his own. In effect, the Catholic was calling the Humanist an "anonymous Catholic," and the Humanist was labelling his opponent an "anonymous Humanist."

"An open mind in an open society": this is the Humanist creed. Actually it is the rejection of any particular creed as absolute or definitive, as Paul Kurtz insists,[26] or of any set program of social action. Humanism deserving of the name is open to diverse viewpoints and to the constant possibility of revising moral stands and political positions in the light of changing experience. *Free thought* is the Humanistic ideal; therefore, Humanism is opposed to any external authority restrictive of free inquiry, whether church or state, and will acknowledge only the internal authority of free human intelligence and reason. Not orthodoxy, but truth sought by the methodical discipline of free unhindered minds is the only norm and value for mature modern men.

The concept of an 'open society' has a specific meaning for the Humanists. It has roots in the Enlightenment, especially in its attitude toward religion as a purely private matter of personal conscience which is not entitled to a direct influence in the public domain. It also derives from the liberal individualistic philosophies of Locke and Mill and their growing conception of toleration of all beliefs within a democratic society.

"By 'an open society' is meant a sharing of institutions, including schools and universities, for all general social purposes, as a common foundation for the coexistence and cooperation within the same polity of communities which differ in their beliefs and ways of life."[27] So. H. J. Blackham, the English Humanist, defines 'an open society' which he opposes to 'a uniform society' (presumably totalitarian in character) and distinguishes from 'a pluriform society.' In the latter, "the diverse communities seek to maintain their own social institutions, sharing only the legal framework and political constitution of the society." The difference is based on one's conception of the rightful range of what is public and what is private. The region of ends is private: that is, every person is an end in himself and may not have his ends dictated to him by society, though he may associate himself with others in a 'private' community of those who accept similar ends, e.g., a church. Thus society is conceived as "an organization of public means to private ends," and can exercise control and sanctions only to insure loyal and active support for those social institutions, e.g., law courts, legislatures, schools, mass media, hospitals, which serve as means to protect or enable the pursuit of private life-goals and styles.

The success of 'an open society' requires the public spirit of its members in arriving at the rules that will govern all, good faith in fulfilling them, and the widest participation in the process of deciding and revising those rules. However, a fully *open* society is an ideal that presupposes great maturity of its adult members. Thus religious believers may insist on their own confessional schools to safeguard the communication of their beliefs to their children in a pluralist society and they cannot be deprived of the freedom to do so. Contrariwise, the ideal would be a universal system of public education in which a general moral and religious education would be provided in an atmosphere in which more specific norms and beliefs could meet in open encounter and discussion.

John Gaine, English Catholic participant, subjects Blackham's description of an 'open society' to a close analysis and critique. Its defense of individual freedom from social constraint through institutions that are neutral toward private ends seems somewhat unrealistic. Can such means be defined without reference to ends? Are there not certain basic humanistic values that serve as ends of social institutions and in the light of which other ends are judged and excluded?

Inasmuch as the open character of a society implies an absence of internal divisions in social institutions such as schools, Gaines questions its validity over against the notion of 'a pluriform society,' in which such divisions are endorsed. Is not a society and its culture enriched precisely by a diversity of its institutions, which may be manifold not only religiously but also as the expression of different heritages or varying concepts of the educational process itself. The insistence on a single system of education is itself an infringement on the freedom to be different. Therefore, Gaines concludes that only distinctions within social institutions that are harmful and discriminatory, creating and maintaining privileged and underprivileged sectors of the population, should be excluded. He opts for 'a pluriform society' which permits the diversity of social institutions on religious and other grounds so long as their existence in particular instances is not harmful to the general welfare or that of specific groups or individuals.

Daniel de Lange, Dutch Catholic spokesman, questions the very possibility of Blackham's proposal of 'an open society.' His judgment is that we are actually locked within 'a uniform society' on a large scale. For those who control the production/consumption system also manipulate the social institutions involved in the political order, in education and in communications and thereby manipulate the populations whose lives they influence and inform. The pluriformity of such institutions is the last remaining defence against this growing monopoly, whereas recourse to the approach of 'an open society' would promote an eventual capitulation.

Wim van Dooren, Dutch Humanist, takes exception to his fellow-Humanist's model of 'an open society' as impracticable since it must presume that common fundamental values are shared by all members of the society. When, as a matter of fact, some advocate contradictory values, the state or society cannot remain neutral, but must intervene. It would appear that Professor van Dooren has the Catholic Church especially in mind as an authoritarian power which is still officially intent on preserving its hold over men's lives, despite the liberalism of a minority of its members. In Blackham's defense, it should be noted that he only allows persons and groups within his 'open society' "to pursue their own ends in their own ways, unless and until any of them constitutes 'a clear and present danger' to the open order in which they maintain one another."[28]

The third set of presentations addresses the issue of "common responsibilities in world policy." Father Caffarena calls attention to the truth that undergirds the entire discussion and provides its underlying motivation: that science and technology have provided mankind with the resources to humanize the world. This confronts humanists of every persuasion with the fateful choice either of grasping this opportunity in a cooperative effort that transcends ideological differences or of betraying their basic commitment by tragic default. What is required is a *world* policy, a need whose urgency cannot afford delays for the battle tactics of contending factions or the protracted resolving of doctrinaire differences.

The humanistic goals shared by both parties implies postulates on the socio-economic and the 'humane' level. The commitment to technological progress and the consequent economic development for the benefit of all people, for example, through fairer distribution of increased production, is one a Catholic can conscientiously make. The thesis of Max Weber and implicitly of Marx that factors indigenous to the 'Catholic mentality' account for the socio-economic underdevelopment of largely Catholic latin nations is not accepted. The obstructive traits pointed to by sociologists have no intrinsic relation to essential Catholic doctrinal or moral beliefs.

On the other hand, the need for an efficacious socio-economic approach is governed by the diverse situations in which the need arises. There seems to be no system, socialistic or other, that applies equally to all. Therefore, allowance for a plurality of solutions is demanded. What hinders efficacy in favor of the many is not pluralism as such, but the fact that it can mask the rise and exploitative operation of selfish group interests.

Any system can nurture selfishness within itself and technological progress cannot of itself insure the equitable distribution of its benefits. Humanists must oppose dehumanizing trends and exploitation in every political and social system. The solution is not to be found in a romantic retreat to a pre-technological 'paradise.' Rather the challenge is to impregnate our technically advanced systems with humanistic values and goals. Caffarena appeals to Erich Fromm's program, offered in his *The Revolution of Hope*. Fundamentally it attempts to humanize the economic system, to plan and manage its functioning to serve human personal development rather than the making of profits or the perpetuation of the system. This implies policies fostering the self-actuation of consumers rather than reducing them to passive receivers and users. Fromm also calls for new equivalents of past religions to nurture man's spirit and his need to expand and express it. Caffarena believes that these suggestions, though generic, provide indispensable postulates for a truly 'humanistic' society on which all can agree.

Paul Kurtz gives an incisive Humanist treatment of similar themes under the title, "Crisis Humanology." He speaks of *Crisis Humanology* in place of a crisis *theology,* because the pressing problem is not the death of God, but the death of Man. Like Caffarena, he insists that any delay in a combined effort of all concerned human beings to forestall the imminent danger of the end of our race would be criminal irresponsibility on a monumental scale.

Kurtz claims that scientific humanism has gained the ascendancy in our technological age over orthodox theism as the dominant human faith. It has advocated the employment of the scientific method and the application of technology to the major human problems, while the Church has unfailingly resisted this trend in the waning cause of its faith in transcendent mystery. The successive shocks of the Copernican, Darwinian and recent behavioristic revolutions have extended the effective range of rational scientific inquiry and shrivelled the domain of the metaphysical and the mysterious. However, scientific humanism must accept responsibility for the perils as well as for the benefits of technological advances. The bright promise of a new epoch of universal well-being could swiftly yield to a more terrible dark age of global extinction. For the dramatic breakthroughs in mechanical, agricultural and medical technology have also brought on the menace of the population explosion, the threat of ecological destruction and a dehumanized technocratic society, not to mention the apocalyptic specter of nuclear annihilation.

At its roots the crisis is a moral one and it demands a moral revolution. "For the scientific humanists the great question is whether man can extend the method of scientific intelligence—fused with compassion—to the solution of the deepest problems of moral decisions."[29] Stumbling blocks are the numberless prejudices and inherited but unreasoned assumptions. Will the Church oppose this revolution as it has opposed those which have preceded it? She is already on record as combatting reforms which the Humanist believes to be imperative: population control through contraception, sterilization and abortion; the working out of a new sexual morality which recognizes the changing character of the family with the possibility of various forms of marriage union, a broader acceptance of divorce and a positive evaluation of homosexual relationships. On the other hand, the Church may be a willing and helpful ally in espousing the cause of the economically under-developed nations, in encompassing the end of nationalism and other forms of separatism, and in fostering the creation of a world society with its system of government and rule of law as the final unconditional need for the justice, peace and happiness of all mankind.

The scientific humanist can hope that the Church, whose cooperation in this global task he recognizes to be indispensable, will not be prevented by its illusory faith in a transcendent God from practical action in behalf of humanistic objectives. That faith expresses poetically the pathos of the human condition which the Humanist also acknowledges, but more realistically accepts. "Nevertheless, since we live in the same world, Catholics and humanists have to work together, whether or not we agree that belief in God is a truth or an illusion"[30].

Abbé Antoine Vergote, Belgian psychologist of religion, and Christopher Macy, editor of the British journal, *New Humanist*, confront the question, "How the Humanist views Christian belief," from their respective viewpoints. Vergote, whose scientific credentials are beyond reproach, chides the Humanists for failing to credit Christians, especially intellectuals, with a minimum of sophistication in the scientific study of religion. Dismissing faith in God, divine revelation, Christ's resurrection and similar beliefs as poetic images symbolizing ethical values and 'mystical' experiences of man's being in his world, they talk to and about Christians as though they were not equally acquainted with the classical critiques of religion and with the literature in the psychology, sociology and philosophy of religion, to much of which they have themselves contributed. They also burden Christians with their own simplistic caricatures of those beliefs and fail to acknowledge or perceive the subtleties and nuances with which they are held by educated persons. Moreover, they tend to overlook the non-rational psychological dynamics at work in their own unbelief.

Macy feels that genuine dialogue requires the clear use of terms. Accordingly, he proposes a distinction between absolute Humanism (atheistic) and relative Humanism (theistic, Christian). The Humanist movement arose within the Christian culture, but cannot be identified with the Christian religion any more than it must be thought incompatible with it. However, its inexorable trend has been away from Christianity and more and more toward its purest and absolute form in atheism.

Unlike the atheistic Humanist, the Christian is caught between the love of God and of man and their possibly conflicting demands. How does he resolve this conflict? The Roman Catholic Church has traditionally stressed love of God over that of man, often to the point of anti-humanist conclusions enforced by its authoritarian rule. Individual Catholics and other Christians have interpreted the twofold commandment of love to favor one's human neighbor. Macy appeals to the New Testament to support this interpretation and makes rather effective use of the Epistle of St. James, especially in its demand for good works as the fruit and criterion of faith. Macy voices the hope that those Catholics who follow this tack (the progressives) will exert the predominant influence in their Church and thereby insure a more fruitful dialogue with atheistic Humanists.

We may fittingly conclude this report of the Brussels meeting on the hopeful note provided by Karel Cuypers, Humanist professor on the faculty of that city's Free University:

> I am trying to find an equivalent of the Christian attitude to God. There must be such an equivalent if we accept that the minds of believing and non-believing men are essentially the same. We could define the 'God' of the atheists (what's in a name?) as (1) the totality of all we do not know or understand; (2) all we cannot express by science or language; (3) all that inspires us to think and to act, or gives us a sense of beauty and rightness. In this sense 'God' is an

object for research and the scientist who is seeking truth is really
seeking after the mystery of such a 'God,' so that an atheist can be a
very religious person even when he does not accept the Christian Lord.
This Lord of the Truth is in us unbelievers, as the kingdom of this
same 'God' is in you, the believers. This 'religious' attitude is one with
morality in the broadest sense.[31]

The first Catholic-Humanist dialogue in North America
took place in New York City, May 5-7, 1972. It turned out
to be somewhat disappointing to a number of its participants,
especially on the Catholic side, and yet perhaps more revealing by its very failures and what those failures uncovered.
For it became obvious that the Humanists approached the
meeting with stereotypes of Catholic positions which were
not verified for the most part by the post-Vatican II mentality and expositions of the largely younger members comprising the Catholic group. The Humanists were under-
standably baffled by this lack of conformity to their expectations and were constrained to ask the question: "Who
speaks for the Church?"[32] On the other hand, the Humanists
displayed a diversity of views and even an antagonism within their own ranks that surprised as well as amused their
dialogue-partners.

The general topic agreed upon was that of conscience
and morality. The first day was devoted to the sources and
sanctions of conscience. Sidney Hook, renowned philosopher
from New York University, and Father James P. Mackey,
Irish theologian at the University of San Francisco, agreed
on the autonomy of the moral order and of the criteria for
the judgment of individual conscience and their independence of a privileged a priori revealed morality.

The principal dissension developed among the Humanists themselves. B. F. Skinner, widely known exponent
of behaviorist psychology, reduced moral conduct generally
to behavior causally explainable in function of one's genetic
history and of patterns of response to reinforced conditioning stimuli originating in one's environment. The sources of
conscience are to be found in punitive sanctions. Men do
not direct themselves interiorly but rather affect and modify
their environment in ways that establish response patterns
in their own behavior. Sidney Hook and his fellow-Human-

ist, Floyd Matson, strongly reacted to Skinner's exposition in defense of man's inner directed freedom as equally capable of causal explanation.

The second day attended to issues of conscience and the state, including civil disobedience and questions of sexual morality. In both areas of discussion, the divisions occurred within the ranks of each side rather than between Humanists and Catholics. Charles Frankel of Columbia University leaned more toward the priority of the citizen's duty to obey the laws of the state over against the right of individual conscience to resort to civil disobedience. His Humanist colleagues, Edward Ericson and Khoren Arisian, were more lenient in allowing individuals the right to disobey the state and were seconded in this view by Catholics, Charles Curran and James Mackey.

Lester A. Kirkendall of Oregon State University catalogued the developments of techniques and methods that have increasingly separated sexual relations from procreation and child-bearing and left them free to be employed in cultivating personal intimacy and communication. Evolving attitudes have kept pace. Subordination of the use of sex to the institutions of marriage and the family has yielded to assertion of the right of individuals to express fully their individual sexuality. Moral priorities for conscience formation should be reordered in line with such developments. Various forms of sexual expression should be accepted as normal modes of behavior in the evolving person and as helpful vehicles for growth in inter-personal communication.

Kirkendall's permissiveness was firmly challenged by some of the elder Humanists including Corliss Lamont, Charles Frankel and Ernest Nagel. Father Richard McCormick, S.J., raised the question whether sex was not being appealed to as a short-range cure for psychological ills and in the process being deprived of its potency for symbolizing as well as nurturing the enduring human relationships of love and friendship.

Father William C. McFadden, S.J., exposed shifting Catholic positions on the theology of sexuality. The resulting pluralism and uncertainty can be disconcerting to a Humanist looking for a settled Catholic teaching as it has been for Catholics themselves. The principal shift has been away from a morality focussed on more or less isolated actions and their objects towards a morality of actions as expressive of various levels of self-engagement within a process of growing self-actualization. The transition in sexual morality has been from an approach centered on procreative intercourse within marriage as the normative sexual act to the developmental process of "conjugal union-in-the-making". This serves as a norm inasmuch as it is a goal to be achieved. The openness to procreation of life would be judged, not as a property of individual acts, but as belonging to the process by which the couple grow by mutual assistance toward the maturity of their shared relationship. The fuller realization of themselves by their developing response to the demands of Christian love rather than the procreative finality of each individual act by which they seek to express that love becomes the moral criterion of their sexual relationship. This approach leaves unresolved the moral evalution of the use of sex outside the context of an enduring marriage, but it points up the broader, more flexible methodology with which many Catholic moral theologians address themselves to all issues of sexual morality.

Paul Kurtz expressed mild appreciation of this evidence of lessening rigidity in the Catholic theology of sex, but still saw it as restrictive in relation to the enjoyment of sex outside of the monogamous union. The Humanist views sex and erotic pleasure as ennobling of human beings and a source of joy legitimately available to responsibly consenting persons. The Church's traditionally repressive attitude toward sex has no plausible sanction in natural law. On the contrary, it has caused untold suffering by making sexual activity an object of pathological guilt feelings and anxiety.

Against the background of the Humanist conviction that the state should remain neutral towards the sexual behavior of its citizens as far as possible, Kurtz sharply critized the Catholic Church for attempting to make its own confining moral code the civil law governing the conduct of all citizens, even those outside its own fold. Moreover, the Church has intransigently stood in the way of any program of effective population control. Despite its efforts to minimize the perils of the problem, the burgeoning growth of the earth's population is a threat to the future welfare of mankind that makes it to be "a moral issue of highest import." It is hoped that progressive Catholics can move the Church from within to a more responsible attitude.

Is the Humanist acting responsibly himself in his lenient attitude toward sexual behavior? Does it not lead itself to accelerating the trend toward total permissiveness? Kurtz insisted that the Humanist favors a *tolerant* and not a permissive society. It acknowledges the right of individuals to develop their own styles of life and would oppose any attempt to impose moral standards. At the same time, it seeks to motivate individuals to cultivate mature attitudes toward sex through the interiorizing of ennobling values and the voluntary acceptance of standards which leave open the possibility of heightening the quality of one's personal life in the long run. It implies respect for the personal dignity of the other in sexual relations.

The Humanist sets an outer limit to the public display or exploitation of sex when it is generally offensive. He sees the need for a responsible humanistic education in morality to accompany the sexual education of the young. He believes that scientific advances in the control of conception and in genetics are potential sources of liberation, especially for women. He hopes that the Church will not obstruct this movement toward greater human freedom.

On the third and final day of the dialogue, each side presented a critique of the other. The Humanists chose Brand and Paul Blanshard, twin brothers who are octogenarians but still unrelenting in their decades-long campaign against the thinking and use of power by the Catholic Church as they perceive them. Brand, a well known philosopher, chose Catholic belief in divine revelation available through scripture, tradition and the teaching authority of the Church as the focus of his critique. Though acknowledging the Catholic respect for reason, he saw it as lacking consistency with the acceptance of the three sources of revelation as inerrant or guaranteed against error. Although he exhibited an acquaintance with much of the pertinent documentation, his presentation was dated. It took no account of the developments in the hermeneutics or inter-pretation of scripture and magisterial statements or authori-tative formulations of Church teaching. Catholic theologians and scripture scholars have with critical honesty confronted all the data and issues raised. His conclusions did not necessarily follow in the light of this altered context.

Paul Blanshard addressed himself to practical aspects of the Church's attitudes toward sex and the family. His treatment covered the questions of birth control, abortion, mixed marriages and divorce. Its contents were fairly pre-dictable, though certainly not to be dismissed for that reason. A number of his objections touched upon areas in which the Church and its representatives are striving for greater flexibility and new approaches, as, for example, in canonical procedures concerning marriage annulments. The main thrust of his argument, however, was in terms of perennial themes of his polemic against the Church in this country: the use of the Church's political power to impose its archaic positions on the American public at large by legislative means and the lack of democratic structures with-in the Church to permit the expression of dissenting opinion by its own members or to allow internal reform arising from the grass-roots level.

Robert J. Roth, S.J. who has written extensively on American Naturalistic philosophy, presented a Catho-lic critique of Humanism. He challenged the Humanist's appeal to reason, empirical evidence and the scientific method as the sources and guarantees of the Humanist option over the theistic one. He saw an inconsistency between the Humanist ideal and the appeal to scientific method. Rather than being rooted in an objective empirical method, acceptance of the ideal, viz., that the goal of man is human happiness to be achieved in the present life, follows from a series of options which are based on a kind of integrating intuition rather than on scientifically verifiable empirical evidence. This applies, for example, to the term, 'happiness.' Who is the 'happy' man? The answer is likely to be that he is "one who tries to do what is beneficial to others, or who engages in a cooperative effort to promote social well-being."[33] Altruism or the willingness to sacrifice oneself for the sake of others hardly seems to be firmly grounded in empirical data that are objectively verifiable, either by an appeal to common consent or by the test of consequences. There seems to be a good supply of contented egocentrists. Moreover, the claim that "effort for the benefit of mankind," that is, activity that leads to *good* social consequences, is the criterion of human happiness, cannot be validated by a mere appeal to reason and to its inferences from scientifically verifiable evidence, e.g., in terms of its testable consequences. Rather the Humanist ethical ideal is accepted on the strength of an insight or intuition into the efficacy of the ideal as able to integrate the otherwise fragmented elements of one's life in such a manner as to bring about a sense of fulfillment. Ultimately any attempt to justify the ideal is reducible to a belief or faith which is tested by its consequences of producing this integration and satisfaction. Thus it becomes "reasonable" to believe in and live by this ideal.

If adherence to the Humanistic ideal is based on faith, then why could not someone come to believe in another ideal that serves to integrate his life and provide personal fulfillment? This faith can be in another form of 'this-worldly' goal or in one that transcends the conditions of this world and furnishes a definitive guarantee against human inclinations to self-idolatry. Humanist faith occupies no privileged status in the gallery of faiths.

After the dialogue had occurred, a number of the participants were invited to express their reflections on the significance of the experience that they had shared. All were agreed that something less than a satisfactory meeting of minds had taken place, but all were equally insistent that further such meetings should be arranged that might benefit from the mistakes and miscalculations of this initial encounter.

John C. Haughey, S.J., in an independent report and commentary published in *America* concluded, "By the time it was over I was sure that it had dealt with the wrong subject, engaged the wrong participants and employed the wrong approach."[34] As the title of his article would indicate, he felt that the Humanists in particular approached the meeting with stereotyped models emanating from the pole-mics of the pre-conciliar period. He was joined in this re-action by John Cogley, Louis Dupré and John A. Oesterle, Catholic co-participants who were asked to respond to his evaluation. As Dupré put it, "Time and again Humanists were disconcerted to see that carefully prepared attacks upon officially established positions missed their mark al-together, because the enemy was no longer where he was supposed to be."[35]

The sharing by both sides of a firm confidence in the capacity of human reason to achieve truth was perhaps the strongest link between them and therefore a telling basis for mutual exchange. But the Humanists seemed com-mitted to the competency of reason in an absolute manner that approached rigidity, especially in some of their older spokesmen. The Catholics presented themselves as more flexible in this regard and more sensitive to the historical relativity of man's grasp on truth. As John Cogley inter-preted the situation:

> I believe it was a case of a fluid tradition (as Catholicism has once more proved to be) up against a fairly frozen one (as the Humanists at the meeting seemed to interpret their tradition). . . . By and large, the Catholics at the meeting talked like contemporary men plugged into the uncertainties of the time; the Humanists too often repeated the kind of certitudes which in dear, dead days used to make life less difficult for all of us.[36]

In fairness, however it has to be additionally observed that the Humanists were much more open to even a radical refashioning of moral norms to a degree a Catholic could not ratify. On the other hand, the Humanists disagreed among themselves as to how drastic a change individuals are will-ing to concede as reasonable. This very pluralism was one of the major discoveries of the conference.

The sum-total of the meeting was positive. Protagonists of each side may have frequently been talking past or around where the others were at, but they were actually engaged in an effort to talk with each other. As Madalyn Murray O'Hair, militant atheist spokeswoman and the one perhaps least enchanted by the proceedings, remarked in her concluding reflection: "In this first encounter positions were shown, evaluations were made. We were no longer speaking each to his own group; we were speaking (the representatives of) each (group) to the other. The Dialogue did not heal the breach, but it was informative. It could be a beginning, not an end. And, in the last analysis, we could not have hoped for more."[37]

Achievements and Prospects: A Resumé

The attempt has been made to present the preceding discussions of Christians with Marxists and Secular Humanists as objectively as possible. Value judgments were avoided or at least kept to a minimum except insofar as they were made within the conversations themselves. This was imperative if the reports were to achieve their purpose: a genuine meeting of the differing viewpoints as they were actually presented and were intended to express the interior beliefs of the protagonists.

In a real as distinguished from a contrived dialogue, none is the victor, but hopefully everyone is the gainer. It is not a debate or an exercise in proselytizing. It is a mutual quest for truth, as the *Directory* for dialogue published by the Secretariat for Nonbelievers makes quite clear. As distinguished from the form of dialogue spoken of by Pope Paul VI in his encyclical, *Ecclesiam Suam,* which he understood as a facet of the Church's mission "to proclaim the Gospel to all men," the Directory adopts the type of dialogue advocated in the Pastoral Constitution, *Gaudium et Spes,* which "treats primarily of dialogue between the Church and the world, a dialogue that does not aim directly at proclaiming the Gospel. In fact the Constitution deals with a dialogue which Christians intend to establish with all men who do not share the same faith, either in order to join them in the quest for truth in various fields, or to collaborate in finding solutions to the great problems facing mankind today."[38]

What is looked for is a removal of misconceptions by each regarding the alternate position, a gradual uncovering of the other perspective as it is honestly understood and adhered to by its proponents. Only then can its authentic values be perceived and shared. Dialogue is not teaching, which presumes the inequality of the teacher and the one taught, although it can be instructive. It is certainly not polemics or controversy which is intended to defend a position and demonstrate the error of its opposite, yet it does involve the dialectical tension of differing views encountering each other. It is not directed explicitly toward converting the other to one's own view, but more toward reciprocal growth in knowledge of the truth. Thus in addition to the shared search for truth, it is sensitive to the dignity of the human persons involved and the freedom required for effective inquiry and inherent in the personal assent to the truth all seek cooperatively.[39]

The *Directory* recognizes three planes on which dialogue can take place: "on the plane of simple human relations or that of a quest for the truth or of collaboration to attain ends of a practical nature."[40] All three are found in the different types of dialogue, but as one or the other predominates, three forms of dialogue can be distinguished:

> —encounter on the plane of simple human relations, with a view to drawing the interlocutors out of their isolation and mutual mistrust, and creating an atmosphere of deeper understanding, mutual esteem, and respect;
> —encounter on the plane of search for the truth, regarding questions of the greatest importance to the persons involved, but striving in common to attain to a deeper grasp of the truth and to a fuller knowledge of reality;
> —encounter on the plane of action, which aims at establishing the conditions for collaboration towards fixed practical objectives, despite doctrinal differences.[41]

The Christian-Marxist dialogue is certainly furthest along the way. Quickly enough it broke through the first plane to the second. Because of the unusual high caliber of the thinkers who exerted the strongest influence within it, it achieved a profound level of reciprocal understanding and insight into the alternate positions and of mutual enrichment as a consequence. This did not remove all areas of disagreement, but it did rather effectually delimit and define those areas. As a result Christians and Marxists, by and large, are quite clear about where they can agree and where they must disagree. This introduces the possibility of dealing with each other with honesty and openness and with a minimum danger of misunderstanding. Of course this somewhat ideal situation is depleted and rendered less actual as the influence of those participants who achieved this impressive meeting of minds is itself lessened. In principle, at least, they have established the opening to further more fruitful dialogues and to the plane of effective collaboration in the mutual striving for desirable practical goals.

Its briefer history has not permitted the Christian-Secular Humanist dialogue the same degree of progress. There is a discernible difference, however, between the European and American encounters and the extent to which they have moved toward a meeting of minds. With considerably more experience behind them, the former are well beyond the point of setting a climate congenial to trustful and meaningful exchange. The Americans, on the other hand, are scarcely beyond the awkward stage of making first acquaintance with erstwhile foes. But the future is promising. Forthcoming meetings, earnestly desired by both sides, should benefit from the removal of misconceptions and previously unchallenged prejudices. Progress should be impressive since there is so great a distance yet to be traversed. It is important, moreover, that Catholics be joined in future meetings by representatives of other Christian viewpoints if the growth in understanding and cooperative action is to have the widest possible impact.

The sense of urgency in joining forces for effective action in the common behalf is keenly felt by all. However, the impatience with which the Humanists, especially in this country, want to get down to practical moral and social issues and their implementation in action could prove disadvantageous in the long run. For the sometimes contrary views held on these issues are in function of basic underlying philosophical differences. If these differences are not honestly and thoroughly confronted, then the measure of mutual understanding arrived at in discussing the practical issues would be too superficial to sustain a genuine and enduring commitment to cooperative action towards the goals all recognize as imperative.

As the ecumenical movement among the Christian Churches and the Christian-Marxist dialogue itself have demonstrated, neither centuries of distrust and acrimonious controversy nor fundamental philosophical differences can preclude the discovery of significant areas of broad agreement or the possibility of fruitful collaboration in practical programs of common concern. All that is needed is mutual respect, a sincere desire to place the quest for truth above partisan considerations, the openness and breadth of mind and heart to credit the others with a similar honesty and esteem for the powers of rational inquiry and the value of the human enterprise. With these attitudes presupposed, one can face what seem to be irreducible divergences in premises and postulates and entertain some hope of narrowing the gap, or even better of moving towards a more comprehensive viewpoint within which both can grasp the truth more fully and discern more clearly the values present in the other position. The basic differences will remain, but now they stand out more distinctly and their real strength is more securely acknowledged.

If all parties involved scrupulously observe the rules and conditions of authentic dialogue, none can be the loser. Everyone should gain a broader, deeper and firmer apprehension of truth as well as a more enriching commitment to his own distinctive faith. Especially here in the United States, we can look forward with great expectations to the outcomes of future meetings between Humanists and Christians. Too long we have isolated ourselves from one another behind barricades of half-truths; we have hardened our hearts and closed our minds to the truths and values others have achieved without us. We cannot afford any more to deny that what we have in common far exceeds the differences that have kept us apart.

The spirited engagement in a continuing dialogue with atheistic Humanists, Marxist and non-Marxist, should strengthen those of us who are Christian believers in our own faith. We should benefit from the broader and brighter vision of truth which any such encounter should engender by its widening of our perspective. We should also gain in confidence in the validity of our own faith as it proves its robustness and vitality as well as its undiminished relevance to contemporary life in the face of similar doubts, confusion, divergence in interpretations, and patent inability to provide ready answers to all problems on the part of those burdened with upholding the other side of our discussion.

The meetings we have reported on in this chapter are single events in an on-going and developing history whose deepest meaning, as we have already observed, is the central dynamic of the process of man's salvation by God through Jesus Christ. Our desire to provide fair and objective accounts of other faiths which deny this fundamental truth of Christian Faith does not compromise our own profound commitment to it. The dialogue as we have tried to practice it is not directly a form of preaching the Gospel, but it is a form of giving witness to it. At its heart is the conviction that ultimately truth, that is, what really is, will conquer. We believe that Jesus Christ is the meaning of what Man really is. Since our dialogue with atheists is based on our common belief in the meaningfulness of Man, this is the angle from which we participate in the on-going conversation. In the final chapter we shall draw out the implications of this faith of ours for contemporary men, living as we do in a pluralistic, evolutionary world.

Notes and references

1 H. W. Richardson, **Toward an American Theology** (New York: Harper & Row, 1967), p. 1.

2 We take the liberty of applying Richardson's distinctions in our own way and for our own purposes, thereby taking full responsibility for the validity of the applications. We do not for that reason pronounce a judgment, favorable or unfavorable, on his own application which indeed stands on its own merits.

3 **Actus credentis terminatur non in enuntiabile sed in rem. S. Th.,** II-II, 1, 2, ad 2.

4 Emerich Coreth, **Metaphysics,** trans. by Joseph Donceel (New York: Herder & Herder, 1968), p. 183. ". . . (man) really knows God, although he can never enclose him in a concept or a definition. Whatever he conceives about God is hopelessly inadequate, yet what he basically means or intends through his concepts comes up to some extent, dynamically not statically, to what the Absolute really is."

5 Leslie Dewart, **The Future of Belief** (New York: Herder & Herder, 1968), pp. 52ff.

6 Roger Garaudy has expressed very well the attitude with which

one should enter the dialogue. "We offer a dialogue without prejudice or hindrance. We do not ask anyone to stop being what he is. What we ask is, on the contrary, that he be it more and that he be it better. We hope that those who engage in dialogue with us will demand the same of us. Dialogue with Christians implies, on their part, no religious concession whatever." **From Anathema to Dialogue** (New York: Herder & Herder, 1966), p. 122.

[7] For the main ideas summarized here, cf. Karl Rahner, "Christian Humanism," **Journal of Ecumenical Studies** 4 (Summer, 1967), pp. 369-384.

[8] Cf. Ingo Herman, "Total Humanism." **Is God Dead?** Concilium, Vol. 16 (New York: Paulist, 1966), pp. 166-167.

[9] **Ibid.**, p. 171.

[10] Cf. supra, ch. 2 pp. 84-85.

[11] Cf. J. Metz, "The Future of Man," **Journal of Ecumenical Studies,** 4 (Spring, 1967), pp. 224-227.

[12] Cf. supra, ch. 2 pp. 81-82.

[13] Roger Garaudy and Quentin Lauer, S.J., **A Christian-Communist Dialogue** (Garden City, N.Y.: Doubleday, 1968).

[14] **Ibid.**, p. 46.

[15] **Ibid.**, p. 54.

[16] **Ibid.**, p. 59.

[17] **Ibid.**, p. 62.

[18] **Ibid.**, p. 65.

[19] Paul Kurtz, in Introduction to "A Catholic/Humanist Dialogue," **The Humanist** 31(May-June, 1971), p. 30.

[19a] The American counterpart of the Vatican Secretariat for Nonbelievers is now called the Secretariat for Human Values and operates under the Interreligious Affairs Committee of the National Conference of Catholic Bishops. (NCCB).

[20] Paul Kurtz and Albert Dondeyne, eds., **A Catholic-Humanist Dialogue** (Buffalo: Prometheus Books, 1972), pp. 3-9.

[21] **Ibid.**, p. 6.

[22] **Ibid.**, p. 61.

[23] **Ibid.**, p. 14.

[24] **Ibid.**, p. 105.

[25] **Ibid.**, pp. 91ff.

[26] **Ibid.**, p. 68.

[27] **Ibid.**, p. 18.

[28] **Ibid.**, p. 21.

[29] **Ibid.**, p. 51.

[30] **Ibid.**, p. 58.

[31] **Ibid.**, p. 102.

[32] Paul Kurtz, "Notes from the Editor," **The Humanist** 32 (July/August, 1972), p. 4.

[33] Robert J. Roth, S.J. "Reflections on the Dialogue," **The Humanist** 32 (July/August, 1972), p. 28.

[34] John C. Haughey, S.J. "Humanists Encounter a 'Pilgrim' Church," **America**, 126(May 27, 1972), p. 564.

[35] Louis Dupré, "Reflections on a Catholic-Humanist Dialogue," **America** 126(June 24, 1972), p. 653.

[36] **Ibid.**, p. 653.

[37] Madalyn Murray O'Hair, "Reflections on the Dialogue," **The Humanist** 32, (July-August, 1972), p. 39.

38 **Directory,** Secretariat for Non-Believers, Introduction, published in English Translation in: **Talking with Unbelievers,** Vol. IV, ed. by Peter Hebblethwaite, S.J. (Isle of Man: The Month, 1971), p. 121.

39Cf. "Declaration on Religious Freedom," #3, **The Documents of Vatican II,** W. M. Abbott, ed., pp. 680-81.

40 **Directory, Talking** with **Unbelievers,** IV, p. 121.

41 **Ibid.,** pp. 121-22.

Aptheker, Herbert. *The Urgency of Marxist-Christian Dialogue.* New York: Harper & Row, 1970.

A Catholic-Humanist Dialogue. Ed. Paul Kurtz and Albert Dondeyne. Buffalo: Prometheus, 1972.

"A Catholic-Humanist Dialogue," *The Humanist* 31 (May/June, 1971) pp. 30-35.

Christian-Marxist Dialogue, The Ed. P. Oestreicher. New York: Macmillan, 1969.

Garaudy, Roger, and Lauer, Quentin, S.J. *A Christian-Communist Dialogue.* Garden City, N.Y.: Doubleday, 1968.

Garaudy, Roger. "Christian-Marxist Dialogue," *Journal of Ecumenical Studies* 4 (1967), pp. 207-22.

Garaudy, Roger. "The Christian-Marxist Dialogue: Possibilities, Problems, Necessity," *Continuum* 3 (1966), pp. 403-17.

Haughey, John C. "Humanists encounter a 'Pilgrim' Church," *America* 126 (May 27, 1972), pp. 564-67.

"Humanist Manifesto, II," *The Humanist* 33 (Sept.-Oct., 1973), pp. 4-9.

"Humanists and Catholics: The First US Dialogue," *The Humanist* 32 (July/August, 1972) pp. 24-40.

Machovec, M., Metz, J. B., and Rahner, K. *Can a Christian be a Marxist?* Chicago: Argus Communications, Inc., 1969.

Marxism and Christianity. Ed. Herbert Aptheker. New York: Humanities, 1968.

Metz, Johannes B. "The Future of Man," *Journal of Ecumenical Studies* 4 (1967), pp. 224-27.

Norris, Russell B. *Transcendence and Futility: Dialogue with Roger Garaudy.* Philadelphia: Fortress Press, 1974.

Norris. Russell B. "Transcendence and the Future: Dialogue with Roger Garaudy," *The Journal of Ecumenical Studies* 10 (Summer, 1973), pp. 498-514.

Openings for Christian-Marxist Dialogue. Ed. T. W. Ogletree. Nashville: Abingdon, 1969.

Rahner, Karl. "Christian Humanism," *Journal of Ecumenical Studies* 4 (1967), pp. 369-84.

Rahner, Karl. "The Concept of Mystery in Catholic Theology," *Theological Investigations,* IV. Baltimore: Helicon, 1966, pp. 36-63, esp. 48-60.

"Reflections on a Catholic-Humanist Dialogue," *America* 126 (June 24, 1972), pp. 652-54.

Richardson, Herbert W. *Toward an American Theology.* New York: Harper & Row, 1967.

Schillebeeckx, Edward, O.P. *God and Man.* New York: Sheed & Ward, 1969, esp. pp. 41-84.

Talking With Unbelievers. Parts 3 & 4 Ed. Peter Hebblethwaite, S.J. Isle of Man: The Month, A Times Longbook, 1970, 1971. Part 4 contains an English translation of the Directory of the Secretariat for Non-Believers, Franziskus Cardinal Koenig, President, and Rev. Vincent Miano, Secretary, given at Rome, August 28, 1968, pp. 117-34, along with a commentary on the Directory by Peter Hebblethwaite, pp. 137-45. The Directory is also to be found in *Herder Correspondence* 5 (1968), pp. 367-72, and was released by the Documentary Service of the U.S. Catholic Conference, Oct. 15, 1968.

Christian Faith and the Future of Man as Believer:
CHRISTIAN FAITH IN A PLURALISTIC, EVOLUTIONARY WORLD.

Many Christians, above all, many Catholics, have lost their nerve. They face the future with doubt and anxiety because they find themselves unable to live with the present and the many new forces that are at work within it. For them they are or seem to be alien forces, hostile to all they have previously found meaningful and precise, solvent of the Church and the world in which they were secure with their reassuring familiar forms. Where once stability ruled, now change is threateningly rampant; in place of unity and uniformity, only diversity is visible.

Is their faith able to survive this ordeal? We can hope. Is their faith what Christian Faith ought to be? Certainly not. For they have fallen into the perennial temptation to which we are all prone: to identify the faith with a particular cultural form it had assumed in an age that is already on its way out.

We dare not live in the past. As Christians, we cannot do so and remain committed to the faith we have received and are responsible for passing on alive to those after us. For it is a faith in Him Who makes all things new, Whose dying and rising have made of all of us a continually New Creation.

Marxists, like Garaudy, accuse us of being untrue to what we ourselves have taught them: confidence in a wholly open future, the self-transcendence of a subjectivity that is free to create an ever new universe, the capacity for a love that surpasses all limitations inasmuch as it realizes its love for the infinite God in one's brother whoever and whatever he may be, but especially the one whose poverty and need are most exacting of our concern and our service. Is our faith vital and large enough to practice what we profess? Is the Church which we are as the earthly Body of Christ, Who is the Savior of all mankind and the Absolute Future of all new ages, willing and able to live with ever-accelerating change and proliferating diversity? Not only able to live with them but to become the vanguard of change as the heralds of its future and the center of diversity as the norm of its unity?

I. CHRISTIAN FAITH AS THE DI-
VINELY GUARANTEED NORM OF
MULTIPLE HUMAN FAITHS
Unity in Diversity: One Truth, Many Faiths

The Christian theologian is the spokesman for the Christian believer at least to the extent that he is the Christian believer seeking to arrive at the fullest self-understanding and self-articulation. As such he strives before all else to ascertain the truth as the goal of his inquiries and reflections, a motivation which he assumes is shared with all men of good will. For himself he is convinced that his Christian faith is the strongest reason for his commitment to that objective, whatever the cost. For he believes that truth is ultimately identical with the Absolute Person to Whom he has dedicated his life and all his energies. Moreover, he believes that the Personal Truth Whom he worships is the God of and for all men and therefore the One Whom they all seek, wittingly or unwittingly, as they strive for self-realization. To avow a dedication to the truth before all else then is required of him by the very faith with which he proclaims what that truth actually is.

Christian Faith presents itself as the absolute truth about man. Especially in Chapter Five, we tried to express the reasoning in faith that purports to validate that claim.

It is a highly pretentious claim, but for one who is in conscience convinced of its validity, it would be a disservice to the truth and an exercise in dishonesty not to put it forward. In essence, it asserts that Christianity is the explicit articulation of what man really *is and is for* whether he recognizes it or not; therefore that it formulates in word and thematizes in sacrament and symbol with divinely guaranteed authenticity what all the other religions and all the ideologies strive to express with varying success and with an inevitable admixture of error and corruption.

As the absolute faith, it is the norm of all human faiths. Especially in Jesus Christ, the revelation of creative divine truth in human form, Christian Faith has as its object and motive the unconditioned standard by which every affirmation about the meaning of man must be judged. He is The Man, the One Who God defined by becoming.

As a matter of fact, most men do not acknowledge the Christian claim and they relegate Christianity to another niche in the gallery of the many religions of man. It is, they say, just one more among the diverse ideologies or world-views to which men pay allegiance, and, as we observed in the first chapter, it has lost its grip among all but a dwindling minority of our contemporaries who regard such issues as even worthy of their concern. We have concluded from our study that, indeed, all men are believers, whether they say so or not. Even the dilettante and the most skeptical have assumed a world-view or life-stance which is at least implicit in their very style of life. Without exception, they-we— are all believers. Every man has some sort of faith.

We have finally gotten around, officially as a Church, to admit not only the reality of pluralism, but to a certain extent its legitimacy, its right to exist; and we have taken the next step of trying to enter into dialogue with these other faiths as a profession of our very mission as the Church of Christ. Somewhat as the Exile was for Israel, so the vast spread and influence of other than Christian, indeed, other than religious faiths in our age is a significant turn in the on-going history of man's salvation. It must not only be acknowledged, it clamors for theological explanation in the light of the universal mission of Christ and His Church.

What is theologically significant about the present situation of the Church? Religious and ideological pluralism, at least in the western world, is the result of a drastic shift in the socio-political and cultural situation. The modern era began when the sacralized society and culture of the Middle Ages began to break up. After the collapse of the Roman Empire, the Church by default had to take over many of the civilizing functions of the secular power with the result that the secular realm became largely sacralized, as it had been under pagan auspices in the early centuries of the Church's existence. With the rise of the Holy Roman Empire in Europe, there was a redistribution of functions. However, there was not a genuine autonomy of the secular order vis-a-vis the sacred. The Church was the more dominant and pervasive partner in relation to the State and the society was quite clearly ecclesiastical in power and form.

In the fourteenth century, this ecclesiastically dominated partnership began to dissolve as the nation-states took over the empire and the great western schism led to conciliarism, that is, the supremacy of the General Council representing all the factions within the Church over the papal office, as its apparently logical solution. The Council of Constance (1417), which seemed to mark the triumph of conciliarism, actually signaled its eventual defeat within the Church. But Luther arrived on the scene a century later (1517) to catalyze the historical processes which seemed bent on destroying the unity of Christianity and the dismembering of Christendom as a socio-political entity. The religious pluralism that resulted not only limited and discredited the absolute claims of the Papacy or any ecclesiastical authority to speak for all Christians, it also gradually produced a social and cultural environment in which the individual was left free in his choice of churchly affiliation.

The time was to come, and has indeed arrived in our age, when the culture would be no longer Christian, but post-Christian; when it would be within the bounds of respectability not merely to be a Christian of any stamp, but to opt for not being a Christian at all. In such a society as ours, one's religious affiliation or lack thereof is tabulated as a neutral statistic along with one's sex and marital status. It marks the final stage in the emancipation of the state from the ecclesiastical and of the desacralization of the secular order which the state embodies. It is the process which we have come to call: Secularization.

The theological interpretation of secularization is a task to which we shall address ourselves later. For the moment, it is the current pluralism of faiths of which it has been a major cause with which we are concerned. How do we understand the Church and the absolute claims of its Christian faith in a world of many faiths?

The momentum of historical change appears to favor diversification of beliefs or world-views. This is true at least to the extent that it is biased against any foreseeable triumph of Christianity or indeed of any faith as the single unifying world-view of all men. This is true also of Communism as its recent history testifies. For neither the objective truth of a faith, such as we claim for Christianity, nor its overwhelming socio-political power as it is exercised in Communist countries, can assure the uniform interior allegiance of any population to that faith.

The subverting counter-force is freedom, not as an abstract ideal, but as the inner dynamism of the evolving subjectivities of men. For more and more men everywhere are advancing toward that stage of human psychological evolution where they are determined to take over their own lives, and whether for their good or ill, to resist any *overt* attempt to impose a global viewpoint on them as their own personal attitude toward themselves and the world they live in. *Overt* is an important word in the context, because along with this development, there has also grown the scientific capacity of men to control the stimuli that excite our feelings and provide the data for our judgments. Covertly, we are in grave danger of being manipulated. Over the long run, however, even this possibility is subject to the transcending drive of the human spirit, man's boredom with sameness, his inborn resistance to "being had" perpetually, and his indomitable desire for change.[1]

Until recently the attitude of the Church to pluralism was baldly negative. In the name of integral truth, the focus was trained exclusively on the error in other faiths that rendered their possession of the truth only partial. With the acknowledgment of freedom of conscience as an authentically Christian value along with truth, a more positive judgment is able to be made. This does not involve a capitulation to error or lessening of one's own commitment to the fuller measure of truth that he is convinced he possesses. As we have tried to illustrate in practice, rather than demanding the surrender to the other's position, genuine dialogue requires that one represent one's own position with its greatest strength. All that is asked is openness to the presence of truth in the belief of the dialogue partner and the consequent enhancing of its presence in one's own.

In the conciliar documents of the Church in the modern world and on its relations with the non-Christian religions as well as those dealing with ecumenism and religious freedom, the new attitude of openness to the truth in other traditions was embraced. It is a more Christ-like attitude in the Body of Christ: a loving solicitude for these others which exacts patience, forebearance that flees the precipitous hurtful judgment, even though errors may distort and conceal the precious core of truth. Only thus is it likely that men who have grasped the truth in part may be gently drawn to the fuller vision.

The hopefulness of this attitude is certainly well justified by the theory of an anonymous or implicit Christianity. For in that perspective the Church approaches those outside its visible fold not as aliens to its message, but as those to whom the saving grace of Christ is already present and consistently provoking their response. The faith by which they live, though burdened with sin as ours also is, to the degree that it is a positive response to the pressure of God's saving will, is a saving faith. The truths that it enunciates are founded on His Self-revelation, the same source as the Church's own divinely guaranteed teaching. The errors which vitiate it are like those from which we are not individually exempt due to human fallibility and sinfulness.

The plurality of human faiths is a predictable consequence of human finiteness and of the historicity of salvation. It has characterized the history of salvation from the beginning. Israel often had to learn the will of Yahweh from its pagan neighbors, from their wisdom as well as their hostility. The Church itself is not excused from its human limitations. Though it embodies Him Who is the Truth, it is through the mutations of its historical experience that it brings to successive focus new facets of the self-same Infinite Mystery. For the community of explicit Christian faith participates in and learns from the larger community of mankind, whose faith is implicitly Christian.

No age of the Church should be more aware of that fact than ours. We have had to confess our faults and short-comings: our anti-Semitism, our share in obstructing the unity of all Christians, our violations of the dignity and freedom of the individual conscience. By the grace of God, we have also proclaimed before the world our dependence upon it to discern His will for us, reading It in "the signs of the times," fresh intuitions triggered by the new insights of science as well as by the traditions of ancient faiths, a deeper self-understanding of the Church stimulated by social changes which require a different kind of living the truth that it bears within.

If the Church is truly "the sacrament of the world's salvation," it is the servant of the world within which it treads its pilgrim way· It is dedicated to the world of mankind, humbly learning from it as well as being its teacher. For all truth is God's truth and therefore it is ultimately one. To serve men in His Name, it must listen for His voice and attend to His presence wherever He, in His sovereign freedom, chooses to manifest them. We might say in freely accommodating the initial statements in the letter to the Hebrews: "In many and various ways, He speaks to us by a Son, whom He appointed the heir of *all* things, through whom also He created the world" (cf. Heb 1:1-2.).

To acknowledge that religious pluralism has a positive role to play in the history of salvation does not, at least it should not, result in a flabby relativism which resigns itself to the position that one man's religious convictions are as good as another's. This would be a repudiation of the mandate of Christ to His Church to preach His gospel to all nations and a rejection of Christ Himself as the source of salvation and the standard of its truth. Religious pluralism is a fact of salvation history in whose unyielding presence the Church must come to understand itself within that history. Yet the goal remains: religious pluralism must be overcome in the unceasing effort toward unity in the one faith in Jesus Christ, even if that goal may never be wholly realized short of the Parousia.

Although religious pluralism may always be with us, its internal dynamic even now, as we discussed in chapter five, is toward that unity of faith in God revealed in His Christ which in every age achieves its fullest expression and earthly actualization in Christ's Church. That Church in its faith, therefore, is the norm by which the truth and authenticity of the many faiths are to be judged. Its own unity is, to put it mildly, imperfect, and yet in its imperfection, it still is the focus of that unity toward which all human faiths are pointing insofar as they are a faithful response to the God Who reveals Himself in His Self-gift to all men. Meanwhile, through sustained ecumenical effort and a greater readiness for plurality in the expression of its own faith the Church must labor tirelessly to realize in itself a fuller unity in Christ as the most effective witness of the Spirit Who draws all men into one.

II. The Church and the World

In recent years theological trends have passed on and off the scene with increasing swiftness. They resemble moods and fashions in their brief prominence more than serious thoughtful reflections of faith on the human situation, which they have usually been. One of the more momentous and apparently enduring of these theologies was that which argued for a 'secular Christianity.' It achieved great popularity in this country, particularly in the writings of Harvey Cox and the various 'death of God' theologians. It found its inspiration, among other sources, in the later thought of Dietrich Bonhoeffer in which that heroic man advocated a 'religionless Christianity.' In effect, it proposed that the time for a 'churchly Christianity' had passed, and that man had matured sufficiently to the point where the Christianity he practiced in Christ-like service of his fellow-man was better left anonymous. Cox had suggested that the appropriate arena of this service as a pursuit of the Kingdom of God was the City of Man. The 'death of God' theologians, like Altizer and Hamilton, had caught Bonhoeffer's hint that God was indeed teaching us to grow toward the full stature of Christ by learning to do without Him and had translated it into the actual passing of any transcendent deity who distracted us from our worldly tasks.

The enthusiasm for a secular Christianity has ebbed in the receding wave of the optimism which it expressed. For the bright promise of 'man come of age,' grasping firm control of his own destiny and that of his world, was all but lost within a few short years darkened by successive failures of secular man: a soul-destroying war, racial conflict, blighted cities, ecological suicide, and the massive self-exile of the youth from our society and its institutions. The City of Man had become the tomb of scarce-born hopes.

A Theology of Christian Secularity

Secular Christianity was a serious attempt to face the fact that we live now as Christian believers in a secularized world that has declared its independence of the Church and of any religious agency that would threaten any more to sacralize it and to take it out of man's control. It is a striking fact that the process of secularization has taken place only in the Christian West, and where it is occurring elsewhere, its origins can be traced to our culture. Many Christian theologians see this as more than a coincidence.

These theologians discern in our secularized society the end-product of a process which is truly biblical in its origins and Christian in its inspiration. For secularization can be described as the dedivinizing and demythologizing of nature, man and society, the growing acknowledgment of the autonomy of the secular over against the sacred and the broadening of its scope. This can be recognized as the other side of the process recorded in scripture wherein God asserted His transcendent uniqueness over against the world.

"I am the Lord your God. There is no other." He forbade images or idols, for no earthly thing could contain His presence or constrain His power. From Moses onward, the prophets fought every effort on the part of the Israelites to reduce God to the form of one of His creatures, to identify Him with a part of His world. Jesus brought this movement to its final phase when He said to the Samaritan woman: "The hour is coming when neither on this mountain nor in Jerusalem will you worship the Father . . . The hour is coming and is now here, when the true worshippers will worship the Father in spirit and in truth . . . God is spirit and they who worship Him must worship in spirit and in truth." (Jn 4:21, 23-24.) When God insists on His unique Godness, the world, which is His creation and infinitely other, is left free to be itself in its worldliness, its secularity.

It is apparent then that secularization need not be interpreted as equivalent to deChristianization, even though it has often given that appearance. It can be welcomed rather than resisted by the Christian. It is not necessarily convertible with secularism, which is the exclusion of the sacred from the central concern of modern man or its reduction to irrelevance.

The interior thrust of Christian faith to desacralize the world and to free it to be itself was given a tentative doctrinal formulation in the synthesis of St. Thomas whose attempt is called by Josef Pieper "a theologically grounded worldliness." However, the initiative toward achieving the governing formulae and guidelines for the historical process of secularization was lost to the Church in the ideologies of the Renaissance and more especially of the Enlightenment with the revolutionary programs that it fostered in England, America and France, in the Industrial Revolution and the proletarian movements it provoked, and finally in the rise of the natural sciences with the technological revolution that they have borne. The history of western man has thus witnessed a step-by-step isolation of the Church from the mainstream of ideas and movements that have formed his world-outlook. Even the progress toward the recognition of individual dignity and fundamental human rights, inconceivable outside the Christian family of cultures, has been attributed to other than Christian parentage. The process of secularization has been all but captured by the secularists, who ignore or dismiss the Church as irrelevant when they do not actively oppose it as an out-dated obstruction to the achievement of man's goals.

At Vatican II the Church began to reverse its direction and it has since taken constructive steps toward re-entering the world from which it seemed bent on banning itself. Christian theologians have attempted to show the Christian roots of the process of secularization and the resulting obligation of Christians to engage actively in it as a vocation to which faith itself calls them. This effort toward elaborating a theology of Christian secularity has assumed various forms: a theology of hope (Moltmann, Pannenberg) and a political theology (Metz) among others.

One of the most incisive and influential of Catholic contributors to the discussion about Christian secularity is Johannes Baptist Metz, erstwhile disciple of Karl Rahner who has passed beyond the position of his master and his own former position when he was still dominated by Rahner's thought. In fact, the master has become to a considerable degree a pupil of his former disciple, at least in this area of his theology. Metz has been engaged in an attempt to develop a theology that is post-metaphysical, critical and social. It was in his grappling with the problem of secularization that he began to develop a theology of hope, akin to that of Jürgen Moltmann, strongly eschatological and oriented toward the future as the direction of transcendence and of man's creative freedom. More recently, he has moved in the direction of what he calls a 'political theology' as a reaction against what he designates the "privatizing" tendencies of Bultmann's hermeneutic, of personalism and even of the transcendental philosophical outlook which he previously shared with Rahner.

In confronting Christian faith with the new conditions of a secularized world, he proposes the following thesis: "the historical situation with which faith is faced today and in which it must prove itself as hope, is that of the transition from a divinized to a hominized world."[2] This situation arose out of a change in man's own attitude toward his world away from a 'cosmocentric' in the direction of an 'anthropocentric' way of thinking.

> Here man grasps himself in his free historical subjectivity. He experiences and fulfills himself no longer as an existent beside other existents in the world, but as the world's subjectivity, to whom the modes of the world's being, nature, culture, society, are ever more available and who now draws this world ever more profoundly into the history of his own free subjectivity . . . The understanding of the world changes from seeing it as nature to seeing it as history . . . The experience of man as a speculative world-subject moves out of its inner life to involve itself actively with the world, thus leading to that transition from the divinized or numinized world to a hominized one that we experience today as the crisis and the future of our faith.[3]

In his formerly 'divinized' world, man was encompassed by nature, at once sheltered and intimidated by it. It was a numinous world, embossed with divine features, the medium of his religious experience, for its indomitable power with its immutable laws could impress him as the very power of God, the *mysterium fascinans et tremendum.* But all this has changed in the modern era. Human life is no longer enfolded within nature. Rather civilizing man has taken nature into his own hands. "In relation to nature man sees himself as a demiurge, a master-builder of the world, who creates *his* world out of the material of nature, the world of man, a *hominized* world."[4]

The hominizing of the world has seemed to many to rob it of its character as a divine creation. God seems to have been deprived of his world, driven out of it. Metz feels that this experience is at the root of much of today's unbelief and that atheism is one of its misinterpretations, for it sees the anthropocentric world-experience as contradicting theocentric faith and demanding the eschatology of a humanism without God.

Like many other Christian thinkers, Metz insists that this hominizing and secularizing of the world has taken place not in opposition to but on account of Christianity, that the change in man's thinking from a cosmocentric to an anthropocentric perspective took place through and not against the Christian mind. Therefore Christians should insert themselves into the heart of this change and face any crisis it may occasion with hope.

He tries to support his stand by pointing to some facets

of the Christian message that suggested and inaugurated the process of hominizing the world. Thus the Christian believer stands before his Creator, a completely transcendent God, Who "dwells in unapproachable light" (1 Tm 6:16). Man's faith in his God Who is infinitely superior to the world manifests the world's own finiteness, its non-divine and non-numinous character. But it also frees the world to be itself in man's consciousness, to be man's world, so that it may be absorbed into the movement of human freedom, brought under man's explanation and control. Thus Christian faith establishes the secular experience of the world. By the same token, where faith in a transcendent Creator is lacking, the divine enters as an element in the world picture, nature is apotheosized, so that the world is something less than world because God is someone less than God.

The Christian gospel also contributed to the inauguration of hominization by setting man free, acknowledging his unique personal worth, and setting him incomparably higher than nature or his world setting. Thereby he was enabled to become a more active subject toward the world, "his footstool," as it were.

It is the Incarnation, however, that furnishes the most profound Christian impetus to hominization. For by it God turned to the world in man who became the only mediator for God's irrevocable acceptance of the world and its history, the meeting place between them and God. In the Incarnation, we have the ultimate expression of biblical anthropocentrism by which the world loses its own aura of divinity and achieves its proper worldly character as man's charge and responsibility.

However, the question still insistently confronts us: how can we speak of Christ as the Lord of history and the master of its future when even the incarnate God seems to be "edged out of his world" by the process of secularization? Metz's reply is a compound one: negatively, the cross is always a sign of contradiction which the world protests and the secularized world is the cosmic expression of its opposition to God and His Christ, which is always to be expected in a Christian view of history. This is, nevertheless, only a corrective to the positive Christian value which the process of secularization has as the historical manifestation of God's acceptance of the world in Christ. The first truth assures the permanent distinction between the sacred and the secular in the present dispensation. The latter truth anticipates their ultimate reconciliation.

"In his son, Jesus Christ, God accepted the world with eschatological definitiveness . . . The Church which he founded is the historically tangible and effective sign, the sacrament of the eschatologically final acceptance of the world by God."[5] The world itself would have been the actuality of its own acceptance by God, but because it culpably rejected its acceptance in Christ, it is distinct from the Church which exists as the sign of its actual acceptance and the promise of its eventual definitive acceptance and reconciliation.

God acts on the world in history. His transcendence is not infinitely distant and supra-historical. It has become an event implying the definitive and inescapable future of man already present and effective within history. He is Lord of history because He has constituted history in its very origins and in its absolute future. Yet the world as history is free and contingent in its divine origins, and as man's world it is subjected to man's understanding and man's free action. It is eschatological in as much as, under man, it must seek its own reality in order to become that which through Jesus Christ it already is: "the new heaven and the new earth" (Rv 21:1), the single kingdom of God and man. Thus the Incarnation is not an extrinsic principle of history, applied *a posteriori* to certain phenomena of history. It is an intrinsic principle of history constituting it in its origins and in its definitive future already operative in its present process towards that future. Christ is the Alpha and the Omega, drawing man and his world towards its final rendezvous with Him.

"God acts in such a way in relation to the world that he accepts it irrevocably in His Son."[6] In His sovereign and transcendent freedom, God constitutes the other precisely as other in so far as He unites it to Himself. By virtue of the hypostatic union, Jesus Christ was constituted other, that is, man, more fully than any other creature could be. Thereby He became the center and basis whereby every creature would be itself. By His acceptance of the world in Christ, God sets the world and man free for their own authentic mode of being, to be that by which they are precisely not divine, but rather human and worldly. In other words, God "is not in competition with, but the 'guarantor' of the world."[7]

The analogy is with human friendship. The more a person is accepted by his friend, the more does he come to know himself and possess himself, the more free does he become to grow and be himself more fully. Thus acceptance and independence and self-realization are not opposed in friendship, rather they complement and reinforce each other. Similarly the world becomes itself most deeply because it is accepted into the divine life through man its center, and man through Christ realizes himself in freedom most fully because he has been accepted as son and friend by the Father.

In his acceptance of man and his world, God remains Himself, the only basis and reason for the diversity from Himself, differentiating Himself from the non-divine-other in His radical transcendence as its creator. Thus God's descent into the world does not compromise His transcendence; rather descent and transcendence grow in the same proportion. Therefore, the Christian who understands the world through salvation history grasps in sharpest terms not only God's uniqueness, but the non-divine, finite worldliness of the world. And so, the first effect of the Incarnation is not a divinization of the world, but instead the clearest demarcation of the world in its secular otherness from the divine, in its proper integrity. Thus distinction precedes eventual union and reconciliation. Realistically, of course, we recognize that the acceptance of the world is a suffering acceptance, under the saving and liberating sign of the cross, always to some degree a mark of contradiction.

Although it was a truly Christian event, the secularization of the world was misunderstood and opposed by the Church, often in the face of genuine concrete dangers and errors. For that reason among others, secularization has tended toward being anti-Christian and secularistic. As a consequence, the Christian, while welcoming it as providential, must recognize that the modern process of secularization and the world-view it frequently projects are less than the adequate expression of the secularization engendered by the Christ-event.

In the light of what we have seen, what should be the attitude of the Christian in faith toward the increasing secularizing of the world? Basically, it should represent "the faithful imitation of God's descent into the world, of the liberating acceptance of the world in Jesus Christ."[8] Often the Christian finds himself living an ambivalent existence, torn between the apparently conflicting demands of his faith and the world. This discrepancy is a real one and cannot be resolved by simply making the world the theme of an act of faith in the God-centered character of worldly events. No, the Christian should imitate Christ and accept in faith those elements of our worldly existence not yet assimilated into it, thereby leaving them free to be what they are.

Metz gives the example of a young man whose plan to be an engineer is not initially motivated by faith and he feels an inward discrepancy between his faith and his worldly ambition. Actually his very faith can resolve the dilemma by guaranteeing the secular character of his existence as an engineer without feeling a bad conscience about it. As St. Paul makes quite clear: "For all things are yours, whether Paul or Apollos or Cephas or the world or life or death or the present or the future, all are yours; and you are Christ's and Christ is God's" (1 Cor 3:21ff).

We cannot forget, however, that our relationship to the world has two sides. Since it was not we, but the Father in His incarnate Son, Who accepted and thereby freed the world, the secular appears as something beyond our control, not penetrated by faith, and in this sense something truly pagan and profane. Although it is already definitively accepted in Christ, for us the acceptance of the world in its worldliness remains an eschatological event towards which we move in hope. Meanwhile we shall continue to have to suffer from it and bear it as a cross of our faith, confessing with St. Paul: "I am crucified to the world and the world to me" (Gal 6:14).

Yet it remains true that the Christian faith, seeing the world in the perspective of its acceptance in Christ, is alone able to take the world as it is in itself without altering it or setting up new gods within or above it. The unbelieving non-Christian will in the end always falsify this worldliness, either in a naive utopian belief in progress, or in an earthly paradise, or in a tragic nihilism and resigned skepticism. On the contrary, the Christian is free by his faith to be the truly worldly or secular man who can let the worldliness of the world be, by re-enacting in faith God's liberating acceptance of the world in Jesus Christ. Our faith is "the victory that has overcome the world" (1 Jn 5:4), which means here that by our faith we are enabled to emulate Christ's acceptance of the world, to take it to ourselves in its worldliness.

Thus to Christianize the world is not to change it to something else, to make it unworldly; rather it means to make the world more worldly, to liberate it from the hidden obstructions of sin which enslave and alienate it from itself, to allow it to be itself most fully. In this sense, grace perfects nature because it frees the secular order to be uninhibitedly secular. "And that is why the Church or the historically tangible sign and the institution of this grace within the world is not the opponent but the guarantor of the world. The Church exists for the world . . . (It) bears witness to, and makes present, the power of that will made flesh in which God finally makes the world over to himself, but precisely in doing so releases it to find its own deepest being."[9] It is true that the fullness of this guaranteed worldliness will not be achieved within history as process, but only eschatologically at the end of the as yet incomplete history of the world.

Meanwhile, the secularized or hominized world is in danger of becoming a *dehumanized* world. Not only nature but man himself is threatened with being manipulated. The subject of the hominizing process is menaced with being degraded into the object of its regimentation. Yet this is not an inevitable consequence. Hominization leaves an opening for a deeper and broader humanization, for treating the individual person more responsibly. By placing man more clearly in the center of nature as its subject, as the one who structures and gives meaning to his world, it lends at once greater urgency and scope to the central Christian message, that God Himself encounters us in every brother. In accepting our brother-man in his uniqueness and mystery, as one who may not be reduced to a mere object, but who is truly the Thou, the other subject, the mystery of God, the Absolute Other, is made present. Thus, in place of nature, the other who is our brother becomes a center of numinous experience and the focus of revelatory experience. Many today practice this brotherhood (we can call them 'anonymous Christians'), who do not realize that thereby they have begun to believe in God Who willed to be our brother and thus to be found, at once revealed and concealed, in human encounter. It is in this heightening of the worth of every brother and the revolutionary indignation it unleashes against every degradation of man that the threat of dehumanization may yet be vanquished. At the same time the Christian can hopefully work to intensify the experience of God's nearness in the sanctity of man and the community of brothers.

The role of the Church, which is the locus and bearer of the sacred in a world from which it is distinct because of sin and man's chronic rejection of God's acceptance, is to further their eventual reconciliation and union. But it may never again be by way of sacralization of the world which is a denial of the distinction and a rejection of the autonomy of the secular order. Now it is rather a sanctifying, a liberating and disclosing of man and his world as already Christified, that is, already in process of being drawn into the divine life by the redemptive Incarnation of the Word of God which establishes the reintegration of all things in Christ as their absolute future.

The Church's role in the world is becoming clarified in our secular, post-Christian age. The liberation of the City of Man has also freed the City of God for its essential task. It is no different from the charge: "Go, therefore, make disciples of all nations." "Repent, the kingdom of God is at hand." It is our less distracted vision of what this entails, of the mission of the Church unencumbered by the social and political and cultural functions with which history saddled it and with which it grew accustomed to confuse and even identify its central vocation for man. Now it can become again, though the restoring transformation will be a slow and painful process, what it was at the beginning: the witness to the glorified Christ in Whom "all things hold together" (Col 1:17), and through Whom all things are to be reconciled to the Father, "whether on earth, or in heaven, making peace by the blood of his cross" (Col 1:20). Now it can return to its iconoclastic task of pronouncing judgment on and of destroying idols men substitute for God, above all the idol which is man himself. This will presuppose on the part of the Church a relentless self-criticism and a perpetual reformation under the probing light of the Gospel with which it dares to judge the world, for the kingdom of God which it preaches is a goal to which it advances in pilgrimage with faltering steps.

We live in an age when mankind is fast progressing toward a more intimate unity than was ever possible before. It is truly providential that at such a uniquely opportune moment in human history the process of secularization is divorcing Christianity from its identification with the culture of the West and revealing in undisguised splendor its intrinsic catholicity "as a sign set before *all* the nations." By a happy and equally providential coincidence, as Charles Davis has pointed out, a secular West, no longer identified with Christianity, is serving as an unwitting vanguard for the Christian mission. For in accepting western science and technology, the sacralized Eastern cultures, hitherto impermeable to Christian faith, will themselves undergo the same desacralization and transformation "into an open, pluralist social order, where ultimate beliefs are freely considered without a cultural exclusiveness. In which case, conditions will have been created that are suitable for the presentation of the Christian message."[10]

The other and inner side of the coin engraved by the secularization of the West is the loss of its identity as a Christian culture and the loss of masses of men whose allegiance to Christianity was cultural rather than based on a living faith able to stand on its own and to withstand adversity. This has made the Church a minority in peoples and nations it once claimed wholly for its own. It has created an open and pluralist society where men differ widely about ultimate truth and are free in an atmosphere of unhampered discussion to make their own personal commitments without compulsion from society or the state. The Second Vatican Council's Declaration on Religious Liberty was a somewhat belated recognition of this present inescapable fact as well as of its hopeful potentialities for the future.

These two facts of contemporary life: the presence of the Church as a diminishing minority in a unifying world whose non-Christian majority is fast coming into its own, and the accelerating loss of former Christian populations to rival ideologies, provide the dramatic setting against which the Church must prosecute its perennial mission. Were we limited to the theological developments of past centuries, it might present depressing prospects. But the very developments in the world around us have provoked theological developments in the Church's consciousness of its own nature and its mission to mankind to match and comprehend the more prepossessing problems of our more complex age.

Political Theology

In developing his Political Theology as a further stage of his theology of Christian Secularity, Metz has criticized modern existential and personalist theologies, even in their transcendental version, for remaining in the private sphere of inter-personal encounter and ignoring the social dimension of the Christian message. This move inevitably involves a certain criticism of the earlier stages of his own thought. He charges these theologians with neglecting to meet the religious critique stemming from the Enlightenment and evolved in Marxism. This critique judges religious thought and forms to be merely a particular cultural superstructure of the prevailing socio-political base and the religious subject as a false consciousness which has not yet achieved adequate self-understanding as a component of the social body. Metz focuses his attack especially on Bultmann whose demytho-logizing of the Gospel terminated in an existentialist inter-pretation which limited itself to the private categories of personal encounter and decision. In doing so he misread the essence of the Christian kerygma which is public proclama-tion of God's revelation directed to the human community. It also tends to treat the individual person abstractly since it does not situate him in his actual social context. There-fore demythologizing must be supplemented by a *depri-vatizing* of theology.

Christian faith is an eschatological and therefore a prophetic faith, which pronounces critical judgment not merely on the life of the individual but also on human society itself. In His proclamation of the Kingdom, Jesus came into open conflict with the public authorities because His Gospel was a judgment on the collective sinfulness of men as well as the decisive disclosure of God's plan for the salvation of the body of mankind. It could not be restricted to the purely private sphere of the individual human con-science.

The Enlightenment attempted to reduce Christian faith to a particular human phenomenon by removing religion from the social and political realm to the purely private and therefore to a matter of public indifference. Marx and his followers carried this trend to the point where religious belief and practice were no more than the symptoms of a particular socio-economic system and its attempted rational-ization. Metz emphasizes that a version of Christian faith that does not assume 'political' proportions is unable to respond to this still prevailing criticism and is in fact un-faithful to the politicalness and social magnitude of the Gospel. This does not mean that Christianity should be identified with the current political system, an historical mistake of the Church which he repudiates with most contemporary Christian thinkers, but rather that the Church has to perform its essential prophetic role in the public forum.

The eschatological character or future-directedness of the Gospel has been revived and heightened in recent times, partly, at least, in view of the modern transformation of man's consciousness. The change has been from the classical mentality which stressed the past as the source of traditions that provided the paradigms for the present to the modern obsession with the future as the open end toward which man can direct his present programs and efforts for the re-making of his world and himself. There has also occurred a corresponding shift from the purely contemplative attitude of theoretical reason to the operative stance of practical reason. Thus Marx insists that the goal of philosophy is not merely to explain the world, but rather to change it.

Metz, like Rahner and many others, assumes a positive posture toward modern philosophy and political thought. For them it represents the reflections of men who are 'anonymously Christian' and for that reason it can be assimilated into the body of Chirstian theology rather than be rejected *in toto,* once the task of criticism in the light of the Gospel has been performed. This implies a positive relationship with modern movements like Marxism, as we have already seen illustrated in our dialogue, which can welcome their authentic values and expose their compatibility with Christianity; and, indeed, in many instances as in that of secularization, their Christian origins. Accordingly he accepts the Marxist and modern pragmatic position of the primacy of public practical reason over purely theoretical reason. It follows that if theology is to fulfill its contemporary task of confronting modern man and his society with the values and critical demands of Christian faith, it must enlist a human reason that is practical and directed toward human action in the public sphere. In other words, it must be a 'political theology.'[11]

What is the relation of the Church and the world in the light of a 'political theology'? First of all, the transformation of the meaning of 'world' from nature to history must be kept in mind.[12] Moreover, the significance of world as 'man's world' in as much as it is understood anthropocentrically as the arena of man's history must not be understood of man merely as person, but in his full social reality. 'Church' must be understood as Vatican II began to understand it in its pastoral constitution, viz., as an institutional reality within the world, though distinct from it in its essential function of prophetic criticism.

As political, theology operates on the post-critical level of a "second reflection," that is, it brings the faith to bear on the condition of man not only by virtue of its self-awareness as an eschatological judgment on sinful mankind of any age, but precisely in terms of its contemporary understanding of the societal dimension of man and of itself as a human institution. Because the Church has as its goal the establishment of the Kingdom of God among men, its perennial prophetic role is performed in view of an 'eschatological proviso.' This involves a distancing of itself from any current structure of society or any political system. For its goal, and therefore the force of its criticism, is transcendent as well as immanent to human history. In terms of its own finality towards the Kingdom which is the transhistorical end of all ages, it must judge the human condition of any age of history as provisional and subject to the always superior norm of the Gospel of the Kingdom. In that context every age is a *kairos* or compelling opportunity for Christian faith in which it must find the incentive to preach and give witness to those values which constitute the promises of the Kingdom: freedom, justice, peace and reconciling love, and to judge every society in so far as it fails to reach for them as its goals.

A political theology perceives the necessity of the Church as *"the institution of the critical liberty of faith."*[13] The perduring function of criticizing social institutions in the light of the Gospel cannot be sustained by individuals. They cannot bear the weight of being over-against the very institutions within which they live out their existence. The socialization of man that has progressed so rapidly in our time makes all the more imperative the institutionalization of the prophetic office. But is this possible? Is not the very history of the Church an argument against it?

Certainly the Church has failed, often lamentably, to fulfill this role. Too often it has either identified itself with the culture it was supposed to judge or it has neglected in itself the very Gospel norms with which the judgment was to be made. Can any institution be sufficiently self-critical to be itself the free subject of critical judgment?

The Church has both the grace and the mission to fulfill this role. Its *raison d'être* is to be the servant of the Kingdom, to exist not for itself but for the salvation of all men. Its very being-in-the-world is to incarnate the eschatological proviso, to be the living historical proof of history's own impermanence and of the self-insufficiency of every human institution; in a word, to be a pilgrim Church.

In the past the Church identified itself with the Kingdom. It is this triumphalism which was put aside by the Second Vatican Council. By being faithful to its divinely appointed role as the servant of the Kingdom, it is assured of the presence of the Spirit Who will work through it to bring that Kingdom about. In our age especially, the Church is needed to fulfill that role to safeguard the freedom of the individual, to protect him against every purely historical institution, humanistic or otherwise, which would reduce man to this-worldly phenomenon and subordinate him to "the building of a completely rationalized technological future."[14] The Church is indeed the unique institution, whose constituting horizon is transhistorical and which therefore by its very character is empowered and compelled to evaluate every program wthin history as transitory and particular. The ambition of any historical movement to encompass the entire history of man is bound to be not only totalitarian but eventually anti-human. As man's transcendence would begin to outstrip its limited range, it would become a prison from which man's spirit would strain to escape. Though Marxists rely on a negative exercise of that very transcendence to provide against such a confining of man by social institutions, their very commitment to a human goal immanent to history deprives them of the distance from such a goal which critical freedom would require.

In fact, the very danger of both Marxism and Secular Humanism is their dedication to a policy of scientific and technological 'triumphalism.' Thus, for example, Secular Humanism could only mount and sustain a social criticism of society by becoming itself 'church,' that is, an institution that is transcendent in the sense of being distinct from the world and its historical structures, which continually merit and require criticism, in order to be freely and perseveringly critical of it. Almost by its self-definition, this possibility is excluded. It is not surprising that both movements have lost their appeal to a generation that is rebelling against the regimentation of a technological society.

The final and greatest resource of the Church as the community of Christian faith is its infused capacity for loving divinely. This is the power as well as the ever-insistent challenge that proceeds from the Spirit within to love not only friends but enemies, to pray for persecutors rather than seek to vanquish and dominate by appeal to power. This demands a universal concern for all men without exception, but especially for the weak and persecuted. Above all, it requires a persistent criticism of undisciplined power. The unconditional character of this love for those who suffer injustice may even require, thinks Metz, a willingness to resort to revolutionary action, if a proportionate evil could thereby be averted.

Quite evidently the Church must undergo a radical change if it is to be an institutional subject of critical freedom. It is *not yet* so transformed, but it gives signs of making the move. Thus in the conciliar postoral constitution and in Pope Paul's *Populorum Progressio*, it has initiated a new language and style into such statements which are both more concrete and more tentative than is customary, reliant in these instances on the less self-assured method as well as on the information of the social sciences. Moreover, in order to exercise its critical function toward the world around it, it must encourage a courageous and enlightened critical public opinion within its own ranks, even when it is the object of criticism. This is a necessary form of the self-criticism to which the Church must subject itself, if it is to approach its own critical function with a clear conscience.

As a critic of particular socio-political institutions, the Church may not betray itself by canonizing a particular political ideology or authority structure. Rather it must maintain its aloofness from any special position in order to be the free critic of all. By the same token, it is able to cooperate with any other group, whether Christian or not, in opposing any threat to justice, peace and freedom even while there may be differences in the positive content of those threatened human values as they are interpreted in the various world-views.

Metz's Political Theology has met severe criticism and he has tried to take account of it in the on-going project of developing his thought. He is charged with insufficient acquaintance with both political science and history, with a consequent tendency to over-simplification. To the degree that he attempts to translate his theological positions into the concrete terms of political practice, he is in danger of lapsing into the proper field of politics itself. Even with regard to the apologetic value of political theology, it is questioned whether it really contributes anything beyond the older argument of the social utility of Christianity.[15]

Metz himself acknowledges the unfinished condition of his theological project and its resulting ambiguity. However, it must be judged within the larger unity of his whole theology which would include his earlier reflections on the relations of the Church and the world in the context of a theology of Christian Secularity as well as his elaboration of an eschatological theology of hope which we shall consider shortly. In that larger setting, it cannot be denied that he has made necessary corrections of emphasis in favor of recognizing the inescapably public character of salvation, an emphasis that is strong in the Catholic tradition, and therefore the essential role of the Church over against the world as the institution of the critical liberty of faith.

Theology of Liberation

The *Theology of Liberation* is a form of political theology and is in part indebted to the Political Theology developed by Metz along with Moltmann, Pannenberg and others as a dimension of the theology of hope. There is therefore a certain continuity between the two, and yet there is a distinct discontinuity as well. For the Theology of Liberation is largely the product of the Third World, the collectivity of those countries which have been called "under-developed" in contradistinction to the "developed" or affluent nations of both East and West.

There has been growing among these peoples, among their intellectual leaders and theologians, especially in Latin America, a new consciousness, what Rubem Alves calls a "proletarian consciousness." It is the awareness that their plight is not merely due to their lagging behind the other parts of the world in technological and economic progress. Rather they interpret their predicament as a form of oppression imposed upon them by the exploitative economic policies of the affluent nations and the selfishly inspired collaboration of their own political leaders. The cure that is to be striven for, therefore, is not "development," the concerted and more conscientious effort to overtake the wealthier countries economically in order that they may belong among the "haves" instead of the "have-nots." It is rather the struggle for "liberation," for freeing themselves that they may become the creative subjects of their own destiny and not merely objects of a history which others are creating for them.

The wider significance of this movement is that the same diagnosis and the emergence of the same sort of consciousness are attributed to minorities and other categories among the populations of the developed nations who feel themselves culturally as well as economically deprived. Thus there have arisen movements for liberation not only among Blacks, Indians and other disadvantaged groups in the United States, but also among women, young students and others who may be economically well-situated, but who feel oppressed and impotent, because denied an adequate voice and initiative in the making of their own lives and the construction of their own futures.[16]

Gustavo Gutierrez discloses the inadequacy of Metz's Political Theology as a theological approach to the problems of the Third World and especially of Latin America. It originated in conditions peculiar to the developed countries of Western Europe and North America and takes a properly critical prophetic stance towards them. Thus it rejects the secularist position which would reduce religious faith and the role of the Church to the purely private sphere. The technological society which immerses the individual in a dehumanizing materialistic environment requires the counterbalance of the Church as an institution of prophetic criticism. What is more the very mission of the Church requires its 'political' presence in a sinful society.

The fact is that Latin America realizes neither the completely secularized society nor the 'privatized' faith and Church which Metz presupposes. On the contrary, the historically Catholic culture of Latin America is one in which the Church has played an influential public role and has until recently been rather uniformly identified with the dominant ruling classes. That trend is being reversed to some degree especially since the Second Vatican Council. Some of the most inspired and thrilling affirmations of the freedom of the Church and its responsibility to give forthright prophetic witness to Gospel values and the social teachings founded on them have come forth from the Latin American hierarchy. These have proclaimed anew the dignity and liberty of all men, the demands of universal justice and the right of everyone to decent working standards, economic opportunity and to participate in the decisions that shape their political future. Pope Paul's encyclical, *Populorum Progressio* (1967), has served as a charter and an especially powerful impetus to the declarations as well as the actions of the bishops, priests, religious and laity of the various countries involved.[17]

Gutierrez sees theology as "a critical reflection—in the light of the Word accepted in faith—on historical praxis and therefore on the presence of Christians in the world."[18] It arises in this instance from the consciousness of Christians immersed in an unjust and alienating situation. Inevitably it takes the form of a theology of *liberation* as it reflects on the radical incompatibility between the "institutionalized violence" of an unjust society and the demands of the Gospel.

It presupposes the birth of a new consciousness in the oppressed. Indeed the oppression remains, but it no longer holds the spirits of the oppressed in bondage, in the passivity of inaction. They are no longer willing to allow others to create their history. They will take over the reins of their own destinies. They will be creators of their own history.[19]

A theology which reflects within such a consciousness is a 'political theology.' It perceives a necessary union of thought and action, of reflection and praxis. For it sees the need of translating Christian conviction into social initiatives. To paraphrase Marx, the point of theology is not merely to interpret the world in the light of faith, but rather to shed the light of faith on the process of its transformation.

It is also a 'theology of hope.' Though it negates the inhumanity of the present situation, it projects the positive possibility of a different future. In Christian hope, it takes up the perennial human task within salvation history of creating the "new man" and a "new earth." Thus the theology of liberation sees its own roots in the closest possible identification of the biblical themes of creation and salvation.

Theologians of liberation understand God before all else as Savior and Liberator. This conforms with the development of the biblical revelation itself. For it would appear that Israel learned that Yahweh was creator of all from the universality of His saving power. Thus creation is not separate from salvation but is rather the first salvific event. Thenceforward God acts within man's history which He constitutes as a salvation history.

The archetypal event is the Exodus which is an act of political liberation. The God Who creates cosmos out of chaos is the same God Who creates His People Israel by freeing them from salvery in Egypt. He brings them from alienation to liberation, forming them into His covenanted nation. Thus He is a God of history more than a God of nature.

Salvation is a re-creation, but it is not instantaneous or once for all. It involves the tortuous struggle of leading a people from an alienated condition to genuine freedom. A passage must be made from an oppressed consciousness to a liberated one. There are many falls on the way. Israel wandering in the wilderness yearned often for the flesh-pots of Egypt. She recoiled in self-doubt and in mistrust of Yahweh as she faced the insecure future of the freedom He promised her. She would have returned gladly to the security of servitude.

Even after the entrance into the Promised Land, Israel alternated between faithfulness and infidelity. The pedagogy of the oppressed is a drawn-out affair. The raising of consciousness from submission to the powers that enslave within and without to the full acceptance of the responsibility of freedom requires a radical conversion. Ultimately it parallels the soul-searing transformation from bondage to the Law to the self-disciplined freedom of the sons of the Spirit. Consequently the liberation to which Yahweh called His People waited for its fulfillment on the death and resurrection of His Son and the sending of His Spirit.

The salvation wrought by Jesus Christ is a "new creation." "All things were created through him and for him . . . God wanted . . . all things to be reconciled through him and for him" (Col 1:16, 19-20). In Christ creation and salvation are one. God re-creates the whole of humanity into His People by freeing them from bondage to sin and making with them a new and everlasting covenant.

Man, redeemed by Christ, carries on His saving creative work. This is the heart and meaning of the process by which man creates himself in the work of transforming his world. It is a salvific task. Therefore its effect is not only to build a world but to build human community. The grace of salvation institutes the unity of mankind founded on his communion with God. Through Christ and in Him, man labors toward realizing God's Kingdom on earth: "a kingdom of truth and life, . . . a kingdom of justice, love and peace" (Preface of Christ the King).

To liberate men from exploitation and poverty and to build a just and peaceful society are works of salvation and not merely of human progress. In struggling for these goals, men are responding to God's initiative in making theirs a history of salvation and are implementing the gradual fulfillment of His eschatological promises. Therefore, man as co-creator with God is not merely humanizing the world, but participating in on-going salvation: freeing himself in the process of freeing his world and his society to be themselves, always by virtue of the gift of God's saving grace in Christ.

Theologians of liberation like Gutierrez consider the

bulk of theology that emanates from the developed countries as under-developed and politically naive. It sees the work of man in transforming his world mainly as the task of humanizing nature through his science and technology. When it is not politically neutral, as Teilhard de Chardin seems to be in his preoccupation with man's scientific progress, its concern with social issues is largely expressed in terms of progress and development. Theologians of the Third World see no reality in the promise of human progress for those who live in a dehumanizing society. One must first reject the alienating and exploitative situation and undertake the struggle of liberation from oppression.

In theological reflection within such a context, the reality of sin and therefore of the need of salvation is obtrusive. But sin is especially perceived as a social, historical fact in the form of unjust social structures and institutional selfishness. The fundamental alienation of man from God and his fellow-man which sin is takes these concrete historical forms.

Redemption from this sinfulness originates in the saving grace of Christ's death and resurrection. On man's part, it requires a radical conversion to God and his neighbor in a love that overcomes selfishness. But it must also take the form of a political liberation from the oppressive structures which institutionalize the selfishness and perpetuate the injustice. Thus the growth of the Kingdom of God on earth and the victory of Christ's saving grace over sin must in this instance assume the very mundane shape of an act of political liberation as the pre-condition for a more just society within which men can authentically realize themselves.

Conversion to God demands conversion to the neighbor, above all, to the poor and oppressed, the least brothers in whom Christ is particularly present. But this involves more than the adopting of a private attitude of charity to unfortunate individuals. It requires commitment to the struggle for a more just society, with concrete plans and strategies to oppose and overcome the sins of institutional selfishness and social injustice.

Thus the spirituality of liberation is grounded in the

spirituality of the poor, the *anawim*. They who are the oppressed will teach us true liberation in the very act of achieving it for themselves. Those who are not poor must learn to be poor in imitation of God the Son Who emptied Himself and became a slave in order to liberate us from our slavery· We become poor by identifying ourselves with their cause at the same time that we protest and oppose their poverty which degrades and dehumanizes them.

Mary, the greatest of the *anawim* who prepared for and awaited the coming of the Liberator, has provided in her Magnificat the charter for a program of liberation.

> He has mercy on those who fear him in every generation.
> He has shown the strength of his arm, he has scattered the proud in their conceit.
> He has cast down the mighty from their thrones, and has lifted up the lowly.
> He has filled the hungry with good things, and sent the rich away empty-handed.

Theologies of Liberation in The United States

The theology of liberation as it comes from Latin America is not univocally applicable to the situation in the United States or other areas. However, it deals with universal themes and concerns. It arises from a biblical source and inspiration that are shared by all Christians. Since it envisages theology as "a critical reflection—in the light of the Word accepted in faith—on historical praxis and therefore on the presence of Christians in the world," it will assume varying modes and forms according to the concrete situation in which Christians find themselves. There are as many potential theologies of liberation as there are social historical contexts calling for liberation. In the final analysis, however, it is as universal as the pervasive presence of sin and the need for salvation.

In the United States, the most prominent and developed theology of liberation is Black Theology. Though it speaks out of the black experience in this country, its ramifications are not limited to blacks only. It can be an exemplar for any American theology of liberation. But more importantly, it implicates all Americans, especially whites, who participate in the tight network of human relationships that constitutes American society.

The black struggle for liberation has passed through and beyond the civil rights phase when the ideal was integration with the white community. In the dialectic of the struggle, this stage had to be surpassed, if the blacks were to throw off the "oppressed consciousness." For integration *then* would have occurred in a mentality of white superiority shared by whites and blacks. True liberation requires an acknowledged relationship between equals: person with person. The black had first to recognize his own dignity as a black human being. This necessary shift in consciousness exploded in the rage and militant self-assertiveness of Black Power.

Black Theology currently reflects this stage of black consciousness, although it is not locked into it. However, it is caught in a tension between universality and particularity. Put more concretely, in affirming forcefully the *humanity* of the black, it is tempted to limit humanity to the black, to identify the species—Man—with the class—Black. Black theologians differ in the exclusiveness with which they identify black with good and white with evil. However, all of them regard their theologies as so many prescriptions for black liberation.

The biblical themes appealed to by the black theology of liberation are very like those of the Latin American version. The Exodus is the primal event by which God liberates His People whom He constitutes as His own definitively by His Covenant. Thus God identifies Himself with the oppressed and makes their cause His own. In our age and in our country, He identifies Himself with the black people because they are the oppressed victims of white racism. In this sense God is black!

James H. Cone is perhaps the most forceful and passionate of the black theologians. In his words, "the task of Black Theology . . . is *to analyze the black man's condition in the light of God's revelation in Jesus Christ with the purpose of creating a new understanding of black dignity among black people, and providing the necessary soul in that people, to destroy white racism* . . . The purpose of Black Theology is to analyze the nature of Christian faith in such a way that black people can say Yes to blackness and No to whiteness and mean it."[20]

His theology is situational or contextual in the sense that it applies the biblical themes and Gospel message very directly to the social and political situation of the American blacks. "Black theology is a theology of the black community and is thus opposed to any idea which alienates it from that community."[21] A Christian theology which is white in origin cannot apply to the blacks, since the oppressor cannot adopt the existence or the consciousness of the oppressed.

The message of the New as of the Old Testament is that of liberation from slavery and oppression. Jesus is the Liberator Who first identifies Himself with the poor and the oppressed. He preaches the Kingdom of God which is the pledge of freedom and justice for the downtrodden. It is a revolutionary message and the Risen Christ conveys the grace and power to achieve its revolutionary aims by sending His Spirit upon the poor and oppressed of every age who appeal for it. "The Spirit of the Lord is upon me, because he has anointed me to preach the good news to the poor. He has sent me to proclaim release to the captives . . . to set at liberty those who are oppressed . . ." (Lk 4:18-19). Through Christ the poor man is freed and empowered to rebel against what dehumanizes him.

In America today, Christ is black because it is the black man who is dehumanized by white racism and for whom the liberating message and power of the Gospel is intended. Thus the cause of Black Power is the cause of Christ because it is the power by which the black man repels the forces that would dehumanize him. This power for freedom, that is, to be human, to be one's true self, is the power purchased for us and pledged to us by Christ.

In order to achieve this freedom for himself, the white man must become black, the racist must be absolved of his sin. For he too is in bondage: to his own alienating ego and his will to oppressive power. This possibility for the white man to become black implies that "blackness" has a wider connotation than that of a particular race. At this point,

Black Theology, whether of Cone or of others, begins to break out of its racial boundaries and assume a more universal significance.

For Albert Cleage, who is more prophet and preacher than theologian, "black" refers first and foremost to his own people, but also in a wider sense to all non-white peoples anywhere who have in one way or another been victims of white racism.[22] Cone distinguishes blackness as a *physiological* trait and an *ontological* symbol. The first refers specifically to the American blacks who carry "the scars that bear witness to the inhumanity committed against them. Black Theology believes that they are the *only* key that can open the door to divine revelation. Therefore, no American theology can even tend in the direction of Christian theology without coming to terms with the black-skinned people of America." The second meaning is deeper and wider. It denotes "all people who participate in the liberation of man from oppression. This is the universal note of Black Theology. It believes that all men were created for freedom, and that God always sides with the oppressed against the oppressors."[23] It is in this sense that the white man must become black.

As an ontological symbol, blackness can signify the situation of those who are oppressed and of those who struggle against it. It is also synonymous with salvation or redemption and with resurrection. In this context, whiteness is the symbol of evil and of the demonic lust for power, somewhat as Babylon and Rome are in Sacred Scripture.

This contrast of images lends sharpness to the black consciousness of white oppression. It can also lead to a blurring of metaphor and reality. The insistent identifying of black with good and with the oppressed and of white with evil and with the oppressor is understandable as a dramatic device. When it is taken literally, as it often enough is in concrete instances, it tends to over-simplify the whole problem of human sinfulness and to provide provocation and an opening for a species of black racism. The fact is that many others besides blacks are among the oppressed in this country, including American Indians, Mexicans and Puerto

Ricans, even many whites. Women too can and do claim that they are an oppressed class in a long male-dominated society.

It is not inappropriate that the term, "black," refers in general to all those who are among the oppressed in a society dominated by whites. For whites are wont to identify being white with the normative expression of humanity according to which all others must be judged and are usually found wanting. No one social or racial group can claim identification with authentic humanity or exemption of its members from being inauthentic. This is true of any human category, whether based on race, nationality or sex. One invalidates one's own authenticity when one repudiates another group in its very humanity rather than for its inhumanity.

In order to avoid being racist itself, Black Theology must be contextual and not exclusive, to adopt the helpful distinction of Rosemary Ruether.[24] The Gospel of Christ is the Gospel of and for all men, but it is received into and interpreted within the concrete particular context of each age and of each distinctive human community. It is indeed imperative that blacks embrace Jesus as their Redeemer, as the One Who comes to identify Himself with them in their needfulness in order to free them to achieve their authentic selfhood and their full stature in the Kingdom of His Father. It is also inevitable that His Gospel, the charter of their freedom, assume the dynamic in their consciousness of a theology of protest and rebellion against the injustice and unfreedom to which they have been subjected by whites. However, their response can be a genuine salvation-event for themselves only if it includes within its redeeming scope those who have been their oppressors. The liberation of the black cannot take place except in solidarity with the liberation of the white. Otherwise, it becomes merely another page in the sordid history of man's alienation from man and therefore from the God Who calls us to unity in Himself.

Black Theology comes to full maturity when its particular form of the gospel message achieves universal validity because it unambiguously affirms the freedom and dignity of all men as sons of the Father. This need not muffle, much less stifle, the shrillness of its anguished cry or the power of its indignation. Jesus unbridled His fury against those who profaned His Father's dwelling. But He commended them to the same Father as He reconciled us all in His redeeming death.

We are all sinners. We are all called to be sons and brothers. Even rebellion is successful only when it eventuates in the greater freedom of the oppressor as well as of the oppressed.

This is the ultimate promise and value of Black Theology and of any theology of liberation. It must reflect the stages by which those whose humanity has been debased recover their dignity and their freedom. Therefore, it must say an impassioned No to their exploiters. It must with equal passion bellow the affirmation of their own distinctive worth and beauty. But then if it is to be a *Christian* theology of redemption, it must pass beyond the antithesis of oppressor and oppressed.

When the exploited have retrieved their dignity and freedom and are able to face those who have despoiled them as confident equals, they must be willing to conspire with Christ to free their former masters. For theirs was the deeper and more corrupting slavery. The recovery of their humanity requires a more profound conversion which they cannot even begin without the support and understanding of those against whom they have sinned.

The Black Church has been the heart and the voice of its people since their early years on this continent. It was a segregated church in a segregated society, and to a large extent it still is. But by the same token, it preserved and nurtured their cultural distinctiveness and was the womb within which Black Power and the renewed sense of black identity could be born.

Many black militants have abandoned their church as too closely wedded to the system of values of their white counterparts to lead or motivate a true black liberation movement. Some black churchmen are seeking to counter this charge by becoming even more stridently militant than their accusers. Such chauvinism is understandable, but in the long run it must be tempered by the superior demands of the Gospel which must be preached in the face of every pressure to divide men against their brothers.

The Church is torn between the demands for revolution and the need for reconciliation. It cannot settle exclusively for either. It must live in the tension between both. For the black as for the dispossessed of Latin America or of any part of the world, the Church must lean very heavily to the side of the poor. It must preach a new Exodus out of their condition of bondage. To become one with the Christ Who suffers in them, it must die to its own privileged security and wealth in order to rise with them to the new life of their freedom. But it may not become so identified with any cause, however worthy, that it surrenders its prophetic duty to judge every human enterprise, including its own, in the light of the Gospel.

This cuts both ways of course. Justice demands that the reconciliation which the Church must also preach be genuine. It must presuppose the equality of those it calls to reconciliation. This means that the consciousness of the one who has been deprived has been raised to the point of full self-acceptance and self-love as a member of his own distinctive community. It also means that he is unqualifiedly received as an equal and a brother who has been wrongfully demeaned.

This implies that the members of the oppressive community have undergone the conversion by which they also have broken through to a new consciousness. Now they recognize that they have violated the humanity which they share with all men in debasing the humanity of any of their brothers. Though the guilt may not be incurred by direct personal actions, it has to be exorcized to the extent that it has deformed a consciousness that has acquiesced in injustices that others in one's own community have inflicted. When we have repented of sins committed in the name which we identify as our own and have the will to make reparation to those who have been sinned against, then and only then, may we be accepted as equals by those brothers of Christ who have been excluded from our family circle.

Those who are oppressors in relation to one group are oppressed with reference to others or to the system under which they live and work. So-called "Middle America," the great mass of middle class whites who are supposed to constitute the majority in this country, are usually charged with being bigoted towards blacks and other minorities. Actually of course Middle America itself is interlaced with numerous brands of bias arising from ethnic and socio-economic differences. Beyond this extensive network of tribalism, snobbery and intolerance, there is the universal malaise which hardly anyone escapes: the dehumanizing impact of a thing-oriented, profit-motivated economic system on the persons who comprise the society it generates. A whole literature has arisen to report on and document this developing social malady. Another has been born out of the counter-culture which has grown as a huge anti-body within the afflicted organism. It is not surprising therefore that there should be appearing among the various theologies of liberation one dedicated to "the liberation of Middle America."[25]

The inference to be drawn from all this is that liberation (read: salvation) is a universal need and that we are all sinned against. The Pharaoh who resisted the divine appeal spoken by Moses: Let My people go! was the slave of his own hardened heart. It is no less true of the rich and powerful of all ages who turn a deaf ear to Moses and the Prophets and will not even listen if someone were to return from the dead. The poor have the Gospel preached to them, but the wealthy will with difficulty enter the kingdom of heaven. They do not recognize their own poverty.

The theology of liberation expresses perhaps the deepest penetration of the Church and Christian faith into the world and its fallenness. It thematizes in concrete political terms the continual drama of salvation history: man's sin and God's redeeming act in Jesus Christ. The Church must preach the gospel of liberation in and out of every season, but it had better practice what it preaches. It too is in need of unrelenting reformation and conversion. It cannot credibly preach freedom if it gives the appearance of unfreedom. It cannot offer itself as "the sacrament of the unity of mankind," if it addresses itself to all in the accents and dialects of the few. Although an effort has been made to internationalize the central administration of the Roman Catholic Church, it is still true that for the most part those who speak officially in its name are elderly white Western European males. This is in a world where the urge for liberation is felt most strongly among the young, the women, the non-whites and outside the North Atlantic community of nations. Obviously a number of Church windows yet remain to be opened.

In every age the Church must judge and amend itself in the light of the Kingdom whose Gospel it proclaims and towards which it is supposed to lead all mankind. It is that kingdom where no distinctions will finally prevail: where "there is neither Jew nor Greek, there is neither slave nor free, there is neither male nor female; for you are all one in Christ Jesus" (Gal 3:28).

III. Christian Faith as the Vision of the Absolute Future of Man's Evolution

The Future as a Dimension of Christian Faith

Except for a rear-guard action by a diminishing remnant of fundamentalists, the combat between official Christian spokesmen and scientists over the question of evolution is well over. Rather the evolutionary view of man and of his universe has provided Christian thinkers with a more majestic backdrop for the depicting of the divine work of creation and the history of man's salvation. Since the last century, man has come to perceive himself in relation to the unimaginably vast reaches of space and to understand himself as temporal in his very essence. He exists as an individual project within the world-project and he is responsible for both. Taking as his raw material his own nature and cosmic Nature, the residue of past evolution, he constitutes himself as free personal subject and remakes Nature into his own world, assimilating it into the collective personal project that is his history.

History is made in the present, but man has come to see it more and more as powered by the future which is its incentive. It is especially concerning man's future, the shape of it and how it is to be shaped, that the plural faiths of man come into contention and are having to learn to engage in mutual dialogue. With respect to the future of man as to the very fact of pluralism itself, Christian faith has something to say. What it has to say is equivalently decisive: just as Christian faith is the divinely guaranteed norm of the plurality of human faiths, so is it the definitive vision of the absolute future of man's evolution.

Man is taking over the process of evolution, his own and the world's. This act of appropriation is still in its early stages, but it is being planned and gradually, yet quite surely, being implemented. Cybernetics, genetic engineering, the synthesizing of the elements of life, the conquering of space: these are a few intimations of man's growing capacity to program much of his own future and that of the universe around him. Marxists and other humanists see these as so many progressive steps in the quickening process by which man is repossessing the prerogatives he alienated from himself and predicated of God. What does Christian Faith have to say about it?

Much has already been said in the terms of a theology of Christian Secularity and the relations of the Church and the world. The secularizing process by which man comes more and more to take over the control of his world and the making of himself is able to be interpreted as a fulfillment of basic Christian beliefs. For the Creator by accepting man and the world irrevocably in the Incarnation of His Son freed the world of man to be itself, to be through man the agent of its own continuous creation. It is only to the extent that this is pursued in sinful opposition to and as though in isolation from its Divine Maker that it tends to self-alienation and the prideful fall of man. In so far as it does, it is unassimilable to Christian faith.

The Christian attitude toward the future is in continuity with the attitude toward the world at any moment of its history. Just as the Christ-event is the foundation of our faith that God has decisively accepted the world in its non-divine otherness by the Incarnation of His Son as His divine otherness, so is it the guarantee of our faith and hope that the absolute future of man and his universe is already actual at the heart of this world, recreating and liberating it to become most fully itself by progressing toward final reconciling union with the creative Mystery Who will make it to be "a new heaven and a new earth." God, the End of His Creation, became its Absolute Future when He entered His creation in Jesus Christ. Yet though immanent to the world in His incarnate Son and interiorly drawing it toward Himself, He is transcendent to the world. As its absolute future His redeeming action cannot be finally identified with any world happening, even though it is operative at the heart of every historical event, transforming it into salvation history.

Christianity offers no blue-prints for constructing man's future in this world. As an eschatological faith, it relates every intra-mundane plan and action in man's history to his absolute future in the Infinite Who is beyond the world and its history. Therefore the Christian is like everyone else. He faces a future within this world that is uncertain, often threatening, yet in its very unfinished and tentative condition a constantly exhilarating and challenging incentive to creative action. His future is not already settled, but rather must be forged and made by his exertion and intelligence contributed to the common effort of all men to humanize the world, to make of it the best possible arena for man's making of man himself.

Atheist humanism expressly limits its horizon of man's future to this world and its history. Its view is utopian in the sense that it projects a future that is always within history, but which is never approached except asymptotically. It is promethean in as much as it attributes a kind of infinity to man which is man's own predicate and not derived by participation from a Being that is Himself infinite. The fact is of course that man and his situation are quite decidedly finite, though the length and breadth and depth of the course ahead might seem boundless. There are his limitations of space and time, especially as he confronts the light-years immensity of the universe. There are the biological limits within which his life and its processes can alone flourish; the psychological boundaries established by the limiting range of his necessarily selective mental functions, granted the broadening and accelerating of these through computerization. There is the final and most fateful frontier of death. Even in the hypothesis of an indefinite lengthening of life, death seems to have the last word in the deadening finiteness of an existence prolonged in the direction of diminishing return. Even cultures and civilizations are subject to the finite limitedness of the individuals who create and maintain them.

The pathetic grandeur of humanist utopias is rooted in the spiritual personhood of man, for it requests each generation to find the value of its own efforts in building a better world for the generations that will come afterward. Implicitly it is affirming its own unconditional value in the free affirmation of its own self-sacrifice. As Rahner interprets it,

> Any conception which regards the future as something which does not simply come about by itself but must be conquered by sacrifice, acknowledges implicitly what Christianity affirms explicitly: the future of the human spiritual person in no way only lies in that future which will be present at some later date but is the eternity which is brought about as the result of the spiritual act of the person.[26]

The foundation of a limitless future within this world and its history is in the unlimited scope of the free spirit of man. The value of a future that will belong to others beyond one's own life-span for which one will sacrifice himself is derived from the same source and becomes intelligible only within a more expansive horizon. The man of the present can dream of an intra-mundane future for others because he, as spirit, lives within a supra-mundane future above the flux of time, in an eternal life which has already begun in this historical moment or in any moment when the human spirit can transcend its limits in a free act of loving faith which is itself a divine gift.

What makes the future genuinely 'new'? Can it arise wholly out of man's creative imagination, even when it is joined in fertile union with the vastly varied potentialities of the world around him? Christianity claims for man a newness that is astonishingly more profound than these resources could account for. It is the newness of a future begotten by the entrance of the infinite divine Mystery into the finite flesh of man. It is the intimate personal encounter of man with the One Who is the creative source of his being and the Absolute Reality toward which every finite being advances in its self-realization. This meeting with the Absolute does not devalue man's finite step-by-step progress into his earthly future; rather it gives it an infinite depth and significance. What Nietzsche sought vainly with his myth of the eternal recurrence is realized here: every human moment dedicated to the better future of man is speeding the advent of the Kingdom of God and is therefore weighted with the eternity into which the Father is drawing us by that saving love made efficaciously present among us through His Son.

Though Christian faith can offer no concrete program for creating man's worldly future, since that is the proper business of man's world left to itself, it calls upon every believer to spend himself within the world for the world. Thus he reenacts in his own life the self-giving of the God-man Who is our absolute future calling us not outside our world, but in our world, our flesh, our history.

Catholic Christianity has recovered its essential eschatological orientation, its sense of the forward movement of salvation history dominated by the end-event of Christ's victory which is already governing that history, but not yet fully triumphant over the recalcitrant freedom of men. All those who formally profess an authentic Christian faith believe in the God Who can be called the Absolute Future of His creation: man and the world. Thereby they proclaim their hope in the future in the face of every human failure and cosmic catastrophe, for they are convinced that they live and move and have their being in loving union with Him Who is their Absolute Future, calling them and all men to the ultimate consummation of that union which He has already initiated. They are not advancing into an emptiness which they alone can fill. Rather they are responding to a perpetual summons to enter ever more deeply into infinite fullness in a process for which they exercise individual and collective co-responsibility, but whose outcome they cannot finally frustrate.

Mankind is already God's Other in Christ. In Him men's Absolute Future is already actualized. He is the pledge that it will also be their future, if they translate His total acceptance of that future into the developing structure of their lives, into the personal initiatives by which they engage in the continual making of themselves and their world. His Paschal Mystery is not only the ground and assurance of their eventual participation in His triumph. It is the revelation of the only way in which man's building of his worldly future will issue in a truly new and enduring creation.

The Church and the Future of Man

What is the role of the Church in the making of man's future? In a world of men who are implicitly Christian, at least by vocation, and consequently of a plurality of religions and faiths which are able to be for their followers the latent and disguised presence of the saving grace of Christ, the Church is the manifest presence of that grace made permanently available in man's history. Christ is the full and definitive revelation of God's saving Self-gift to man. He is therefore the Head of mankind and the Lord of history Whose permanent visible presence among men and Whose redeeming formative influence on human history are signified by the Church or assembly of those who formally profess their faith in Him as Savior and Lord.

The Church is a people dedicated to the explicit task of witnessing to the actuality of God's saving acceptance of man and his world in Christ. It is "the epiphany of the sacred, the consecrated reality set apart to constitute the visibility of grace."[27] The subsuming of human life into the divine life is a universal vocation or calling mediated within history by the Church which gives formal thematic expression to this divine call experienced often unknowingly within the consciousness of every man. Therefore the Church must proclaim and ceaselessly witness to the explicit revelation of God's Self-gift before men in order that they may be led to an appropriate response in faith which is truly personal because fully conscious and free. Thus is it engaged in the mission of building the Body of Christ to the fullness of its stature until He comes.

"Until He Comes":—that, in a sense, is the keynote of the Church's mission in the world. The Church is the sacrament of the eschatologically definitive acceptance of the world by God in Christ. Inevitably the gaze of the Church is toward the future and it is in the light of that future, already realized in the glorified humanity of Christ, that it is able to judge both itself and the world in the present.

This orientation toward the future is the characteristic of Salvation History since the beginning and has in consequence marked the enduring posture of the church of the Old as well as of the New Testament. Thus "the words of Revelation of the Old Testament are not primarily words of statement or of information, nor are they mainly words of appeal or of personal Self-communication by God, but they are *words of promise* . . . This . . . word of promise initiates the future: it establishes the covenant as the solidarity of the Israelites who hope, and who thereby experience the world for the first time as a history which is oriented to the future."[28]

The New Testament did not alter, but rather reinforced and gave a definitive form to this orientation to the future, this eschatological posture of hope in Him Who is to come. For the Gospel revelation teaches us that the new aeon, the future time, has already begun in this time. The final future for man was actualized in the Resurrection and exists now in the glorified Christ. But the entrance of the saving grace of Christ which invites us and draws all men toward the New Creation is not out of the past, not even primarily in the present, except in so far as the present is constituted by being drawn toward the future to which Christ beckons us. And so in that action in which the Church as the community of faith and hope realizes itself as an ever renewed event in the history of salvation, namely, in the Eucharistic celebration, we commemorate the death of the now glorified Christ until He comes. We are then most fully an eschatological community.

The Marxists criticize the Christians for being too saddled with structures and doctrinal commitments coming out of the past and stifling man's potentialities for the future. The Christians reply that the Marxists have so blue-printed the future by their ideological commitments that they tend to ignore the contingency of the future and too stringently circumscribe man's freedom to constitute himself and to improvise his future. The Marxist vision wants to spell out man's future in earthly terms within history. The Christian vision presents man's Absolute Future in the Christ Who is to come at the end of history. It leaves intact the contingency of man's historical future and therefore the scope of his freedom to create his future in this world within the horizon of a New Creation, whose ultimate realization is already achieved in the Risen Savior, but whose detailed implementation in this aeon is radically undetermined.

The task of the Church in the world, therefore, is to witness to this faith and hope in man's Absolute Future, already actualized in Christ. But it is to be achieved by man, sinful and alienated, yet redeemed, by the gradual conquest of himself and his world through the power of Christ's Spirit but also by the exertion of his own labor and genius. As man works to construct his world and to project himself into an uncertain future, the Church in the world must incarnate and give witness to the God Who is before us, Whose irruption into man's existence constitutes man's historicity precisely by calling him unceasingly out of his present situation into a newer, more fully actualized redeemed creation. As his Absolute Future, embodied in Christ and thereby immanent in history, God draws man forward and so constitutes always the goal and horizon of his present efforts and the source of his hope. For men individually and for the race in general, the End is already realized in Christ and therefore the power by which we shall attain that goal is necessarily derived through Christ. Yet the way by which we shall avail ourselves of that power in our secular worldly tasks to reach that goal is radically contingent.

God has given us no detailed plans for building our world. He has given us only hints and suggestions and general pointers by way of His revealed word whose implications for the shape of our lives and their direction we can grow to learn as we confront each new situation with His word informing our minds and our hearts. It is thus that we are able to "read the signs of the times" as intimations of His will in the midst of secular events and projects.

The Church and the world, distinct now and always within man's history because of sin, are nevertheless on a converging course which will reach the point of absolute unity only in the Eschaton, the Parousia of Christ. It is the *world* that He claims; the Church is already His in principle, though actually only in part, since it too is burdened with the sins of men who are of the world and it is always merely on the way to the Kingdom whose advent it proclaims. The Church exists therefore for no purpose but to serve the world, to help it realize its own true identity and destiny, to criticize it and therefore to suffer with it, for it and on account of it. It must seek to manifest in itself the redeeming and renewing grace of Christ which is always at least latently present wherever man is and therefore throughout man's world.

The Church may never lose its distinction from the world, may never become completely secularized. Otherwise, it could not remain the servant of the world, often the suffering servant, humbly standing over against the world in judgment, even if only by mute witness of what the future of man should be in contrast with his present.

As the eschatological community of those who profess faith and hope in the Absolute Future of man made always present in the victory of Christ, the Church shares in the invincibility, the indefectibility of Him Whom it continually embodies within man's world. As a part of man's world sharing in the mutations of his history, the Church is also relative and contingent, subject to obsolescence and the need for periodic renewal, especially in its structures and symbols.

The faith by which the Church confesses the definitive victory of God's saving grace in Christ is itself an element in that victory, for the grace of God's Self-gift is one with the grace that empowers man's receptivity for that gift in faith. The Church as the community of faith and hope which makes Christ's justifying victory available to each and to every historical age is guaranteed against final failure and defeat by the victorious grace which it embodies and mediates. Therefore the Church is indefectible in its faith and as a means of salvation.

This indefectibility must characterize the Church in its total reality, that is, in its worldly presence as structured and symbolizing as well as in its hidden divinizing life perpetually fed and supplied by the indwelling Spirit of God. As a consequence it is a property of the Church as institution and in its official ministry whereby its salvific presence is inserted into the action and structure of the world of men and its history. Were this not so, that is, if it could be that the Church as the community of salvation were able to be separated from the truth and love of Christ by the very offices and functions by which it makes them historically available, then the Church in its essence would cease to be indefectible.

It is evident that the expression of its indefectibility in its ministerial offices and institutional structures is a participation wholly derived from its primal character as the eschatological community of salvation and therefore as itself a fruit of Christ's own victory. This fact is also an indication of the limits of the indefectibility of the Church's ministry in its teaching, pastoral and sanctifying offices: that is, it extends as far as the Church's guaranteed historical witness to Christ would otherwise be substantially jeopardized. Such a contingency would occur if the Church were to invoke the fullest exercise of its teaching and pastoral office as binding on the consciences of all believers and in doing so impose a belief opposed to Christ's truth or a course of conduct contrary to His saving will. This would in effect establish the Church in contradiction to Christ Who founded it precisely to make His truth and redeeming grace unfailingly available to men.

> Where it is not a question of a definitively and irreversibly posited official act of the universal Church it does not necessarily and with the certitude of faith have in itself the prerogative of indefectibility of the Church. And in so far as the Church as still in a pilgrim-state, waiting, hoping, must also be the tempted and tried Church in order that her relationship to the realization of salvation which is already given in her should be one of faith and of hope, in fact tempted by her pilgrim existence itself, the acts which do not possess this indefectibility necessarily and inevitably belong to her pilgrim existence in faith and hope.[29]

We are dealing with the question of the indefectibility

of the Church solely as a dimension of the future of the Church. It is not within the scope of that limited intention to explore the various thorny issues associated with infallibility which is the specific realization of the Church's indefectibility in its preaching and teaching office. However, it is pertinent to acknowledge and to emphasize that infallibility is an attribute of that ecclesial ministry not only because it is implied in Christ's promise to be with His Church in the presence of His Spirit of Truth in perpetuity, but because it is an inescapable corollary of the eschatological character of the Church's mission to the world. To affirm the opposite would amount to denying the definitiveness of the victory of the truth of Christ over the sin and error of man, that victory which the Church was instituted precisely to make available within man's history.

The balancing fact is of course the very historicity of the Church in its ministry and institutional elements. It is the worldly presence of the glorified Christ in our unglorified condition. As a consequence, it is a sociological entity subject to the limitedness and relativity of all corporate human enterprises. Were it not, it would fail its very reason for being, namely, to make the divine mystery of salvation historically available to men. This paradox with the tension that results from it is of the very essence of the Church.

> The Church, at once a visible assembly and a spiritual community, goes forward together with humanity and experiences the same earthly lot which the world does. She serves as a leaven and as a kind of soul for human society as it is to be renewed in Christ and transformed into God's family.[30]

There are risks and tensions indigenous to the Church's mission as servant of the world, a world that evolves toward fulfillment in anguish and ambiguity. This same price the Church itself must pay. As herald of the world's Absolute Future, the Church often enough sounds an uncertain trumpet. We look for the bread of decisive leadership and guidance and we get the stone of pious platitudes. But then often enough we look for what the Church cannot or ought not give. If we acknowledge the autonomy of the world, then we should not find fault with the Church when it abides by that modern truth. As Rahner observes, "In this secularization, the Church's own enterprise, she offers to the world her grace, her principles, and her ultimate horizons, but it is the world itself which must bring forth human and Christian action on its own terrain and on its own real responsibility."[31]

In our new world oriented more and more toward the future which it has the capacity and the will to create, the Church certainly has a more specific function than to enunciate general principles to serve as guidelines and pointers to contain that future within a horizon of Christian faith. It is not to create a new Christian culture or an up-dated version of the Christendom we have left behind. Cultural as well as religious pluralism, as we have discussed, is a fact of the foreseeable future which must be confronted and not evaded or explained away. It is rather a return to the originating mission assigned to the Church by its divine Founder, a prophetic task of proclaiming and giving historical witness to the Gospel of the Kingdom intended for all nations. The building of a world which will incorporate those Gospel values in its own fabric or that will at least provide an environment in which those values can flourish in the lives of individuals and human communities must be the task of those members of the Church whose vocation is specifically secular. Their formation into a thoroughly Christian community is the primary and indispensable responsibility for the service of the wider human family whose universal calling is to become the family of God.

The Church is the nucleus of that family, the gathering of those who respond consciously and deliberately in faith and hope to the promises of Him Who calls all to Himself as our shared Absolute Future. It is a People that explicitly professes and witnesses to the reality of Christ's Lordship and God's Fatherhood and therefore to man's brotherhood in Christ. It is also a People, indeed a Body, whose teaching, pastoral and sanctifying functions are distributed within it diversely and hierarchically. Still if it is to be, as it must be, a "sign to the nations," it must exercise those functions humbly for the service of men in the spirit of brothers as Christ has given us the example, not lording it over one another as the pagan rulers do.

It is in the laity that the Church is most intimately present to the world, as the Constitution on the Church affirms.

What specifically characterizes the laity is their secular nature. It is true that those in holy orders can at times be engaged in secular activities and even have a secular profession. But they are by reason of their particular vocation, especially and professedly ordained to the sacred ministry. Similarly, by their state in life, religious give splendid and striking testimony that the world cannot be transformed and offered to God without the spirit of the beatitudes. The laity, by their special vocation, seek the kingdom of God by engaging in temporal affairs and by ordering them according to the plan of God. They live in the world, that is, in each and in all of the secular professions and occupations. They live in the ordinary circumstances of family and social life, from which the very web of their existence is woven. Today they are called by God that by exercising their proper function, and led by the Spirit of the Gospel, they may work for the sanctification of the world from within as a leaven. In this way they may make Christ known to others, especially by the testimony of a life resplendent in faith, hope and charity. Therefore, since they are tightly bound up in all types of temporal affairs, it is their special task to order and to throw light upon these affairs in such a way that they may always start out, develop, and persist according to Christ's mind, to the praise of the Creator and the Redeemer.[32]

In the layman, the Church is most properly the servant of the world and able to be the harbinger of its future. In the distribution of ministries or functions within the Church, the clergy and the religious are the servants of the servants of the world. The performance and shape of these diverse ministries are undergoing transformation in our increasingly secularized society and perhaps they will never again settle into a permanent, in the sense of a static, structure and stance. For the time being, the once sharp distinction of their functions may become blurred by virtue of the fluidity and uncertainty of our present relationship as Church to the new secular forms that are emerging. But the distinct character of the ordained priestly and of the religious ministries and of their indispensable contributions to the life and mission of the Church ought to be maintained. For the priest's essential function is the ministry of Word and Sacrament whereby the manifest presence of Christ's redeeming grace is made perennially available to all and whereby the Church, as the embodiment of the glorified

Christ in the world, is unceasingly constituted as Event and Mission.

The religious, whatever specific service may be the vehicle of their commitment, by lives consecrated to incarnating the highest demands of the Gospel, are necessary present reminders in human flesh and spirit of the Absolute Future to which we are all called and of the eschatological kingdom in which men and women will not be given in marriage because world and Church will be fused in the conjugal union of God and man. Priests and religious, by life-long commitment through self-donation to the Church's mission, must be free to embody in the world in unequivocal fashion the Church's service to the world. It will indeed often be as signs of contradiction to the current standards of the world, so that being "crucified to the world," they may unveil in high relief its sinfulness and yet its hope, founded in God's acceptance through Christ, Whose definitive victory as man's Absolute Future incarnate, is proclaimed under the sign of the cross.

Man: His World and his Future

Christian faith provides man a vision of the Absolute Future that is his goal as an individual and as a species. But that Absolute Future, which is God historically incarnated in Jesus Christ, is beyond history as transcendent to all creation. Even Jesus' triumphant return at the Parousia will mark the end of human history. Does this mean that the future of man of which faith speaks is removed from the warp and woof of his historical present and indeed of his future as it lies within history? Is it a matter of the future for man only as an ever receding horizon toward which man is drawn as to a goal but which will never be actual for him until he relinquishes his historical task of creating himself and his world?

The Incarnation is the decisive resolution of such doubts. For in Christ God not only committed Himself to man and the whole of His creation. He enacted in Him in a definitive fashion His perpetual entering into man's world as His unfailing Self-gift which is ever transforming it into the arena in which His future Kingdom is coming into being. In fact it is this very movement which constitutes history. For history is precisely the active response of man to God's incessant summons to become His other by appropriating His creative activity in the constituting of himself and his world. It is a redemptive activity inasmuch as the Redeemer is already at the heart of the universe and its cosmic and human energies, harnessing them to the extension and the implementation of His paschal victory since the first Pentecost.

The Church does not bring Christ to a universe that has hitherto lacked Him. It discloses the Christ Who is hidden within. The Christian does not preach the good news of an Incarnate God as man's Absolute Future in order to change the direction of human history. In every human effort to build a more just, free, humane, peaceful and loving world, men have been hastening the coming of the Kingdom of Him Who is that Absolute Future and thus have been implicitly accepting the meaning of their history as a history of salvation. For in all those ways by which a better world is being made, the salvific power of Christ already interior to history and the cosmos is released to produce a specifically new creation.

The most powerful creative force in the world is that of love. It is in love that all other forces and energies are focussed and brought to their peak. Love at once unifies and elicits from each being the expression of its uniqueness. God creates out of love and recreates out of redeeming love. Man shares in God's creative love in that *caritas* which is the fullness of the faith and the hope by which we begin to live His life as His gift.

The Law, the Prophets and the Gospel are summed up in the two-fold law of the love of God and of one's neighbor; but actually these two are one. Our Lord intimated this when He identified Himself with the least of His brethren (Mt 25:40). St. Paul asserted it when he stated that the love of neighbor is the fulfilling of the law (Rom 13:10) and then spelled out its implications in his lyrical hymn to charity (1 Cor 13). St. John interpreted the new commandment of Jesus to His disciples (Jn 13:34) as meaning that the God Who is Love has loved us not so much that we love Him directly but that we love Him in our brother (1 Jn 4:11-12). It is thus that "God abides in us and His love is perfected in us."

The infused theological virtue of Charity is that God-given power by which we are able to love as God loves. How does God love? With utter selflessness. He loves the one whom He created as other precisely to have someone to give Himself to in love. We exercise His love when we love the one whom He created to love. This does not mean we cannot or should not love Him in Himself. It does mean that we cannot genuinely love our neighbor without being a vehicle of His Love, and indeed without loving Him at least implicitly.

The unity of the love of God and of our neighbor is such that when one is authentically present the other is essentially implicated, whichever of the two is formally intended. This can be explained transcendentally. Just as we affirm God, the Absolute Truth, implicitly as the co-known non-objective condition or horizon of every act of knowing and affirming a determinate object, so we co-intend God, the Absolute Good, as the non-objective condition or horizon of every act of willing a particular good or of loving someone in response to such a good encountered in him. In faith we profess that the God so known, willed and loved has given Himself to us as divinizing grace which transforms every act we perform in accord with its acceptance or rejection by us.

All this is true of any morally good act since it is also a saving act performed by virtue of the supernaturally divinizing grace offered to all men by the God Who wills all men to be saved. It is uniquely true of the love of our neighbor which is the basis of human morality as such. For every moral value, in whatever object it may reside, is person-oriented. The world of things has moral value only because it belongs to the world of persons which it enters as the object of human knowledge and freedom. Men achieve themselves precisely in going out to the personal other, the Thou. For thereby they come to themselves in growing self-knowledge as persons culminating in the freedom which is measured by their capacity for self-possession and self-disposal in relation to the personal other.

Thus the love of one's neighbor is the fundamental act of man toward which all others are referred. It is the act in which his humanity as essential transcendence toward the Infinite Mystery is perpetually engaged in the process of its own achievement. *De facto* it is the basic act by which man responds to the unfailing initiative of God's loving Self-gift and therefore the vehicle by which we love God with His own power of love, His Spirit. Moreover, it is not that we are in effect disguising our love for God in the form of love of our neighbor. Rather it is the very love of our fellow-man in which our love for God is realized and expressed.

It is possible and indeed desirable to make of God a direct object of our love. But that is not how He originally enters into the dynamic of our loving, viz., as one object among others. Rather He is the transcendental a priori condition of every act of loving another in this world, the non-objectified goal towards which the spirit of man transcends in each loving communication with another person in his world. This experience of God as the ground of our subjectivity, even when not recognized as such, is the source of our power to love our fellow-man and to embrace our this-worldly tasks. Although the explicit religious act by which God becomes for us a reflex object of our knowledge and love is of higher dignity than the loving act of which our neighbor is the object, "yet this does not alter the fact that the primary basic act of man who is always already 'in the world' is always an act of the love of his neighbor and *in this* the original love of God is realized in so far as in this basic act are also accepted the conditions of its possibility, one of which is the reference of man to God when supernaturally elevated by grace."[33]

The unity of the love of neighbor and of God is such

that we can affirm that the formal love of our neighbor is the primary act of our love of God. We cannot love God without loving our neighbor. The implications of this for the integrity of the Christian's commitment to this world and its future are evident and profound. On the other hand, we cannot truly love our neighbor without at least implicitly but necessarily loving God. The implications of this are even more astounding. For it uncovers the theocentric, indeed the Christocentric dynamism of every authentic human relationship and every worthwhile worldly endeavor.

Teilhard de Chardin strove for, and before his death believed he had achieved, a union between his faith in God and his faith in the world. The convergent center of this union was his faith in the Universal Christ, the personalizing Omega Point toward which the evolutionary process is progressing. Cosmogenesis, the coming into being of a world, is thus transformed into Christogenesis, the coming into being of the total Christ, that is, of a world centered in man evolving toward more and more total union with God in Christ. For God, having entered His creation personally in Christ incarnate is constantly drawing that world into closer union with Himself through the cosmic Christ.

> With cosmogenesis being transformed, as we said, into Christogenesis, it is the stuff, the main stream, the very being of the world which is now being personalized. Someone, and no longer something, is in gestation in the universe. To believe and to serve was not enough: we now find that is is becoming not only possible but imperative literally to love evolution.[34]

For Teilhard, love is the fundamental force drawing all the components of the evolving universe towards their ultimate union in Christ. He also affirms the underlying unity of the two commandments of the love of God and of our neighbor, but he gives it a bold cosmic significance. "Thou shalt love God in and through the genesis of the universe and of mankind."[35] For him, therefore, this 'super-charity,' this love of God which powers our love of fellow-man is also the energy by which we enter most deeply into the evolutionary dynamic itself in which our world and ourselves are in constant process of creation. Thus loving commitment to our world and its progress, like love of our neighbor, is a performance of our love of God.

One does not have to embrace unconditionally the 'cosmic optimism' of Teilhard (indeed it may require considerable tempering) to catch the exciting vision it opens up for the man of Christian faith, for the contemporary man of any faith. The superficial signs of our epoch point to a religious recession, an eclipse of Christianity. But stirring beneath the surface are growing rumblings which a prophetic genius like Teilhard has interpreted as omens of a major breakthrough to new heights of spiritual consciousness. For they arise from a new, rapidly developing awareness of the oneness of our species and of our destiny. More and more indivisibly, we share common perils of unprecedented magnitude and common opportunities of unparalleled promise. Which road will mankind travel: toward universal annihilation, whether sudden or lingering, or toward ever fuller unity with his kind and with his world?

Teilhard has scarce doubt that it will be the way of universal convergence. The contemporary Christian man of faith, whether Teilhardian or not, founds his hope ultimately on the Paschal victory of Christ Who has made Himself one with man's universe. More proximately, and in this context more practically, he bases his expectations of a nobler future on the willingness of himself and his fellow-men to serve one another and the building of their world with a creative love that is one with the Creator's love. The Gospel which preaches the unity of the love of God, of neighbor and of the universe is the final divine word that sustains our hope in the future of man and his world.

CONCLUSION

In Christian Faith, man has a self-understanding which comprehends others as less ultimate. Anyone that would be equally ultimate would be identical with it, although expressed categorically in different terms.[36] As the founding contemporary man in his pluralistic, evolutionary world, it furnishes him with a self-understanding which is not only not disharmonious with his own experience of himself, but is one that provides a horizon within which he can confidently assert his own meaningfulness and absolute value. At the same time it secures his real freedom and responsibility for his own destiny and that of his world in summoning him constantly to co-create himself and his world towards a future that is open, unpredetermined and full of hope. That hope is based not only on the infinite potentialities of his own transcendence, but on the immanence of his Absolute Future within his own history and human condition in the universal Christ Who continually redeems him from the counter-weight and inertia of his sinfulness and despair.

In the final analysis, the Christian who understands his Faith and lives it authentically cannot escape being 'contemporary' in any age. By his fundamental life-option, he has committed himself to the loving service of his fellow-man and to the building of a more humane world in every today that he lives. Doing so, he is constituting himself in growing solidarity with others in his world as he is, in effect, responding through them and the tasks they share to that Other Who incessantly summons His whole creation to share His Life as its Absolute Future.

Notes and references

[1] "The presence of a pluralistic society is a persistent fact, today and in the future, because the grounds for a non-pluralistic society do not consist apriorily in the absolute, objective correctness of a system or a world view, but in historically conditioned social causes which have been suppressed and could reappear just as they once were only if the unity of the history of the world, or the freedom present in a rational and technical society and the social possibility of making this freedom objective, were to disappear. If the Christian, on theological grounds, cannot expect the global victory of Christianity in the social dimension, within the concrete limits of history, then Christianity can only expect a pluralistic society in its future, and accept it as its context of existence, or it will set up the conditions for a non-Christian, totalitarian society." Karl Rahner, **Handbuch der Pastoraltheologie** II/I, p. 214, as quoted in Heinrich Fries, **Faith Under Challenge**, (New York: Herder & Herder, 1969), p. 141.

[2] J. B. Metz, "The Future of Faith in a Hominized World," **Theology of the World**, (New York: Herder & Herder, 1969), p. 57.

3 Ibid., pp. 57-58.

4 Ibid., p. 60.

5 "How Faith Sees the World," ibid., p. 21.

6 Ibid., p. 22.

7 Ibid., p. 27.

8 Ibid., p. 42.

9 Ibid., pp. 49-50.

10 Charles Davis, **God's Grace in History** (New York: Sheed & Ward, 1966), p. 112.

11 Metz does not equate political theology with the whole of the theological enterprise. It is rather the application of fundamental theology in its critical and prophetic function. Cf. Henri de Lavalette, S.J., "The Political Theology of J. B. Metz," **Theology Digest** 20 (Spring, 1972), p. 4, a digested translation of "La 'theologie politique' de Jean-Baptiste Metz," **Recherches de Science Religieuse**, 59 (1970), pp. 321-350. For de Lavalette's further thoughts on Metz's Political Theology, cf. also his: "Ambiguités de la théologie politique," ibid., v. 59 (1971), pp. 545-562.

12 Karl Rahner, "The Church and the Parousia of Christ," **Theological Investigations, VI**, p. 311.

13 Metz, **Theology of the World**, p. 116.

14 Ibid., p. 118.

15 Cf. de Lavalette's two articles cited above; also Helmut Peukert, editor, **Diskussion zur 'politischen Theologie'**, Mainz-Munich, 1969.

16 Ruben A. Alves, **A Theology of Human Hope** (St. Meinrad, Ind.: Abbey Press, 1972), pp. 5-17.

17 Gustavo Gutierrez, **A Theology of Liberation** trans. and ed. Sister Caridad Inda and John Eagleson (Maryknoll, N.Y.: Orbis Books, 1973), pp. 220-25. Cf. **Between Honesty and Hope: Documents from and about the Church in Latin America, Issued at Lima by the Peruvian Bishops' Commission for Social Action**, trans. John Drury (Maryknoll, N.Y.: Maryknoll Publications, 1970).

18 Ibid., p. 145.

19 The classical treatment of the raising of the consciousness of the oppressed and the process of "conscientization" by which it is to be accomplished is the influential work of the Brazilian, Paolo Freire, **The Pedagogy of the Oppressed**, trans. Myra Bergman Ramos (New York: Herder & Herder, 1972). The original Portugese edition was published in 1967.

20 James H. Cone, **Black Theology and Black Power** (New York: Seabury Press, 1969), p. 117. Cone's own italics.

21 Ibid., pp. 130-31.

22 Albert B. Cleage, Jr., **The Black Messiah** (New York: Sheed & Ward, 1968) p. 38 and passim.

23 James H. Cone, **A Black Theology of Liberation** (New York: Lippincott, 1970), p. 32, n.

24 Rosemary Ruether, **Liberation Theology** (New York: Paulist Press, 1972), p. 131.

25 Cf., for example, Gabriel J. Fackre, **Liberation in Middle America** (Philadelphia: Pilgrim Press, 1971).

26 Karl Rahner, "Christianity and the New Man," **Theological Investigations V**, p. 144.

27 Charles Davis, **God's Grace in History**, 1966, p. 115.

28 J. B. Metz, "An Eschatological View of the Church and the

World," **Theology of the World**, p. 87.

29 Karl Rahner, "The Church and the Parousia of Christ," **Theological Investigations**, VI, p. 308.

30 "Pastoral Constitution on the Church in the Modern World," 40, in **The Documents of Vatican II**, p. 239.

31 Karl Rahner, "Theological Reflections on the Problem of Secularization," **Theology of Renewal, I** (New York: Herder & Herder, 1968), p. 172.

32 "Dogmatic Constitution on the Church," 31, **Documents of Vatican II**, 57-58.

33 Karl Rahner, "Reflections on the Unity of the Love of Neighbor and the Love of God," **Theological Investigations**, VI, p. 246. This whole article has been the primary source of the foregoing considerations. Cf. also, Rahner's article "Marxist Utopia and the Christian Future of Man" in the same volume pp. 64, ff.

34 Pierre Teilhard de Chardin, "Suggestions for a New Theology," in **Christianity and Evolution**, (New York: Harcourt Brace Jovanovich, Inc., 1971), p. 184.

35 **Ibid.**

36 To make such a claim seems monumentally presumptuous and patronizing, reducing all other faiths, to the extent that they are authentic, to implicit or anonymous forms of Christian Faith. We have tried to show that the Christian understanding of man corresponds with the total reality man is and experiences and understands himself to be. The success of that effort will decide the credibility of that claim.

Alves, Rubem A. *A Theology of Human Hope*. St. Meinrad, Ind.: Abbey Press, 1972.

Berryman, Philip E. "Latin American Liberation Theology," *Theological Studies* 34 (Sept., 1973), pp. 357-95.
Between Honesty and Hope: Documents from and about the Church in Latin America. Issued at Lima by the Peruvian Bishops' Commission for Social Action. Tr. John Drury. Maryknoll, N. Y.: Maryknoll Publications, 1970.
Braaten, Carl E. *Christ and Counter-Christ*. Philadelphia: Fortress, 1972.
Braaten, Carl E. *The Future of God: The Revolutionary Dynamics of Hope*. New York: Harper & Row, 1969.

Carey, John J. "Black Theology: An Appraisal of the Internal and External Issues," *Theological Studies* 33 (1972), pp. 684-97.
Christian and the World, The: Readings in Theology. Compiled at the Canisianum, Innsbruck. New York: Kenedy, 1965.
Cleage, Albert B., Jr. *The Black Messiah*. New York: Sheed & Ward, 1968.
Cone, James H. *Black Theology and Black Power*. New York: Seabury, 1969.
Cone, James H. *A Black Theology of Liberation*. New York: Lippincott, 1970.

Dimension of Future in Our Faith, The. Ed. Josef Goldbrunner. Tr. Sister M. Veronica Riedl, O.S.F. Notre Dame, Ind.: University of Notre Dame Press, 1966.
Dogma and Pluralism. Ed. Edward Schillebeeckx. New York: Herder & Herder, 1970.
Dulles, Avery, S.J. *The Survival of Dogma*. Garden City, N.Y.: Doubleday, 1971.

Fackre, Gabriel J. *Liberation in Middle America*. Philadelphia: Pilgrim, 1971.
Faith and the World of Politics. Ed. J. B. Metz. New York: Paulist, 1968.
Freedom and Unfreedom in the Americas: Towards a Theology of Liberation. Ed. Thomas E. Quigley. New York: IDOC, 1971.
Freire, Paolo. *Pedagogy of the Oppressed*. Tr. Myra Bergman Ramos. New York: Herder & Herder, 1972.
Fries, Heinrich. *Faith Under Challenge*. Tr. William D. Seidensticker. New York: Herder & Herder, 1969.
Future of Hope, The Ed. Walter H. Capps. Philadelphia: Fortress, 1970.
Future of Hope, The. Theology as Eschatology. Ed. Frederick Herzog. New York: Herder & Herder, 1970.

Gilkey, Langdon. *Religion and the Scientific Future*. London: SCM Press, 1970.
God Experience, The. Essays in Hope. Ed. Joseph P. Whelan, S.J. New York: Newman, 1971.
Greeley, Andrew. *Religion in the Year 2000*. New York: Sheed & Ward, 1969.

Gutierrez, Gustavo. *A Theology of Liberation.* Tr. and ed. Sister Caridad Inda and John Eagleson. Maryknoll, N.Y.: Orbis, 1973.
Gutierrez, Gustavo. "Notes for a Theology of Liberation," *Theological Studies* 31 (1970), pp. 243-61.

Häring, Bernard. *A Theology of Protest.* New York: Farrar, Straus and Giroux, 1970.
Herzog, Frederick. *Liberation Theology.* New York: Seabury, 1972.
Hope and the Future of Man. Ed. Ewert H. Cousins. Philadelphia: Fortress, 1972.
Houtart, Francois, and Rousseau, André. *The Church and Revolution,* Maryknoll, New York: Orbis, 1971.

Jones, Major J. *Black Awareness: a Theology of Hope.* Nashville: Abingdon, 1971.

Knowledge and the Future of Man. Ed. Walter J. Ong, S.J. New York: Holt, Rinehart and Winston, 1968.
Komonchak, Joseph A. "A Theology of Liberation," *Catholic Mind* 71 (1973), pp. 21-29.

"Latin America in Search of Liberation." Ed. Gary MacEoin. *Cross Currents* 21 (1971), pp 341-62.
Laurentin, René. *Liberation, Development and Salvation.* Tr. Charles U. Quinn. Maryknoll, N.Y.: Orbis, 1972.
Lavalette, Henri de, S.J. "The 'political theology' of J. B. Metz," *Theology Digest* 20 (1972), pp. 4-12.
Lonergan, Bernard. "Theology and Man's Future," *Cross Currents* 19 (1969), pp. 452-61.

Mascall, E. L. *The Secularization of Christianity.* New York: Holt, Rinehart & Winston, 1965.
Metz, Johannes, B. *Theology of the World.* Tr. William Glen-Doepel. New York: Herder & Herder, 1969.
Moltmann, Jürgen. *Hope and Planning.* Tr. Margaret Clarkeson. New York: Harper & Row, 1971.
Moltmann, Jürgen. *Religion, Revolution and the Future.* Tr. M. Douglas Meeks. New York: Scribner's 1969.
Moltmann, Jürgen. *Theology of Hope.* Tr. James W. Leitch. London: SCM Press; New York: Harper & Row, 1967.
Mooney, Christopher F., S.J. *The Making of Man.* New York: Paulist, 1971.

O'Collins, Gerald, S.J. *Man and His New Hopes.* New York: Herder & Herder, 1969.
Oglesby, Carl, and Shaull, Richard. *Containment and Change.* New York: Macmillan, 1967.
O'Grady, Colm, M.S.C. "Change in Theology," *Louvain Studies* 4. (1973), pp. 209-28.

Paupert, Jean-Marie. *The Politics of the Gospel.* New York: Holt, Rinehart & Winston, 1969.
Perspectives of a Political Ecclesiology. Ed. J. B. Metz. New York: Herder & Herder, 1971.
Pieper, Josef. *Hope and History.* Tr. Richard & Clara Winston. New York: Herder & Herder, 1969.
Political Commitment and Christian Community. Ed. A. Muller & N. Greinacher. New York: Herder & Herder, 1973.
Projections: Shaping an American Theology for the Future. Ed. T. F. O'Meara & D. M. Weisser, Garden City, N.Y.: Doubleday, 1970.

Quest for a Black Theology. Ed. J. Deotis Roberts & James J. Gardiner, S.A. Philadelphia: Pilgrim, 1971.

Rahner, Karl. *The Christian of the Future.* Tr. W. J. O'Hara. New York: Herder & Herder, 1967.
Rahner, Karl. "Christianity and the New Earth," *Theology Digest* 15 (1967), pp. 275-82. Also in *Knowledge and the Future of Man.* Ed. W. J. Ong, S.J. New York: Holt, Rinehart & Winston, 1968.
Rahner, Karl. "Christianity and the New Man," *Theological Investigations,* V. Baltimore: Helicon, 1966, pp. 135-53.
Rahner, Karl. "Christology within an evolutionary view of the world," *Theological Investigations,* V, pp. 157-92.
Rahner, Karl. "The Church and the Parousia of Christ," *Theological Investigations,* VI. Tr. Karl-H. & Boniface Kruger. Baltimore: Helicon, 1969, pp. 295-312.
Rahner, Karl et al. *The Future of Man and Christianity.* Chicago: Argus Communications Co., 1969.
Rahner, Karl. "The hermeneutics of eschatological assertions," *Theological Investigations,* IV. Tr. Kevin Smyth. Baltimore: Helicon, 1966, pp. 323-46.
Rahner, Karl. "The Historicity of Theology," *Theological Investigations,* IX. Tr. Graham Harrison. New York: Herder & Herder, 1972, pp. 64-82.
Rahner, Karl. *Hominisation: The Evolutionary Origin of Man as a Theological Problem.* Tr. W. T. O'Hara. New York: Herder & Herder, 1965.
Rahner, Karl. "Marxist Utopia and the Christian Future of Man," *Theological Investigations,* VI, pp. 59-68.

Rahner, Karl. "Pluralism in Theology and the Oneness of the Church's Profession of Faith," in *The Development of Fundamental Theology.* Ed. J. B. Metz. New York: Paulist, 1969, pp. 103-23.

Rahner, Karl. "Reflections on Dialogue within a Pluralistic Society," *Theological Investigations,* VI, pp. 31-42.

Rahner, Karl. "Reflections on the unity of the love of neighbor and the love of God," *Theological Investigations,* VI, pp. 231-49.

Rahner, Karl. "The Second Vatican Council's Challenge to Theology," *Theological Investigations,* IX, pp. 3-27.

Rahner, Karl. "A Small Question Regarding the Contemporary Pluralism in the Intellectual Situation of Catholics and the Church," *Theological Investigations,* VI, pp. 21-42.

Rahner, Karl. "Theological reflections on the problem of secularization," in *Theology of Renewal,* I, (Ed. L. K. Shook, 1968), pp. 167-92.

Rahner, Karl. "Theology and the Church's Teaching Authority after the Council," *Theological Investigations,* IX, pp. 83-100.

Richard, Robert L. *Secularization Theology.* New York: Herder & Herder, 1967.

Roberts, J. Deotis. *Liberation and Reconciliation: A Black Theology.* Philadelphia: Westminster, 1972.

Ruether, Rosemary. *Liberation Theology.* New York: Paulist, 1972.

Schillebeeckx, Edward, O.P. *God the Future of Man.* Tr. N. D. Smith. New York: Sheed & Ward, 1968.

Schillebeeckx, Edward, O.P. *World and Church.* Tr. N. D. Smith. New York: Sheed & Ward, 1971.

Segundo, Juan Luis, S.J. *A Theology for Artisans of a New Humanity.* 5 vols. Tr. John Drury. Vol. 1. *The Community Called Church.* Vol. 2. *Grace and the Human condition.* Maryknoll, N.Y.: Orbis, 1973.

Sleeper, C. Freeman. *Black Power and Christian Responsibility.* Nashville: Abingdon, 1969.

Social Message of the Gospels, The Ed. Franz Böckle. New York: Paulist, 1968.

Spirit and Power of Christian Secularity, The. Ed. Albert L. Schlitzer, C.S.C. Notre Dame, Ind.: University of Notre Dame Press, 1969.

Teilhard de Chardin, P. *Christianity and Evolution.* Tr. R. Hague. New York: Harcourt Brace Jovanovich, 1971.

Theology of Renewal. Ed. L. K. Shook. 2 vols. New York: Herder & Herder, 1968.

Thompson, William M. "Rahner's Theology of Pluralism," *The Ecumenist* 11 (1973), pp. 17-22.

Toinet, P. "Le Problème théologique du pluralisme," *Revue Thomiste* 72 (1972), pp. 5-32.

Truth and Certainty. Ed. Edward Schillebeeckx & Bas Van Iersel. New York: Herder & Herder, 1973.

Walgrave, J. H., "Change in Christian Dogmatic Language," *Louvain Studies* 4 (1973), pp. 245-53.

Washington, Joseph. *Black Religion.* Boston: Beacon, 1964.

Washington, Joseph. *The Politics of God.* Boston: Beacon, 1969.

Weber, Paul J. "Daniel Berrigan: Political Theology in the Post-War Years," *Chicago Studies* 12 (1973), pp. 77-90.

Williams, Colin. *Faith in a Secular Age.* New York: Harper & Row, 1966.

Wilmore, Gayraud S. *Black Religion and Black Radicalism.* Garden City, N.Y.: Doubleday, 1972.

"World Congress on the Future of the Church, Brussels, 1970," *Catholic Mind* 68 (Dec., 1970), pp. 1-51.

INDEX

absolute (God) vii, 5, 7f., 13-29, 31, 36, 38ff., 51, 58, 60, 62, 64ff., 78, 82ff., 86, 90ff., 92, 98, 111, 117-122, 128-131, 135-138, 142ff., 154-157, 160, 162ff., 173-175, 178, 181, 184-187, 193-207, 208, 211f., 217n., 211-230, 231, 233f., 236f., 240-263, 266, 281, 283f., 292f., 299n., 303ff., 312ff., 323, 339f., 348f., 355, 358-367, 379, 387f., 390-405

ALFARO, J. 256
ALTIZER, T. 25, 354f.
ALVES, R. 373
anonymous Christian 255-262, 268, 273f., 275, 364
anthropology (Christian) 6, 15f., 39, 109ff., 197-262, 276n., 283f., 302f., 309, 317
apologetics vi-vii, 6-8, 19, 109, 123, 133f., 140, 141ff., 222, 306
AQUINAS, ST. THOMAS vi, 17, 172f., 174, 176, 178, 179ff., 196, 208f., 217n., 241, 242f., 246ff., 286ff., 296, 303f., 356
ARISTOTLE vi, 19, 52, 177, 247, 286
atheism 7, 21, 25, 28, 40, 51, 62, 74, 78, 85, 109, 256, 301, 332
AUGUSTINE, ST. 177, 211, 228, 245, 266, 286

Bainism 208, 218n.
BARTH, K. 15-16, 265f., 318
belief 5, 7, 9, 44, 89f., 97, 120, 158, 243, 281-299, 303, 307f., 323, 327, 338, 347-405
BERGER, P. 44, 46-47
BERGSON, H. 141

BERKELEY, G. 18
BINSWANGER, L. 57
BLACKHAM, H.J. 326ff.
BLANSHARD, B.P. 336f.
BLOCH, E. 78-82, 311, 315f.
BLONDEL, M. 110, 122-140, 141, 143, 159, 162f., 170, 172, 189, 208f., 211
BONHOEFFER, D. 318, 354f.
BRENTANO, F. 52
BUBER, M. 110
Buddhism 91, 159, 262, 367
BULTMANN, R. 128, 318, 357,

CAFFARENA, J.G. 322f., 328ff.
CAJETAN, CARD. 208
Chalcedon 226
CHRIST 5f., 9, 36, 58, 64, 77, 82f., 97, 121, 131, 139, 141, 144, 157, 160-164, 197, 207f., 222, 234-236, 238-276, 281, 292, 297f., 303, 307, 311, 313, 323, 331, 344, 384f., 352, 354ff., 359-366, 367, 377ff., 380f., 382f., 387ff., 390-405
Church 5, 9, 109, 161f., 240-262, 264, 268, 271, 273f., 275f., 295, 303, 347, 348, 350-405
CLEAGE, A. 381
COGLEY, J. 339
cognitive minority 44
COMTE, A. 29-31
concupiscence 294-299
CONE, J. 379f.,
conversion 203
CORETH, E. 187-195, 324n.
COX, H. 45f., 354f.
CURRAN, C. 334
CUYPERS, K. 332f.

DARWIN, C. 31, 87, 91

Dasein 54-59
DAVIS, C. 365
death of God 13f., 17, 21-24, 28f., 38, 51, 330, 354f.,
De Ecclesia 398
DE CHARDIN, TEILHARD 6, 110f., 122, 140-162, 164, 379, 405f.
Dei Verbum 241
DE LANGE, P. 328
DE LUBAC, H. 16, 211f., 214
demythologization 45, 58, 355, 367
DESCARTES, R. 17f., 52, 176
DE SOLAGES, B. 142
DEWART, L. 318
DEWEY, J. 87-91, 93, 95
dialectics vii, 62, 88, 111, 129, 133, 137, 143, 189
dialectical theology 265ff.
DILTHEY, W. 31-34, 55
Directory 340
DONDEYNE, A. 324
DUPRE, L. 339
DURWELL, F.X. 279n.

ENGLES, F. 66f.
EBELING, G. 58
eschatology 46
evolution 30ff., 87, 94, 101, 141-163, 170, 386, 405
existentialism 14, 51, 67ff., 86, 98, 110f., 120, 122, 124
experience 178

faith viff., 5, 9, 14, 20, 25, 33, 38f., 41, 45, 47f., 66, 87ff., 92ff., 95, 120ff., 131, 133, 139, 141ff., 152, 157-164, 208f., 221ff., 224ff., 231, 233f., 236f., 239-262, 270, 281-299, 301, 313, 317, 338, 340, 344, 347-405, 407n.
FATHER (GOD THE) 242, 244, 246f., 249f., 252, 261, 275, 281, 292f., 297, 307, 323, 361, 365, 384, 390
FEUERBACH, L. 15f., 24-26 36, 38ff., 60, 78, 314
FICHTE, J. 21f., 134
FREUD, S. 35-39, 80f., 306
FROMM, E. 95, 329f.
FUCHS, 58
fundamental (foundational) theology v-viii, 8, 196, 207-255

GAINE, J. 327f.
GALILEO 31
GARAUDY, R. 78, 83-85, 311ff., 314ff., 334n., 347f.
Gaudium et Spes 324, 340, 352
grace 121, 207-215, 232ff., 236, 241, 247ff., 250, 256-262, 268-276, 281, 283, 293f., 337, 392, 394
actual 278n.
created 258
habitual 278n.
uncreated 258
GUTIERREZ, G. 373-378

HAECKEL, E. 31
HAMILTON W. 355
HAUGHEY, J. 338
HEGEL, E. 16ff., 21-28, 30f., 40, 55, 79, 88, 111, 125, 134, 137, 172, 190
HEIDEGGER, M. 34, 54-60, 62, 64ff., 70, 117, 170, 176f., 180
Hinduism 159, 262
historicism 31-34
HOOK, S. 333f.
humanism 51, 109, 124, 159, 301ff.,
atheistic 306-320, 332, 399f.
evolutionary 92-94

Marxist 66-85, 311-320
scientific 86f., 91-95, 111, 330f.
secular 86-96, 100ff., 262, 320-340, 342, 371f.
HUME, D. 19
HUSSERL, E. 51-54, 58, 64, 70, 170
HUXLEY, J. 87, 91-95, 144f., 150, 152
HUXLEY, T. 31, 91
hypostatic union 225f., 233

idealism 53, 134, 170

JAMES, W. 122
Jansenism 208
JASPERS, K. 55
JOHN OF THE CROSS, ST. 305
Judaism 82, 262-270
judgment 171f., 178
justification 291-294
JUSTIN MARTYR, ST. 226

KAEHLER, M. 291
KAHLER, E. 47
KANT, I. 19ff., 32f., 51, 170ff., 176, 178, 182
KAUFMANN, W. 95
KIERKEGAARD, S. 16, 24f., 28
KIRKENDALL, L. 334
KOLAKOWSKI, L. 68f.
KOSIC, K. 70f.
KRAEMER, H. 266
KUNG, H. 263f.
KURTZ, D. 321, 325f., 330, 335f.

LAMONT, C. 95, 334
LAUER, Q. 316f., 319
LEIBNITZ, G. 18f.
LENIN, N. 66f., 75
  Marxist-Leninism 66f., 74f.

liberalism 98
linguistic analysis 14
LOCKE, J. 19, 326
logical positivists 70
LONERGAN, B. vif., 170
Lumen Gentium 256
LUTHER, M. 350

MCBRIEN, R. 278n.
MCFADDEN, W. 334f.
MCCORMICK, H. 334
MACY, C. 325, 331f.
MALEBRANCHE, N. 18
mana 91
MAO TSE-TUNG 73-77
MARCEL, G. 110-122, 124, 162
MARECHAL, J. 171-176, 178, 188, 211
MARX, K. 16, 24, 26-28, 36, 66ff., 72, 74f., 78, 306, 329, 369, 375
Marxism 7, 69-86, 111, 306-321, 340f., 347f., 366, 369f., 387, 392
  Marxist humanism 66-85
  institutional Marxism 68
  intellectual Marxism 68
MATSON, F. 334
MENCIUS 74
MERLEAU-PONTY, M. 53, 58, 60-66
METZ, J.B. 176, 207, 276n., 314f., 319, 357-374, 406n.
MIANO, V. 333
MILL, J.S. 31, 326
MOLTMANN, J. 357, 372
morality (civil, sexual) 334ff.
MOSES 36, 82, 356
Moslemism 262
MURY, G. 313f.
Mystici Corporis 256

nature 207-215, 218n., 226f., 232, 241
neo-orthodoxy 15
NEWTON, I. 18
NIEBUHR, R. 14
NIETZSCHE, F. 13, 16, 28f., 36, 306, 340

OCKHAM, W. 17
OESTERLE, J. 337
O'HAIR, M.M. 339f.

PANNENBERG, W. 357, 372
PAUL, ST. 264f., 362, 400f.
PAUL VI 122, 348, 371, 374
PETROVIC, G. 72f.
phenomenology 51ff., 58, 80, 144, 174
PIEPER, J. 356
PIUS XII 122
pluralism 43, 347-405
Populorum Progressio 371, 374
positivism 29-31
psychologism 35-38

RAHNER, K. vi, 175-187, 196-207, 209-215, 224, 226-230, 234f., 249, 255ff., 268, 270, 276n., 278n., 294f., 312ff., 319, 357, 389, 396f., 405n.
realism 53, 171, 174
real symbol, theory of 226ff.
religion vii, 14ff., 20f., 24ff., 30ff., 39f., 41ff., 46, 67, 78f., 82f., 85ff., 90ff., 121, 131, 139, 158-162, 196, 203, 207f., 235, 262-276, 314, 317, 324, 327, 331, 333, 349, 391
redemption 232, 245, 265, 373
REUTHER, R. 382
revelation vii, 9, 15, 17, 20, 200, 203-208, 221, 223-231, 233f.,

236-262, 265f., 268-276, 281, 331, 392
RICOEUR, P. 35
RICHARDSON, H.W. 301f., 334n.
ROTH, R. 335
RUIZ, G. 318

sacrament, Church as 260f., 356f., 387, 391f.
salvation 232-239, 241f., 251, 253f., 256-262f., 268-276, 293f., 323, 353, 370, 375f., 394ff.
SARTRE, J.P. 58-60, 65, 68f., 110
SCHAFF, A. 69f.
SCHELLING, F. 21, 134
SCHILLEBEECKZ, P. 256, 278n.
SCHLEIERMACHER, F. 15
SCHLETTE, H.R. 268
scholasticism 19, 169
SCHOPENHAUER, K. 29
SCOTUS, J. 17
secular Christianity 354-366, 387
secularism 7, 42, 351-405
SKINNER, B.F. 333
SPINOZA, B. 18
SPIRIT, HOLY 242, 244, 246-293, 354, 371, 385f.
STACE W.T. 41
STALIN, J. 67
SUN YAT SEN 74f.
supernatural existential 213ff., 234, 236, 239, 258
SZCZESNY, G. 95-100

Taoism 262
theology, black 378-386
of fulfillment 265ff.
of liberation 373-386
political 366-372
TILLICH, P. v, 14, 289-291 296

transcendental method vif., 187-195, 198ff.
transcendental Thomism 169f., 175f., 226ff.
Trent, Council of 240, 282, 291, 293
TRINITY 244-230
TOYNBEE, A. 263

unbelief 7, 9, 38, 95-100, 140, 143, 221, 281-299, 301, 307f.
understanding 178

VAHANIAN, G. 14
VALENSIN, A. 140

VAN DOOREN, W. 328
VAN PRANG, J.P. 322ff.
Vatican I 240f.
Vatican II 110, 241f., 256, 262, 309, 324f., 340, 352, 357, 366, 368f., 374, 398
VERGOTE, A. 331f.

WANG FU-CHIH 74
WEBER, M. 329
WOLFF, C. 19

Yoga 46

Zen 46